Techniques of
Organizational Change

Techniques of Organizational Change

Stephen R. Michael

Fred Luthans

George S. Odiorne

W. Warner Burke

Spencer Hayden

McGraw-Hill Book Company

New York St. Louis San Francisco Auckland
Bogotá Hamburg Johannesburg London Madrid Mexico
Montreal New Delhi Panama Paris São Paulo
Singapore Sydney Tokyo Toronto

Library of Congress Cataloging in Publication Data

Main entry under title:
    Techniques of organizational change.

    Includes index.
    1. Organizational change—Addresses, essays, lectures.
I. Michael, Stephen R.
HD58.8.T42   658.4'06   80-16243
ISBN   0-07-041775-X

 234567890   DODO   898765432

The editors for this book were William R. Newton and Esther
Gelatt, the designer was Mark E. Safran, and the production
supervisor was Teresa F. Leaden. It was set in Melior by Heffernan
Press, Inc.

Printed and bound by R. R. Donnelley & Sons Company.

Contents

About the Contributors . . .

Stephen R. Michael

Stephen R. Michael is Professor of Management at the School of Business Administration, University of Massachusetts at Amherst. Prior to his 15 years of service there, he spent an equivalent amount of time in business line and staff positions. He is the author of *Appraising Management Practices and Performance*, coauthor of *Organizational Management*, and the author of many articles and papers on a variety of business topics. Currently his interest centers on organizational change, and he is doing research and writing on the subject of planning and control. Professor Michael is a member of the Academy of Management and the American Society for Public Administration and consults on planning, control, and related subjects.

Fred Luthans

Fred Luthans is Regents Professor of Management, University of Nebraska. He received his Ph.D. from the University of Iowa and taught at West Point while serving in the U.S. Army. He is the author or coauthor of over a dozen books and numerous articles and papers. His book *Organizational Behavior,* now in its third edition, is a widely used textbook and *Organizational Behavior Modification* (with Robert Kreitner) recently won the annual A.S.P.A. award for outstanding contribution to human resource management. A consulting coeditor for the McGraw-Hill Management Series, Professor Luthans also is on the editorial boards of a number of journals and is currently president of the Midwest Academy of Management. He is an active consultant in the area of behavioral management.

George S. Odiorne

George S. Odiorne is Professor of Management and former Dean of the School of Business Administration at the University of Massachusetts at Amherst. He was also Dean of the College of Business and Professor of Management at the University of Utah, was affiliated with the University of Michigan, and taught management and economics at Rutgers University and New York University. His business experience has included associations with major American firms, and he has served as a consultant to major American corporations. He received the Ph.D. degree from New York University. Dr. Odiorne serves on several boards of directors of corporations and civic institutions. He is a member of several learned societies and is the author of 10 books and over 100 articles. His most current books include: *MBO II, a System of Managerial Leadership* (1979), *Management and the Activity Trap* (1974), and *Personnel Administration* (1972).

W. Warner Burke

W. Warner Burke is Professor of Psychology and Education and Principal Adviser for the graduate program in organizational psychology in the Department of Psychology at Teachers College, Columbia University. He is also editor of *Organizational Dynamics*. Prior to going to Columbia University, Dr. Burke was Professor and Chairman, Department of Management, Clark University. He is a consultant to a variety of organizations in business-industry in the United States and abroad, and to NASA. He is the author of more than 40 articles and book chapters, and is author, coauthor, editor, or coeditor of ten books.

Spencer Hayden

Spencer Hayden is the founder and president of The Spencer Hayden Company, Inc., management consultants. Earlier Dr. Hayden had spent several years with other major consulting firms. He has also had management experience in a variety of companies. Dr. Hayden has been a full professor at Rensselaer Polytechnic Institute and the New York University Graduate School of Engineering. He has written a book and numerous articles on business topics and is a member of many professional societies.

Preface

Current economic, political, and social events are bringing the "future shock" of environmental change to bear on organizations at an exponential rate. The energy crisis, inflation, severe international competition, drastic change and improvement in technology, the rapid spawning of new products and the abrupt obsolescence of old ones—these are a few only of the problems and opportunities that confront the managers of organizations and challenge them to update their organizations for more efficient and effective results.

As managers move into the 1980s, therefore, they will find themselves faced with more—not fewer—challenges to survival and growth than they were in the 1970s. Their major task will be continually to accommodate their organizations to an ever-changing environment. Consequently, managers must increasingly become *agents of organizational change.*

But even the concept of organizational change is undergoing modification. It appears subject to fads and fashions just like automobile and clothing design. The result is that only some techniques of organizational change are promoted in the literature and taught in business schools and professionally sponsored seminars. Unlike car and clothing styles, however, management techniques do not lose their appeal merely because they may be temporarily out of style. Some techniques may be more seductive because they are new and others less attractive because they are old. To achieve efficient results, nevertheless, managers must be familiar with both old and new techniques of organizational change. Nothing less will facilitate the right choice when change is necessary.

To facilitate such choice, my colleagues and I have brought together a review of all the known and useful techniques of organizational change. Each of us has practiced, consulted, taught, and written about one or more of these techniques over a period of many years. In successive chapters, Fred Luthans describes Organizational Behavior Modification, George S. Odiorne discusses Management by Objectives and Management Development, W. Warner Burke reviews Organization Development, Spencer Hayden explains Management Auditing, and I cover the

Control Cycle of planning and associated processes. In each case we have defined the technique, illustrated its use, detailed the procedures involved, and attempted to appraise its usefulness by citing research and other data available.

The explanation of the techniques is preceded by a chapter on the subject of organizational change to provide a context for the subsequent chapters. The chapters on the various techniques are followed by a summary chapter which compares and contrasts the applicability of the techniques to specific kinds of situations. Such treatment is in accord with the widely accepted *contingency approach to management,* which holds that the correct solution to a management problem is a function of the situational variables.

We believe that a knowledge of the techniques of organizational change will be a necessary minimum qualification for effective managers of the 1980s. My colleagues and I hope that we will have made some contribution to helping them to achieve proficiency in their developing role of change agents.

Stephen R. Michael

Techniques of
Organizational Change

Part 1

Organizational Change

Organizational Change and the Contingency Approach to Management

Stephen R. Michael

Professor of Management
University of Massachusetts/Amherst

Two themes dominate the teaching and the practice of management today. They are *organizational change* and the *contingency approach to management.*

The former is concerned with adapting the organization to the changing demands made upon it by the environment in which it operates. The latter is the increasing recognition that the correct solution to a management problem depends upon the situation. For example, the proper structure for an organization is that which enables it to deal with its environment in an optimal mode.

These two themes are merged in this book to help a manager choose the technique of organizational change most appropriate for a particular problem or situation. This chapter will focus on the nature of organizational change and preview the techniques to deal with it. Subsequent chapters will provide details of the techniques.

Much has been written about change in the history of mankind. One insightful nineteenth-century remark was that the more things change, the more they remain the same. It may have been true for that period.

For the late twentieth century, however, it would be better to say that the more things change, the more different they become. One important change has been a tremendous transformation in organizations. Since the days when the textile mill and the railroad epitomized the height of organizational size and structural elegance, we have gone through an organizational revolution unparalleled in history. Now, references to organizations in society usually include some comment about "big business," "big government," or "big labor."

Organizations have grown large and successful because they have learned to deal with their environments by engaging in organizational change. Simply put, they have adjusted on a continuing basis to the demands made upon them by their environments. These adjustments have consisted of two kinds of actions: (1) changes in the resource mix which the organizations have procured from the environment and also in the products, programs, and services they have supplied back to the environment and (2) changes in their internal structure, their processes, and the behavior of their members to environmental demands.

The adjustments or changes have been the products of managerial decision making. The origins of such actions are lost in history, but during the past 75 years—especially since World War II—a number of specific techniques have been developed and expanded. It seems that successful organizational change does not come about through a series of isolated, uncoordinated decisions. What seems to be needed, instead, is a series of *integrated* decisions representing a *collective* solution to an organizational problem.

TECHNIQUES OF ORGANIZATIONAL CHANGE

As of now, we have a number of major techniques of organizational change:

Organizational Behavior Modification (O.B.Mod.)

Management by Objectives (MBO)

Management Development

Organization Development (OD)

Management Auditing

Control Cycle

These techniques have been developed and formalized at various times in this century. The concept of the Control Cycle of planning, directing implementation, and evaluating the results of plans took shape in the "management science" of Frederick Winslow Taylor[1] and the attempt of Henri Fayol, a French industrialist, to summarize his experiences as a manager,[2] both of them writing after the turn of the century.

The origins of Management Development and Management Auditing are somewhat more obscure. The former grew in part out of the special courses for managers offered by business schools and organizations such as the American Management Association. The latter resulted from the formation of management consulting firms. When and how rapidly these two techniques developed is not entirely clear.

Management by Objectives seems to have had its beginnings in the writings of Peter Drucker after World War II. Drucker emphasized the idea that managerial behavior is meaningful only if directed toward the accomplishment of business objectives.[3]

Organization Development and Organizational Behavior Modification are the most recent additions to the repertoire of techniques of organizational change. Organization Development evolved from the early work in sensitivity training in the 1950s. Organizational Behavior Modification, based upon the operant conditioning theories of B. F. Skinner, has become prominent in the last decade or so.

Organizational change has been a major concern in management theory and practice for several decades. It will likely be an abiding—and even growing—preoccupation in management for the foreseeable future. However, because the various techniques of change have appeared at different times and in response to different needs, they are not equally publicized and used at any given point in time. For example, the Control Cycle today is frequently not even discussed in books on organizational management, while Organization Development, in turn, may be superseded in the limelight by Organizational Behavior Modification, the newest of the techniques.

CONTINGENCY APPROACH TO MANAGEMENT

As both theory and practice shift from one technique of organizational change to another, we can see that the concept of how to bring about organizational change is itself undergoing change. Thus, organizational change, like so many other aspects of management theory and practice, appears to be subject to fads and fashions, just like hemlines and hairdos. Unlike older hemline and hairdo styles, however, older ideas about organizational change are not necessarily bad because they have been superseded by newer ideas. Nor are new ideas better than old ones merely because they are current.

It is easy, nevertheless, to be intrigued by new approaches to management. They are usually publicized by academicians as the consequence of their search for new knowledge. The new approaches, like new cars, appear more seductive to managers than the old approaches. But, of course, it should be remembered that academicians can afford to concentrate on new ideas because they are not concerned with the practical problems of managing an enterprise. Practicing managers are just so concerned. They cannot ignore new ideas, but neither can they afford to forget old ones. Managers must be concerned with both the old and the new. The reason is an obvious one: An organization does not exist for the purpose of testing new ideas. Rather, it exists to benefit its mission and to achieve its objectives. Ideas, whether old or new, should be utilized if they further the organization's mission and objectives. If one theory or practice is more appropriate than others, logic dictates its use whether or not it is fashionable. That, in essence, constitutes the contingency approach to organizational change.[4]

Recognition that the contingency approach was superior to single universal solutions for management problems came out of Fred Fiedler's studies of leadership.[5] Prior to Fiedler's publication, most research and advocacy stressed the superiority of one style of leadership—participative or people-oriented. Authoritarian or task-oriented leadership was assumed to be inferior and a holdover from a more primitive industrial era.

Fiedler showed that the successful or effective style of leadership was one that complemented the situation. The "situation" consisted of three factors: leader-follower relations, the degree of structure of the task, and the position power of the leader. To summarize Fiedler's results, when these three variables had high values or low values, task-oriented leadership was more effective. When they had intermediate or mixed values, a participative style was more effective. Research with work groups, athletic teams, bomber crews, and many other forms of collective effort appeared to give quite consistent results, though the theory is said to still have shortcomings in explaining leadership.

Following Fiedler's publications, writers began to find contingency approaches everywhere, both in new studies and in reinterpretation of older ones. Today it is quite clear that there is probably no one best way to do anything in the realm of management. Whether the problem is one of leadership, of organizational structure, of planning practices, of control techniques, or anything else, there are generally two or more options facing the manager who has to make a decision. It is the same with organizational change. Managers who have to decide how to go about adapting their organizations have a half-dozen alternative techniques from which to choose.

EXAMPLES OF ORGANIZATIONAL CHANGE

One of the most obvious indications of how well organizations adapt to their environments is found in *Fortune*'s annual Directory of the 500 Largest Industrial Corporations. The list of companies changes from year to year, in terms of both relative rankings and inclusion-exclusion. While there are many reasons why a firm may be listed one year and not the next, a perusal of the names on the list in previous years—but no longer listed—would certainly show that some firms were dropped partly because they were unable to cope with the environmental changes that overtook them and thus fell to a lower ranking.

A current success story is Texas Instruments, Inc. (TI), which has moved up in rank from 133d in 1976 to 124th in 1977.[6] It has developed a method of managing which places separate emphasis upon current operational tasks and upon innovative activities. This emphasis is founded upon separate strategic and operating budgets and upon differentiated structure for this "bimodal" view of the organization: a project-oriented management group for innovation and an operating hierarchy for more routine work. As a consequence, the company is able not only to survive but even to prosper in the dynamic electronics business. One of the major innovations it has undergone in the past decade has been to move from its basic business of manufacturing electronic components into consumer markets, including hand-held calculators and electronic watches. More recently, it has begun to market a series of learning aids, including three that teach math, spelling, and how to tell time.

So successful has TI been that it not only has become fearsome competition for American firms in the electronic industrial and consumer markets, but it is apparently keeping the Japanese industry at bay. It has been able to do so because it has used the Control Cycle as the organizational change technique to spot and solve problems and take advantage of opportunities it finds in its environment. TI also engages in an "objectives-strategies-tactics" program which is essentially Management by Objectives in disguise. Finally, TI has had a long-standing program of *job enrichment,* one of the methods of Organization Development.[7]

A startling contrast to TI was the behavior of Non-Linear Systems, Inc., a small manufacturer of technical instruments. For no reason discernible in its environment, the president decided to reorganize the firm in accordance with some current theories of motivation and group dynamics. The hierarchy was stripped of its control and coordinating function and given the role of staff advisers. Workers were to be motivated by freedom to be creative and productive.

Initial reports seemed to confirm the value of such developments. But in a few years, the overall results of operations began to threaten the survival of the firm; finally the president reversed the organizational design. He conceded that the company would have to pay attention to its environment and not adopt universal, esoteric ideas of management simply because they appeared seductive.[8]

General Electric and Westinghouse present an even more useful contrast of differing abilities to adjust to the environment because of their many apparent similarities. They have been lifelong competitors in household appliances, industrial electric products, and utility power equipment, among other markets.

But the differences are stark indeed. As *Business Week* noted, "GE is growing rapidly as a result of its strong financial controls and marketing strategies. Westinghouse, with huge potential losses hanging over it, is lagging further and further behind."[9]

General Electric (GE) has done so well in some markets—consumer goods and aerospace—that Westinghouse has abandoned them. The latter has tried to recoup its fortunes in other fields—soft-drink bottling, real estate, and educational services. Perhaps because they are unrelated to its major markets, the contribution to profits has been extremely low. The biggest problem that Westinghouse has been wrestling with, however, is its uranium contracts. These long-term contracts involve a potential loss equal to the book value of Westinghouse's assets. The differing fortunes of these two firms appear to be the consequence of different approaches to adjusting their organizations to their environments.

General Electric has a sophisticated Management Development program in conjunction with delegation of responsibilities which makes managers thoroughly aware of organizational objectives, policies, and procedures. This program is coupled with the Control Cycle. Top management, with the assistance of planning experts, prepares plans. Implementation of plans is delegated to middle management. Implementation and the results of plans are continually monitored and evaluated. For example, when a new venture does not live up to expectations, it is canceled, curtailed, or sold.

Westinghouse does otherwise. To the extent that the Control Cycle is used, planning is a computer-based, middle-management-input operation. Risk is ignored if a market appears alluring. That happened in the uranium market and in the real estate market also. There seems to be no monitoring of the implementation of plans, and results are evaluated only when crises and disasters are impending. For example, Westinghouse ignored the growth of the mass merchandisers in the household appliance markets and had to sell that part of its business when it became unprofitable. There seems to be no comprehensive Management Development program at Westinghouse comparable to the one at GE. As *Business Week* notes, because of these differences towards organizational change between the two companies, "GE grows while Westinghouse shrinks."[10]

MODEL OF ORGANIZATIONAL CHANGE

It is possible to present a simplified model of organizational change, showing the basic steps that are involved in adjusting the organization to its environment. Figure 1-1 details the following aspects of the process.

1 The *environment* consists of a bundle of *opportunities* and *problems* These impact upon the organization as a set of *demands.*

2 The organization has some characteristic *strengths* and *weaknesses.* These characteristics all determine the ability of the organization to *supply products, programs,* and *services* to the environment.

3 The ability or inability of the organization to respond to demand with supply can be seen as indicating a *good, fair, or poor fit between* the *environment* and the *organization.*

4 To the extent that there is an *inadequate fit* between the organization and its environment, there is a need for a *problem definition.*

5 The problem definition leads to a *set of alternative strategic solutions* which specify ways in which the organization can seek a better fit with its environment.

6 One of the alternatives is chosen as the *strategic solution* which *will maximize* the *fit between organization and environment.*

7 The chosen *strategic* solution is *implemented.*

8 The organizational change required by the strategic solution should result in *a better fit between organization and environment.*

ILLUSTRATION OF MODEL

This model of organizational change can be illustrated with the relatively simple story of Emery Air Freight Corporation.[11] Luthans discusses the

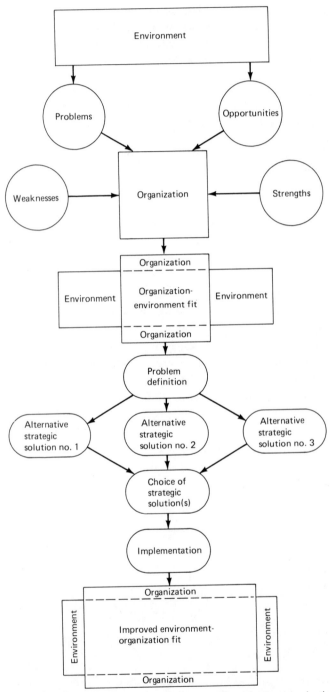

Fig. 1-1 Model of organizational change: adjusting the organization to its environment.

Emery case critically in Chapter 2. We will use the firm's experience in an uncritical fashion here because the purpose is to illustrate the model rather than evaluate the efficiency of Organizational Behavior Modification. In fact, we may have to supplement the known facts to make the example fully useful for our purposes.

In terms of our model, we can describe the environment as constituting an opportunity rather than a problem. There was considerable demand for air freight services and Emery Air Freight was a leading supplier in the market.

Yet Vice President Edward J. Feeney felt that the company exhibited weaknesses in dealing with its environment. For example, their salespeople were not being trained adequately to take advantage of the demand. Training programs seemed to consist of pumping them full of selling techniques and evangelical lectures from supersalespeople. Their productivity in the field appeared low.

Inability to respond to demand was evident elsewhere in the company. The customer service department was expected to respond to customer inquiries within 90 minutes. Department personnel estimated that they did so 90 percent of the time. But the goal was met only 30 percent of the time according to an audit of the operation.

Similarly, the containerized shipment operation was apparently effective in that the company assumed that consolidation of many small shipments into single containers was the practice about 90 percent of the time. Again, the actual achievement was about 45 *percent* of the potential.

Here, then, were three instances where the company exhibited weaknesses in supplying the demand for its services:

1 The salespeople did not take advantage of the opportunity of getting a larger share of the market.

2 Service personnel did not respond efficiently to customers' "demands" for information about orders.

3 Shipping personnel did not supply the company's services as efficiently as the environment permitted.

Note that we have not specified any organizational strengths for Emery Air Freight Corporation. That is not to say that there weren't any. In fact, the firm was and is a leader in the field of air freight service. Rather, the sources on which this analysis is based simply did not include information about its strengths. Judging from its performance generally, Emery was probably doing many things that were right. If our analysis were based upon intimate knowledge of the organization, a listing of strengths would be a necessary and extremely useful kind of information and would assist materially in deciding how to bring about change. We can, however, proceed without such information since this is merely an *illustration* of organization change.

Having completed the examination of the environment and the organization, it is time now to attempt a *problem definition*. We could, for example, make a generalized statement, such as, "The company is unable to take advantage of the sales opportunities in the economic environment and does not supply its services efficiently in response to existing demand."

However, the problem definition should provide clues as to strategic solutions, and this definition is too general to help in that respect. It is usually necessary to attempt successive, more specific approximations at stating the problem until one is reached which suggests possible resolutions. The definition should stop short of merely reiterating the separate, detailed components of the problem, such as the three weaknesses cited above.

After a few more attempts, we might come up with something like the following problem definition: "The company is unable to take advantage of the demand for its services from the perspectives of sales revenues and processing costs because the personnel engaged in selling, order processing, and shipping do not get adequate feedback to tell them how well or badly they are performing."

We now have a more useful statement because it isolates a common thread in the three substandard operations: ignorance of, or indifference to, performance levels due to lack of feedback. Moreover, the problem definition identifies a deficiency in management in terms of which there are solutions. The deficiency is lack of feedback upon which control depends. Simply put, if you don't know or don't care about substandard performance, you are not likely to improve.

Now we can proceed to developing alternative strategic solutions to the problem. As in all kinds of decision making, it is possible to engage in what is called "satisficing." This is the tendency of decision makers to settle for the first reasonably attractive or apparently adequate solution to a problem. The result is that better solutions are often not found because of this premature termination of searching. We will propose several alternative solutions.

One standard alternative is to *remain as is*. It is an alternative to changing something and, occasionally at least, turns out to be a reasonable resolution of the problem. In such instances, it is the best solution because of obvious inability to implement other solutions (for example, inordinate costs), because of great risks associated with other solutions, or because of extreme uncertainty associated with the outcomes of other solutions.

A second alternative is to put *supervisory pressure on personnel to improve performance.* This too, is a fairly standard solution, and may work when the problem is sheer laziness of personnel. The expectation is that exhortation and the implied threat of firing for substandard performance will bring about improvement.

Monetary incentives for improved performance is a third alternative that can be considered. Increasingly larger payments can be made for closer approaches to standards. Salespeople's commissions can be a larger percentage as sales increase; order processing clerks can be given incentive increments for each *x* percent of on-time performance above some baseline; shipping clerks similarly could be given increasingly larger incentive payments as they performed at levels above a baseline or as they approached a set standard.

Closer supervision is a fourth alternative that can be considered as a solution to the problem. The expectation here is that, as in the supervisory pressure solution in the second alternative, personnel will perform better if pressured, especially if the person who is the source of pressure breathes down their necks and watches their behavior at close range.

A fifth alternative would be to have *each person keep a performance log* in which actual performance would be recorded. The record would provide immediate feedback as to how well a person was meeting, exceeding, or undersubscribing standards.

Finally, a last alternative might be to institute a practice of *positive reinforcement by supervisors.* Personnel would be given supervisory approval whenever they performed according to procedures and/or standards. There would be no punishment if they did not.

Not enough is known about the events at Emery Air Freight Corporation to know whether a list of alternatives such as the above was ever drawn up or contemplated. The probability is low, since Vice President Feeney had attended a seminar on Organizational Behavior Modification—the application of B. F. Skinner's theory of operant conditioning. This theory led to the view that to get people to behave in desired ways, their behavior should be reinforced positively (rewarded) whenever they emitted the desired behavior. Feeney had become a devoted convert to that view.

Nor will we attempt an evaluation of the various alternatives to see which one might be the best strategic solution for the problem. We do not really have enough information about the situation to do that. We can note the procedures necessary to evaluate the possible courses of action. The basic technique of evaluation is *cost-benefit analysis.* Given a desired objective or outcome, the analysis should show which of the alternatives will provide the best pattern of low costs and high benefits.

Evaluation should begin with a screening of the alternatives to see if any of them are impossible to implement because of uncontrollable elements in the environment. For example, the personnel involved might be represented by a union which is unalterably opposed to monetary incentive systems. In that case, the third strategic solution must be deleted from the list to be considered.

The remaining alternatives then should be carefully examined in terms of their costs and benefits using common criteria wherever possible—dollar revenues and costs, motivational effects, and payout period, for example. An attempt should be made to assess the probability of success of each alternative when properly implemented. One alternative with a lower payout than another may be chosen because it has a higher estimated probability of success.

During the cost-benefit analysis, it may also become clear that some alternatives appear to zero in more accurately than others upon the objective sought in the organizational change. Finally, some alternatives may be easier to implement than others. This is a topic that will be dealt with at greater length in a subsequent section of this chapter.

In summary, then, alternative strategic solutions need to be compared and contrasted in terms of costs and benefits, possibility of implementation, probability of success, accuracy of resolving the problem of reaching the intended objective, and relative feasibility of implementation.

As already noted, the record provided about events at Emery Air Freight Corporation does not include any information about the consideration of alternative strategic solutions. We do know that Vice President Feeney was convinced that positive reinforcement was the means to the company's salvation and enhancement. Perhaps there was no consideration of alternatives. The proposed solution for the problem in any case, was positive reinforcement, or in our terms, Organizational Behavior Modification.

Specific tactics of implementation had to be included for each of the three operations slated for improvement. With respect to the salespersons, the tactics were to convert the sales training program from the conventional seminar-type training to programmed learning. The new technique provided the sales staff with constant feedback on how well they were doing, a kind of built-in positive reinforcement. The end objective of the training was to get the customer to respond to a salesperson's call by making a commitment to take some positive action leading to the use of Emery's services. These commitments were self-reinforcing, and the sales manager could also reinforce positively when reviewing the performance of the sales force.

To provide the basis for performance improvement in customer service operations, clerks kept daily checklists on which they indicated the calls that had been returned within the standard of 90 minutes. The direct feedback from the checklist was further reinforced by praise and recognition from supervisory personnel.

A similar tactic was used with the containerized shipping operation. Here, too, a checklist provided feedback for reinforcement. Unlike the experiences of most organizations which undergo change, Emery Air Freight Corporation personnel apparently did not resist the changed behavior required by the implementation of Organizational Behavior Modification. Perhaps that aspect of change was simply left out of the narrative provided. Resistance is quite normal and should be expected. As already noted, this topic will be treated at length later.

The end result of the organizational changes made at Emery were significant improvements which brought about a better fit between the environment and the organization. For example, sales during the first years after the change in sales-force training and positive reinforcement for results went to $79.8 million from $62.4 million, a 28 percent increase. In the previous years, the sales increase had been only 11 percent. In the customer service operation, on-time performance went from 30 percent to 95 percent. The 45 percent achievement of standard in the containerized shipping operation escalated to 95 percent also. All in all, Emery Air Freight Corporation appears to have achieved an improved fit between itself and its environment as the consequence of organizational change.

With a different situation facing some other company, of course, we would have illustrated organizational change with one of the other techniques. To reiterate the point of the contingency approach to management, the technique to use depends upon the situation.

ANALYSIS OF MODEL

Let us take a more detailed look at the components of the model of organizational change. The intent here is to identify characteristics of these that logic and experience have shown to be universal.

The Environment

Take the first component of the model: *environment.* From this environment arise the external demands which are made upon the organization. These demands, in the broadest interpretation of that term, include opportunities and problems or constraints. *Opportunities* are those events, trends, and possible future states which facilitate carrying out the mission of the organization and enable it to achieve its objectives. The most desirable opportunity, of course, is demand for the organization's products, programs, and services. *Constraints* include problems, threats, and imposed requirements which, conversely, may retard achievement of mission and objectives. An economic recession, for example, is usually seen as an environmental constraint. Opportunities and constraints abound in the three major sections of the environment: social, political, and economic.

The Social Environment   Events and trends in the social environment can have immediate or delayed impacts upon the organization. Probable future states, of course, will have future impacts. The first announcement of a new, completely safe, and foolproof birth control technique can have an immediate impact on the producers of inferior control techniques; a trend toward delayed family formation will have different short- and long-term implications for the furniture and leisure industries; expected changes in age composition in the population will seriously affect all organizations at some future date. Furthermore, what is an opportunity today may become a problem tomorrow, especially if an organization's competitors seize the advantages first.

In general, one can look for a variety of forms of social environmental change. Population change is one of these. The center of population gravity has been moving west for many decades, and now it seems to be taking a detour to the south. Elderly age groups are increasing as a percentage of the total population and almost one of every two marriages contracted ends in divorce. Social norms are changing, also. We are entering a more egalitarian era in social relations. Lower voting and drinking ages, unconventional clothing and hairstyles, and a preference for pot over alcohol and rock over classical music increasingly characterize young people. The young are also increasingly better educated than the elderly. Older men jog and older women have facelifts, all to keep in tune with the health and beauty norms increasingly established by the younger set. Environmental conservation, consumerism, and gun control also originate in the social environment.[12]

The Political Environment   Phenomena in the social environment can affect the organization directly or may be mediated by the political environment. Changing life-styles will have a direct and immediate economic impact upon organization in terms of the demands for different kinds of products. On the other hand, conservation, product standards, and gun control are the kinds of social demands that are legislatively imposed upon the organization.

Most if not all of the demands originating in the political environment probably have some social antecedents. But they can be spontaneous also. And, of course, the economic environment can pressure the political powers to pass legislation that will affect the social or economic environments.

The more obvious political demands include the regulation of wages and hours, working conditions (for example, the requirements of the

Occupational, Safety, and Health Act), unionization, product standards, and environmental pollution. Legislation and administrative regulation define the nature and character of corporate organization, impose constraints on the behavior of corporate offices, and establish standards for financial accountability. Most important of all, the fiscal and monetary powers of the federal government have impacts upon the economic environment and therefore upon organizations.

The Economic Environment   Gross national product (GNP) is the central fact of the economic environment for most organizations, whether profit or not-for-profit, since it may have the single greatest influence on revenues and expenditures. By-products of GNP include personal disposable income and the attendant standard of living, price levels, availability of capital, etc. There is a reverse effect here, also.

It is changes in the economic environment that usually have the most dramatic and drastic effects upon organizations. The energy crisis, the deterioration of the dollar in international money markets, foreign and domestic competition—such events and trends tend to change the demands made upon the organization in terms of opportunities and constraints with which it is faced.

The most immediate subsector of the economic environment which affects the organization is the industry in which it operates. Changes in the industry such as in price, in the size of markets, the introduction of new products by competitors, the development of new technology, a sudden dearth or surplus of raw materials, mergers and acquisitions of competitors, and a host of similar transitions leave little room for an organization to survive and prosper if it is indifferent to such happenings.

Events, trends, and possible future states of the environment, then, constitute a set of challenges that face the organization. These demands upon the organization, seen as opportunities and constraints, require reactions that will maximize gains and minimize losses.

Organizational Structure and Weaknesses

To respond effectively to the challenges in its environment, an organization needs to exploit its strengths and bolster, if it can, its weaknesses. To do these things, it must know what they are.

To help in their identification, we can define strengths as those organizational attributes which enable it to perform well and weaknesses as those attributes which force it to perform poorly. Organizational strengths and weaknesses can best be understood in the context of a brief review of organizational design and control.

Essentially, there are two forces at work in any organization—

bureaucratization and *innovation*. They tend to have opposite but complementary effects. The former tends to make the organization stable; the latter, flexible. Although complementary, the two processes nevertheless conflict to a certain degree. Both of them are designed to reduce the effects of uncertainty. Bureaucratization reduces the uncertainty in the *internal environment* of the organization, and innovation reduces the uncertainty in the *external environment*. Let us see how.

Bureaucratization   Bureaucratization means establishing habitual ways of doing the organization's work.[13] What that work is is given by the organization's mission. The scope and depth of the work will be determined by the ability of the organization to achieve its objectives as it interacts with its environment.

After its inception, the members of an organization discover, if they do not already know, that there are four basic functions that an organization must engage in if it is to be a viable entity in its environment. It must *procure* resources for its activities; it must *produce* goods or services; it must *market* its products; and it must *finance and account* for its activities.

Chaos will result if everybody tries to do everything. Hence, there is an initial division of labor with respect to these functions. As the organizational members go on about their work, they learn how to do things better. Their skills improve; they gain additional knowledge about the transformation processes involved in their work; they discover that some ways of doing things are better than others; they find that some combination of resources—labor, machinery, and materials—results in greater efficiency. They are experiencing the benefits of the *learning or experience curve*. To put it simply, productivity increases as a person's or organization's experience in doing specified work increases.

What managers learn from experience is structured into the organizational design. The initial division of labor is modified and refined as workers and managers carry out their specialized roles. As demand and output increase, new jobs and additional positions, and even new organizational units, are established. The new organizational units and new jobs in turn may be modified in the light of further experience. Personnel also enjoy or suffer the consequences of experience. They are promoted, demoted, transferred, or given raises as they perform over time.

Experience also shows managers that some decision guidelines are better than others. Organizational mission is clarified; targets for objectives become more realistic over time; recurring decision situations suggest the formulation of specific policies to facilitate operational decision making; task experience shows that some sequences or methods of operations give greater yields than others and these become standard procedures; task experience also results in the determination of output and operational work standards which signal to personnel what is expected of them as they go about their jobs; finally, rules of individual and interpersonal behavior develop in the form of "thou shalt . . ." and "thou shalt not. . . ." These decision rules or norms become, in effect, the customs of the organizational society.

The structure of jobs and job relationships resulting from the division of labor and the development of decision-making guidelines or the normative pattern result in both differences and similarities in the behavior of organizational members.

Division of labor in an organization has the effect of differentiating the behavior of people. That is the consequence of specialization. One person's job is different from another's. By contrast, common norms of behavior represented by the decision-making guidelines have the effect of making the behaviors of personnel more nearly alike. Although these different outcomes appear to have countervailing consequences, that is not actually the case. For the total effect of organizational design—the job structure and the normative pattern—is to make behavior more predictable.

It is reasonable to expect the behavior of a person in the manufacturing division to be directed toward production at low unit costs. Similarly, a person in the marketing division can be expected to focus on increasing sales volume or sales profitability. Objectives, policies, and procedures also arouse predictable expectations in behavior. If it is company policy to offer a six-month warranty on appliances, then we can reasonably expect that personnel involved in customer relations will abide by that decision rule if anything goes wrong with an appliance.

The set patterns of behavior which result from the process of bureaucratization described above under normal circumstances has predictable results: a decrease in the unit cost of outputs. For example, in the production function, the Boston Consulting Group has found that doubling the volume of output over time can result in unit cost reductions of from 20 to 30 percent.[14]

There is another, more subtle, and equally predictable result of bureaucratization. To a greater or lesser extent personnel tend to internalize their job role requirements and the normative guidelines for decision making. That is, habituated to the requirements of their job and the relevant decision-making guidelines, they do what they do not merely because at one time it seemed to be the best way to do it; now they may do it that way because they have done it that way in the past. In effect, means have become ends.

Innovation Meanwhile, the environment has been knocking ceaselessly on the organizational door. The demand for the organization's products, programs, or services has gone up or gone down; new competitors have entered and old competitors exited from the industrial arena; great strides have been made in technology; legislation or an administrative regulation has changed the minimum wage, product standards, or shop safety requirements; changing life-styles have compounded the problems of recruiting and motivating employees in the factory and office.

The organization cannot and does not remain completely oblivious of environmental demands. It responds with innovation to at least some of the demands made upon it. Innovation occurs when an organization responds to an environmental demand by changing organizational structure, process, or behavior—or any combination of these factors—so as to be able to supply the demand which it perceives. A change in structure might involve the establishment of an industrial relations unit in the personnel department to deal with the newly recognized union; a change in the communication process might be required by government demands that the organization report certain information quarterly; a change in behavior is exemplified by a switch in leadership style by one or more managers as they perceive changes in the life-styles of newly recruited organizational members. Any of these kinds of innovations might require change in one or both of the other factors.

The most obvious innovative response is to fluctuations in product demand. The organization allocates more resources when it wants to increase its supply or withdraws resources if it wishes to curtail the supply. The organization is also likely to respond to legal demands, such as avoiding discrimination in hiring and meeting new product safety requirements. These kinds of responses may require varying degrees of innovation, from a little to a lot.

An organization may fail to respond to its environment, however, with respect to other, not-so-obvious changes in demand. For example, there may be potential, untapped segments of a product market awaiting recognition in the form of product innovation. Or a firm may have the opportunity to enter a market when the product is in the growth stage of the product life cycle, as an electronics component manufacturer had some years ago. The firm produced components for a hand-calculator manufacturer but did not seriously entertain the thought of producing calculators itself at that time. When it finally began to think seriously of the venture, the firm decided it could not compete with the companies already entrenched in the market.

Contributions of Bureaucratization and Innovation   Both bureaucratization and innovation contribute to the strengths and weaknesses of an organization. They are neither good nor bad as such, but only as they increase or decrease the organization's prospects of surviving and prospering.

Bureaucratization contributes to the strengths of the organization insofar as the resulting organizational design reflects efficient and effective ways of fulfilling its mission and achieving its objectives. For example, a company with a single homogeneous product line can operate best under a functional division of labor. But if an organization has multiple, heterogeneous product lines, it will do better with product division of labor. Similarly, a company that has fine-tuned its customer service policies to an existing buyers' market should do well as a consequence. Overall, if an organization has learned its lessons from its experiences it should be able to design an efficient and effective structure for operations.

But not every organization learns equally well, and failure to learn the right lessons results in organizational weaknesses. A firm may have excessive or inadequate specialization in the division of labor; its production procedures may be outmoded, its salespeople improperly motivated, its accounting practices limited to recording revenues and expenditures when it should also be engaged in cost accounting.

In a similar way, the process of innovation may also contribute to the strengths and weaknesses of the organization. Innovative activities will yield strengths when they are based upon accurate perceptions of events, trends, and likely future occurrences in the environment, with the nature of the responses accurately geared to the organization's capabilities. For example, a firm may be in a market highly responsive to new product introduction. Its strength is that it endeavors to be the leader in new product introduction. When it is not the leader, it attempts to enter the market during the growth stage of the product life cycle; whenever it cannot do this, it wisely refrains from entering that product market altogether. Another company may emphasize production technology because low profit margins in the industry require low unit costs. The firm may, therefore, be constantly on the alert for new developments in technology so as to keep constant downward pressure on costs. Still another company may be adept at horizontal integration, and will successfully buy out struggling firms and infuse them with the right amount of capital and controls to make them more productive.

Improperly carried out, innovative activities can result in organizational weaknesses. They can be the consequence of horizontal integration, as in the preceding example, but with an inability of the parent firm to provide sufficient capital or establish adequate controls over the subsidiary. Indeed, many of the acquisitions and mergers of the 1960s and 1970s, meant to be innovative practices, ended up as disasters or at least failures because of organizational indigestion.

Environment-Organization Fit

Whenever the environmental opportunities and problems are juxtaposed with the organization's strengths and weaknesses, we can determine whether there is a good or poor fit between the environment and the organization. A good fit means that the organization is able to satisfy the demands made upon it with an adequate supply of outputs while making little or no change in its structure, processes, and behaviors. Thus, the organization might discover that the demand for its product will be quite stable for the foreseeable future and that it will be able to supply what it sees as its share of the market for the forecast period, perhaps five years. There would be a poor fit between the environment and organization, conversely, if the forecast period showed a sudden decline in demand at just the time that the firm is bringing a new plant on stream.

Problem Definition

Assuming that there is somewhat of a poor fit between the environment and organization, we need to define the problem and/or opportunity which faces the organization. The most obvious way to do this is to prepare the definition specifically in terms of the gap between the environmental demand and the organization's capacity to supply. Such an approach is tenable if analysis has shown that there is only one area of poor fit, for example, greater potential product demand than supply capability. But unless the organization is quite small and continually and accurately monitors its environments—a combination of very low probability—that outcome is not likely.

Rather, we can assume that, big or small, the organization is unlikely to perceive all problems and opportunities as it scans its environment at any point in time. It may overlook a constraint or an opportunity at one time only to be confronted by it at another, sometimes with larger and more obvious dimensions. There is reason to believe, in fact, that organizations fail to perceive many changes in the environment—or perceiving them, take no action—until the cumulative impact is considerable and change clearly becomes overwhelmingly more desirable than maintaining the status quo.

There is a likelihood, therefore, that when organizational members—or consultants—attempt to summarize the causes of the poor fit between environment and organization, they are likely to have a list of items rather than one or perhaps at most two specific mismatches between organization and environment. It will then frequently be possible to summarize the difficulties as errors in bureaucratization or errors in innovation—or even errors in both.

Errors in bureaucratization typically appear to be inadequacies rather than excesses. There may not be enough structure, for example, rather than too much. The former is more likely to be the case because organizations spend a greater part of their existence in growing and expanding rather than in shrinking and declining. Normally the growth rate is slow and the decline rate is fast. During growth, emphasis will more likely be upon expanding supply capabilities to meet demand as quickly and informally as possible, rather than deliberately and formally, and in due course. It may be more efficient in the long run to make formal changes in structure, process, and behavior, but the demand is immediate and in the short run. Therefore, it is easy to rationalize the responses to be operationally oriented—just do more of the same as quickly as possible—rather than organizational-change-oriented—let's reorganize the manufacturing division before we hire all those new people.

Thus, many organizations tend to evolve in a hodgepodge rather than orderly fashion, generally making only the changes that are absolutely necessary. As already noted it will less likely be the case that there will be excessive bureaucratization, for example, establishing an elaborate, and presently unnecessary, organizational structure or establishing policies and procedures in great detail for trivial concerns of the moment. It does happen sometimes, however.

Inadequacies and excesses can be found in the innovative practices of organizations also. Simple failure to perceive the need to change is perhaps matched by simple failure to bring about change even when recognized as necessary.

For example, a company may over time perceive that it is getting fewer but larger orders from its customers. The paper-processing task may be reduced as a result, but higher management may be blissfully oblivious of the fact that there is now slack time in the sales order processing department. Personnel in the department, by contrast, are blissfully aware of the slack time, and following Parkinson's law, spread the work out to fill up the time. After all, who wants to lose a job?

Even if higher management is aware of the reduced workload of the sales order processing department, it may be reluctant to act. There may be more important things to do, or perhaps all the people in the department have high levels of seniority and management fears the impact on the morale of others from transfer, demotion, or dismissal of departmental personnel.

Excesses in innovation are often the consequences of *prematurity*, of a *haphazard approach*, and of *imitation*. For example, one firm developed an informal policy of getting American rights to foreign technological developments. In a large number of cases, it was very premature. Having paid large licensing fees, the company was frequently unable to interest American firms in sublicensing the developments. As a result, its investments lay fallow for many years. An organization can also approach innovation in a haphazard fashion. One firm developed new products primarily in terms of the interests of the president who doubled in brass as the R & D director. Because of the considerable differences in the resulting products, it was not possible to achieve any economies of scale in the production and marketing functions. Imitation as an excess in innovation is best illustrated by the acquisition of computers by business firms in the late fifties and the decade of the sixties. The capabilities of the computer aside, many firms leased or bought computers because it was the fashionable thing to do. They were usually displayed at headquarters with store-window elegance, and company presidents acted as if they had personally fathered the data processors. Meanwhile, surveys showed that the majority of the acquisitions had negative cost-benefit outcomes in the early years of installation. For example, one company ordered a computer, selected primarily on the basis of early delivery, so that it could join the ranks of computer users in its industry. The computer turned out to be adequate for some data processing operations and not for others—with a negative cost-benefit outcome overall. Only after trading it in for a different computer, more attuned to the company's needs, did the cost-benefit outcome become positive.

The foregoing discussion on problem definition has emphasized the negative aspects of the poor fit between environment and organization. That is, the emphasis has been on the poor adjustment the organization has made both in bureaucratization and innovation as it reacted to its environment. But the poor fit can also presage opportunities as well as problems. Markets may be growing; manufacturing technology may be improving; the economy may be in an upswing; company salesmen may be able to sell faster than the goods can be produced; the local union may have just elected a new president who is a more accommodating negotiator than his predecessor; the list can go on and on. These opportunities become meaningful primarily as the organization has matching strengths which can be brought to bear on the opportunities.

It is possible also, of course, to recognize opportunities which are matched by organizational weaknesses. The product markets, for example, may be changing and the firm's marketing organization is geared to selling rather than doing market research.

To the extent possible, the definition of organizational problems and opportunities should be summarized in the categories of bureaucratization and innovation. The former will include all those shortcomings in organizational design which inhibit the organization from carrying out its operations effectively. These would include such things as ill-defined roles or jobs which lead to jurisdictional disputes or which permit tasks to fall between jobs and remain undone, vague policies which result in inconsistent decisions, inadequate decision-making powers in lower echelons, outmoded management information systems which do not accurately reflect ongoing operations. All of these contribute to the inability of the organization to respond adequately to the current demands made upon it by its environment.

Opportunities for innovation should similarly be grouped together. These could include such things as strategies to capture larger shares of growing markets, a change in government regulations which favor the firm's products or services, the possibility of horizontal or vertical integration, development of new product lines, and so on.

When the *problem/opportunity definition* has been articulated with supporting data ("The organization has an inadequately specialized division of labor, especially in the marketing division, because of continuously increasing demand . . . ." "There are opportunities for sales growth both through internal development and acquisition in the following markets. . . ."), the question of what specifically to do arises.

Alternative Strategic Solution

Tentative answers are broached in the form of alternative strategic solutions. One of these should always be "remain as is." Such an alternative has a comparative and absolute value. By sketching out the future implications of not trying to change the fit between the organization and its environment, the remain-as-is alternative helps to show up the comparative advantages of the other alternatives. The absolute value of the remain-as-is alternative is that it does point up the consequence of not changing. Indeed, sometimes this alternative is eventually chosen when other alternatives prove not to be viable.

In the same way that the definition of problem/opportunity is generalized as concisely as possible, alternative strategic solutions should also be broadly summarized, with specific examples. Thus, instead of saying that "the production manager's job should be divested of responsibility for quality control, the quality-control activity should report directly to the manufacturing vice president, and a committee should be established consisting of . . . to periodically evaluate improvements in quality control," the strategic solution should emphasize what is to be achieved and how to achieve it: "The quality of products should be improved by establishing quality control as a department reporting to the manufacturing vice president and by establishing a committee consisting of . . . to evaluate progress in quality control and make recommendations to . . . ." The second example gives the essence of strategy in a way that the first does not.

Ordinarily, strategies for organizational change will be aimed at improving organizational design (bureaucratization) or changing operations or outputs (innovation) or both. The example above is a combination of these: quality of output (innovation) is to be changed by a change in responsibilities and reporting relationships (organizational design).

While there may be an almost unlimited number of alternatives that can be developed for all imaginable situations, possible changes can probably be categorized as (1) involving *changes in existing relationships* (the transfer of the quality-control function from the production manager to the manufacturing vice president in the example above), (2) *the addition of new ingredients* (establishment of a committee, as in the example above) and (3) the *deletion of an existing ingredient* (abolishing a job, dropping an old product).

The question of how long to search for alternatives inevitably arises at this point. It is more than likely that, to the extent that the problem or opportunity is not unique to the experience of the decision maker, fairly conventional solutions will present themselves at first. While there is nothing wrong with using conventional solutions for conventional problems, there is also something to be said for attempting to go beyond the obvious whenever there is any reason to think that additional effort may bring additional rewards. The tendency to "satisfice"—to settle for the first reasonably adequate-appearing solution—probably should be resisted. Nor is there any magic to the number 3, as exemplified in the number of strategic solutions indicated in Figure 1-1. Sometimes an organization has only a "go–no go" set of alternatives: do only one thing that is open to it or do nothing. At other times there may be literally no limit on the number of alternatives that can be developed.

Yet a limit must be set, and in general it can be done in terms of a cost-benefit approach. Basically, the decision to cut off further search for alternatives should be made when additional alternatives do not suggest benefits equal to the additional cost of searching. Of course, time pressures may also dictate the end of developing additional alternatives.

Choice of Strategic Solution

It is easy enough to say that the alternative strategic solution should be chosen which best improves the fit between the organization and its environment. But every organization is constantly faced with a set of constraints that limit what appears feasible at any point in time. The environment itself may pose obstacles. Demand for the firm's products is increasing and the obvious alternative is to build a new plant. But interest rates are high and stock-price averages are low, making it both difficult to borrow and to issue additional stock to raise capital. Under such conditions, subcontracting may turn out to be more feasible than expanding production facilities.

Internally, too, there may be a variety of constraints which may pose problems for the selection of an alternative strategic solution. One form of reorganization may promise more benefits than another—if personnel changes are ignored. But if the "better" solution is more likely to arouse more antagonisms among personnel than some other, that anticipation may suggest a solution that is more acceptable.

Problems also arise in considering alternatives in terms of *short-range* and *long-range costs and benefits*. Sometimes a solution will give an attractive short-range combination of costs and benefits but a very unattractive long-term combination. The reverse can also occur.

A related form of difficulty arises when a solution appears *ideal* but involves *real* short-term problems which prohibit moving directly to the ideal solution. The apparent impossibility of adopting an ideal solution can sometimes be overcome if it is possible to develop one or more interim steps leading to the desirable state. Assume, for example, that a senior vice president, within a few years of retirement, has not kept up with the changes in his functional specialty. In ordinary circumstances, such a person might be retired early or moved into a consultant's position to get him out of the way. But he is also a major stockholder and a member of the board of directors. Removing him, therefore, is difficult or impossible. The ideal solution will have to be delayed. But it is possible, for example, to create the position of assistant vice president and fill it with a person who has the specialized knowledge plus the ability to take over the vice presidency when the incumbent retires. Major reorganizations of the firm may have to be handled in this way also, since a drastic restructuring cannot be carried out overnight but will require a relatively long period of transformation.

Whenever possible, *common denominators* by which alternatives can be compared should be used. The obvious common denominator is money; others include time, distance, and productivity. Monetary payoffs provide the easiest mode of comparison, as Table 1-1 shows. The alternatives given are solutions for what to do with product demand increasing, with not enough idle capacity to take care of all of the demand.

The *environmental conditions* (or states of nature, as they are frequently called) can affect the payoffs. The assumed environmental condition in Table 1-1 is *certainly*, that is, the assumption that the state of nature will

Table 1-1   Alternative Payoffs under Conditions of Certainty

Strategic alternative	Payoff
Build new plant	$1,000,000
Subcontract	750,000
Do nothing	500,000

not change, that the increased demand will occur with a probability of 1.0.

If there is some unknown chance that the environment will change, then there may be two or more possible states of nature and there will be alternative payoffs for each strategic alternative. Table 1-2 shows payoffs under conditions of *uncertainty*.

In the event that it is possible to attach objective probabilities to the different states of nature, the payoffs occur under conditions of *risk*. It is easier to make a choice under conditions of risk because of what is called *expected value*. For each alternative, each payoff is multiplied by its probability of occurrence. The outcomes are summed and the result is the expected value. Example (probabilities are given in the calculation):

$$(1,000,000 \times 0.6) + (500,000 \times 0.3) + (250,000 \times 0.1)$$
$$= \text{expected value of } \$775,000$$

For the payoffs given in Table 1-2, the first strategic alternative gives the highest expected value.

The final environmental condition under which a decision may have to be made is called *conflict*. This condition is usually associated with strategies aimed at product markets but can happen in connection with any contemplated organizational change in which opposition to change is to be expected. Under conditions of conflict, the competitor or other opponent can be expected to take some countervailing action to offset strategic change. Thus, if one company drops its product price, a competitor may also drop its price and/or extend the warranty period on its product. For all but environmental conditions of certainty, it appears desirable not only to pick the best strategic alternative solution to the problem, but also to pick a contingent alternative if the state of nature should change.

Implementation of Solution

The implementation of an organizational change, like the implementation of any decision having complex implications, should be *programmed*.

Table 1-2   Alternative Payoffs under Conditions of Uncertainty

Strategic alternatives	States of nature and alternative payoffs		
	A	B	C
Build new plant	$1,000,000	$500,000	$250,000
Subcontract	750,000	250,000	0
Do nothing	500,000	0	−250,000

The program will consist of the list of resources that will be required to effect the change, scheduled dates of their procurement, the assignment of responsibilities to organizational members, inclusive dates when the various activities should be carred out, and similar matters. Much of what goes into the program will already be known since these matters will have been discussed during the choice of the strategic solution.

The program, in turn, should be converted into a *budget*. Again, there will have been at least reasonably good approximations of cost made during the comparison of alternatives, but now estimates need to be made even more carefully.

The budget itself will constitute a *standard* which will serve as a benchmark for successful implementation of the organizational change. Other standards are needed also. For example, the schedule may be very important and one or more deadlines can be selected to gauge progress toward completion.

Improved Environment-Organization Fit

Thus, with a program, budget, and deadline dates, the *paperwork* for changing the organization will have been completed. Unfortunately, bringing about organizational change is not as simple as ordering and receiving a new piece of equipment or erecting a building from blue-prints. Instead, it is usually in the implementation stage of organizational change that the greatest difficulties can occur, difficulties that may determine just how much of an improved fit between environment and organization is achieved with the strategic solution. We turn now to that question.

RESISTANCE TO ORGANIZATIONAL CHANGE

The question of fit concerns *organizational design*. The answer can be found in a review of structure and the factors that affect program change.

Organizational Structure

At any point in time, the organizational structure consists of a set of roles and role relationships. The roles—or jobs—reflect the division of labor, and role relationships reflect hierarchical coordination, the familiar set of superior-subordinate relationships which constitute the chain of command. Any change in the organization is likely to affect some if not all roles and role relationships. There is thus potential for any one person to experience any one of the following consequences from organizational change:

1   No change in status
2   An improvement in status
3   A decline in status

It is people's expectations about status outcome that will probably affect their attitude toward organizational change. An expectation of no change in status is likely to result in a neutral stance toward change. Not all roles and role relationships are subject to alteration in organizational change. For example, changes in the marketplace might require changes in the marketing department but leave the personnel department unchanged.

Those who foresee an improvement in their status, of course, will be enthusiastic advocates of change. Whether what is involved is more power, higher salary, promotion, larger office, more subordinates, or whatever, few people can resist the lure of such temptations. Additionally, there may be considerable anxiety, frustration, and other unsettling and negative feelings and attitudes toward the *present* situation. Almost any change may then appear desirable.

Expectations of a decline in status will inevitably bring about resistance. People who are comfortably settled in their jobs, are on top of current operations, and are satisfied with the current level of power, position, and salary may find any intimation of change disturbing. Such people may sense that any change may be for the worse.

Resistance in such cases may be understood from a cost/benefit perspective. Whatever position a person occupies in an organization, achieving that position has involved a set of costs. These include education, prior experience, competition which resulted in getting the job, learning the particular tasks in the present position, developing habitual behavior for discharging the requisite tasks, and the like. These costs can be viewed as an investment in the job. The benefits are whatever the incumbent sees as desirable results of occupying the position: salary, prestige, power, security, etc.

With impending organizational change, people may feel threatened about whatever they see as satisfying in their jobs. Employees' investments in their work may be wiped out if they are fired, or diminished if they are transferred or demoted. Benefits will, accordingly, be lost or decreased. It is not a pleasant prospect. Acquiescence in it is unlikely.

Kurt Lewin has suggested that where the driving forces (read people) for change equal the restraining forces favoring the status quo, there is likely to be, if not stability, at least a situation of equilibrium, perhaps an uneasy one.[15] When a plan for change has been developed, however, it is clear that the driving forces have won out over the restraining forces. But perhaps the concept of winning is inappropriate in organizational matters. Winning could result in a Pyrrhic victory if the losers should sabotage the plan for change.

Consequently a more appropriate strategy, as opposed to strengthening the driving forces for change, is to weaken and win over the restraining forces in the organization. If that is possible, then it is more likely that the eventual relationship between the proponents and opponents of organizational change will be one of cooperation rather than conflict.

It may be "better late than never" to be concerned about opposition to organizational change, but it is *better earlier than later.* Because some resistance by some persons to change is normal, it should be expected and should be a continuous item on the agenda. It is possible to pinpoint the obvious sources of resistance. If a person's job is to be abolished, or if employees will be laid off because they don't have the skills contemplated for their new jobs, or if people will have to be transferred to other departments, then we can automatically expect resistance.

But resistance will crop up in other than the obvious places. This is because all parts of an organization are linked together; because of this interdependence, we can expect that an intended change in one part of an organization will likely have an unintended change in another. For example, if a product or service is discontinued, we know that all personnel directly connected with its production will be affected. But how about the product manager who loses a part of his or her product line or the buyer in the purchasing department who secures the raw materials, or the clerk in the personnel department who handles the records for the people who produce the product? They, too, may suffer some consequences.

Experience also plays a part in the nature and scope of resistance to change. If past programs of change have been unsuccessful and demoralizing, then the likelihood of resistance this time is increased. Conversely, if change experiences have been rewarding, they will be anticipated with some enthusiasm.

How can support for change be generated and encouraged? One condition appears to be the need for support by higher management. Personnel generally look to higher authority to legitimate change. Openly supporting proposals for innovation may be seen as dangerous if upper echelons of managers, especially the senior executives in the organization, do not explicitly espouse the changes. If they do not, lower-level personnel will quite rightly fear to stick their necks out, concerned that premature exposure of their stand may incur the wrath of their superiors.

Thus it is necessary not only for higher management to indicate the need for change but also to be as candid as it possibly can be about impending innovation to generate a high level of trust and acceptance. Probably the surest way to achieve those twin goals is to secure not only the cooperation but also the participation of the personnel who will be affected by the transformations. There is evidence that planning future tasks improves commitments and productivity.

Participation can begin at the highest level and work its way down the organizational ladder. Such an approach reinforces the perception of commitment by higher authority and enhances consistency in the making of major or crucial decisions in the change process. It is important, of course, for higher management not to anticipate or foreclose decisions that should properly be made at lower echelons. Thus, the senior executives can make the major decisions which are properly in their jurisdiction, then invite middle managers to make follow-up and subsidiary decisions, and so on.

Although commitment to change must be manifest in higher echelons for success, it is not necessary for the participative process to work its way down the hierarchy. As an example, some lower-level members in an organization concluded that the firm needed a more comprehensive, integrated data processing system than the company had at that time. The company had espoused a "bottoms-up" approach to management for many years and so after informing higher authority of their conclusion, the lower-level personnel established themselves as a task force and examined the organization's data processing requirements. Their recommendations were submitted to department and then to division heads for review, and eventually the solution for the firm's data processing requirements was approved by the president and board of directors.

Wherever possible, participative activities should be undertaken in small peer groups. A group context provides opportunities for interaction and the exchange of ideas on a spoken basis. Oral communication provides more flexibility for tentative ideas than written communications, which seem to take on a rigid life of their own, independent of those who prepared them. The peer aspect of the group also facilitates communication since people are more likely to voice their opinions in the presence of their equals rather than their superiors.

Factors That Affect Program Change

There are organizational characteristics that apparently affect the rate of program change, that is, the addition of new products or services. These characteristics are complexity, centralization, formalization, stratification, production rate, efficiency, and morale. In addition to these internal characteristics of organization, it appears that the relationship between the organization and its environment has an impact on organizational change.[16] We will examine each of these factors briefly.

Complexity is defined as the variety of occupations and/or professions, especially those involving high levels of knowledge such as engineering, to be found in an organization. The greater the variety or number of occupations/professions, the greater the complexity. Complexity is directly related to the rate of program change. That is, the greater the complexity, the greater the rate of program change. Presumably the variety of knowledge held by organizational members brings a variety of views about what the organization should be doing.

Centralization is defined as the concentration of decision-making power in a limited number of persons at the top of the organizational pyramid. Centralization is inversely related to program change. The greater the centralization, the lower the rate of program change. The rationale here seems to be that where power is concentrated, the power-holders have structured the organization to suit themselves and cannot easily be challenged by subordinates who have very limited decision-making power.

Formalization reflects the degree to which roles and role relationships in the organization are specified by job descriptions and rules, respectively. The enforcement is as important as the existence of specifications and rules. Usually they are published as job descriptions and organizational policies and procedures. There is an inverse relationship between formalization and program change: the greater the formalization, the lower the rate of program change.

The differential distribution of rewards—money and prestige—to personnel results in organizational *stratification*. Monetary rewards may include stock options and special fringe benefits such as a company car. Prestige covers titles, size and location of office (janitors seldom have large corner offices with picture windows on the 18th floor), rugs on the floor and titles on the door. Stratification is inversely related to program change. That is, the greater the stratification, the lower the rate of program change. The logic here may be that those with much money and prestige are reluctant to approve organizational change lest they inadvertently lose some of their rewards.

High volume of production is thought to inhibit program change; that is, the relationship is inverse. *The higher the volume of production, the lower the rate of program change.* However, the evidence for this proposition is very limited and correlational in nature. For example, companies with high levels of output have low research and development budgets and vice versa. Presumably, the larger the R & D budget, the greater the number of innovative ideas and, therefore, the greater the amount of program change.

Efficiency has an effect on program change. Efficiency has to do with relative unit cost of output; the more efficient a process, the lower the unit cost. Hence, efficiency is adversely affected by program change because change introduces initially unpredictable factors into a program and the costs of coping with them increase unit cost. Therefore, the greater the emphasis on efficiency, the lower the rate of program change.

The final internal organizational factor that affects the rate of program change is *morale* or job commitment. The relationship is inverse; the higher the morale the greater the rate of program change. Since change ordinarily introduces stresses and strains due to coming uncertainties, the commitment from higher morale is probably an offsetting factor, making organizational change more palatable.

The external factor in program change, *the relationship between the organization and its environment,* seems to be an amalgam of the seven internal factors discussed above. To keep matters simple, we can characterize the organization-environment relationship as *dynamic* or *static.* In the dynamic relationship the internal factors have values which facilitate change: complexity is high, while centralization, formalization, and the other factors are low. In the static relationship the seven internal factors have opposite values. In other words, the structure and functioning of the organization appear to be responses, and to determine the organization's responsiveness to the environment.

CHANGING BEHAVIOR

As already suggested, it would appear that when a plan of organizational change has been programmed, budgeted, standards set, and resistance overcome, then implementation would be a relatively mechanical task. That is not the case, except with changes in tangible resources such as plant, equipment, materials, and the like. It is quite otherwise with personnel. What is at issue is changing people's behavior.

Schein developed a brief conceptual model of behavioral change which is pertinent here.[17] Three interrelated processes are involved over some period of time. These processes are (1) unfreezing current behavior, (2) substituting new behavior, and (3) refreezing the new behavior.

Current behavior of personnel is likely to be habitual. Habitual behavior is learned or conditioned behavior. Faced with recurrent situations over time, people respond to stimulii in different ways, some of which prove to be fruitful and rewarding. As experience piles up, the fruitful and rewarded behavior tends to move from being fully conscious and reflective to being relatively unreflective and perhaps semiconscious.

Whether concerned with dressing for the shop or office, driving a car, controlling a milling machine, or making business decisions, repetitive behavior tends to freeze into habit. There is considerable utility in this—it leaves a person more time and effort to deal with nonroutine situations. But such behavior is not easy to unfreeze. Unfreezing is accomplished when the behavior is no longer found to be fruitful or rewarding. If a person's behavior no longer produces the intended result, or if the result is no longer wanted, or if the result is unrewarded, then the person may feel inadequate, anxious, and even disoriented.

When these negative reactions reach some critical level, the individual is ready to try substituting new behaviors for old. Generally, it is better for the individual to search for new, appropriate behaviors than to have them imposed. Where imposition cannot be avoided, it may help to have the person work out the details insofar as possible. If complete imposition is necessary, then it may be helpful to provide some extrinsic incentives to secure acceptance of specific required behaviors.

Refreezing of the new behavior into personal habits involves some general principles of learning. The individual must be motivated. The feelings of inadequacy and anxiety about old behavior will help, but typically there should be some obvious, positive incentives. The individual who tries out the new behaviors should be able to get impersonal feedback on results. Positive reinforcement from one's superior and peers will help. Punishment for failure following genuine attempts to change will not help—impersonal feedback from results should be sufficient at this point. The expected behaviors, of course, have to be made clear and unambiguous. Normally this can be done by rewriting job descriptions and revising policies and procedures.

This institutionalization of tasks makes clear on what bases those in higher authority will judge the outcomes of the new behaviors. That such new behaviors are expected to completely replace the old should also be clear. Recognizing that they could not possibly have anticipated and resolved all problems that might arise in the organizational changes planned, those in positions of higher authority also have to be prepared to make alterations as they receive feedback on implementation. In addition to problems, opportunities to improve changed tasks may also arise. Clearly, they should not be overlooked.

If the process of change has been implemented with support, sympathy, and determination on the part of higher authority and with highly motivated behavior and a spirit of cooperation by lower levels, there should now be a *better fit* between the organization and its environment. The fit will not be perfect; indeed, it may never be possible even to know if the fit is perfect. But it should be possible to tell if the adjustment of the organization to the environment has resulted in reduced problems and improved operations. Results can be measured in items of the criteria that led to the choice of the specific strategic changes that were implemented. Success will be judged to the degree that profit has increased, customer service has improved, costs and defects are down, productivity has improved, tardiness and absenteeism have declined, fewer grievances are filed, and the like.

TECHNIQUES OF ORGANIZATIONAL CHANGE

So far we have discussed organizational change as if it were a monolithic process. That is the most likely interpretation by the reader of the model of change that has been elaborated in the preceding pages. That is a reasonable interpretation. Fortunately, that is not the case.

Rather, as noted in the opening pages of this chapter, techniques have been developed which make it possible to deal in different ways with the parts of the whole process of organizational change. They will be described in greater detail in the following chapters. What follows immediately is an overview of these techniques to provide perspective for the detailed explanations.

Organizational Behavior Modification

Organizational change ultimately is a change in the behavior of organizational personnel. Therefore it is appropriate that the first technique of change discussed is Organizational Behavior Modification. We touched upon this technique in discussing the Emery Air Freight case.

Stripped of its details, it is an approach based upon the psychological law of effect: behavior which is rewarded tends to be repeated. Put in another way, behavior is a function of its consequences. If individuals repeat behavior which is rewarded, they also extinguish behavior which is not. Therefore, whether we wish to correct behavior in the sense of directing it toward an established pattern, or wish to redirect it to a new pattern, change can be accomplished by manipulating the environment and by the proper use of positive reinforcement to motivate.

Organizational Behavior Modification (O.B.Mod.), is a process carried out in five steps:

1   Identification of critical behaviors—those which apparently are in need of change. In the case of Emery Air Freight, one of the critical behaviors was the time involved in responding to a customer's request for service.

2 Measurement of initial behaviors. For example, a survey at Emery Air Freight showed that unit personnel failed to call back on time in about 50 percent of the calls checked.

3 Functional analysis of the behavior. This step attempts to analyze the causes, stimuli, and/or symptoms which bring on undesirable behavior. At Emery Air Freight, the cause was ignorance: clerks did not know they were not always responding on time.

4 Development of an intervention strategy. The intervention strategy is a solution for the problem identified in step 3. At Emery Air Freight, clerks were asked to keep a log of customer's calls and were to be positively reinforced only when the log showed an improved percentage of on-time calls.

5 Evaluation of performance to assure improvement. Feedback information needs to be evaluated to determine how well the program is working and to take remedial measures if it is not. The change at Emery air Freight was a shift from under 50 percent on standard to over 90 percent.

This brief review may have already suggested that O.B.Mod. is an organizational change technique especially relevant to changing observable, repetitive behavior, especially the behavior of nonmanagerial employees. That has been its major use so far, as Luthans demonstrates in Chapter 2. It may prove viable for managerial work also, and therefore on an organization-wide basis.

Management by Objectives

Like Organizational Behavior Modification, Management by Objectives (MBO) is also directed to organizational change by changing the specific behavior of individuals. As Odiorne points out in Chapter 3, however, there are many differences.

A major difference is that MBO is more likely to be concerned with managerial, technical, and professional personnel. This is so because their work cannot be programmed as readily as the work of lower-level employees. Therefore, MBO is a collaborative technique. Superiors and subordinates get together to discuss the subordinate's work for some future period of time.

The need for much collaboration stems from conclusions reached on the basis of both experience and research: superiors and subordinates tend to have very different views of the work of the subordinates. They can differ by as much as 25 percent. Hence, by getting together, they can minimize differences in their views of the objectives toward which the subordinates are working and come to mutual agreements on subordinates' objectives and plans for the future. Information on results is fed back to both superiors and subordinates and they discuss these results periodically. Where necessary, changes in plans are made to facilitate on-target achievement. The follow-up meetings are essentially performance appraisals and consequently provide information useful in decisions about raises and promotions for subordinates.

Although MBO as a process takes place between a superior and each of her or his subordinates, the superior coordinates the plans and objectives of the subordinates, as the superior's supervisor coordinates the next higher level of management. This coordination is carried out at both higher and lower levels.

The overall assumption, then, is that, through a process of adjusting managers' objectives and plans to the organization's needs, organizational change will take place on a continuing basis.

Management Development

In many ways, Management Development, elaborated by Odiorne in Chapter 4, is especially complementary to Management by Objectives. While MBO focuses on the operational responsibilities of a manager, Management Development is a technique for creating a better fit between managers and their jobs, present or potential. Thus, the results of Management Development should be an enhanced capability for doing the tasks which are planned under Management by Objectives. Indeed, performance under MBO will usually indicate the fit between manager and job, suggesting the kinds of training and education the manager needs for optimum development.

Development essentially is done both on and off the job. On-the-job training is given for the obvious purpose of improving the performance of the manager in the present position or in preparation for a higher-level one. Coaching and counseling, delegation of new decision-making powers, assignment of special tasks, increases in overall jurisdiction and responsibilities—all these modes of development help prepare the individual to better discharge organizational responsibilities.

However comprehensive the on-the-job training, it may nevertheless, not be enough, for two reasons. The first is that the manager can only be taught what the organization has already experienced. Organizational experiences vary and each organization draws different, and sometimes incorrect, lessons from them. Seldom do any but the largest organizations have the variety of experiences which straddle the industry in which it operates, thereby often denying an individual the opportunity to gain a really comprehensive understanding of the business in which the organization operates.

The second limitation of on-the-job training is the need to become acquainted with new developments in organization and management. New ideas in computer use and technology, increasing emphasis on environmental factors which impact the organization, new knowledge in the behavioral sciences, new concepts in management such as feedforward control: all these events and trends occur outside the organization. The only feasible way, then, to secure such new knowledge is to get off-the-job training and development at industry association meetings and workshops, seminars, and self-study courses by academic and professional organizations.

The basic assumption behind Management Development is the expectation that as people's knowledge increases, they will utilize that knowledge to become more efficient and effective on the job. Exposure to new and different ideas will inevitably result in the application of some of them. The consequence will be organizational change.

Although many or all of an organization's members may be involved in the three preceeding techniques of organizational change, they are essentially designed to change the behavior of individuals as individuals. The next three techniques are different. The successful application of them should result in organization-wide, or at least organizational unit, changes.

Organization Development

Wider changes usually result, for example, with Organization Development (OD). Burke describes this technique in Chapter 5. The focal points of OD are individual behavior *and* interpersonal and group relations. Change in individual behavior is the prelude to change and improvement in interpersonal and between-groups behavior. The need for OD surfaces in the presence of unhealthy interpersonal and intergroup rivalries, destructive conflict, and lack of cooperation in matters that need to be coordinated. In effect, OD is needed when organizational members are not well adjusted to working with one another.

The Organization Development process normally includes six steps:

1 *Entry* occurs when the client organization concludes that it needs help because of interpersonal problems.

2 The call for an OD consultant results in a *contract* specifying what is to be done.

3 The OD consultant *collects data* about the organization from organization members, from organizational documents, and by observation *for diagnosis.*

4 *Feedback* then takes place by the OD consultant reporting the analysis of the data.

5   Feeding back information may result in *intervention,* such as team building, training, and structural changes.

6   Finally, the OD process is *evaluated* for results.

Management Auditing

Like Organization Development, Management Auditing usually involves outside consultants who constitute the profession of management consulting. Management Auditing is also done by inside consultants. Hayden details the process in Chapter 6.

It is possible to suggest a long list of organizational problems that are grist for the Management Auditing mill. But the bulk of them can be categorized as being concerned with organizational *structure* (roles or jobs and role relationships plus the policies and procedures which constitute the organization's norms), organizational *processes* (decision making, communication, control, etc.), and organizational *tasks* (product and functional operations).

Most management consultants follow some kind of routine in analyzing the problems they are called in to resolve. The reason for this routine is that in many ways a Management Audit, in its initial stages, resembles a medical checkup for an individual. Before the doctor can diagnose and prescribe, it is necessary to ascertain the present state of the patient. So, too, the management consultant checks out the present state of the organization. In other respects, a Management Audit resembles a conventional problem-solving activity. The problem to be resolved might be: Why is the new product failure rate so high? Should the company develop products to expand its line or should it acquire firms with such products? How should the long-range planning process be structured into the company's operations? Is functional organization still appropriate for this company?

Management consultants essentially provide services for one or more of a variety of reasons as they go about a Management Audit. One of these is that there may not be any special expertise required to solve the problem within the organization. Alternatively or additionally, there may be no slack time in the ranks of the managers to handle the problems. Sometimes, also, there may be a division of opinion among top management, and an outside, objective opinion is desired. Occasionally, management may have decided what to do but wants an apparently disinterested party to reaffirm its solution and/or implement it.

The Control Cycle

The final technique of organizational change (to be discussed in Chapter 7 by Michael) is the Control Cycle of *planning* operations, *directing* implementation of plans, and *evaluating* results. This is a process of anticipating environmental changes and adapting the organization to those changes. Like Management-by-Objectives, the Control Cycle is a built-in process. It differs from MBO mainly in that it focuses on organizational structure, processes, and tasks rather than on individuals.

Control as a concept deserves emphasis in any preview of the Control Cycle. Control may readily be defined as an attempt to bring about a consequence between organizational means and ends. Means are manipulated to achieve ends. Control is either feedforward or feedback in nature.

Feedforward is synonymous with planning, which is the most essential component of the Control Cycle. Planning is the attempt to anticipate environmental change and to be prepared to adapt the organization in advance as the environment changes. In practice, planning is coupled to a feedback system of control. The coupling is necessary since the feedforward character of planning can only provide estimates of the required organization changes. The feedback from actual results helps to close the remaining gap.

Briefly put, the Control Cycle is used to bring about a dynamic equilibrium between the environmental demand for the organization's products, programs, and services and the organization's supply capabilities. Plans are proposed in terms of the organization's objectives, strengths and weaknesses, estimates of environmental change, forecasts of demand, and the formulation of strategies. A program of action, a budget, and performance standards are developed for one or more years. Higher management directs implementation of the changes required by the plans and then compares actual results with objectives and standards.

Finally, the techniques of organizational change are compared and contrasted in Chapter 8.

NOTES

1   Frederick W. Taylor, *The Principles of Scientific Management*, Harper & Row, New York, 1911.

2   Henri Fayol, *General and Industrial Management*, Constance Storrs (trans.), Sir Isaac Pitman & Sons, London, 1949, orig. publ., 1916.

3   Peter F. Drucker, *The Practice of Management*, Harper & Row, New York, 1954.

4   For a variety of excerpts illustrating the contingency approach to management theory, see F. E. Kast and J. E. Rosenzweig, *Contingency Views of Organization and Management*, Science Research Associates, Chicago, 1973. For specific applications of contingency to the everyday problems of management, see

Stephen R. Michael, "The Contingency Manager: Doing What Comes Naturally," *Management Review*, November 1976, pp. 20–31; and Michael, "Control, Contingency and Delegation in Decision Making," *Training and Development Journal*, February 1979, pp. 36–42.

5 Fred E. Fiedler, *A Theory of Leadership Effectiveness*, McGraw-Hill, New York, 1967.

6 "The *Fortune* Directory of the 500 Largest U.S. Industrial Corporations," *Fortune*, May 8, 1978, p. 238 ff.

7 "Texas Instruments Shows U.S. Business How to Survive in the 1980's," *Business Week*, Sept. 18, 1978, pp. 66–70+.

8 Erwin L. Malone, "The Non-Linear Systems Experiment in Participative Management," *Journal of Business*, vol. 48, January 1975, pp. 52–65.

9 "The Opposites: GE Grows While Westinghouse Shrinks," *Business Week*, Jan. 31, 1977, pp. 60–66.

10 Ibid.

11 The Emery case is discussed in, among other places, "New Tool: 'Reinforcement' for Good Work," *Business Week*, Dec. 18, 1971.

12 For a summary of the opinions of Americans on a variety of issues, see Marketing Concepts Inc., *The Study of American Opinion: 1978 Summary Report* U.S. News and World Report, Washington, D.C., 1978.

13 For a review of the many facets of bureaucracy and its functions, see Alvin W. Gouldner, *Patterns of Industrial Bureaucracy*, Free Press, New York, 1954.

14 "The Experience Curve—Reviewed, I. The Concept," *Perspectives*, The Boston Consulting Group, Boston, 1974.

15 Kenneth D. Benne and M. Birnbaum, "Principles of Changing," in W. Bennis, K. Benne, and R. Chin (eds.), *The Planning of Change*, Holt New York, 1969, pp. 328–335.

16 Jerald Hage and Michael Aiken, *Social Change in Complex Organizations*, Random House, New York, 1970, pp. 30–61.

17 Edgar H. Schein, "The Mechanisms of Change," in Bennis, Benne, and Chin, op. cit., pp. 98–107.

REFERENCES

Abrahamsson, Bengt: *Bureaucracy or Participation*, Sage Publications, Beverly Hills, Calif., 1977.

Albanese, Robert: "Overcoming Resistance to Stability," *Business Horizons*, vol. 13, April 1970, pp. 35–42.

Bennis, W., K. Benne, and R. Chin (eds.): *The Planning of Change*, Holt, New York, 1969.

Boulding, Kenneth E.: *The Organizational Revolution*, Harper & Row, New York, 1953.

Dalton, G., P. Lawrence, and L. Greiner (eds.): *Organizational Change and Development,* Dorsey-Irwin, Homewood, Ill., 1970.

Galbraith, Jay R.: *Organizational Design,* Addison-Wesley, Reading, Mass., 1977.

Greiner, Larry E.: "Evolution and Revolution as Organizations Grow," *Harvard Business Review,* vol. 50, July–August 1972, pp. 37–46.

Guest, Robert H., Paul Hersey, and Kenneth H. Blanchard: *Organizational Change through Effective Leadership,* Prentice-Hall, Englewood Cliffs, N.J., 1977.

Hage, Jerald, and Michael Aiken: *Social Change in Complex Organizations,* Random House, New York, 1970.

Kahn, Herman: *The Future of the Corporation,* Mason & Lipscomb, New York, 1974.

Kaufman, Herbert: *The Limits of Organizational Change,* University of Alabama Press, University, 1971.

Leavitt, Harold: *Managerial Psychology,* 3d ed., University of Chicago Press, Chicago, 1972.

Leavitt, Harold, Lawrence Pinfield, and Eugene Webb (eds.): *Organizations of the Future: Interaction with the External Environment,* Praeger, New York, 1974.

Lippitt, Gordon L.: *Organizational Renewal,* Appleton-Century-Crofts, New York, 1969.

Sashkin, M., W. Morris, and L. Herst: "A Comparison of Social and Organization Change Models," *Psychological Review,* vol. 80, 1973, pp. 510–526.

Shepard, H.: "Innovation-Resisting and Innovation-Producing Organizations," *Journal of Business,* vol. 40, 1967, pp. 470–477.

Skibbins, Gerald J.: *Organizational Evolution: A Program for Managing Radical Change,* AMACOM, New York, 1974.

Toffler, Alvin: *Future Shock,* Random House, New York, 1970.

Viola, Richard H.: *Organizations in a Changing Society,* Saunders, Philadelphia, 1977.

Part 2

Techniques of Organizational Change—Individual Oriented

2

Organizational Behavior Modification[*]

Fred Luthans

Professor of Management
University of Nebraska

Henry Jakel didn't know where to turn. The organization had installed the latest technologically advanced equipment and processes in his department. And yet there was no question that his department was near or at the bottom on all dimensions of performance (quantity and quality) and personnel areas such as tardiness, absenteeism, and turnover. The logical conclusion that Henry drew was that if it wasn't the technological side, then his problems must be the result of the human side of his department.

This was very perplexing to Henry. He had always prided himself in his ability to understand people. After all, he reasoned, he had come up through the ranks and had direct experience with working people practically all his life. Even though his formal education and training had been in his technical specialty, he had always carefully read the articles in the professional periodicals on management of people and, because of his extensive involvement in church and public service activities, he felt a genuine sympathy for people and liked them. In fact, just the other day he had called his staff together

* This chapter is adapted from Chapter 10 of the author's book *Organizational Behavior*, 3d ed., McGraw-Hill, New York, 1981.

to tell them all how much he appreciated their efforts, but that they would have to try harder.

The facts didn't lie; the department was in trouble. Henry had about decided that the only thing left for him to do was to crack down. Although this "hard-nosed" approach was against Henry's nature, he didn't see any alternative solution to his people problems. The "soft" approach obviously hadn't worked; what else was available to manage his human resources that would enable him to turn things around?

The purpose of this chapter is to give an alternative, systematic approach to the management of human resources. Managers like Henry Jakel in the opening illustration should realize that there are technologies to improve human resource management just as there are technologies to improve the physical side. This chapter is specifically devoted to an applied, environmental approach to an individually oriented organizational change effort. Observable employee behaviors and their direct impact on performance effectiveness are the focus of attention. The concepts and techniques presented in this chapter are not proposed as an alternative to the more traditional and widely accepted methods of human resource management presented in other chapters of the book. Instead, the behavioral management of change techniques in this chapter are meant to supplement and to be used in combination with the other approaches.

HISTORY AND DEFINITION OF ORGANIZATIONAL BEHAVIOR MODIFICATION

Organizational Behavior Modification, or simply O.B.Mod., has its roots in behaviorism. Modern behaviorism stems from the significant distinction that B. F. Skinner made between respondent or reflexive behaviors that are the result of classical conditioning and operant behaviors that are the result of operant conditioning. In an organization, very few of the behaviors of employees are the result of classical conditioning; the mechanistic S-R type of behaviorism is of little value to the analysis or change of organizational behaviors. Operant conditioning is a much better basis for the analysis and change of organizational behavior. Very simply, under classical conditioning the person automatically learns to respond to a stimulus, whereas under operant conditioning the person must "operate" (thus the term operant conditioning) on the environment in order to obtain a desired outcome (reward). In other words, in an operant perspective organizational behavior is largely a function of its consequences. This premise is the basis for O.B.Mod.

Behavior Modification in Other Settings

The basic principles of operant conditioning were developed by Skinner and his colleagues mainly with the use of lower-order animal subjects under highly controlled laboratory conditions. The application of Skinner's principles as a behavioral change strategy for humans had its beginnings in the mental health field. Through the systematic management of antecedent and consequent environments, psychologists were able to dramatically change the behaviors of their patients (the mentally retarded, psychotics, and autistic children). For example, mentally retarded patients were systematically taught to take care of themselves, psychotically disturbed patients who had been silent for many years were shaped to the point where they carried on a conversation, and autistic children's self-destructive behaviors were eliminated. Such changes in behaviors were often attained with patients who had had years of traditional psychotherapeutic and medical treatments with no noticeable effect. Few would dispute the fact that behavior modification techniques have had a tremendous impact on the treatment of mental patients in recent years.

The next major thrust of the application of Skinnerian behaviorism has been in education. In particular, applied behavior modification has been used in both classroom instruction techniques and child management problems. For example, it has been successfully used in the acquisition of language and other intellectual skills and in the modification of undesirable behaviors of problem children in the classroom. Many of today's teachers systematically manage their classroom environment to accelerate desirable behaviors and decelerate undesirable behaviors. Although the approach is still controversial, most educators would agree that behavior modification has had, on balance, a positive effect on educational effectiveness.

The Application to Organizational Behavior

The natural extension of the application of behavior modification from mental hospitals and classrooms would be to the more complex, less controlled environment of work organizations. Although suggestions on the use of operant techniques in managing people can be found as far back as twenty years ago,[1] only in the last few years have systematic theory, research, and application of the operant approach to human resource management been attempted. In one of the first comprehensive articles in 1969, Walter Nord pointed to the fact that the work of Skinner had been almost completely ignored by the field of management. He suggested how the operant model could be applied to training and personnel development, job design, compensation, and organization design, and in a follow-up article he described how attendance may be improved.[2] Shortly after, Luthans and White suggested the direct application of behavior modification to human resource management in general, and Adam and Scott reported research results on the application of behavioral conditioning to quality control.[3] With this start, the theoretical underpinnings and practical applications for an operant, environmental approach to human resource management called Organizational Behavior Modification (O.B.Mod.) have been developed.[4]

Figure 2-1 briefly traces the theoretical paths that lead up to O.B.Mod. As shown, O.B.Mod. is the result of two separate paths of development. On the one path is the development of behaviorism into behavior modification and on the other is the development of the behavioral approach to management into organizational behavior. The combination of these two paths of development is O.B.Mod. The approach was first introduced in the first edition of the book *Organizational Behavior* authored by Luthans, but was given only minor attention. The first comprehensive treatment of all aspects of O.B.Mod. (theory, research, and application) appeared in a book by this title authored by Luthans and Kreitner.[5] Obviously, there have been other authors/consultants who have developed behavioral management approaches similar to O.B.Mod. In a recent comprehensive analysis of the literature to date on an operant-based approach to human resources management,[6] in addition to the Luthans-Kreitner book on O.B.Mod., four others are listed:

1 Brethower, D. M.: *Behavioral Analyses in Business and Industry: A Total Performance System,* Behaviordelia, Kalamazoo, Mich., 1972.

This early volume offers a model for analyzing performance in organizations. It includes coverage of the main principles of behavior analysis and provides numerous examples of practical applications. The volume is both entertaining and informative and provides an excellent introduction to O.B.Mod.

2 Brown, P. L., and R. J. Presbie: *Behavior Modification in Business, Industry and Government,* 1976. (Available from Behavior Improvement Associates, P.O. Box 296, New Paltz, NY 12561.)

This volume is correctly subtitled as a resource guide for managers, executives, training directors, and others interested in O.B.Mod. It contains (1) a brief introduction to behavior modification principles and procedures, (2) multiple examples of behavior modification projects, and (3) a bibliography on behavior modification articles, films, and newsletters. It provides a good, brief overview and introduction to the field.

3 Gilbert, T. F.: *Human Competence: Engineering Worthy Performance,* McGraw-Hill, New York, 1978.

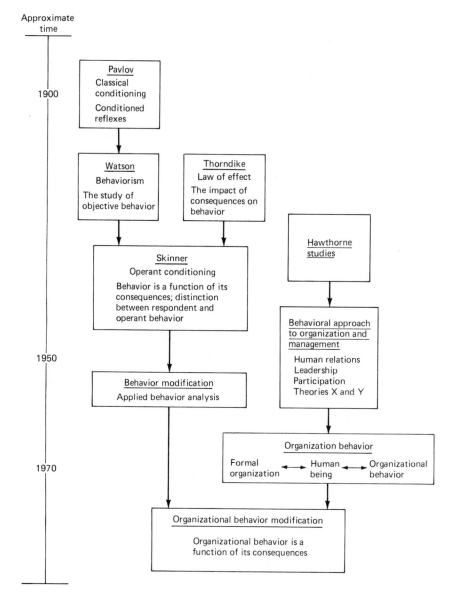

Fig. 2-1   Historical development of Organizational Behavior Modification. SOURCE: Fred Luthans and Robert Kreitner, *Organizational Behavior Modification,* Scott, Foresman and Company, Glenview, Ill., 1975. Reprinted by permission of the publisher.

This book focuses on an analysis of competence rather than behavior per se. The author, a former student of B. F. Skinner, advances the technology of applied behavior analysis by providing a model for appraising performance and evaluating interventions. His Performance Engineering model allows an economic analysis of training and intervention by identifying areas with the greatest potential for improvement. Gilbert presents this sophisticated material in a light and elegant manner. A case study in the appendix details his analysis technique in a business setting.

4   Luthans, F., and R. Kreitner: *Organizational Behavior Modification,* Scott, Foresman, Glenview, Ill., 1975.

This book is one of the earliest and most complete treatments of O.B.Mod. It is frequently cited and can be considered one of the basic references in the area. It includes discussion of the behavioral approach, behavior modification principles and procedures, some case study material, and chapters on ethical issues and preconditions for further development of the field.

5   Miller, L. M.: *Behavior Management: The New Science of Managing People at Work,* Wiley, New York, 1978.

This recent volume is a reasonably comprehensive treatment of O.B.Mod., especially as it applies to business and industry. It includes an introduction to the behavioral approach, a comparison of O.B.Mod. with more traditional approaches to organizational behavior, behavior modification principles and procedures, and chapters on both individual and organization-wide behavior management. The case studies in each chapter, as well as a chapter on frequently asked questions, add a distinctively practical emphasis. Appropriate for managers, students, or professionals, this volume will probably establish itself as one of the classics in the field.

The basic principles underlying the various approaches are largely the same, but the specifics on implementation vary. We have enough research and experience to feel confident that the O.B.Mod. approach, as suggested in this chapter, will lead to more effective human resource management.

GENERAL EXPERIENCE WITH THE APPLICATION OF BEHAVIORAL MANAGEMENT TECHNIQUES

As pointed out earlier, O.B.Mod. and related operant-based approaches to human resource management are relatively new. In 1972 *Business Week* printed an article about a number of companies that were either looking into or using behavior modification techniques,[7] and more recently the magazine has reported even greater popularity of behavior modification methods.[8] Among the 100 or so organizations which are reportedly using the approach are 3M Company, Frito-Lay, Addressograph-Multigraph, B. F. Goodrich, Weyerhaeuser, Warner-Lambert, Ford, American Telephone & Telegraph, Western Airlines, United Air Lines, IBM, International Telephone and Telegraph, Procter and Gamble, Milliken Company, and General Electric. All claim to have experienced considerable cost savings and dramatically increased worker productivity. In addition, *Training Magazine* devoted a recent issue to the behavioral management approach and listed nine consulting firms that specifically deal with this approach.[9] Despite this apparently gaining popularity, the most widely publicized case of behavioral management remains that of Emery Air Freight. The Emery experience has been widely publicized in management practitioner–oriented magazines and training films.[10] Under the direction of Edward Feeney, who was then a vice president of Emery and now has his own consulting firm aimed at implementing his program, the company apparently was able to realize a $2 million savings over a three-year period.

The program at Emery is similar to the O.B.Mod. approach outlined in this chapter in that critical performance-related behaviors are identified and then strengthened by positive reinforcement and feedback. For example, it was determined that a critical behavior was whether the dock workers at Emery were utilizing the air-freight containers to the fullest advantage. The containers have to be full in order for the company to make money. Because the employees on this job were extensively trained and because they were constantly reminded of the importance of full containers, both management and the workers estimated that the containers were being optimally utilized about 90 percent of the time. However, the performance audit team found the actual effective utilization to be 45 percent, or half what they thought. Through feedback and social reinforcers this situation was quickly turned around. This same type of approach was successfully used in many other areas of the company and led to the $2 million savings claim.

Unfortunately, the exact way that this $2 million was saved is not reported. As far as can be determined, there was no methodologically sound evaluation to determine the direct impact of the Feeney program on the publicized results. In other words, all that exists in the body of knowledge is testimonial evidence that the Emery program worked to the tune of $2 million. What is not satisfactorily answered to date is whether these impressive results were due to Feeney's program, to other programs reported in the business periodicals, or to some other factor such as the economy. The same criticism of course, can be made of much of the literature reporting experiences in the application of other human resource management techniques. After detailing the specific steps involved in the O.B.Mod. process, more systematic research results will be reported.

DESCRIPTION OF THE O.B.MOD PROCESS

The basic premise of O.B.Mod. is that organizational behavior is a function of its consequences. As a specific approach to organizational behavior analysis and change, O.B.Mod. can be portrayed as a five-step problem-solving model. Figure 2-2 shows this model. It can be used in a step-by-step process to change performance-related behaviors of personnel in today's organizations. Thus, O.B.Mod. can be thought of as an overall approach to human resource management or as a technique of organizational behavior change. The following sections discuss the specific steps of O.B.Mod. that can be followed to implement the approach.

Step 1:   Identification of Critical Behaviors

In this first step of O.B.Mod. the critical behaviors that make a significant impact on performance (e.g., making or selling widgets or service to clients or customers) are identified. In every organization, regardless of type or level, numerous behaviors are occurring all the time. Some of these behaviors have a significant impact on performance and some do not. The goal of the first step of O.B.Mod. is to identify the critical behaviors—the so-called 20/80 behaviors; meaning those 20 percent of behaviors that may account for up to 80 percent of the performance in the area in question.

Methods of Identifying Critical Behaviors   The process of identifying the critical behaviors can be carried out in a couple of ways. One approach is to have the person closest to the job in question (e.g., the immediate supervisor or actual jobholder) determine the critical behaviors. This goes hand in hand with using O.B.Mod. as a problem-solving approach for the individual manager. Its advantages are that the person who knows the job best can most accurately identify the critical behaviors and, by participating, that person may be more committed to carrying the O.B.Mod. process to its successful completion.

Another approach to identifying critical behaviors would be to conduct a systematic behavioral audit. The audit would use internal staff specialists and/or outside consultants. The audit would systematically analyze—in the manner that jobs are examined in job analysis techniques in personnel management—each job in question. The advantages of the personal approach (the jobholder and/or the immediate supervisor mak-

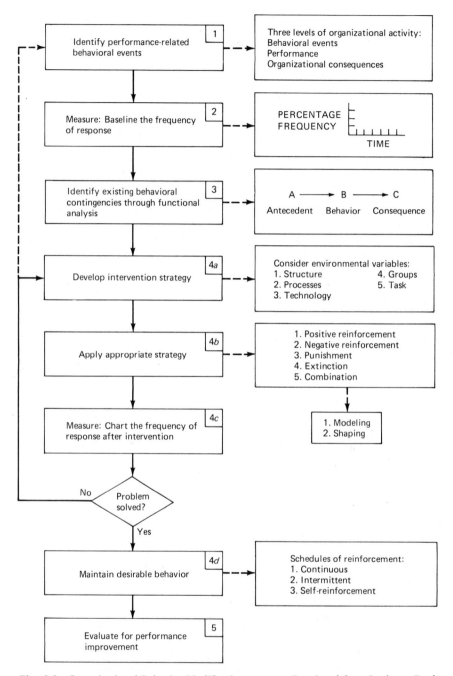

Fig. 2-2 Organizational Behavior Modification. SOURCE: Reprinted from Luthans, Fred, and Robert Kreitner, "The Management of Behavioral Contingencies," *Personnel,* July–August 1974, (New York: ANACOM, a division of American Management Associations, 1974), p. 13.

ing a vital input into the audit) can be realized by the audit. In addition, the advantages of staff expertise and consistency can be gained. Such an audit approach was successfully used in the behavioral management program at Emery Air Freight. Even if an outside audit identifies the critical behaviors, it is usually the supervisor of the area in question who performs the succeeding steps in O.B.Mod. In the future, if an entire organization sets up behavioral systems and takes an O.B.Mod. approach to total organization development,[11] there could be more involvement of staff specialists in the succeeding steps in O.B.Mod.

Guidelines for Identifying Critical Behaviors Regardless of the method used, there are certain guidelines that can be helpful in identifying critical behaviors. First, only observable, countable behaviors are included. An employee's "bad attitude" and continual "goofing off" are unacceptable criteria. Attitudes and a lack of motivation are unobservable inner states of people. Only observables—behaviors that can be seen (e.g., absenteeism or attendance, tardiness or promptness, complaints or constructive comments, and doing or not doing a particular task or procedure that leads to quantity and/or quality outcomes)—play a role in O.B.Mod. Something like "goofing off" is not acceptable because it is not operationally measurable. It could be broken down into observable, measurable behaviors such as not being at the work station, being tardy when returning from breaks, spending time at the water cooler, disrupting coworkers, and even flirting with the opposite sex. To be identified as a critical behavior there must be a positive answer to two questions: (1) Can it be seen? and (2) Can it be measured?

Another helpful guideline for identifying critical behaviors is to work backward from an obvious performance deficiency. Just as not all behaviors contribute to performance (e.g., complaining behavior may have nothing to do with performance), not all performance problems can be traced to behaviors. For example, the cause of poor performance of a production unit in a manufacturing organization may be faulty machinery or poorly trained workers (they do not know the proper procedures) or unrealistically high production standards. Each of these possible causes is not, at least directly, a behavioral problem. The same is true of the person who does not have the ability to produce at an acceptable level. This is a selection problem, not a behavioral problem. However, despite the possibility of nonbehaviorally related performance problems, in general such problems are the exception rather than the rule. Most organizations are not having problems with their technology or the ability of their people, but like Henry Jakel in the opening illustration, they have many behaviorally related performance problems. Desirable performance-related behaviors need to be strengthened and accelerated in frequency, and undesirable performance-related behaviors need to be weakened and decelerated in frequency. Like the initial step in any problem-solving process, the critical behaviors must be properly identified or the subsequent steps of O.B.Mod. become meaningless for attaining the overall goal of behavioral change for performance improvement.

Step 2:   Measurement of the Behaviors

After the critical behaviors have been identified in step 1, they are next measured. A baseline frequency is obtained by determining (either by observing and counting or by extracting from existing records) the number of times that the identified behavior is occurring under present conditions. Often this baseline frequency is in and of itself very revealing. Sometimes it is discovered that the behavior identified in step 1 is occurring much less or much more frequently than anticipated. The baseline measure may indicate that the problem is much smaller or bigger than anyone thought. In some instances the baseline measure may cause the "problem" to be dropped because its low (or high) frequency is now deemed not to need change. For example, attendance may have been identified in step 1 as a critical behavior that needed to be changed. The supervisor reports that her people "never seem to be here." The baseline measure, however, reveals that there is 96 percent attendance, which is deemed to be acceptable. In this example, the baseline measure rules out attendance as being a problem. The reverse, of course, could also have occurred. Attendance might have been a much bigger problem than anticipated.

The purpose of the baseline measure is to provide objective frequency data on the critical behavior. A baseline frequency count is an operational definition of the strength of the critical behavior under existing conditions. Such precise measurement is the hallmark of any scientific endeavor and separates O.B.Mod. from more subjective human resource management approaches such as participation. Although the baseline is established before the intervention to see what happens to the behavior as a result of the intervention, it is important to realize that post-intervention measures are taken as well. Busy managers may feel that they do not have time to record behavioral frequencies objectively, but, at least initially, they must record them in order to effectively use the O.B.Mod. approach. The following discussion of tally sheets and charting point out how to minimize the problems associated with this second step of O.B.Mod.

Tally Sheets   A tailor-made tally sheet should be designed for each behavior. A piece of notebook paper usually is sufficient. Figure 2-3 shows a typical tally sheet. As shown, the tallies record behavioral fre-

| Employee: _____ | | | Behavior: _____ | | | | | | |
| Position: _____ | | | Supervisor: _____ | | | | | | |

	Monday		Tuesday		Wednesday		Thursday		Friday	
Times	Yes	No	Yes	No	Yes	No	Yes	No	Yes	No

Fig. 2-3   Typical tally sheet.

quencies in relation to time. The frequencies are usually broken down in a yes-no type of format, which greatly simplifies the job of the recorder. However, such an approach requires precise definitions of what constitutes a frequency. For example, say that the critical behavior is tardiness in returning from breaks. A decision must be made on what is considered tardy. Say that it is decided (and this may be different from situation to situation) that five minutes or over is tardy. The observer/recorder then has a definite guideline in checking yes or no for frequency of tardiness behavior.

The time dimension on the tally sheet can also follow some specific guidelines to simplify the observer/recorder's job. With some behaviors, such as attendance or complaints, it may be feasible to record every occurrence. However, with many other critical behaviors it would be so time-consuming to record every frequency that it would be practically impossible. On behaviors of the latter type, time-sampling techniques can be effectively used. The approach is similar to the work-sampling techniques that have been successfully used by industrial engineers for years. An example of a time-sampling approach would be to randomly select a time per each working hour to observe the behavior. As in any sampling procedure, if the times are in fact random, confident generalizations can be made to the whole day.

Charting the Behaviors   The data collected on the tally sheets are transferred to a chart or graph like the one shown in Figure 2-4. As shown, the frequencies of behaviors are along the vertical, and time is on the horizontal. Percentage rather than raw frequency is usually used. This practice again simplifies the recorder's job because it permits the recorder to miss a time or two during the day or even entire days without badly distorting the data.

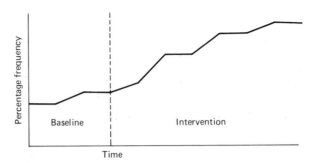

Fig. 2-4   Charting critical behaviors.

Charting of critical behaviors is important to O.B.Mod. because it permits quick, accurate visual inspection of the frequency data. As Kreitner has noted,

> In effect, behavior charts are mini behavioral experiments complete with "before" and "after" measures for control purposes. Baseline data collected under normal conditions later act as a standard for evaluating interventions. Baseline data help answer the pivotal question: Has the intervention strengthened, weakened, or not affected the target behavior?[12]

The Role of the Observer/Recorder   The role assumed by the observer/recorder can be important not only to the measurement step but to the credibility and ethics of the entire approach. There is a growing need for accurate, observational measures in all areas of research and practice in organizational behavior. This need is especially acute in the O.B.Mod. approach. Questionnaire and interview data are highly reactive. However, the mere presence of an observer may also badly distort the behaviors being measured. For this reason, it is important that observational data be gathered as unobtrusively (inconspicuously) as possible.

Advocating the use of unobtrusive observational measures does not mean that hidden observers or hidden audio and/or video equipment should be used. Obviously, such practice gets into ethical and legal problems. With possibly a few exceptions (e.g., security), such hidden or deceptive approaches cannot be justified. On the other hand, straightforward observational techniques that use common sense can minimize the reactive effects of those being measured. The observer should be completely open to any questions that the person being observed may have. Most employees in modern organizations are not sensitive to being measured because industrial engineers and personnel specialists have been doing it for years. There have certainly been abuses of this in the past, but in most cases the lessons have been learned and the abuses can be eliminated.

In addition to observational techniques of data collection, much data on typical critical behaviors (e.g., absenteeism, quantity, and quality data) are already being gathered for other purposes. All that recorders have to do is retrieve these data; they do not have to intervene intrusively. Recently, Johnson et al. have given specific guidelines about the use of behavioral measurement in business.[13] They suggest ways to observe, record, display, interpret, and assure the quality of behavioral measurement. Finally, self-reporting procedures can be employed to gather the data. Having people reinforced for honestly and accurately keeping records on their own targeted behaviors will eliminate the need for an observer/recorder. In the Emery Air Freight program of behavioral management and in our own work such self-reporting has been successfully used.[14]

Step 3:   Functional Analysis of the Behavior

Once the critical behavior has been identified and a baseline measure is obtained, a functional analysis is performed. In an expanded functional analysis both the antecedent (the S in the S $\leftrightarrow$ O $\leftrightarrow$ B $\leftrightarrow$ C model) and the consequent (the C in the model) environments are vital to the understanding, prediction, and control of human behavior in organizations.[15] In Figure 2-2 the abbreviated functional analysis is referred to simply as A——B——C or antecedent—behavior—consequence. The functional analysis brings out the problem-solving nature of O.B.Mod. Both the antecedent cues which emit the behavior and sometimes control it and the consequences which are currently maintaining the behavior must be identified and understood before an effective intervention strategy can be developed.

An example can demonstrate why the functional analysis is so important to O.B.Mod. In an actual case of an O.B.Mod. application, a production supervisor in a large manufacturing firm identified unscheduled breaks as a critical behavior affecting the performance of his department. It seemed that his people were frequently wandering off the job; and when they were not tending their machines, time was lost—a case of lost time production. A baseline measure of this critical behavior showed he was right. The data indicated that unscheduled breaks (defined as leaving the job for reasons other than taking a scheduled break or to obtain materials, etc.) were occurring in his department on a relatively frequent basis. The functional analysis was performed to determine the antecedent(s) and consequence(s) of the unscheduled break behavior. It was found that the clock served as the antecedent cue for the critical behavior. The workers in this department started work at 8 A.M.; at 10 A.M. they had their first scheduled break; they had lunch at 12. They started again at 1 P.M., had a break at 3 P.M., and quit at 5 P.M. The functional analysis revealed that almost precisely at 9 A.M., 11 A.M., 2 P.M., and 4 P.M. the workers were leaving their jobs and going to the rest room. In other words, the clock served as a cue for them to take an unscheduled break midway between starting time and the first scheduled break, between the first scheduled break and lunch, between lunch and the scheduled afternoon break, and between the afternoon break and quitting time. Note that the clock did not cause the behavior; it only served as a cue to emit the behavior. On the other hand, the behavior was under stimulus control of the clock because the clock dictated when the behavior would occur. The consequence, however, was what was maintaining the behavior. The critical behavior was a function of its consequences. The functional analysis revealed that the consequence of the unscheduled break behavior was escape from a dull, boring task (the unscheduled break behavior was being negatively reinforced) and/or meeting with coworkers and friends to socialize and have a cigarette (the unscheduled break behavior was being positively reinforced). Through this functional analysis the antecedents and consequences are identified so that an effective intervention strategy can be developed. The next section on the intervention step will reveal what the production supervisor actually tried in this case.

The functional analysis pinpoints one of the most significant practical problems of using an O.B.Mod. approach to change critical behaviors. Only the contingent consequences have an impact on subsequent behavior. The functional analysis often reveals that there are many competing contingencies for every organizational behavior. For example, a supervisor may be administering what he or she believes to be contingent punishment for the undesirable behavior of subordinates. However, what often happens is that the coworkers are providing a very rewarding consequence for the undesirable behavior. In many cases the persons who are supposedly being punished will allow the coworkers' rewards to be the contingent consequence, and their undesirable behavior will increase in subsequent frequency. In other words, the supervisor's punishment was not contingent; it had no impact on the subordinates' subsequent behavior. The functional analysis must make sure that the contingent consequences are identified, and the analyst must not be deluded by the consequences that on the surface appear to be affecting the critical behavior.

Step 4:   Development of an Intervention Strategy

The first three steps in an O.B.Mod. approach are preliminary to the action step, the intervention. The goal of the intervention is to strengthen and accelerate desirable critical behaviors and/or weaken and decelerate undesirable critical behaviors. There are several strategies that can be used, but the main ones are positive reinforcement, punishment/positive reinforcement, and extinction/positive reinforcement.

Positive Reinforcement Strategy   There is considerable misunderstanding surrounding the concept of reinforcement. A positive reinforcer is defined as a consequence which strengthens the behavior and increases its subsequent frequency. It is important to note that *negative reinforcement* (the termination or withdrawal of an undesirable consequence) has the *same impact* on behavior (strengthens and increases subsequent frequency). Yet, positive and not negative reinforcement is recommended as an effective intervention strategy for O.B.Mod. The reason is that positive reinforcement represents a form of positive control of behavior while negative reinforcement and punishment represent forms of negative control of behavior. Negative reinforcement is actually a type of "blackmail" control of behavior; the person behaves in a certain way in order not to be punished. Most organizations today control participants in this manner. People come to work in order not to be fired and look busy when the supervisor walks by in order not to be punished. Under positive control, the person behaves in a certain way in order to receive the desired consequence. Under positive control people would come to work in order to be recognized for making a contribution to their department's goal of perfect attendance or would keep busy whether the supervisor was around or not in order to receive incentive pay or because they get self-reinforcement from doing a good job. Positive control through a positive-reinforcement intervention strategy is much more effective and long-lasting than negative control. It creates a much healthier and more productive organizational climate.

Identifying Positive Reinforcers   It should be carefully pointed out that a reward becomes a positive reinforcer only if because of its presentation the behavior increases in subsequent frequency. Thus, some of the commonly used organizational rewards are not necessarily positive reinforcers. This is why it is so vitally important that the measures initiated in step 2 be continued after the intervention. The objective measures are the only way to tell whether an intervention is in fact a positive reinforcer.

There are various conceptual categories of rewards (extrinsic/intrinsic and primary/secondary) and each has subtle effects on behavior.[16] There are also available several techniques to help determine potential positive reinforcers.[17] The most accurate method of identifying positive reinforcers, but one often difficult to accomplish, is to analyze empirically each individual's history of reinforcement. Knowledge of a particular person's likes and dislikes gained through experience can help in this regard, and, of course, empirical evidence post-intervention from the charting in step 2 can be used to analyze the history of reinforcement. However, in cases where there is little or no experience with the individual prior to trying an intervention, several self-reporting techniques can be used.

The most straightforward technique is simply to ask what the person finds to be rewarding. Although the person may not always tell the truth, it is nonetheless a logical point of departure for identifying potential reinforcers. A more formal approach is to use test instruments. For example, Blood developed an ipsitive test which identifies the relative importance of several possible job-related reinforcers.[18] Another possible method of identifying reinforcers is the use of contingency questionnaires.[19] The latter tests measure perceived performance-outcome probabilities and can help identify the important outcomes (reinforcers) for employees. Still another way to help identify possible reinforcers is through self-selection techniques: the workers are allowed to select their own reinforcers from a variety of stated possibilities sometimes called "smorgasbords" or "menus."

Contrived Reinforcers   The various techniques discussed above can be used to help identify reinforcers for the positive-reinforcement intervention strategy. Although reinforcers are highly individualized, research and experience have shown that there are several rewards that most organizational participants find positively reinforcing. These can be classified as contrived and natural rewards. The contrived rewards are those that are brought in from outside the natural work environment and generally involve costs for the organization over and above the existing situation.[20] Examples would include the consumables, manipulatables, visual and auditory reinforcers, and tokens found in Table 2-1. The two most widely used and effective contrived rewards would be money and feedback about performance.

The literature on the positive impact that feedback has on organizational participants is quite complete. Feedback played an important role in the Emery Air Freight program[21] and has been shown to have a positively reinforcing impact on employee performance in a variety of applications. There is little question that despite the tremendous amount of data being generated by computerized information systems in all modern organizations, *individuals* still receive very little, if any, feedback

Table 2-1 Classifications of On-the-Job Rewards

Contrived on-the-job rewards				Natural rewards	
Consumables	Manipulatables	Visual and auditory	Tokens	Social	Premack
Coffee-break treats	Desk accessories	Office with a window	Money	Friendly greetings	Job with more responsibility
Free lunches	Wall plaques	Piped-in music	Stocks	Informal recognition	Job rotation
Food baskets	Company car	Redecoration of work environment	Stock options	Formal acknowledgment of achievement	Early time off with pay
Easter hams	Watches	Company literature	Movie passes	Invitations to coffee/lunch	Extended breaks
Christmas turkeys	Trophies	Private office	Trading stamps (green stamps)	Solicitations of suggestions	Extended lunch period
Dinners for the family on the company	Commendations	Popular speakers or lecturers	Paid-up insurance policies	Solicitations of advice	Personal time off with pay
Company picnics	Rings/tiepins	Book club discussions	Dinner and theater tickets	Compliment on work progress	Work on personal project on company time
After-work wine and cheese parties	Appliances and furniture for the home	Feedback about performance	Vacation trips	Recognition in house organ	Use of company machinery or facilities for personal projects
Beer parties	Home shop tools		Coupons redeemable at local stores	Pat on the back	Use of company recreation facilities
	Garden tools		Profit sharing	Smile	
	Clothing			Verbal or nonverbal recognition or praise	
	Club privileges				
	Special assignments				

SOURCE Fred Luthans and Robert Kreitner, *Organizational Behavior Modification*, Scott, Foresman, Glenview, Ill., 1975, p. 101. Used with permission.

about their performance. People generally have an intense desire to know how they are doing, especially if they have some degree of achievement motivation.[22] Feedback, in and of itself, can potentially be very positively reinforcing and thus be an effective O.B.Mod. intervention strategy.[23] The example of the supervisor faced with the problem of his people taking unscheduled breaks used such an intervention. In that case, he could not change the antecedent cue (he could not change time) and he could not change the consequence by preventing his people from going to the bathroom. What he did do was calculate the exact cost for each worker in the unit (in terms of lost group piece-rate pay) every time one of them took an unscheduled break. This information regarding the relatively significant amount of lost pay when any one of them took an unscheduled break was fed back to the employees in his unit. After this feedback intervention, staying on the job increased in frequency and taking unscheduled breaks dramatically decreased. The feedback pointed out the contingency that staying on the job meant more money. At least in this case, the money proved to be a more contingent consequence than the competing contingencies of social rewards with friends at the rest room and withdrawing from the boring job. The feedback in this case merely clarified the monetary contingency, but feedback about performance can by itself be reinforcing.

Money as a Reinforcer Despite the tendency in recent years to downgrade the importance of money as an organizational reward, there is ample evidence that money can be positively reinforcing for most people. The downgrading of money is partly the result of the popular motivation theories of Abraham Maslow and Frederick Herzberg plus the publicity from surveys which consistently place wages and salaries near the middle of the list of employment factors that are important to workers and managers. Although money was probably overemphasized in classical management theory and motivation techniques, the pendulum seems now to have swung too far in the opposite direction. Money remains a very important but admittedly complex potential reinforcer.

In terms of Maslow's "hierarchy of needs" concept of motivation, money is often equated only with the most basic level of needs. It is viewed in the material sense of buying food, clothing, and shelter. Yet money has a symbolic as well as an economic material meaning. It can provide power and status and can be a means to measure achievement. In the latter sense, money can be used as an effective positive-reinforcement intervention strategy.

Accepting the importance of money as a possible reinforcer does not mean that the traditional techniques for dispensing it are adequate. Starting with the scientific management movement at the turn of the century, numerous monetary incentive techniques have been developed. Flippo and Munsinger classify them in three broad categories:

1 Base pay or salary which is given for a job regardless of how it is performed

2 Variable pay which gives recognition to individual differences on the job

3 Supplementary pay which is not directly related to the job or the individual[24]

The base-pay technique provides for minimum compensation for a particular job. Pay by the hour for workers and the base salary for managers are examples. The technique does not reward for above-average, or penalize for below-average, performance, and it is largely controlled by the job rather than the person performing the job. The variable-pay technique attempts to reward according to individual or group differences and is thus more human- than job-controlled. Seniority variable-pay plans recognize age and length-of-service differentials, and merit and individual- or group-incentive plans attempt to make rewards contingent on performance. Incentive plans pay personnel according to piece rate, bonus, or profit sharing. Supplementary monetary techniques have nothing to do with the job or performance per se. The extensive fringe-benefit package received by employees in most modern organizations is an example.

Further refined and newly developed variable-pay or contingent-pay plans seem to be necessary to the effective use of money as a reinforcer. The base- and supplementary-pay plans are adequate for their intended purposes, but the variable-pay plans do not seem to have the desired effects. After an extensive review of relevant research, Filley and House note:

> Although there seems to be little question that incentive programs frequently result in greater productivity, the effects of both individual and group plans have been shown to vary with such factors as the attitudes and background of employees, the nature of the task performed, informal work norms, and the size of the work group.[25]

In other words, monetary incentive plans have many complicating factors. Edward Lawler supports this conclusion in his book devoted specifically to the relationship between pay and organizational effectiveness. At the end of the book he states that "a pay plan must fit the characteristics of an organization if it is to be effective; it must be individualized in terms of organization size, management style, etc."[26] Webber suggests that in order for money to be reinforcing, the individual must believe that:

1   Increased effort would lead to better performance.

2   Your employer can determine the improved performance.

3   Increased money will follow from this performance.

4   You would value the additional money because it would satisfy your needs.

5   You would not have to unduly sacrifice satisfaction of other needs for security, affiliation, and so on.[27]

Analyses of the role of money, such as the points made by Lawler and Webber above, are usually couched in cognitive terms. However, from these cognitive explanations it is very clear that the real key for assessing the use of money as a reinforcer is not whether it satisfies inner needs but rather *how it is administered*. In order for money to be an effective positive-reinforcement intervention strategy for O.B.Mod., it must be administered contingently on the performing of the critical behavior.

About the only reinforcing function that pay currently has in organizations is to reinforce employees for walking up to a pay window or opening an envelope every two weeks or month. With the exception of some piece-rate incentive systems and commissions paid to salespersons, pay is generally not contingent on the performance of critical behaviors. One experimental study clearly demonstrated that money contingently administered can be an effective intervention strategy.[28] A contingently administered monetary bonus plan significantly improved the punctuality of workers in a Mexican division of a large United States corporation. It should be pointed out, however, that the mere fact that money was valued by the Mexican workers in this study does not mean that it would have the same impact on all workers. For example, in a society with an inflationary economy and nonmaterialistic social values, money is much less likely to be a potential reinforcer for critical job behaviors. Money certainly cannot be automatically dismissed as a positive reinforcer, but, because of its complexity, it may also turn out to be a reward but not a reinforcer. Only postintervention measurement will determine if in fact money is an effective positive reinforcer for the critical behavior in question.

Natural Reinforcers   Besides the contrived rewards which most human resource managers tend to depend upon, there are a host of overlooked natural reinforcers available in every organizational setting. Potentially very powerful, these are the rewards that exist in the natural occurrence of events.[29] Table 2-1 categorizes the natural rewards under social and Premack headings.

Social rewards such as recognition, attention, and praise tend to be very reinforcing for most people. In addition, few people become satiated with social rewards. However, similarly to the contrived rewards, the social rewards must be administered on a contingent basis. For example, a pat on the back or verbal praise that is randomly administered (as was the case under the old human relations approach) can have more of a punishing, "boomerang" effect than positive reinforcement. But genuine social rewards, contingently administered to the critical behavior, can be a very effective positive-reinforcement intervention strategy. The added benefit of such a strategy in contrast to the use of contrived rewards is that the cost of social rewards to the organization is absolutely nothing.

Premack rewards are derived from the work of psychologist David Premack.[30] Simply stated, the Premack principle is that high-probability behaviors can be used to reinforce low-probability behaviors. For example, if there are two tasks A and B, and the person prefers A over B, the Premack principle would say that the person should perform B first and then A. In this sequence, task A serves as a contingent reinforcer for completing task B, and the person will perform better on both tasks than if the sequence were reversed. In common practice, people often tend to do the task they like best first and put off the less desired task. This common sequence of doing things is in direct violation of the Premack principle and can contribute to ineffective performance.

As an O.B.Mod. intervention strategy, the Premack principle would suggest that a natural reinforcer could always be found. Certain job activities can invariably be used to reinforce other job activities. No matter how much employees dislike their jobs, there are going to be some things they like to do better than others. Premack sequencing would allow the more desired activities to reinforce less desired activities. The rewards listed under "Premack" in Table 2-1 can be used to reinforce the less desirable activities on a job.

Punishment/Positive-Reinforcement Strategy   The discussion so far has emphasized the positive-reinforcement strategy as the most effective intervention for O.B.Mod. Yet realistically it is recognized that in some cases the use of punishment to weaken and decelerate undesirable behaviors cannot be avoided. This would be true of something like unsafe behaviors that need to be immediately decreased. However, it must be recognized that there are many negative side effects that accompany the use of punishment, and therefore it should be avoided if at all possible. Punished behavior tends to be only temporarily suppressed; for example, if a supervisor reprimands a subordinate for some undesirable behavior, the behavior will decrease in the presence of the supervisor but will surface again when the supervisor is absent. In addition, a punished person becomes very anxious and uptight; thus, reliance on punishment may have a disastrous impact on employee satisfaction. Perhaps the biggest problem with the use of punishment, however, is that it is very difficult for a supervisor to switch roles from punisher to positive reinforcer. Some supervisors/managers rely on punishment so much in dealing with their subordinates that it is almost impossible for them to effectively administer positive reinforcement. This is a bad situation for the management of human resources because the use of positive reinforcement is a much more effective way of changing organizational behavior. If punishment is deemed to be necessary, the desirable alternative behavior (e.g., safe behavior) should be positively reinforced at the first opportunity. By using this combination strategy, the alternative desirable behavior will begin to replace the undesirable behavior in the person's behavioral repertoire. Punishment should never be used alone as an O.B.Mod. intervention. If punishment is absolutely necessary, it should always be used in combination with positive reinforcement.

Extinction/Positive Reinforcement   A much more effective way to decrease undesirable behavior is to use an extinction strategy. Extinction has the same impact on behavior as punishment (though it does not act as fast), but extinction does not have the negative side effects of punishment. Whereas punishment could be thought of as the application of a noxious or aversive consequence or the deliberate withdrawal of a positively reinforcing consequence, extinction can be defined simply as providing no consequence. Obviously, there is a fine line between extinction and the withdrawal of a positive-reinforcer type of punishment. In fact, there is such a fine distinction between the two that some behaviorists do not even deal with extinction. They simply operationally define anything which decreases behavior as punishment. But the important point for human resource management is that undesirable behavior can be decreased without the accompanying negative side effects of punishment. This can be done by making sure the undesirable behavior is not being reinforced, i.e., by putting it on extinction. Remember that behavior is a function of its consequences. The undesirable behavior would not be occurring if it were not being reinforced. Under an extinction strategy you do not simply ignore the undesirable behavior; instead, you make sure that it is no longer being reinforced.

In the functional analysis performed in step 3 of O.B.Mod., the consequences maintaining the critical behavior were identified. The extinction strategy would eliminate those consequences of critical behaviors that were to be decelerated. For example, if complaining was the targeted behavior and the functional analysis revealed that the supervisor's attention to the complaining behavior was maintaining it, the extinction strategy would be to have the supervisor no longer pay attention to it. The supervisor may be able to avoid the complainer. Walking away from the person who is complaining may be punishing; but if handled properly, i.e., in a nonobvious manner, it could be an extinction strategy without the negative side effects. Again, as with any intervention strategy, whether it was effective in reducing the behavior can be known only by what happened to the frequency measures postintervention. Also, similarly to the punishment strategy, extinction should be used only in combination with positive reinforcement. The desirable alternative behavior would be positively reinforced at the first opportunity. The positively reinforced behavior would begin to replace the undesirable behavior. In the example of the complaining behavior, when the person did not complain, the supervisor would notice and give attention to the person for constructive comments and noncomplaining behavior.

Because most organizational behaviors are being reinforced by intermittent schedules, which are very resistant to extinction, the use of the extinction strategy may take time and patience. But as a long-range strategy for weakening undesirable behaviors and decelerating the frequency of occurrence, extinction can be effective. In general, the very simple rule of thumb to follow in employing an O.B.Mod. intervention strategy is to positively reinforce desirable behaviors and nonreinforce undesirable behaviors. This simple guideline may have as big an impact on effective human resource management as any single thing the supervisor/manager can do. But once again it should be pointed out that understanding and using the other concepts and techniques discussed in other chapters of this book are also necessary for the complex, challenging job of effective human resource management and organizational development and change.

Step 5:   Evaluation to Assure Performance Improvement

A glaring weakness of most human resource management techniques is the absence of any systematic, built-in evaluation. For example, one comprehensive survey of 154 selected companies concluded that "most organizations are measuring reaction to training programs. As we consider the more important and difficult steps in the evaluation process (i.e., learning, behavior, and results) we find less and less being done, and many of these efforts are superficial and subjective."[31] In another survey, it was concluded that the typical firm that used job enrichment "believes it has benefited from improvements in employee performance and job satisfaction but has made little effort to formally evaluate the effectiveness of the program, depending on impressions and anecdotal evidence, rather than quantifiable data, for its conclusions."[32] Such haphazard evaluations of human resource management techniques have led to credibility problems. Today all programs dealing with people, whether they are government welfare programs or human resource management programs, are under the pressure of accountability. Donald Campbell has labeled our society under the current climate of accountability the "experimenting society."[33] Human resource managers no longer have the luxury of trying something merely new and different and hoping they can improve performance. Today there is pressure for everything that is tried to have proven value. Just as the validity of selection techniques used in the personnel process had to be demonstrated, systematic evaluations of human resource management techniques should have been done all along.

O.B.Mod. attempts to meet the credibility and accountability problems head-on by including evaluation as an actual part of the process. In this last step of the model, the need for four levels of evaluation (reaction, learning, behavioral change, and performance improvement) is stressed. The reaction level simply refers to whether the people using the approach and those having it used on them like it or not. If O.B.Mod. is well received, if there is a positive reaction to it, there is a better chance of its being used effectively. If it is not well received, there is little chance of its being used effectively. Reaction is obviously important to the evaluation of the O.B.Mod. technique. The second level is learning. This is especially important when first implementing an O.B.Mod. approach. Do the people using the approach understand the theoretical background and underlying assumptions and the meaning and reasons for the steps in the model? If they do not, the model will again tend to be used ineffectively. The third level is aimed at behavioral change. Are behaviors actually being changed? The charting of behaviors gives objective data for this level of evaluation. The fourth and final level, performance improvement, is the most important. The major purpose of O.B.Mod. is not just to receive a favorable reaction, learn the concepts, and change behaviors. The importance of these dimensions is mainly that they contribute to the overriding purpose, which is to improve performance. "Hard" measures (e.g., quantity and quality data, turnover, absenteeism, customer complaints, employee grievances, length of patient stay, number of clients served, and rate of return on investment) and experimental methodology are used whenever possible to evaluate systematically the impact of O.B.Mod. on performance. The next section will report some of this research effort on evaluating O.B.Mod.

RESEARCH RESULTS ON THE USE OF
O.B.MOD.

To date, there have been a number of studies on behavioral management reported in the literature. A recent search of the literature by Professor Charles Snyder of Auburn University uncovered 64 studies, of varying degrees of sophistication, that attempted to evaluate various aspects of behavior modification of employees in actual organizations and an additional half dozen studies that were conducted in laboratory or simulated organizational settings.[34] Although there are many methodological problems with practically all of this research that would threaten both the internal and external validity of the findings,[35] in general the results are extremely positive. Behavior modification techniques reportedly reduced accidents, improved quality, decreased costs, improved performance, increased sales, improved attendance, decreased tardiness, improved service, increased the job openings reported and job placements in an employment service, increased the wearing of safety devices, increased the frequency of staff members following instructions, reduced accounting errors, reduced errors on inventory entry cards, reduced customer complaints, reduced electricity consumption, reduced crime, reduced errors in change making and/or theft by cashiers, reduced the negative comments by supervisors, and increased employee participation in a suggestion program.

The research findings referred to above report on behavior modification in organizations using a variety of approaches and specific facets. Research on the specific five-step O.B.Mod. approach outlined in this chapter has also been conducted by the author and his colleagues. The initial study was conducted in a medium-sized light manufacturing firm located in a large city. Two groups (experimental and control) of nine production-type supervisors were used in the study. The experimental group received training in the O.B.Mod. approach (essentially on the five steps discussed earlier in the chapter). The results showed that O.B.Mod. had a definite positive impact on reaction, behavior change, and performance (learning was not evaluated in this study). Questionnaires administered to the trained supervisors indicated that they liked the O.B.Mod. approach and that their subordinates seemed to react positively. It was clear from the charts kept by each trainee (step 2) that in all cases they were able to change critical behaviors. Examples of behavioral changes accomplished by the supervisors included decreasing the number of complaints, reducing the group scrap rate, decreasing the number of overlooked defective pieces, and reducing the assembly reject rate.[36]

The most important result of the study, however, was the significant impact that the O.B.Mod. approach had on the performance of the supervisor's departments. By using an experimental design with a pretest-posttest control group, it was found that the departments run by members of the experimental group (those supervisors who used O.B.Mod. in their departments) outperformed the control group's departments. Figure 2-5 shows the results. Statistical analysis revealed that the department production rates of supervisors who used O.B.Mod. increased significantly more than the department production rates of the control supervisors (those who were not using O.B.Mod.).[37]

A replication in a larger plant obtained almost identical results to those of the original study on all levels of evaluation (including learning). The following summarize some typical cases of behavioral change that occurred in the production area of the larger manufacturing firm.

1 Use of idle time. One supervisor had a worker with a lot of idle time. Instead of using this time productively by helping others, the worker would pretend to look busy and stretch out the day. After getting a baseline measure and doing a functional analysis, the supervisor intervened by giving the worker social reinforcers (attention, praise, and recognition) contingent upon the worker's helping out at other jobs during idle time. Eventually the supervisor also reinforced the worker through more responsibility. This approach dramatically increased the worker's productive use of idle time.

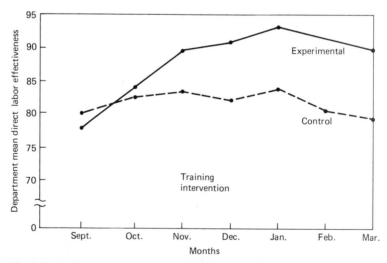

Fig. 2-5 Performance results of experimental (those who received O.B.Mod. training) and control groups. SOURCE: Robert Ottemann and Fred Luthans, "An Experimental Analysis of the Effectiveness of an Organizational Behavior Modification Program in Industry," *Academy of Management Proceedings*, 1975, p. 141.

2   Low performer. A production worker in one of the supervisor's departments was producing way below standard (80.3 percent of standard on a six-month baseline). The low performance was not deemed to be an ability, technical, training, or standards problem. After the functional analysis, the supervisor intervened using feedback and social reinforcers to increase the types of behaviors that would lead to higher output. This intervention resulted in a 93 percent performance level with no decrease in quality.

3   Group quality. One supervisor had a major problem with the quality of work in his department. The baseline measure verified this problem. After the functional analysis, the supervisor used feedback and social reinforcers on the group as a whole. Shortly after use of this intervention strategy the group attained the quality standard for the first time in three years.

4   Group attendance. Another supervisor felt he had an attendance problem in his department. The baseline measure revealed 92 percent attendance, which was not as big a problem as he had thought. However, he established the goal of 100 percent. After using daily feedback and social reinforcers on the group, 100 percent attendance was attained very rapidly. An interesting anecdote told by the supervisor was that one of his workers was riding to work from a small town in a car pool early one morning when they hit a deer. The car was disabled by the accident. Coworkers in the car pool who worked in other departments in the plant called relatives and went back home for the day. The worker in his department, however, not wanting to spoil the 100 percent attendance record, hitchhiked to work by herself and made it on time.

5   Problem with another department. One supervisor felt the performance of his department was being adversely affected by the unrecoverable time of truck-lift operators who were not directly under his supervision. After obtaining baseline data and making a functional analysis, the supervisor decided to apply feedback and social reinforcers on the informal group leader and the supervisor of the truck-lift operators. This intervention substantially reduced the unrecoverable time affecting the operational performance of his department.

The five examples above are representative of the type of behaviors that the supervisors using an O.B.Mod. approach were able to change. Cumulatively such applied behavioral analysis and change were able to improve the performance of these supervisors' departments in both the original study and the follow-up. More recently the O.B.Mod. approach has been extended beyond first-line supervisory training to the total organizational development process and to nonmanufacturing organizations.

The application of O.B.Mod. to total performance improvement was systematically evaluated in a small manufacturing plant.[38] It was implemented in three major phases. The first phase was primarily educational and consisted of training all three levels of management (first the owner/manager, then the four department heads, and finally the eight supervisors) in the principles of O.B.Mod. (basically following the five-step model discussed in this chapter). The second stage involved a simulation/experiential approach. At first, the participants analyzed case studies and developed intervention strategies. Then, once both the participants and the researchers/trainers had developed confidence in the participants' skills, the participants applied O.B.Mod. principles to their own work areas in a manner similar to that already described in the other manufacturing studies. The third and final phase of the intervention involved the development of a total organizational performance management system. In this phase, all levels of management collaborated to identify key behaviors and performance indexes. An organization-wide feedback system was then developed based on key behaviors and performance measures. In addition, programs for specific problem areas were developed.

The results of this comprehensive, *total organization* intervention indicated that there were significant improvements in both productivity and quality. In fact, record performance was attained. Statistical analyses demonstrated the significance of these changes, and simple inspection of the graphical representation of the data in Figure 2-6 shows the impact that the O.B.Mod. program had in this company. The left-hand portion of the graph depicts the average levels and variability of both productivity and quality prior to the intervention. The next segment of the graph displays the effects of a contingent time-off intervention on productivity when no consequences were being applied to quality. As evidenced by the changes illustrated, productivity improved with the application of the contingent time-off consequences while the quality level, for which consequences were not changed, remained about the same. The third segment then demonstrates the positive impact of the contingent application of social reinforcers on quality, while the productivity levels remained about the same. Finally, the last segment demonstrates improved levels of both quality and productivity under the control of the feedback system and contingent social reinforcement. Whereas the first study used a control group design, in this study, where the total organization was being impacted by the O.B.Mod. intervention, the multiple baseline design was deemed to be more appropriate for the evaluation. Such

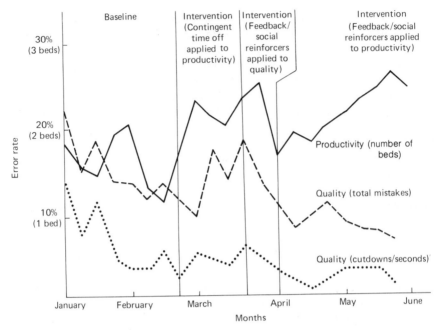

Fig. 2-6 The impact of O.B.Mod. on the total performance improvement of a small factory. SOURCE: Reprinted from Luthans, Fred, and Jason Schweizer, "O.B.Mod. in a Small Factory: How Behavior Modification Techniques Can Improve Total Organizational Performance," *Management Review,* September 1979 (New York: ANACOM, a division of American Management Associations, 1979), p. 49.

designs give considerable confidence to the conclusion that the O.B.Mod. approach did indeed cause the total performance of this organization to improve.

Nonmanufacturing Applications

The studies discussed above do provide considerable evidence that an O.B.Mod. approach can have a positive impact on employee performance, at least in a relatively structured environment such as that found in most manufacturing plants. But what about less structured, nonmanufacturing organizations? Preliminary research indicates that similar results are possible in nonmanufacturing organizations as well.

In a large hospital eleven supervisors from medical service units, business, and operations were given O.B.Mod. training in eight sessions covering a two-month period.[39] During the O.B.Mod. training these hospital supervisors learned the principles of O.B.Mod. and used the five-step approach; i.e., they identified, measured, functionally analyzed, and intervened to change key performance behaviors of their subordinates in their respective areas of responsibility. The results of this program are shown in Table 2-2. Although the researchers were unable to employ an experimental design in this study (and therefore cause-and-effect conclusions are not warranted), the simple before and after analysis provides a rather convincing argument that the O.B.Mod. intervention was effective in modifying a broad range of performance-related behaviors in a hospital setting. The O.B.Mod. program seemed to affect both the quality and quantity performance measures. Moreover, the data indicate that each of the O.B.Mod.-trained supervisors was successful in applying the intervention despite the wide variety of situations encountered.

In another nonmanufacturing organization, a little different type of O.B.Mod. application was tried.[40] Instead of training supervisors to use an O.B.Mod. approach, the researchers themselves did the steps normally done by the supervisors. An experiment (an A-B-A compared to a control group, i.e., a true experimental design) was conducted in a major metropolitan department store. Critical performance behaviors of 82 retail clerks from 16 randomly selected departments were identified. These included selling, stockwork, idle behaviors, absenteeism from the work station, and miscellaneous behaviors. Next, the baseline measure of these behaviors was obtained by observational and work sampling techniques. An analysis was then conducted to determine the appropriate performance goals for these behaviors. For example, based upon job descriptions, organizational goals/policies, direct observations, and role plays, it was determined that: (1) the salespersons, except for excused absence, should be present in the department (within 3 feet of displayed merchandise) during assigned working hours; (2) a customer who comes to the department should be offered assistance (or acknowledged and promised aid momentarily) within five seconds; and (3) the display shelf should be filled to at least 70 percent capacity. Then, prior to the positive reinforcement intervention, an informational session spelling out the objectives, logic, and performance objectives was held with the subjects. The intervention consisted of contingently applying time-off with pay or equivalent cash and an opportunity to compete for a free vacation for two for attaining the performance goals. The observationally gathered behavioral data was kept during and after this intervention. For computational and graphic presentation, the selling, stockwork, and miscellaneous behaviors were collapsed into a single category called aggregate retailing behavior, and absence from the work station and idle time were also combined. Figure 2-7 shows the results.

The baseline frequency of these behaviors was not significantly different, but immediately upon the first day of the intervention the aggregate retailing behavior of the experimental group dramatically increased

Table 2-2 Performance Measures Before and After an O.B.Mod. Training Program in a Large Hospital

Unit	Measure(s)	Pre-intervention	Post-intervention	Percent change
Emergency room clerks	Registration errors (per day)	19.16	4.53	76.1
Hardware engineer group, HIS	Average time to repair (minutes)	92.53	33.25	61.4
Medical records file clerks	Errors in filing (per person per audit)	2.87	.078	97.3
Medical records	Complaints	8.0	1.0	875.0
Transcriptionists	Average errors	2.07	1.4	33.0
	Average output	2,258.0	2,303.33	2.0
Heart station	EKG procedures accomplished (ave.)	1,263.0	1,398.97	11.0
	Overdue procedures	7.0*	4.0	42.8
Eye clinic	Daily patient throughput	19.0	23.0	21.0
	Daily patient teaching documentation	1.0	2.8	130.0
	Protocols produced	0	2.0	200
Pharmacy technicians	Drug output (doses)	348.8	422.1	21.0
	Posting errors	3.67	1.43	59.7
	Product waste (percent)	5.8	4.35	25.0
Radiology technicians	Average patient throughput (procedural)	3,849.5	4,049.0	5.0
	Retake rate (percent)	11.2	9.95	11.2
Patient accounting	Average monthly billings	2,561.0	3,424.5	33.7
Admitting office	Time to admit (minutes)	45.73	13.57	68.97
	Average cost	$ 15.05	$ 11.73	22.0
Data center operations	Systems log-on (time)	1:54	1:43	13.4

* Estimate

NOTE   All averages are arithmetic means.

SOURCE   Charles A. Snyder and Fred Luthans, "The Application of O.B.Mod. to Increase the Productivity of Hospital Personnel," *Personnel Administrator* (in press). Used with permission.

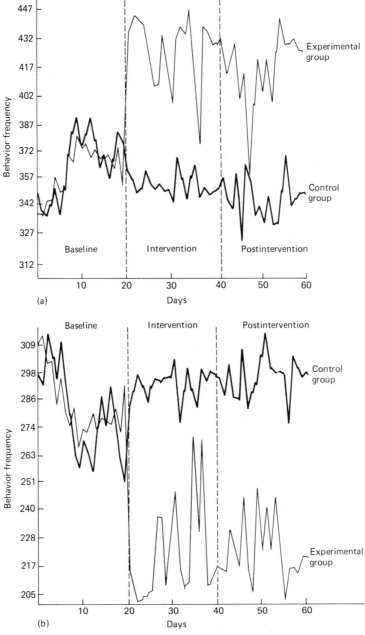

Fig. 2-7 Results of a positive reinforcement intervention on salespersons' performance behaviors: (*a*) aggregate retailing behavior; (*b*) absenteeism from work station. SOURCE: Fred Luthans, Robert Paul, and Douglas Baker, "An Experimental Analysis of the Impact of O.B.Mod. on Salespersons' Performance Behaviors," working paper, Department of Management, University of Nebraska, Lincoln, 1980.

and there was a huge decline in the average incidence of absence from the work station and idleness. As shown, this frequency maintained itself even after the intervention was withdrawn. This suggests that other more natural reinforcers in the environment and perhaps self-reinforcement had taken over.

Obviously, more research in more settings is needed before any definitive conclusions and broad generalizations about O.B.Mod. can be drawn. But, at least for now, it does seem to hold considerable potential for the effective management of human resources.

The Need for New Research Methodologies

The standard control group experimental design—as used in the first reported manufacturing study and the retail store study—is certainly a powerful, and needed, way to evaluate behavioral management techniques such as O.B.Mod. Unfortunately, it is often difficult to obtain matched control groups in field settings. There is a definite need for alternate methodologies such as reversal and multiple-baseline designs (as used in the total organizational study) to test the effectiveness of O.B.Mod.[41] The reversal, sometimes called the ABAB design, is performed in the following manner.

1   First a baseline measure is obtained on the individual or group in question (A).

2   Then an intervention is made and the behavior is measured until the change stabilizes (B).

3   Then the intervention is withdrawn and baseline conditions are reestablished (A).

4   Once the behavior under baseline conditions stabilizes, the intervention is made again (B).

In this ABAB design the subjects serve as their own control. The problem of intersubject variability inherent in a control group design is eliminated. The drawback of this potentially powerful design, however, is that it assumes that the behaviors are capable of being reversed when baseline conditions are reintroduced. Intermittent schedules which are resistant to extinction and the movement from the intervention to a self-reinforcing contingency may undermine this assumption. In addition, a very practical problem in using a reversal design is how to persuade results-minded management to return to baseline conditions if an intervention is working in the desired direction. Few managers are willing to sacrifice results in order to help prove a cause-and-effect relationship. To test the feasibility of this reversal design, seven cases of

O.B.Mod. interventions were analyzed.[42] In all seven cases (targeted behaviors included specifically defined evidence of leadership, job knowledge/interest, tardiness, dysfunctional interruptions, quality, and two cases of productivity) the behaviors moved in the desired direction after the O.B.Mod. intervention, but in only four cases did the behaviors reverse when baseline conditions were reintroduced. The three did not reverse for reasons outlined above.

To get around some limitations of reversals, especially the practical problem of reversing desired results, a multiple-baseline design may be more effective. In this design, baseline data are gathered across behaviors, individuals, or situations. The design is implemented as follows:

1   Baseline data are obtained on two or more behaviors (or individuals or situations).

2   An intervention is then made on one of the behaviors, but baseline conditions are maintained on the other(s).

3   Once the behavior has stabilized after the intervention, the next behavior is given the intervention.

4   This continues until all the behaviors are brought under the intervention.

This design has advantages similar to the reversal and eliminates the practical problem of reversing the behavior, but it makes the assumption of noninterdependence. In some cases changing one behavior (or individual or situation) may cause others to change. To test the feasibility of the multiple-baseline design as a way of evaluating the O.B.Mod. intervention, five cases were utilized.[43] For consistency, all five cases used a critical behavior (attendance, staying at the work station, contribution to performance, being productive in the work station, and improved service) across two individuals. The results were very encouraging for the use of multiple-baseline designs. In all cases the design was very adaptable and relevant and overcame the problems encountered in the reversal design. The multiple-baseline design was then successfully used in the total organization study reported earlier and does seem to be a viable alternative to more conventional control group research strategies.

ANALYSIS OF THE POSSIBLE ETHICAL ISSUES[44]

Skinner's work in general and some of the behavior modification applications made in mental hospitals, clinics, classrooms, and especially prisons have generated emotional criticism and much controversy. Surprisingly, this concern has not yet seemed to carry over to the applications in management. To date there are only a few scattered criticisms, on ethical grounds, reported in the literature,[45] but there are probably many managers and potential managers who feel uneasy about using an O.B.Mod. type of approach. Most of these agree that it works but feel that it is somehow wrong. Such concerns must be fully aired and constructively analyzed if O.B.Mod. is going to be a viable human resource management approach in the future. The ethical problems must be anticipated and discussed rather than simply reacted to.

Popular Criticism of Behavior Modification

Much of the popular criticism of Skinner's work revolves around his heavy dependence on the use of lower animals (especially the white rat) in developing the operant learning principles. The criticism that behavior modification tends to equate rats with humans is unfounded. The behaviorist would be the first to admit that rat and human behaviors are not the same. But at the same time they would point out that the mechanism of behavioral control is the same. From the operant perspective, all behaviors, animal and human, depend on their consequences. The appropriateness of the transition that behaviorism has made from animals to the mentally retarded to children to normal adults has been sufficiently demonstrated by both empirical research and practical application.

Besides the "applied ratamorphism" charge, another problem stems from the villainous portrayal of behavior control in popular literature, television, and the movies. The simple fact is that although the behavior control techniques portrayed in popular movies like *A Clockwork Orange* may be entertaining (if sinister manipulation and sadistic punishment can be called entertaining) and theoretically possible, they have nothing to do with the approach discussed in this chapter. Aversive conditioning and severe forms of punishment have no more chance of being used in human resource management than does any other preposterous diabolical scheme.

Legitimate Ethical Concerns

Getting the popular and spectacular but highly unreasonable ethical charges out of the way leaves the more legitimate ethical concerns surrounding control per se, particularly individual freedom and dignity, and the question of who controls the controllers. First of all it should be recognized that control of behavior has existed, does exist, and will continue to exist regardless of whether it is purposeful or not. The primary concern should probably not be with control per se but instead with the beneficiary of the behavioral control. If behavioral control is misapplied for selfish purposes, the charge of being unethical seems legitimate. On the other hand, if the control is used for more effective management with mutually beneficial consequences for both the person being controlled and the organization, it would seem to be on ethical grounds.

The individual-freedom-and-dignity issue popularized by Skinner's book *Beyond Freedom and Dignity* largely boils down to a philosophical discussion of relative ethics. The O.B.Mod. approach, which emphasizes positive control and creating a reinforcing organization environment, can increase rather than decrease an employee's freedom and dignity. This is especially true relative to the existing dependence on negative control found in most of today's organizations. The same can be said of the question of who controls the controllers. This is certainly not as big a problem in management application as it is in other applications. Whether in a public or private organization, the authority structure would always make the controller responsible to someone higher in the hierarchy. In addition, through countercontrol, subordinates can control their supervisors as well as be controlled by them. A major goal of O.B.Mod. is to create a mutually reinforcing environment so that participants may be self-reinforced for pursuing organizational objectives.

The Charge of Limited Application and Manipulation

Those who argue that an O.B.Mod. approach can have only very limited application in a complex organizational setting must recognize that the underlying theory and mechanisms hold in very simple or in very complex environments. The previous section demonstrated how O.B.Mod. has been and can be applied in complex organizational settings. Certainly O.B.Mod. is not the only approach to effective human resource management, and there is a challenge for more research and broader application. This is why O.B.Mod. is exciting; it is relatively new in terms of application, and to date there is a need for more research support, but it is built on a very well-developed, sound theoretical base.

As far as being manipulative, the same charges could be leveled at the techniques discussed in other chapters of this book. O.B.Mod. seems to be no more and no less manipulative than other human resource management approaches. It is important to note that in O.B.Mod. it is the environmental contingencies that are manipulated, not the individual.

A Final Word on Ethical Implications

Issues such as measuring on-the-job behaviors cannot be automatically dismissed. However, such measurement is certainly not new with O.B.Mod. (industrial engineers have been doing this since the turn of the century), and, as discussed earlier, there are ways of obtaining behavioral data without contaminating the data or compromising the individual's privacy. In the final analysis, the ethical answer to O.B.Mod. or any other technique lies in the professional integrity of the manager using the approach and the value of the results to both the organization and the individual. O.B.Mod. should in no way attempt to be secretive or manipulative. If O.B.Mod. is to be an effective human resource management approach, it must be completely ethical from a societal, organizational, and individual standpoint.

NOTES

1 Owen Aldis, "Of Pigeons and Men," *Harvard Business Review*, July–August 1961, pp. 59–63.

2 Walter R. Nord, "Beyond the Teaching Machine: The Neglected Area of Operant Conditioning in the Theory and Practice of Management," *Organizational Behavior and Human Performance*, November 1969, pp. 375–401; and Nord, "Improving Attendance through Rewards," *Personnel Administration*, vol. 33, no. 6, 1970, pp. 37–41.

3 Fred Luthans and Donald White, "Behavior Modification: Application to Manpower Management," *Personnel Administration*, July–August 1971, pp. 41–47; and E. E. Adam and William E. Scott, "The Application of Behavior Conditioning to the Problems of Quality Control," *Academy of Management Journal*, June 1971, pp. 175–193.

4 See Fred Luthans and Robert Kreitner, "The Role of Punishment in Organizational Behavior Modification (O.B.Mod.)," *Public Personnel Management*, May–June 1973, pp. 156–161; Fred Luthans and David Lyman, "Training Supervisors to Use Organizational Behavior Modification," *Personnel*, September–October 1973, pp. 38–44; Fred Luthans and Robert Ottemann, "Motivation vs. Learning Approaches to Organizational Behavior," *Business Horizons*, December 1973, pp. 55–62; Fred Luthans and Robert Kreitner, "The Management of Behavioral Contingencies," *Personnel*, July–August 1974, pp. 7–16; Fred Luthans and Mark Martinko, "An O.B.Mod. Analysis of Absenteeism," *Human Resource Management*, vol. 15, no. 3, Fall 1976, pp. 11–18; and Fred Luthans, "An Organizational Behavior Modification (O.B.Mod.) Approach to O.D.," *Organization and Administrative Sciences*, Winter 1975/1976, pp. 47–53. For a comprehensive review of other related approaches see Craig E. Schneier, "Behavior Modification in Management: A Review and Critique," *Academy of Management Journal*, September 1974, pp. 528–548, and Donald M. Prue, Lee W. Frederiksen, and Ansley Bacon, "Organizational Behavior Management: An Annotated Bib-

liography," *Journal of Organizational Behavior Management,* vol. 1, no. 4, Summer 1978, pp. 216–257.

5 Fred Luthans and Robert Kreitner, *Organizational Behavior Modification,* Scott, Foresman, Glenview, Ill., 1975.

6 Prue, et al., op. cit.

7 "Where Skinner's Theories Work," *Business Week,* Dec. 2, 1972, pp. 64–65.

8 "Productivity Gains from a Pat on the Back," *Business Week,* Jan. 23, 1978, pp. 56–62.

9 "Special Report: Performance Feedback and Positive Reinforcement," *Training,* December 1976, pp. 15–56.

10 "Performance Audit, Feedback, and Positive Reinforcement," *Training and Development Journal,* November 1972, pp. 8–13; and "At Emery Air Freight: Positive Reinforcement Boosts Performance," *Organizational Dynamics,* Winter 1973, pp. 41–50. The film on the Emery experience is "Business, Behaviorism, and the Bottom-Line," CRM McGraw-Hill Films, Del Mar, Calif.

11 An example of such a total organization development approach can be found in Luthans and Kreitner, *Organizational Behavior Modification,* pp. 164–170.

12 Robert Kreitner, "PM—A New Method of Behavior Change," *Business Horizons,* December 1975, p. 82.

13 James M. Johnston, Phillip K. Duncan, Craig Monroe, and Albert Stoerziner, "Tactics and Benefits of Behavioral Measurement in Business," *Journal of Organizational Behavior Management,* vol. 1, no. 3, Spring 1978, pp. 164–178.

14 "Performance Audit, Feedback, and Positive Reinforcement," and "At Emery Air Freight."

15 An expanded functional analysis includes provision for cognitive mediating processes (O in the model) and recognizes both overt (observable) and covert (unobservable) behaviors (B) and environmental contingencies (S and C). The more traditional Skinnerian functional analysis gives recognition to a three-term contingency of observable antecedent—behavior—consequence or simply A—B—C. It is this latter functional analysis that is presently used in O.B.Mod. In the future, however, when self-control is better understood, the expanded S ↔ O ↔ B ↔ C functional analysis may be applied. See Fred Luthans, *Organizational Behavior,* 1981 ed., McGraw-Hill, 1973; and Fred Luthans, "Leadership: A Proposal for a Social Learning Theory Base and Observational and Functional Analysis Techniques to Measure Leadership Behavior," in J. G. Hunt and L. Larson (eds.), *Crosscurrents in Leadership,* Southern Illinois University Press, Carbondale, 1979, pp. 201–208.

16 See Luthans, *Organizational Behavior,* chap. 9.

17 See Luthans and Kreitner, *Organizational Behavior Modification,* pp. 91–99.

18 Milton R. Blood, "Intergroup Comparisons of Intraperson Differences: Rewards from the Job," *Personnel Psychology,* Spring 1973, pp. 1–9.

19 For example, see H. Joseph Reitz, "Managerial Attitudes and Perceived

Contingencies between Performance and Organizational Response," *Academy of Management Proceedings*, 1971, pp. 227–238.

20 Luthans and Kreitner, *Organizational Behavior Modification*, p. 102.

21 "Performance Audit, Feedback, and Positive Reinforcement," and "At Emery Air Freight."

22 High achievers have been shown to have an intense desire for immediate feedback. See David C. McClelland, *The Achieving Society*, Van Nostrand, Princeton, N.J., 1961.

23 Studies showing the positive impact that feedback has on the performance of workers in industrial settings include L. Miller, *The Use of Knowledge of Results in Improving the Performance of Hourly Operations*, Behavioral Research Service, General Electric Company, 1965; and P. S. Hundal, "Knowledge of Performance as an Incentive in Repetitive Industrial Work," *Journal of Applied Psychology*, June 1969, pp. 224–226.

24 Edwin B. Flippo and Gary Munsinger, *Management: A Behavioral Approach*, 3d ed., Allyn and Bacon, Boston, 1975, p. 334.

25 Alan C. Filley and Robert J. House, *Managerial Process and Organizational Behavior*, Scott, Foresman, Glenview, Ill., 1969, p. 371.

26 Edward E. Lawler, *Pay and Organizational Effectiveness: A Psychological View*, McGraw-Hill, New York, 1971, p. 284.

27 Ross A. Webber, *Management*, Irwin, Homewood, Ill., 1975, p. 108.

28 Jaime A. Hermann, Ana I. deMontes, Benjamin Dominguez, Francisco deMontes, and B. L. Hopkins, "Effects of Bonuses for Punctuality on the Tardiness of Industrial Workers," *Journal of Applied Behavioral Analysis*, Winter 1973, pp. 563–570.

29 Luthans and Kreitner, *Organizational Behavior Modification*, p. 103.

30 David Premack, "Reinforcement Theory," in David Levine (ed.), *Nebraska Symposium on Motivation*, University of Nebraska Press, Lincoln, 1965, pp. 123–180.

31 Ralph F. Cantalanello and Donald L. Kirkpatrick, "Evaluating Training Programs—The State of the Art," *Training and Development Journal*, May 1968, p. 9.

32 Fred Luthans and William E. Reif, "Job Enrichment: Long on Theory, Short on Practice," *Organizational Dynamics*, Winter 1974, p. 33.

33 Carol Tavris, "The Experimenting Society: A Conversation with Donald T. Campbell," *Psychology Today*, September 1975, pp. 47–56.

34 Charles Snyder, *Application of Organizational Behavior Modification in the Public Sector: Case Studies in a Hospital Environment*, unpublished doctoral dissertation, University of Nebraska, Lincoln, 1978.

35 See D. T. Campbell and J. C. Stanley, *Experimental and Quasi-Experimental Designs for Research*, Rand McNally, Chicago, 1963.

36 These examples are reported in detail, including the charts, in Luthans and Kreitner, *Organizational Behavior Modification*, pp. 153–157.

37   Robert Ottemann and Fred Luthans, "An Experimental Analysis of the Effectiveness of an Organizational Behavior Modification Program in Industry," *Academy of Management Proceedings,* 1975, pp. 140–142.

38   Fred Luthans and Jason Schweizer, "O.B.Mod. in a Small Factory: How the Behavior Modification Technique Can Improve Total Organizational Performance," *Management Review,* September 1979, pp. 43–50.

39   Charles A. Snyder and Fred Luthans, "The Application of O.B.Mod. To Increase the Productivity of Hospital Personnel," *Personnel Administrator* (in press).

40   Fred Luthans, Robert Paul, and Douglas Baker, "An Experimental Analysis of the Impact of O.B.Mod. on Salespersons' Performance Behaviors," Working Paper, Department of Management, University of Nebraska, Lincoln, 1980. Presented at the Academy of Management Meeting, Detroit, 1980.

41   See Alan E. Kazdin, "Methodological and Assessment Considerations in Evaluating Reinforcement Programs in Applied Settings," *Journal of Applied Behavioral Analysis,* Fall 1973, pp. 517–531; and Michel Herson and David Barlow, *Single Case Experimental Designs,* Pergamon, New York, 1976.

42   Fred Luthans and Kenneth M. Bond, "The Use of Reversal Designs in Organizational Behavior Research," *Academy of Management Proceedings,* 1977, pp. 86–90.

43   Peter W. Van Ness and Fred Luthans, "Multiple-Baseline Designs: An Alternative Strategy for Organizational Behavior Research," *Proceedings of the Midwest Academy of Management,* Cleveland, Ohio, 1979.

44   The author is indebted to Professor Robert Kreitner for many of the thoughts expressed in this section.

45   For example, see M. Hammer, "The Application of Behavior Conditioning Procedures to the Problems of Quality Control: Comment," *Academy of Management Journal,* December 1971, pp. 529–532; Fred Fry, "Operant Conditioning and O.B.Mod.: Of Mice and Men," *Personnel,* July–August 1974, pp. 17–24; and Edwin A. Locke, "The Myths of Behavior Mod. in Organizations," *Academy of Management Review,* October 1977, pp. 543–553.

REFERENCES

Adam, Everett E., Jr.: "Behavior Modification in Quality Control," *Academy of Management Journal,* December 1975, pp. 662–679.

"At Emery Air Freight: Positive Reinforcement Boosts Performance," *Organizational Dynamics,* Winter 1973, pp. 41–50.

Beatty, Richard W., and Craig Eric Schneier: "A Case for Positive Reinforcement," *Business Horizons,* April 1975, pp. 57–66.

Fry, Fred: "Operant Conditioning and O.B.Mod.: Of Mice and Men," *Personnel,* July–August 1974, pp. 17–24.

Goldstein, Arnold P., and Melvin Sorcher: "Changing Managerial Behavior by

Applied Learning Techniques," *Training and Development Journal,* March 1973, pp. 36–39.

Kreitner, Robert: "PM—A New Method of Behavior Change," *Business Horizons,* December 1975, pp. 79–86.

Luthans, Fred: "An Organizational Behavior Modification (O.B.Mod.) Approach to O.D.," *Organization and Administrative Sciences,* Winter 1975/1976, pp. 47–53.

Luthans, Fred, and Robert Kreitner: "The Management of Behavioral Contingencies," *Personnel,* July–August 1974, pp. 7–16.

Luthans, Fred, and Robert Kreitner: *Organizational Behavior Modification,* Scott, Foresman, Glenview, Ill., 1975.

Luthans, Fred, and Robert Kreitner: "The Role of Punishment in Organizational Behavior Modification," *Public Personnel Management,* May–June 1973, pp. 156–161.

Luthans, Fred, and David Lyman: "Training Supervisors to Use Organizational Behavior Modification," *Personnel,* September–October 1973, pp. 38–44.

Luthans, Fred, and Mark Martinko: "An Organizational Behavior Modification Analysis of Absenteeism," *Human Resource Management,* Fall 1976, pp. 11–18.

Luthans, Fred, and Mark Martinko: *The Power of Positive Reinforcement,* McGraw-Hill, New York, 1978.

Luthans, Fred, and Robert Ottemann: "Motivation versus Learning Approaches to Organizational Behavior," *Business Horizons,* December 1973, pp. 55–62.

Luthans, Fred, and Jason Schweizer: "O.B.Mod. in a Small Factory: How Behavior Modification Techniques Can Improve Total Organizational Performance," *Management Review,* September 1979, pp. 43–50.

Luthans, Fred and Donald D. White, Jr.: "Behavior Modification: Application to Manpower Management," *Personnel Administration,* July–August 1971, pp. 41–47.

Miller, L. M.: *Behavior Management,* John Wiley, New York, 1978.

Nord, Walter R.: "Beyond the Teaching Machine: The Neglected Area of Operant Conditioning in the Theory and Practice of Management," *Organizational Behavior and Human Performance,* November 1969, pp. 375–401.

Ottemann, Robert, and Fred Luthans: "An Experimental Analysis of the Effectiveness of an Organizational Behavior Modification Program in Industry," *Academy of Management Proceedings,* 1975, pp. 140–142.

Schneier, Craig Eric: "Behavior Modification in Management: A Review and Critique," *Academy of Management Journal,* September 1974, pp. 528–548.

Snyder, Charles A., and Fred Luthans, "The Application of O.B.Mod. to Increase the Productivity of Hospital Personnel," *Personnel Administrator* (in press).

Yukl, Gary A., and Gary P. Latham: "Consequences of Reinforcement Schedules and Incentive Magnitudes for Employee Performance: Problems Encountered in an Industrial Setting," *Journal of Applied Psychology,* June 1975, pp. 294–298.

Management by Objectives

George S. Odiorne

Professor of Management
University of Massachusetts/Amherst

The McDonnell-Douglas Company was formed through the merger of the McDonnell Aircraft Company of St. Louis and Douglas Aircraft of California. In theory at least, the two companies should have been nearly identical in performance. Yet McDonnell was profitable and had a sizable cash surplus, whereas Douglas was in serious trouble. After the preliminary negotiations, some study of the situation at Douglas convinced the top management at McDonnell that it could make the necessary changes to turn Douglas around and make it a productive and profitable part of its operation. During the preliminary studies, executives and managers from St. Louis had toured the Douglas plant, talking to workers and supervisors. They came back with a fundamental conclusion: the people at Douglas simply didn't know how to do their jobs. There were welders who couldn't weld, riveters who couldn't rivet, typists who couldn't type, and many others who were far below the skill levels ordinarily found in the St. Louis operation of McDonnell. Nevertheless McDonnell decided to proceed with the deal.

Shortly after the merger was consummated, planeloads of employees from St. Louis flew to California and trained their counterparts at Douglas in how to do their jobs. Schools, coaching situations, and extensive tutoring and job training sessions went on at the same time. As a result a dramatic turnaround was reported.

This description illustrates, in a dramatic way, how training, development, and knowledge of basic job objectives constitute a change program for an organization.

Job Experience Ranked Top in Management Development

The Autumn 1978 issue of *Organizational Dynamics* includes an article by Lester A. Digman, "How Well-Managed Organizations Develop Their Executive," which reports on a study of 10 companies in depth and a survey of 59 others. Some of the interesting findings can be seen in Table 3-1, which is adapted from that data.

Other findings and conclusions from the article:

There is no one best way to develop managers.

There is a common philosophy that development occurs on the job.

Management development gets the attention of top management in all the companies studied.

In-house training is preferred by companies with training populations large enough to make it cost-effective. Out-of-company programs are being used less and less.

The experience from McDonnell-Douglas and elsewhere, however, makes it clear that simply showing up for work every day doesn't constitute being trained. An employee might be doing the wrong things repetitively or learning the wrong way of doing things. Employees might be obtaining on-the-job experience in making a mess of things and, even worse, being rewarded for that effort. Organizational change occurs

Table 3-1 Importance of Developmental Means as Ranked by Respondents

	Percent ranking means in importance as		
Means of development	1st	2d	3d
On-the-job experience	74	10	8
Coaching by superiors	12	42	0
Rotational assignments	6	20	0
In-house classroom	4	24	44
University programs	0	4	10
Others	4	0	2

mainly on the job, but only when the purposes of the job are crystal clear and there is a basis for improvement.

Jean Baptiste Lamarck (1815) after a lifetime of studying biological processes, arrived at some conclusions about evolution and change. Change has, he said, four major component elements:

1 A striving for perfection
2 An ability to adapt to outside change
3 An ability to make major changes of a major nature
4 The condition of being a product of its own history

While this terse summary, of course, hardly does justice to Lamarck, it fairly represents his overall perception of change, and perhaps it is a worthy guide to the organization that would produce change, especially through changing the behavior of its people.

The management process known as Management by Objectives is clearly a conscious attempt to change the organization for the better by focusing its attention constantly, unremittingly, and systematically on its goals and purposes and attempting to get every member of the organization to do likewise for his or her own job.

THE DIFFICULTIES IN STRIVING FOR PERFECTION

Perfection is, of course, never attained, but as a goal it lends an organization and its people purposes and aims. Even when a logical statement is agreed to by all concerned, it is not a simple matter to find specific goals and pursue them unrelentingly. This is especially true in large organizations where the bureaucratic pathology takes over and people continue their pursuit of goals (or perfection) through what psychologist T. A. Ryan has called "intentional behavior." This goal-seeking behavior, which is ubiquitous in most all human behavior, gets diverted because of the difficulty in identifying the proper goals and then continuing the pursuit of those goals without diversion. One of the major influences of diversion is the *activity trap*.

The Activity Trap

Some of the largest and most affluent corporations are caught in an insidious trap. It is called the "activity trap," and it afflicts small corporations as well. It extends beyond the business world into governments, schools, hospitals, churches, even families. Unless victims are aware of it, the activity trap will ensnare the wisest, most experienced old hands.

What is the activity trap? It's the abysmal situation in which people find themselves when they start out for what once was an important and clear objective but, in an amazingly short time, become so enmeshed in the activity of getting there that they forget where they are going.

Every business started out to achieve some objective, usually an increasing profit. Resources were assembled from stockholders, loans, or savings and poured into the enterprise. Everyone got busy, engaging in *activity* designed to carry the organization toward its objectives. But once-clear goals somehow evolved into something else, while the activity remained the same—and became an end in itself.

In other words, in most businesses the goal moves, but the activity persists and becomes a false goal. This false goal becomes the criterion for making decisions, and the decisions get progressively worse.

If this seems complicated, look at some examples of the activity trap:

- Quality-control directors act as if the enterprise were created so that they could shut it down and hold up everything produced yesterday.

- The accountant acts as if the business were created so that she could keep books on it. No longer does she keep books so that the boss can run it better.

- The sales manager acts as if there were no problems that couldn't be solved by more volume. Sales go up, but profits fall.

- Production supervisors get tonnage out the back gate by shipping junk, or using wrong labels and faulty addresses, then ride the backs of the help to get more production out tomorrow.

- Personnel managers behave as if the entire purpose of hiring all those people, providing them with tools and equipment, and building a plant was so that the personnel department could make them happy.

- The labor relations director acts as if the company were formed so he could fight with union officers.

Meanwhile, the stockholders and the president sit atop the mess wondering where the profit went.

The activity trap is a self-feeding mechanism if you don't turn it around. Everybody becomes emotionally attached to some irrelevancy, and does the job *too well*. Its ultimate stage is reached when even the president loses sight of the reasons for being in business, and demands more and more activity, rather than results. Layers of professionals are added to help control the activity. Large corporations have acres of lawyers, each outstripping the other in preventing everybody from producing anything. Profits decline and the president adds a battery of accountants. So what happens? Considerable accounting is produced; costs go up. Engineers fight engineering problems by hiring more engineers, each with a technical opinion designed to prevent something from happening someplace else in the firm. Many professionals spend their entire working life taking in one another's administrative laundry, creating jobs and administrative hierarchies to generate more activity that is increasingly unrelated to the purpose of the company's existence.

Churches, too, become enmeshed with covered-dish suppers and basketball leagues—activities generating little other than indigestion and flat feet. Families get so entangled in the mechanical process of living that they forget what families were started for. (There is the story of the perfect homemaker whose child got up at night to go to the bathroom. When he came back to his bed, he found it had been made.) Service clubs spend more and more time exhorting the members to "support this activity" with no hint of a worthwhile payoff.

Meanwhile, all this activity eats up resources, money, space, budgets, savings, and human energy like a mammoth tapeworm. While it's apparent that the activity trap cuts profits, loses ball games, and fails to achieve missions, it has an equally dangerous side effect on people: they *shrink* personally and professionally.

Take any boss and any subordinate. Ask the employee to write down what specific results are expected by the boss in the next quarter. Now ask the boss, "What results would you like to see that person produce next quarter?" The average manager and subordinate won't agree on results sought, while they may be reasonably close on activities to be conducted. Answers will differ, and the differences will cause the subordinate to shrink essentially in potential. Research shows that:

1   On regular, ongoing responsibilities, the average boss and subordinate, caught in the activity trap, will fail to agree on expected outputs at a level of 25 percent.

2   At the same time, resulting from this failure to agree on regular responsibilities, they will disagree on what the subordinate's major problems are at a level of 50 percent.

3   The worst gap of all is the failure of boss and subordinate to agree on how the subordinate's job should be improved. On this latter count, they fail to agree at a level of 90 percent.

As a result, nothing really changes in the way things are done. The environment changes, the customers' tastes change, the values of employees change. But the methods remain static and the organization is crippled by the outdated acts of its own employees.

The human consequence is that employees shrink. The organization drains its people of their zap and finds itself employing pygmies. They look like real people, wear suits, drive cars, and pay taxes, but they are performance midgets. They nod their heads when the boss chastises them, but know they have been cheated. They are stabbed daily in duals they didn't know were underway. Trees fall upon them, and *then* somebody yells "timber." Their defensive recourse? Keep *active*.

Employees redouble their energy when they have lost sight of their goal. They may be reprimanded, or even fired, for doing something wrong when they didn't know what "right" was to begin with. They run a race without knowing how long the track is. They wonder if it's time to sprint for the wire, but they can't guess when, because it might be a 100-yard dash or the Boston Marathon.

The effect is cumulative. Because people don't know the ordinary objectives of their jobs they are hit for failures growing out of ignorance of successful measures. This produces a reluctance to discover shortcomings. Suggesting something new in such an environment is risky. Better to stick with the old activity. Looking busy becomes safer than being productive.

This tendency toward activity is not inevitable, if top people try to circumvent it. The law of gravity is always with us, but some people build bridges. In America's best-managed organizations, the management has leadership systems that concentrate on output and results. In such organizations, every manager and subordinate manager periodically sit down and talk about what the latter is going to produce next quarter or next year. The two talk about objectives, outputs, results, and indicators until they agree on what the future shall hold. One of the parties then confirms the agreement with a memo. Now when the curtain goes up, both actors have the same script: this improves the quality of the acting considerably.

- The emphasis is on output, not activity.
- Both people know what is expected of them and can tell immediately how well they are doing.
- Each is responsible for results and is committed to trying to achieve them.
- Each feels free to make necessary decisions and take necessary actions to achieve the objectives.
- At the end of the period, the manager and subordinate sit down once more and talk again. "Here is what you said you were going to produce. How well did you do, and what are you going to do next quarter?"

The key figure in this type of productive organization is the top person. This individual determines that the organization will be managed by objectives, not activity, and also determines the corporate objectives and strategic goals. The subordinate managers define their operational objectives to fit those top-level goals and strategies. The top person should not be involved in day-to-day operations, but should manage them by selected objectives.

Nonbusiness organizations need explicit objectives, too. Families with defined objectives can get off the backs of their offspring, permitting wider latitudes in activity and behavior if the end result is good. Service clubs find that definite objectives attract resources and manpower for their achievement.

Virtually any organization can get caught in the activity trap, because the bait is so alluring. But the security of the trap is inherently false and the rewards diminish at an accelerated rate. Organization, after all, is not an end in itself; it is a means of achieving specific objectives. To accomplish this, the participants—if they themselves are to survive—must eventually get down to business rather than the "busyness" of the activity trap.

MANAGEMENT BY OBJECTIVES

General Introduction

1 Management by Objectives is a way of getting improved results in managerial action. It's not an addition to a manager's job, it's *a way of doing it.*

2 It's based on observations of what successful executives do in many companies and organizations (General Mills, General Motors, Minneapolis-Honeywell, IBM, and General Electric, to name a few).

3 It is especially pertinent in *managing managers,* and most applications have been limited to upper levels of management. Management by Objectives can extend down as far as first-line supervision, provided top management endorses and supports it through using it.

4 It relates to several key problems in the management of an organization.

    a What is expected—in terms of *objectives.*

    b Obtaining teamwork—by identifying common goals.

    c Programming work—by setting *terminal dates* for tasks.

    d Recognizing process—through mutual agreement on goals and measuring accomplishments against them.

e Salary administration—how would increases be allocated?

f Assessing promotability—by identifying *potential* for it.

5 In its briefest form, Management by Objectives can be described as a managerial method whereby the superior and the subordinate managers in an organization identify major areas of responsibility in which the employee will work, set some standards for good—or bad—performance, and plan for the measurement of results against those standards.

6 The advantages of this kind of management are better results, lower costs, improved performance, larger number of promotable people, improved quality of service, more businesslike management of salaries, and the development of subordinates' best abilities.

Management By Objectives as a Managerial Strategy

Management by Objectives should provide a realistic tie between immediate operational controls and long-range planning, making them different dimensions of the same process.

1 The entire process of management includes the following ingredients:

   a A five-year plan adjusted annually. That is, when the first year has been completed and reviewed, the entire process is repeated. Thus, the five-year plan is produced every year by dropping the prior year and adding the next in order.

   b The first year calls for tighter controls and commitments from every manager.

   c It requires quarterly review of results of interim adjustments of activities to adhere to the year's objectives (see Figure 3-1).

   d It calls for some indicators or criteria for decisions. These are

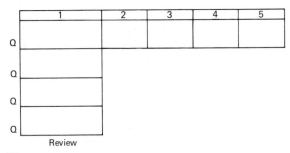

Review

Fig. 3-1 Five-year plan and quarterly review.

the overall guides, such as Return on Investment (ROI), which are the basic decision criteria against which company performance is measured.

2 Management by Objectives is not a top-down-only process. That is, the top management five-year plan is not made rigidly without room for accommodation for operating experience. Nor is it exclusively a bottom-up process in which short-run goals of people are added together and thus become the five-year plan. It provides that yearly goals and the budgeting for each year will meld with long-run plans through dialogue and acceptance of one another's conclusions. This often occurs at the budget-making level of responsibility.

3 This strategy implies that the following conditions must exist over the whole matrix of management.

   a The business will be stable, that is, under control during the first year, and commitments made by people in manufacturing, selling, and staff work will be observed and the results used for decisions and action in managing managers.

   b It implies that deviations from standard will be dealt with by responsible committed persons to restore normality when committed objectives are not being met.

   c It places innovation and improvement of regular operations, as well as strategic changes which affect the character of the organization, high in the system of values which are rewarded and approved.

4 Its major function in operational management, the first year of the five-year plan, is the management of managers. Thus objectives agreed upon between manager and boss become the criteria for pay, bonus, promotion, coaching, training, and selection.

5 Staff work, especially at the corporate level, becomes that of "making and selling intangible products to internal captive markets." The major product line produced by staff departments includes the following outputs:

   a Advice—case load units, billable hours, and similar indicators.

   b Service—doing something for line departments or other staff units that they cannot do as efficiently as the staff service unit, which has expert knowhow or special tools.

   c Controls—producing information which will assist in error prevention, error correction, and restoration of norms.

   d Research—including new products, new ideas, trade advantages, monopolies, cost reductions, or answers to questions requiring analytical effort.

TWO PARTS TO MBO

In brief, we've noted that the system of Management by Objectives (MBO) can be described as a process whereby the superior and subordinate managers of an organization jointly identify its common goals, define each individual's major areas of responsibility in terms of results expected, and use these measures as guides for operating the unit and assessing the contribution of each of its members. The logical beginning point in the organization for MBO is at the top. The sequence in which objectives will be set and reviewed comprises a rudimentary calendar of events that occur in the organization over a two-year cycle on a continuing basis.

How to Set Objectives

The first step in goal setting is to define the ordinary calendar of events which must occur in the organization where MBO is to become the prevailing management system. This entails, as is shown in Table 3-2 and Figure 3-2, scheduling some events that occur prior to the beginning of the target year, and some events which will occur during that year.

Management by Anticipation   This term is used to describe goal-setting actions which are required of staff departments such as personnel, accounting, legal, traffic, finance, controller, and other staff functions.

Audit Information   This information, which includes program audits and overall review of the major strengths and weaknesses of each staff responsibility, should be reviewed to provide a basis for finding major opportunities and problems.

Five-Year Plan   The annual edition of the company five-year plan should be prepared for each of the major areas of responsibility. Thus the annual edition of the five-year personnel plan, financial plan, technical plan, and the like should be prepared at a period some three months in advance of budget submission. For a company on a fiscal year starting January, the close-off date for the annual five-year plan thus would be about July 1 of the prior year. This permits opportunity to revise budgetary planning, move resources to new uses, find new funding requirements, and make decisions about the abandonment of programs or plans.

Annual Budgets   With audit information reviewed and the annual edition of the five-year plan written and circulated, the allocation of resources can occur. It permits more rational commitments of resources, including the use of zero-based budgeting for support services, and of cost effectiveness methods for facility and program decisions.

Table 3-2   A Rudimentary MBO Strategic Planning Cycle for Business or Other Organization on a Calendar-Year Operation Basis

Date	Event	Comments
July 1	Annual edition of the five-year plan and review of prior year's five-year plan	Responsibility of the top person and all major functional (staff) heads, assembled by planning department
October 1	Budgetary submission to budget decision group (for the following year)	Upward from all units starting with sales forecast, cost estimates, and profit forecast to budgeteer
	Review, revise, approve final budget figures	Executive Committee
January 1	Start the new budget year, release resources	Issue detailed, approved financial targets in final form
January 15 to February 1	Completion of individual operational objectives at all levels	Sets standards for managerial performance for the year
	Annual goals conference by managers of departments	To share goals and devise teamwork
	Annual message of the president	To give a challenge
April to July 1 October 1	Quarterly reviews of individual results against goals and adjustments as required	All managers at all levels
April 15	Audits—including program	Staff departments
Monthly	Meetings of the Executive and Finance Committee to note exceptions and make corrective moves	
Passim:	Position papers for circulation and discussion and policy committee actions as major issues are noted	By staff experts or any responsible manager or professional or functional group
July 1	Process repeated	

These three steps in management by anticipation are essential in the effective functioning of MBO in an organization. They provide for sound strategic objectives being in hand before efficient operational

1. Should be prepared three months in advance of budgeting decisions
2. Should come up from below as proposed alternative strategies
3. Should be prepared annually at *half-year*

Outline	Comments
I Describe the present condition, statistically and verbally (add your professional opinion) on: **A.** Internally: Strengths, weaknesses, problems? **B.** Externally: What are the threats, risks, and opportunities you see? **II** Trends: If we didn't do anything differently in this area, where would we be in 1, 2, 5 years? (Do you like this possible outcome?) **III** WHAT ARE THE MAJOR MISSIONS? What are we in business for? Who are our clients? What is our product? What should it be?	

IV WHAT ARE SOME OPTIONAL STRATEGIES?	What would the consequences be?		
	Contribution	Costs	Feasibility
A. Do nothing differently			
B. _____			
C. _____			
D. _____			
E. _____			
F. _____			
(Press for multiple options)			

Recommended action plan: To be turned into OBJECTIVES

Fig. 3-2   Format for annual strategic objectives statements.

objectives are chosen. *Without strategic objectives stated in advance, measurable operational objectives may not be valid. You may simply be running a well-run bankruptcy.*

In formulating strategic objectives, the following points should be considered:

Strategic objectives should be stated in advance of budgetary decisions.

Strategic objectives should define strengths, weaknesses, problems, threats, risks, and opportunities.

Strategic objectives should note trends and missions and define strategic options, including consequences of each option.

Good strategic objectives will answer the question "are we doing the right things" in contrast with the operational objectives which define "how to do things right."

The emphasis in strategic anticipation staff goals need not necessarily be measurable but should use both words and numbers with clarity to define long-run outcomes sought. They are often established by groups such as the board of directors, management committee, personnel policy committee, and the like. For example: "Apex corporation will become the leading seller of solid state monitoring devices in the field by 1983."

There are some specific questions which will be included in the strategic goals statement of every staff department and major business unit. These key questions, to be answered in defining strategic objectives, are as follows:

1 *Market orientation.* Are we market centered or technology centered? Do we make things for the sales department to sell, or do we find market opportunities and invent things to fit?

2 *Service.* How completely do we wish to follow up our product?

3 *Top down or bottom up?* Do we have the top management (board, etc.) come up with the numbers for sales and growth and work back from the numbers at lower levels? Or do we collect the bottom-up goals and cumulate them to find the corporate goals?

4 *Indicators.* What is the best indicator (or indicators) of total organizational success? Dollar profit? Percent profit? Earnings per share? Return on investment? Return on gross assets? Market share?

5 *Pricing.* Are we a market skimmer? A price cutter? Are we in price competition or nonprice competition?

6 *Ethics.* Are we a "straight arrow" company, or do we consider ourselves "rough and tough" in dealing with competitors, suppliers, employees, customers?

7 *Systematic.* Do we rely more on experience and personal knowhow of managers, or upon systems such as computers, analytical work?

8 *Incentives.* Do we aim at sharing our profits and successes widely with employees, with just a few managers, or not at all?

9 *Employee growth.* Do we spend resources to grow our own people, or do we let them take care of that themselves, and hire others from outside when a new demand for talent crops up?

10 *Technology.* Are we a basic inventor and exploiter of our own research, or do we wait for others, and assume a second-bite-of-the-apple approach to new technology?

11 *Products.* Are we a company with a Cadillac, a medium-price, or a low-price product, or with all of them?

12 *Compensation.* Where do we wish to stand with respect to the community and competitive firms? Higher, the same, or lower?

13 *Community relations.* Are we a community leader, a middle-of-the-road citizen, or do we remain silent with a low profile?

14 *Government relations.* Do we respond when required, do we permit some affirmative actions toward government, or do we assume positive leadership and work to affect government?

How to Set Objectives/Operational Goals

At the beginning of the operational year, each manager and subordinate manager sits down and conducts a dialogue on specific operational objectives for the coming year for the subordinate position. Prior to the discussion each reviews the present situation, the results of the previous year, and some of the more likely requirements for change. Each thus comes to the discussion prepared to arrive at commitments and to assume and delegate responsibilities.

The boss is armed with information about budget limitations, strategic goals which have been agreed upon above, plus some information about actual results obtained the prior period.

The subordinate comes with some expectations and self-knowledge of particular performance strengths, weaknesses, and problems as well as threats, risks, and opportunities.

Management by Commitment   Operational management by objectives adds to the previous management-by-anticipation a new dimension which is a face-to-face relationship with the superior, and through that superior the organization itself—management by commitment.

Commitment means that the person makes some promises to somebody else whose opinion is important. This commitment is not general but specific, explicit, measurable, and worthwhile.

Responsibility means that the person accepts full accountability for the outcomes which will be produced during the commitment period without reference to excuses or exculpatory explanations. This doesn't guarantee that the responsible person can't fail for reasons beyond control, but regardless, assumes a responsibility for the results. This implies a kind of adult behavior, professional effort, and mature self-control in engaging one's work.

The superior is also committed. If the superior agrees in advance that the proposed operating goals are meritorious in advance, then those objectives must be the criteria for judging performance at the end of the period. Such judgments could include salary adjustments and merit pay recommendations, bonus awards, appraisal, promotability notations, and similar rewards for achievement. In accepting objectives in the beginning, the superior thus cannot apply capricious or *ex post* judgments.

The key to management by commitment is that the hard bargaining about what constitutes excellence of performance is done up front, before the period begins, not after a year or so of effort.

The process by which the operating goals (commitments) are established consists of a dialogue and a memorandum. The dialogue is one to which each person brings something. It is neither solely top down nor solely bottom up, but is a genuine two-way discussion. It is most satisfactory when it is conducted on an adult-to-adult level rather than on a parent-child model.

How to Write Objectives for Commitment

Operating objectives should comprise an ascending scale of excellence, by which the manager can administer certain ongoing concerns in managing managers. For the subordinate it should comprise a series of levels of excellence. As shown in Table 3-3, this is best accomplished when the superior has criteria for making year-end decisions for purposes of compensation, personnel records, defining promotability and assignments, coaching and training subordinates, and the administration of discipline and delegation.

For the subordinate, these five questions should have been answered or resolved:

1   What is expected of me? (Let me know in advance.)

2   What help and resources will be available to me in my work?

Table 3-3   The Respective Roles of Boss and Subordinate in Goal Setting

Subordinate proposes	Superior's actions
Sets standards for job	Insists upon realistic ones that challenge ability
Defines measures for results	Asks how arrived at
Does detailed analysis	Questions methods
Suggests alternative actions	Suggests other possible actions where germane
Proposes one course of action	Forces a recommendation from subordinate
Predicts effect of goals	Gets commitments and makes them to subordinate

3 How much freedom may I expect, and what reporting times and forms should I assume?

4 How can I tell how well I am doing in my work while I am doing it?

5 Upon what performance bases will rewards be issued?

This is best achieved by writing goals in three categories as shown in Fig. 3-3. Goals are defined in three major categories and should be written to cover all three.

Category 1 *What will be the regular responsibilities* of the position? These are the ongoing, recurring, repetitive, and measurable objectives of the job such as dollar volume of sales or units per shift.

Category 2 *What are the major problems* which should be attacked and solved in this position during the coming period? A problem is a deviation from a standard which persists or which somebody important wants to have fixed.

Category 3 *What innovations will be attempted?* These are not reactive but proactive goals. They are improvements, betterments: projects which will cause the organization under the subordinate's control to operate better, cheaper, faster, safer, at higher quality, or with greater dignity to people.

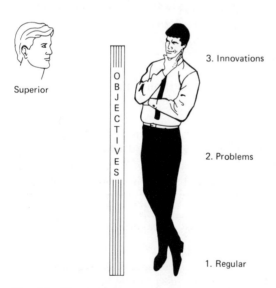

Superior

OBJECTIVES

3. Innovations

2. Problems

1. Regular

Fig. 3-3 The divisional general manager's objectives.

What Are Some Typical Performance Measures?

Starting with the regular objectives (Category 1) of the general manager and key subordinates, the goals should lock the organization together through some key indicators. Figure 3-4 shows some sample objectives of an ongoing, recurring character of the division general manager. The indicators of the regular category for this position include the following:

Dollar volume of revenue per month

Return on investment per quarter

Cash on hand at quarter end

Receivables, average age in days per quarters

Inventory, average dollar level over the quarter

Budget deviations as percent on capital budgets

Growth in dollar volume per quarter

Labor stoppages per year

The indicators are never standard, but those listed were found to be common among a sample of 50 general managers. A study of Figure 3-4 should highlight some of the features of operating regular objectives.

1   Objectives are stated as outputs for a time period. Statements of activities are not objectives but means.

2   The actual number chosen as objectives should be stated in ranges. Start by defining the middle figure first, "normal realistic." Let the subordinate set the optimistic or stretch objectives. The superior chooses the pessimistic figure. This figure comprises the exception point at which the subordinate should *notify* the superior that things are not going according to plan. The middle point is based upon history, upon estimates, industrial engineering studies, or sales forecasts.

3   When deviations occur, the subordinate should know it before anyone else, know why the deviation has occurred, have taken corrective action where possible, and notified and requested help from above early enough.

4   On the other hand if the subordinate is attaining the middle level (normal-realistic goals), he or she should be left alone to operate without interference.

Name_____ Period _____
General Manager
Regular–Basic Indicator Objectives

Responsibility		Level of result sought		
			(Normal)	
Output indicator	Time period	Pessi- mistic	Real- istic	Opti- mistic
1 Dollar volume of revenue per mo.	Qtr.			
2 Profit: ROI	Qtr.			
Dollar volume per mo.	Qtr.			
3 Cash at mo. end, $	Qtr.			
4 Receivables: Mo. end, $	Qtr.			
Days	Qtr.			
5 Inventory: Mo. end, $	Qtr.			
Turnover days	Qtr.			
6 Capital budget percent deviation	Qtr.			
7 Labor problems—step 4 grievances	Qtr.			
8 Share of market, percent	Qtr.			
9 (Other)_____—........	—			
_____—........	—			
_____—........	—			

Results Score Sheet

Target no.	1st qtr.	2d qtr.	3d qtr.	4th qtr.	Total
1					
2					
3					
4					
5					
6					
7					
8					

Fig. 3-4 Operating objectives.

2 Statement of problem-solving objective

    a Present condition or situation
    b Desired condition or objective of the problem if solved satisfactorily
    c Time commitments (always state as a range: pessimistic, realistic, optimistic)

3 Statement of innovative project commitment

    a The present condition or situation
    b Innovation to be attempted
    c Results sought (condition which would exist if the innovation were to work well)
    d Time commitment (state dates: optimistic, pessimistic, realistic)

Fig. 3-5 Problem-solving and innovative objectives.

Figure 3-5 shows what a page of written problem-solving objectives (Category 2) might look like. This usually involves committing oneself to one or two major problems defining:

The present level or condition

The desired level or condition

The time when it is to be corrected (brought to the desired level)

Category 2 objectives are also shown in Fig. 3-5. This is a statement of the present condition, the desired condition, and some time frame for the proactive, innovative goals, perhaps including some stages of study or development.

Organizational objectives The example given of the general manager's objectives, of course, must be supplemented by specific and explicit objectives for each of the key subordinates reporting to the general manager. The manufacturing manager might have these regular (Category 1) objectives to which she is committed:

Average daily output per month

Units per shift per month

Indirect labor as a percent of direct per month

Factory overhead as a percent of total per month

Average quality reject rate per month

Warranty and policy costs per month

Step 4 grievances per quarter

Overtime hours per week per quarter

Hours of supervisory training per quarter

The sales manager, on the other hand, doesn't have the same objectives as the general manager—except for a few key result areas—but rather defines the indicators that will cover the major indicators of output for a time period for his responsibility areas. These might include such indicators as the following:

Dollar volume per month per quarter

Costs of producing the revenue per month per quarter

New products introduced

Dollar level of bad debts per quarter

Days of sales training conducted per quarter

New customers added per quarter

Lost accounts per quarter

For each person reporting to the general manager, there would be indicators which are special to that position, but following a similar format. Included would be indicators of output for the time period, stated in ranges, and problem-solving and innovative goals.

How to Audit and Review Objectives

Periodic Audits Two forms of review and audit are important in MBO. The first kind of audit is the periodic audit. This is a financial audit of a comprehensive nature usually based upon a sampling of the realities of the situation. It can be done by professional internal auditors, or by an outside audit group, such as a CPA firm. Program audits should be performed periodically not only for financial results and practices but for *program* operations as well.

Personnel audits and manpower audits for such matters as affirmative action, replacements of key persons, compliance with company or organizational personnel policy, and similar matters including labor relations should be included in periodic audits. Safety audits against Occupational Safety and Health Administration (OSHA) standards done internally may prevent unfavorable audits by OSHA inspectors from enforcement agencies.

Other current practices of the best-run organizations include new forms of audit of programs. They might include technical audit, community relations audit, public responsibility audits, purchasing practices audits, and legal compliance audits for antitrust or patent protection.

Continuing Review Having made commitments, all managers should continually review their own performance. Reviews consist of observing and notating actual results against the statements of objectives to which managers are committed. They are of shorter time period and relate to the shorter time periods in which supervisory management gets daily, weekly, monthly, and quarterly reports of outputs.

One major advantage of MBO is that it permits self-control by the manager against objectives agreed upon in advance. Self-control has some powerful motivational effects, for it is the tightest and most perfect form of control. Commitment is a means of motivation which is considerably enhanced when self-correction is built into the system.

As shown at the bottom of Figure 3-4, the manager should be able to post her or his own actual outcomes on the original objectives; the superior receives a copy. The function of the superior is to respond with help and resources when requested, or when notified that exceptions are present.

Annual Review At the end of each year, the superior and subordinate pull out the objectives prepared in advance and review actual results. This is a preface to defining new objectives for the coming year. Such discussion should be treated as an important event. It should be done free from distraction and should deal with objectives, results, problems, deviations, and improvements needed. The two participants should avoid personality discussions or adopting a manner which is exacting, hostile, judgmental, or punitive. With actual results against objectives in hand, the superior can make such personnel decisions as are required.

HANDLING BEHAVIOR CHANGE IN DISCIPLINARY CASES ACCORDING TO DISCIPLINE BY OBJECTIVES[1]

The material heretofore discussed on coaching is perfectly fine for most situations. But what of situations faced by every manager in which employees simply aren't sticking within the rules of the road, the ordinary policies and practice, rules and regulations of the business? The manager is then faced with the most difficult managerial situation known, turning wrongdoing into good behavior.

In such cases, following one's instincts and even common practice can get the manager into trouble. Applying disciplinary practice inequitably can cause difficulties. Potentially good employees will be lost because they were not changed into good ones. Even if discipline is applied equitably and competently using behavioral principles, a number of bad effects may follow.

- If the disciplined person is a member of a minority group or a woman, the employer may be charged with discrimination.

- If wrongdoing is allowed to persist and is ignored, the good performers will in all likelihood take a lackadaisical attitude toward necessary rules.
- If a stern and schoolmasterish approach to minor infractions occurs, the good performers as well as the bad performers will be adversely affected.
- If the employees have a union, the number of grievances will rise.

The foregoing materials in this book outlining the principles of behavior modification can, however, be applied along with an MBO approach to bring about a new and more progressive kind of organizational discipline.

Discipline by Objectives

Modern discipline is not punishment but a shaper of behavior. It requires rules to be reviewed periodically against objectives to see if they are still productive in changing conditions, and it allows the exceptional performer who is achieving exceptional results to be treated with far greater tolerance when it comes to violations.

The old-fashioned approach to discipline was that of the Old Testament dictum "An eye for an eye and a tooth for a tooth." The purpose of such discipline was to exact punishment for sins, maintain conformity to old customs, and sustain the authority of the old over the young. Punishment was designed to fit the crime. Retributive justice drew upon a kind of natural law which provided that certain actions were forbidden by lower classes of persons, and when such offenses occurred and were proved, the guilty party would naturally be subjected to the punishment which had been designated for that crime. In the Far East, theft was punishable by amputation of a hand; in the American West, theft of a horse was punishable by hanging, and so on. Aboard the old British Navy sailing ships the punishment was generally the lash, with a specified number of strokes for specific offenses, and hanging for another group of crimes including murder, mutiny, and combat cowardice.

While it is entirely conceivable that such a system in its origin may have had some behavior-change objectives, over time such exacting kinds of punishments acquired a character quite apart from the behavior-change effect and became an almost divinely inspired system of cause and effect, as if the crime itself produced the punishment.

Modern discipline is forced to meet a number of new requirements beyond punishment. Modern values tend away from excessively physical forms of punishment. The decline of capital punishment in many states and foreign nations is matched in declining levels of physical punishment for lesser levels of offense. Greater protection of the rights of the accused is being developed. The belief that it is better to allow many guilty persons to escape than to punish one innocent person prevails in society at large, in our courts and policy system, and in industrial and business discipline.

The decline of arbitrary individual judgments and the movement toward group judgments of guilt or innocence (those requiring disciplinary procedures) is rising, even in the school system, the last bastion of dictatorship. The trial by jury of one's peers, the right to counsel, the right to confront accusers, the right to cross-examine witnesses, and the use of evidence in systematic fashion are now widespread.

The right to protect unilateral judgments is also rising in disciplinary cases. Even in those cases where no labor union exists, the skeletal outline of the arbitration system, the grievance procedures, and the right to appeal are increasingly being used in disciplinary cases.

Two major segments make up the modern behavioral approach to discipline.

1 Defining a list of actions, regulations, rules, behaviors, or offenses which shall trigger the corrective and remedial process.

2 Providing a set of procedures which shall be put into action when such offenses occur. This may also include investing certain persons with disciplinary powers and creating groups to deal with and apply the procedures.

In all human organizations there will be kinds of behavior which cannot be permitted, for they keep the organization from going toward its objectives, bar individual members from being free to do their own work, or interfere with the personal rights of others. Traditionally, listing such offenses is done in order of seriousness and according to the severity of the ultimate punishments which might be used in the corrective process. These offenses generally fall into categories such as "major," "moderate," and "minor" or some such classification.

Traditionally, lists of offenses are posted in places where they can be seen and referred to by employees, without flaunting them in a threatening manner. They are reviewed at the time of employment as part of the induction process. They are available to every manager and discussed with all supervisors from time to time. Notes or memoranda regarding their interpretation are circulated to all managers who have responsibility for their application.

Traditional Discipline Systems

At this point, we can see little to differentiate the rules and regulations of the modern factory or office from the work force of the pharaohs in their structure or application. The rules were different and the punishments certainly more severe, but the basic design of the disciplinary system was similar. List the crimes, note the punishments attached to each, and promulgate and apply the rules. This old-fashioned discipline had several basic assumptions which require updating in the new climate for discipline. These assumptions could be listed as follows:

1   Discipline is what superiors apply to subordinates and never the reverse.

2   The past is the arbiter of present and future actions.

3   Discipline is punishment for forbidden actions, and the severity of the punishment should, when practical, be equivalent to the severity of the offense.

4   The end effect of punishment is deterrence of others who have not sinned, who will be halted in their tendencies to do so by the example of those who have sinned, been caught and punished accordingly. Punishment for "principles" should be more severe than punishment for the act itself.

5   Where the prevalence of wrong behavior increases in the entire group, it may be necessary to accelerate the severity of the punishment for the next person caught violating a rule in order to set an especially impressive example for the others.

6   When a single individual cannot be isolated who will admit responsibility for the violation, the entire group should be punished; this will strike the guilty individual's conscience, as well as motivate the group to turn in the violator, or perhaps even mete out the punishment themselves.

7   Absolute consistency in punishment should be maintained *at all times* in all cases. If this is not done, the group will protest, feel that injustice is being done, and seek ways of circumventing the disciplinary system.

8   The severity of the punishment for a second offense should always be much more severe than for the first offense, even though the offense is identical to the first in nature and severity.

9   The announcement of punishment and its administration should be given the maximum possible visibility and exposure, in order that the deterrent effect shall be maximized.

While there are, of course, many other specific details which could be noted, these are illustrative of the traditional philosophy and the format and structure of the traditional disciplinary system. It has permeated the school system, the workplace, and the life of the citizen.

Discipline by Objectives in the Workplace

While the systems of discipline in law enforcement and in school systems would be worthy of some discussion, the applications of interest to the personnel manager relate to the workplace and to the personnel policies regarding the discipline of people at work. Discipline in such an environment has some special features which are not characteristic of discipline elsewhere, such as the home or the church. This difference centers around the objectives and purposes of the business firm. The presumptions of discipline by objectives in the work environment could be listed as follows:

1 Discipline at work is for the most part voluntarily accepted, and if not voluntarily accepted is not legitimate.

The recruit aboard a whaler out of New Bedford in the early 1800s was subjected to ferocious standards of discipline, which could be considered voluntary if the seaman signed the articles and was fully aware of the strict requirement of being a sailor on a whaler. If he were shanghaied aboard, however, or beguiled by lies from a recruiter, or were forced into accepting such a job because he was starving ashore and could find only this alternative to starving, he could hardly be identified as a volunteer.

Such a voluntary bargain implies that the person entered it freely and willingly, with full knowledge of the demands to be made upon him and of the rewards and punishments for success and failure. Yet, if he understood and accepted the stringent requirements, the need for barbaric punishment is questionable. The discipline thus becomes a harsh reminder of the penalties for trying to escape a trap into which he unwittingly stepped.

The human memory is fallible, but the young accountant who was reminded again and again during the hiring interview that her position with the accounting firm entailed extensive travel and long hours at certain times of the year cannot expect to remake the bargain after employment to which the employer has committed funds and time. If after entering the business she sees more clearly what she did not foresee with clarity, she cannot selectively break the bargain without penalties of one kind or another.

2 Discipline is not a punishment system, but a shaper of behavior.

Like the operant conditioning of B. F. Skinner, the disciplinary action should serve to provide unfavorable consequences for the wrong kind of behavior. This means that not only are verbal or physical punishments used in a response, but all the elements in the system which can be conveniently arranged to produce the desired behavior will be employed, and not merely the judicial-like system of accused, prosecutor, judge, crime, and punishment.

On a military base it was noted that young soldiers were slipping over the fence after hours in violation of regulations. Some officers proposed stiff courts-martial. Others proposed issuing live ammunition to sentries. The wise commanding officer, however, discovered that the soldiers were visiting local bars. He ordered that beer be sold in the PX throughout the entire evening. The rate of fence jumping dropped considerably.

While we really don't care about the details of the case, the principle behind the solution is important. One must find the causes of the behavior and arrange the situation so that it won't occur. In this case, nobody was punished, for that was not the objective. The objective was to keep the soldiers in camp. The difference is the avoidance of principles to be upheld, and a concentration upon behavior and results.

3 The past provides useful experience in defining and changing behavior, but it is not an infallible guide to right and wrong.

The fact that something has been done consistently in the past is, of course, no assurance that it is the best behavior for the present. While it often is, the greatest use of precedents is in positions where danger, high cost, or excessive losses could result from failure to use the right principle voluntarily the first time. The boss who suggests "Do it my way the first time; then, after thinking about it, introduce improvements if you can" is sensing the importance of using experience while encouraging innovation. He is providing a base point for departure.

4 Contribution to objectives is a reasonable guide as to when to depart from rules and regulations.

When subordinates are well aware of their own objectives and those of their units, variations from rules and regulations become a part of their professional or occupational skills. The engineer who knows when to depart from rules and when not to is a better engineer than the one who adheres slavishly to every rule simply because it is a rule. The breaking of a rule, however, when such violation has the effect of being counterproductive, and carries the person or the organization away from the desired objectives, should be the subject of some unfavorable attention on the part of the superior. Equally culpable is the individual who adheres strictly to regulations, when the effect of the behavior is such that the organization is served poorly and its movement toward its objectives is impeded or halted.

The tiny voice of the bureaucrat inevitably cries out to establish the presence and presumably sacred nature of the rule and regulation.

When the bureaucrat is in charge, people are punished or reprimanded for offenses according to consistency, precedent, or rules for rules' sake. The bureaucrat's memory for the details of such rules is formidable. Such a person's belief in their sanctity is impressive, but the contribution to objectives is marginal, perhaps ranging as high as nominal.

Yet, persons who break the rules do so at their own risk. They may do so without full knowledge of objectives, either their own or the organization's. They might make a change for what seems to be a contribution to objectives when, in fact, they are diminishing the total contribution. They may, indeed, on occasion hash the whole plan. It is this latter unseen possibility that should deter responsible people from casual variation for its own sake, just to be different. Not to worship laws and rules as having a special mystique of their own is excellent. Not to hate them blindly is equally sound.

5 Charts, lists, and compendiums of rules and regulations should be reviewed periodically against organization objectives to see if they are still productive.

In organizations where the system of Management by Objectives is being utilized, it makes good sense to review the rules periodically and revise the regulations of the organization to prevent absurdities in behavior being enforced upon employees. Where there are no stated objectives, then, of course, such review against them becomes impossible, and the mere listing of activity guides is perfectly logical. Organizations tend to conduct their affairs in a way that is activity-centered, or input-centered rather than output-centered. For such organizations, it thus seems important to keep all the activity under control.

Input-centered organizations emphasize discipline to prevent nonconforming use of inputs. The control of expense accounts is the most common application of an input-centered system of management. The manager who makes a trip to New York City where meals and lodging are higher than in Dodge City, Kansas, for example, will be bound by identical regulations for both locations. The possibilities that the gains attributable to the New York expenses may be far greater than those for the Dodge City trip, and therefore should be treated as having different requirements, is contrary to every traditional rule. To the office manager who would prevent such variances, the ultimate logic lies in a statement: "But we simply can't have everybody setting their own expense rates. We would be victimized by excessive expenditures." To which the response might well be, "We expect everyone to set and achieve his own objectives; otherwise we would not achieve breakthroughs and innovations to new heights of organizational achievement."

6 The application of individual discipline by objectives makes each individual responsible for output, and the individual differences are explainable in individual results.

It is reported that Alfred P. Sloan, for 28 years chief executive officer of General Motors Corporation, used the expression "Did he [she] get the job done?" in response to ordinary complaints that individuals had varied from customary practice or rules on the job. Abraham Lincoln, when told that General Ulysses S. Grant drank whiskey regularly in large amounts, is reported to have replied: "Tell me what kind he drinks. I should like to buy a case for my other generals. I can't spare this man; he fights!"

The point is clear. The exceptional performer in achieving exceptional results should be treated with far greater tolerance when it comes to violation of rules and regulations. This implies a converse rule. Ordinary and below ordinary people should adhere to the rules until their exceptional excellence has been demonstrated. The exceptional should be given greater tolerance.

Are All Forms of Discipline Obsolete?

The steps of short-cutting to reach a goal can be constructive for one person, whereas for another they can be destructive. Having made this distinction, we now face the procedural matters in dealing with destructive kinds of variation. About 2 million crimes take place in this country each year. Every day over 300 people are killed or feloniously assaulted. Over 3000 reported thefts occur in an average day, in addition to over 500 car thefts. Clearly this is destructive behavior, and law enforcement is a growing problem.

While the rates of crime in the workplace are proportionately less than in the population at large, where crimes are committed mainly by unemployed and underemployed persons, there is needed a legal system inside the plant and office comparable to the one outside. At the same time, this system of legal codes should draw sharp distinctions between customary antisocial behavior and the finely honed requirements of conformity to the will of the boss on the job.

The Requirements of Discipline

To make the disciplinary process into a teaching and behavior-change action, some conditions must be met:

1 Rules and regulations should be devised and made known as outlined in the section above.

2 When an apparent violation has occurred, the action taken should occur as close to the time of the violation as is feasible. Holding off discussion of personal behavioral lapses until the annual performance review or some future time lessens the behavior-change effect.

3 The accused person should be presented with the facts and the source of those facts. "Mr. Smith of the Eliot Store called this morning and stated that you have not taken inventory in his store for two months."

4 If a specific rule is broken, that rule should be stated. In the above case, for example: "As you know our rules call for an on-site inventory every two weeks, with a signed report turned in certifying the inventory."

5 The reason for the rule should be given, for example, "Three things can occur if this rule isn't followed. First, the company could lose money because it puts goods in stores on consignment, and the store could go out of business and leave us a big bad debt. Second, the store managers like to have their billings accurate, based upon inventory and not on estimates. Finally, we need the accurate inventory to schedule our production for the month ahead."

6 Ask the apparent offender if the facts as stated are correct. Then ask what the objective was for the demonstrated behavior. Asking an apparent offender for an "excuse" or "alibi" or even for the reasons places that person on the defensive and can quickly lead to a fight. Eliciting the objectives for the behavior opens the door to future improvement. By wording, we turn the context from backward-looking to forward-looking behavior.

7 State the corrective action in positive and forward-looking form: "'Given your objective of covering more stores in the territory, how can you do that and at the same time meet my three objectives for getting inventory taken?"

Periodic Review of Shop or Office Rules

A continuing source of discontent, especially among young employees, is the existence and enforcement of rules which apparently have no reason. Rules which were made for a long-forgotten purpose continue to be enforced, without noticing that the objective for which the rule was devised has long since become outmoded and forgotten.

Development of sound disciplinary policy requires that the personnel department initiate and maintain a review of rules of conduct for the plant or office. Such a review should deal with two specific categories for each rule. In the first column, the rule as it now exists should be stated. In the second column a brief statement of the contribution of the rule to objectives should be listed. Where the rule makes a contribution, or prevents something from happening which could diminish contribution, it stays.

Some typical contributions to objectives of work rules could be the following:

The rule stated as it presently exists	The contribution to objectives which this rule makes
1.	1.
2.	2.

Prevents line shutdown

Prevents spoilage and repair costs

Prevents customer complaints for quality

Ensures safety of fellow workers

Ensures safety of the employee

Improves yield of line

Prevents tool breakage

Prevents overexpenditure for small tools

There are, however, certain rules which have vast powers of survival for which only the following responses can be found; these should be eliminated unless further study shows them making a contribution to objectives:

We've always done it that way.

It's our policy

That rule was made out of many, many years of experience.

The boss (now retired) installed that one.

Because I want it, dammit.

It's generally a good thing.

You wouldn't really know why, so let's not discuss it.

Don't make waves.

I don't have time to explain it to you just do it.

Further study might well reveal a legitimate reason, in the form of a contribution to objectives. It might even be found that rules that are absolutely necessary in one location or department won't be necessary in another. Smoking is not allowed in the plant where volatile liquids are used, but may be allowed in the office. Creative development of discretionary and selectively applied rules is evidence of good management, not bad management. Just as was the case with the no smoking rule, there may be discretionary application of rules affecting attendance, starting and stopping times, time cards, and other matters. There is no inherent and automatic virtue to consistency in the making of rules. Consistency of application among all those employees covered by the same rule is, however, necessary to avoid charges of injustice and disputes between employees. You might, for example, suspend the attendance-keeping rules for engineers by eliminating time cards, if it is done for all engineers. You can't selectively single out Jim and make a rule for him alone (unless he is a Steinmetz, a Shockley, or other genius).

Using Progressive Discipline

For certain kinds of offenses, such as murder, rape, felonious assault, major thefts, deliberate damage to company property and the like, the first offense is the last since it is a cause for immediate discharge.

Another category of offense which is worthy of disciplinary attention is less than a cause for immediate discharge, and here the use of progressive discipline applies. Progressive discipline means that the employee is subjected to several stages, each one moving closer to the separation stage, but each one in turn designed to effect a behavior change prior to that move. The stages used in many firms, such as General Motors, Ford, Chrysler, and numerous other large firms, have grown for the most part out of successive tests of their effectiveness, as reviewed by arbitrators for equity and fairness to the employee. These steps generally include:

Step 1 First offense: Instruct the employee in the proper method, explain the rule and its reasons, and explain what the next level of discipline will be for a recurrence. Write the incident in the employee's personnel record.

Step 2 Second offense: This could be a repeat of the first, or it could be a different offense of a similar magnitude. If a repeat of the first, summarize the instructions, tell the individual that this is a second offense, that this is a reprimand, and that the third step will be a temporary layoff without pay. Explain the reason for this rule. Write the incident in the employee's personnel record. If the offense is a second offense of a similar magnitude, but different in specifics, give instructions for the proper method and a warning of the next step which follows a third offense. Write the incident in the employee's personnel record.

Step 3   Third offense: The first-line supervisor should at this stage consult with superiors and the personnel department since the issue might become subject to arbitration. If the stage is clear, the individual is instructed and given a layoff of two to five days without pay, with the warning that a repeat of any similar level offense will result in discharge and a record marked to prevent reemployment. Write the incident in the employee's personnel record.

Step 4   Discharge: Following a confirmation from the supervisor's superior and the personnel department, the supervisor should tell the person he or she is discharged. This should be written up in the employee's personnel record, with recommendation for rehiring or not rehiring.

This brief description of the stages of discipline is based upon successful experience of employers in unionized situations and in government supervision who have discharged employees and been upheld. Throughout the entire process it should be borne in mind that each move may be subsequently subjected to the close scrutiny of an arbitrator, a review board, or a top manager.

Some Umbrella Rules for Discipline

In addition to knowing the general stages, the supervisor should now apply certain rules which hang over the entire disciplinary process itself like an umbrella. Failure in any of these rules could result in the action being reversed.

1   Be certain that the rule exists, is clear, and that the employees know the rule.

2   Use a statute-of-limitations rule for writing up disciplinary incidents. For example, if a person breaks a rule and has this entered in the record, after six months of good performance without further incidents, remove the record from the file and clear the slate. Do not carry minor incidents over from year to year. Layoff reports could be kept for periods of two to three years.

3   Avoid behavior which creates further incidents. Using profanity (even where it is the ordinary language of the shop) in disciplinary proceedings or physically touching the person invites explosions, anger, and physical responses.

4   Don't apply the procedure inconsistently to individuals, such as adding a step between two and three, or shortening the layoff period for one person unless the facts are sufficiently different to permit toleration.

5 Listen carefully to what the other person says at all times, and note the substance of those remarks in the record.

6 Be certain of your facts before making your decision. In the rushed life of the business world wrong perceptions, garbled information, and errors in fact will come easily. Dig as deeply as is necessary to get all the necessary facts before moving into action.

7 Don't jump the stages for less-than-discharge offenses under emotional pressures. This is the most likely cause of reversal by an arbitrator, who will reduce the penalty to the level at which the offense should have been handled. To discharge an employee for spoiling work twice would probably result in the person's being reinstated with full pay since ordinary practice would call for an intermediate stage first, before jumping to the ultimate punishment.

8 When the laid-off employee returns to work, don't continue the punishment. She or he has been instructed and warned and has seen the effects of the behavior. Treat such employees like all the others; don't spend any special amount of time checking on them. Be businesslike, neither clubby nor aloof.

9 Avoid entrapment. Setting snares to encourage employees to violate rules in order that the boss may administer the next stage of discipline is bad business. It breeds distrust in the equity and justice of the whole system.

Handling the Nonrule Offense

Certain kinds of behavior requiring supervisory attention do not fall clearly into the rule book but nevertheless need correction. Take the case of a salesperson who habitually tells racist jokes. This offends certain of the customers, and the president of one large company calls to tell you of the person's behavior.

1 If no rule has been broken, don't invent one to cover the situation.

2 Treat nonrule violations as behavioral problems which need coaching and training rather than discipline.

3 Use feedback and discussion of objectives to effect a behavior change.

In the case of the salesman the dialogue might go something as follows:

"Joe, I received a call from Mr. X, President of the Apex Company this morning. He said that you have offended several of his people because you tell jokes about Jews, blacks, and Italians while you are on their premises. He says, further, that they have many such employees, and that they are insulted by what you say."

"I don't mean anything; it's just a joke. Where is their sense of humor?"

"I wanted you to know that Mr. X had called, and exactly what he said."

"It's only a joke."

"What would you say your objective is in calling upon Apex?"

"To get orders, of course, but you know you have to have good relations with people, and a sense of humor and being cheerful is part of getting good relations."

"Given your objective of getting orders through being cheerful, using jokes, how would you say your action is working in getting you to your objectives?"

Notice what the boss didn't say or do:

- He didn't teach about racism.
- He didn't lecture Joe on his stupidity.
- He didn't use satire or sarcasm.
- He didn't agree or sympathize with Joe.
- He didn't prescribe by saying, "Now here is what you must do. . . ."

The emphasis here is upon behavior change, through concentrating on responsible behavior in the future. The manager presented the facts as he had heard them, avoided generalizations and sweeping charges, and used a Socratic discussion to permit Joe to obtain insight by seeing his own problem. Once Joe sees the objective and the problem he can start discussing some optional plans for solving the problem.

"What do you think you should do next, Joe?"

"Well, I guess I better quit using jokes, even become a sourpuss if that's what they want."

"All jokes?"

"Well, at least the ones about race and religion. I guess I could also apologize over there to some of the people I run into. Maybe I could get a new stock of jokes too."

"Sounds as if you have a good plan, Joe. Now is there anything you think I can do to help?"

"Sure, Apex is a big account and makes up a large hunk of my business. If you could call the president and tell him you talked to me, and I was startled and plan to apologize and lay off the bum jokes in the future, that might help. Tell him I appreciated the call too."

The details of the case are, of course, more complex, but it illustrates the principle. What appears to be a discipline case becomes a teaching and coaching incident. There is no useful purpose to writing up this incident. The personnel-centered manager who builds his or her subordinates through coaching has hundreds of such incidents each year. They comprise the ordinary fabric of management and should not be treated as disciplinary incidents.

This blending of discipline and coaching, or remedial rather than punitive discipline, is centered around the achievement of objectives rather than the extermination of sin.

THE POLITICS OF IMPLEMENTING MBO[2]

It is not likely today that many managers will object to Management by Objectives as a concept of philosophy. The question of available alternatives seems unanswerable in the face of such an eminently logical developmental system. Why, then, do people seem to have reservations about committing themselves to it? Why, indeed, do some people find it impossible to make it work, while others report great success in its application and enthusiasm for its effects?

One of the major reasons for the failure of MBO in many organizations is that those in charge fail to recognize the political character of the implementation process. MBO is indeed logical and systematic, but it also must deal with a number of factors, including power and authority, the organization's form, and the values and expectations of the people. MBO implementers, therefore, must recognize the reality of political constraints and manage them during the process of implementation.

If they fail to do so, MBO may start off with a flourish but gradually fade away; begin well, reach a certain level, and stall; or start well but produce a dramatic failure and be dropped, becoming a taboo subject thereafter. Success, on the other hand, results when MBO begins at a sound level of acceptance, gains from its own successes, continues to flourish and expand its influence and contributions, and is widely appreciated and supported.

Case studies of successful and unsuccessful implementation plans show that there are three major avenues currently used for implementation of MBO and that all three must be modified by political constraints characteristic of every organization. This section will briefly illustrate the three approaches, and then describe the political considerations that must guide them.

Three Approaches

Methods of implementing MBO may rely on the use of raw power and direct orders, persuasion, or education (see Figure 3-6). Case studies indicate that no one route is best; instead, analysis of the organizational

MEANS:

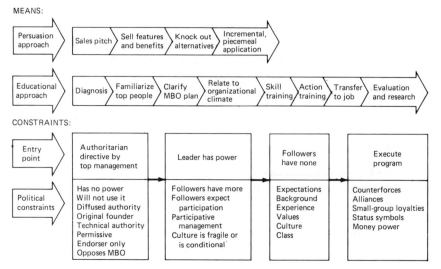

Fig. 3-6 The alternatives and constraints in implementing MBO.

climate and the situation will indicate the best approach—one alone or perhaps a combination of all of them. A specific set of steps in linear form would be highly desirable, but such a method would probably miss the mark and lead to an implementation that fails in one or more respects.

Authoritarian Directives   It is an article of faith, supported by some research evidence, that the installation of MBO must start at the top. In part, such a beginning is justified. The purpose of the business flows down and the methods of getting there flow up. The strategies of the business are chosen by persons with high-level responsibility, whereas the operational objectives are the responsibility of lower levels. This might lead to the conclusion that the power of the higher ranks must be invoked to direct implementation. This approach, which Joseph Juran has labeled the "king's ear" approach,[3] is founded upon the assumption that if the staff person can get the president to listen and to issue the right directives, everybody below will obey. The concept is that of the self-executing order, a rare phenomenon.

Behavioral scientists deplore such autocratic methods, but they are used in some organizations where tight technical organization and discipline are the modes of operation. Where the following conditions exist in the organization, such authoritarian methods will indeed work:

The leader has absolute power and is willing to use it.

The followers need the leader more than that person needs them, because the leader has knowledge, skills, or resources which they need but that the leader can withhold.

The followers have lived under unexplained orders for some time, perhaps for their entire working lifetime, and have learned to expect them, even when the subject is MBO.

The situation requires autocratic orders. The leader is expected to state orders quickly and clearly whether in charge of a ship at sea in a storm, a plane in distress or a temporary work force.

Under proper circumstances, autocratic implementation of MBO has been successful. That is not to say that all situations demand it; many are not suitable for autocracy—the college faculty or the volunteer group, for example. The major limitations of the use of force to implement MBO lie in the situation in which it is applied. Where the boss has no power or has power and will not use it, the followers expect to be consulted and have something important to withhold (and will do so). Under these circumstances, the authoritarian directive will produce counterresponses that block MBO.

Persuasion   One reason for the failure of MBO to achieve its full potential has been the misguided reliance upon persuasion as a means of implementation. The guru or inspirational speaker comes to a meeting of management and through hortatory lectures persuades everyone that MBO will be beneficial. Persuasion methods ordinarily can be distinguished by their content.

First, they appear to be balanced; that is, they explain all the advantages of MBO, then turn and judiciously explain the disadvantages of not managing by objectives. This is clearly an advocacy approach designed to persuade. Second, features and benefits are grist for the persuader's mill. A description of the features and a discussion of the usefulness of each are persuasive tactics.

Third, in this debater's form of persuasion, all the alternatives for solving some chronic problems are noted. Then each is knocked out in turn, excepting the MBO solution. The fourth form of persuasion, incrementalism, is probably the most risky. It consists of starting with a simple segment of the whole program and selling it. "You simply sit down once a year with all of your subordinates and talk to them about their objectives" would be an incremental approach. Many instances of MBO failure have been caused by incrementalism in the introduction. The concept began as a change in the company performance-appraisal system or as a salary-review plan, but lost favor when the full implications of the time and effort demanded were realized.

Persuasion is the favorite method of hortatory speakers and consultants. It is detested and avoided by academics who would prefer an approach that relies almost wholly upon education, particularly in the underlying theory. As a complete method of installation, it obviously leads to disillusionment. Yet it has a useful part in implementation in the early stages, if only to get people to submit to education.

Educational Programs   One of the more successful patterns for installing an MBO program is a continuous educational effort that teaches the concepts, philosophy, and procedures of MBO in detail. As a training subject, MBO has many excellent features.

Training should produce behavior change, and training in MBO is measurable. It can be readily determined if the training worked: Did the trainees set objectives or didn't they?

The quality of the results can be noted clearly. The course may suggest, for example, that a manager should establish three classes of objectives. The effect on the manager can be checked by examining sample goals statements.

MBO comprises a sound basis for relating training to the job. Some training sessions require students to set objectives on their job as part of the course; they learn by doing what they are being taught.

MBO provides a vehicle for teaching more general management education. It can be the framework for teaching motivational methods, management functions (organizing, planning, and controlling), and such interpersonal skills as coaching, counseling, and listening.

MBO can teach interpersonal skills that can be applied on the job, rather than skills which the boss will not permit or endorse when the trainee returns to the desk or plant floor. This is especially true if the boss attends the session or is used as a trainer.

MBO can reinforce company objectives rather than become, as it does in many behavioral courses, an internal reform movement to overcome the organization's autocratic or bureaucratic tendencies or to produce some new kind of organizational form.

MBO is capable of maintaining a high level of trainee interest, since it deals with the real world of work and its problems, and with interpersonal and group relations problems.

Conceptually, it is easy to learn, for MBO training courses ask people to "talk shop"; they have a tendency to do this whether they are in training or not. Except for courses in which the trainers have worked hard at obscuring the obvious, the language is operational and practical.

The basic framework of MBO permits it to take a behavioral or logical systems direction without appearing contradictory or mutually exclusive. This means that it can appeal to the personnel section and trainers in the organization, as well as to the engineer, controllers, and dollar-centered managers.

Both insiders and outsiders can be used as trainers. The insiders have more knowledge of the business and can deal with real problems, and the outsiders can be briefed sufficiently to relate to the world of the trainee.

The Politics of Implementation

The constraint of organizational politics is a formidable barrier to implementation. Unless it is taken into account, it will outweigh the logical and behavioral efforts that go into directing, persuading, or educating people to accept a new management system. Several political factors must be considered.

The Power Structure An often overlooked political factor affecting the implementation of MBO is the power structure of the organization. MBO is rightly seen as having the potential for shifting the locus of power within the organization, and accordingly will meet political resistance from those who might be affected adversely.

The resistance of such persons as corporate attorneys or other executive staff members is frequently rooted in the probability of shifting power. A person who has developed a strong personal relationship with the top officers, in which they draw upon his counsel in all sorts of matters other than law or his specialty, is clearly threatened by systematic management. In one large firm, the corporate purchasing director had performed numerous personal favors for the president and his family, and had attained the status of a family favorite. When MBO was suggested, this family retainer saw immediately that his status could be threatened and he greeted the proposal with a flurry of cluckings and exceptions. He noted its flaws and limitations, insisted that it was nothing new, and adopted other delaying and obstructive tactics familiar to the MBO administrator.

In another firm it was the tax manager who headed up the political resistance movement against MBO. The manager had helped the family with the controlling interest to minimize their personal estate taxes over the years, and she hoped to retain her personal position of favor.

The Diffusion of Authority In many modern corporations there has been a blurring of the decision-making power. Starting at the top, where the charismatic leader or dynamic chief has been supplanted by "the office of the president" generally occupied by two or three officers, it is difficult to identify a single channel for decisions. This has some advantage in gaining acceptance for decisions, but it also generates political maneuvering in order to get objectives decided upon. In other organizations, the key committees of the board may produce some mutually exclusive objectives which they are pushing. These require some political tacking and hauling in order to make a particular position dominant.

In government, of course, the basic motivator of the system and its servants is political power, and the diffusion of power is well understood by most of the people who share in it. Cabinet members know that bureau chiefs ostensibly under their control can lobby their congressional representatives to protect a job or program. A letter from a member of Congress can always sway a bureaucrat. At the same time, the large departmental public relations sections in government can swing public opinion to press Congress for increased space or increased military and welfare appropriations.

Such a political climate requires more patience, continuous effort, and persuasion to get a management-style change such as MBO into effect. Even some trading of favors and arm twisting may be necessary.

The Fragility of Participation   Even in those organizations where participation of the lower levels has been designated as the mode of operation, it is possible that it can be withdrawn. Where the possibilities of power exist, there is a possibility that power once withheld will be reasserted.

Take the case of the governor of a state who was enthusiastic about MBO and employed a participative style of management. He delegated responsibility extensively and pressed decisions down to the lowest possible level. This produced high morale at lower levels. But the governor left office, and his successor immediately suspended all the mechanics of participative management and centralized everything in the governor's office. In the process, this governor declared support of MBO but in fact killed it by locating total control in the governor's office.

Similar experiences abound. A humanistic president of a corporation installed a participative MBO program. Upon his retirement his successor, a four-star general, promptly applied autocratic controls. He eliminated certain policy committees, scuttled meetings which had been the major vehicle for MBO, and ordered the appraisal form abandoned and training programs stopped. He did so for a plausible reason. The company had been in market trouble, and a lax style of MBO had made the corporation an easygoing but unprofitable place. After a turnaround, he retired. Major promotions were made from within, the earlier participative management style of MBO was restored, and the results were excellent.

It is a hard political fact about organizations, public and private, that a form of MBO which is inextricably tied to participative management may be damaged if an autocratic boss gets on top. MBO that is top down and somewhat autocratic to begin with suffers no such setback. On the other hand, it never had the developmental and humanistic benefits of participative management in the first place.

The Problem of Countermoves   A strong move to produce an MBO program that would change the behavior of people or the arrangement of the organization, and how it does its work, can be counted on to produce an equal and opposite reaction somewhere. It may be expressed by scoffing, by wisecracks, by definitions of MBO ("Massive Bowel Obstruction" or "Mr. Big's Obsession" to name two), or by overintellectualizing the obvious.

In other cases, the reaction produces some fairly stiff fights, scuffles, and corporate infighting. This is not peculiar to MBO, but is characteristic of political response to changes that will shuffle the power structure and power alignments in the organization. Changes in cost accounting or market research, a new salary system, or simply reassignment of parking places will trigger similar counterresponse.

Predicting the reaction and pinpointing its source is one of the arts of the organization politician, who is then able to take corrective, remedial, or ameliorative action before the problem arises. In some instances, these sources of reaction are found by testing a first idea in tentative form, sending out position papers, and holding discussions in order to elicit the expected responses. If the trouble spots surface after installation, they can be patched up through trading, arm twisting, or muscle, or by changing the program.

Even though most politically aware persons realize the advantages of option *b* over option *a,* it is often impossible to get complete support. Therefore, the need to modify and amend the MBO program after it is underway, for example in the second go-around, should be considered one of the political realities. Running roughshod over those who would resist a new idea not only stiffens the backbone of the resisters, but makes all changes less likely to be accepted.

Unit Loyalty   A rule of allegiance often overlooked is that people center their loyalties around the smallest unit of which they are a member rather than around the overall organization. The basic unit for the soldier is his squad, not the armed forces or the free world. It is the engineering project for the engineer, rather than the entire firm. The personnel expert is often more centered in her staff department's goals than the corporation's.

This fact has great significance for implementing MBO. It means that the objectives must be related to this person, this job, in this unit, this year. Expecting people to be motivated by grand designs and overall global strategies is unrealistic and contrary to political realities.

In one large oil company, the MBO program met poor acceptance in the engineering and development departments, even though it was a smashing success in the refinery and the marketing department. The resistance in the two departments was not only embarrassing, but threatened to weaken the program in other areas as well. A wise MBO administrator suggested a conference in which the people in engineering designed their own MBO system, with special salmon-colored forms and a different kind of calendar of events. The program immediately began to operate smoothly.

Diversity in applications of the MBO program may be necessary for the political reasons of unit loyalty. Permitting variances in details, in application, in timing, and in sequencing of events may assist implementation.

The Individualists   One of the greatest potential sources of political opposition to an MBO program is the uniformity and conformity imposed by some systems. When the MBO program is seen as a set of forms to be filed—a cookbook set of procedures—it will run into individuals who resist.

The reasons lie in the value systems of technical, managerial, and professional people, who possess primarily middle-class values. They are most often the educated professionals, though a degree or college experience is not necessarily the sole criterion for the job or the values. People without degrees who have associated with such educated persons at work have often acquired their values. They cherish their own professional individuality, and while an objective observer might see this individuality as insignificant, it has an important bearing upon the behavior of the person. The desire to participate in decisions is strongly held by the middle-class employee, and denial of the wish will produce political effort contrary to the whole idea.

Sometimes the individualists will object to the name of a program. Some of the best MBO programs have found it necessary to adopt another label, calling it "goals management" or permitting major subunits to use their own names or acronyms. The fetish of maintaining a single unified program with a common label, often adhered to by corporate staffs, can work to the disadvantage of the program.

The image of being "unprofessional" or requiring unprofessional behavior can be the kiss of death to any kind of new procedure. The unexplained and seemingly pointless order or the cold memo not accompanied by a dialogue increases the likelihood that the program will be seen as an indignity or as unprofessional. This perception can be extended to the specifics of the standards of performance which are produced from the goals-setting process ultimately installed. If it seems to be enforcing conformity and attaching present eccentricities, the whole program becomes suspect.

One major feature of MBO that makes it politically palatable to professionals is its indifference to activities but its deep concern about output. This assurance of the protection of individual idiosyncracies is important to professionals.

Status Symbols   Attention must be paid to the effect of the new system on the present structure of status in the organization. Status symbols are the subtle indicators of a person's standing in relation to others. In some instances, these are the physical symbols of office, such as uniforms, desks, office fittings, parking places, and the like, and they are quite standardized. In other instances, more probably in an MBO program, the effect on the status system will be reflected in the reduction in influence or authority for some persons, as the center of decision making moves to a lower level. In one bank where MBO was installed, the power to make certain equipment-purchase decisions was delegated. Yet when the new equipment arrived the president was shocked. "My feelings were hurt that they hadn't consulted me," he reported later.

Social and status significance is attached also to certain prerequisites or roles. If an MBO system robs a person of such status symbols as authority to conduct the annual performance review or to award raises, resistance from the deprived can be expected. People so affected may, in their own minds, be forced to downgrade, depreciate, or even attack MBO. However, the true reasons for the opposition will not be revealed. Such an attack is not conducted openly, of course, for the losses would appear to be a trivial, and perhaps even an immature, reason for attacking something as logical as MBO. The attack may be couched in terms that are eminently logical and rational in language, even though the basis is far from being rational.

Organization Form

Among the more sophisticated approaches to political maneuvering to get an MBO system in operation is that of organizational planning. Decentralization, for example, is ostensibly an organizational structure change, but it also forces MBO into being. Decentralization is also a political action, for it represents a shifting of power within the organization. It is a blending of the bureaucratic form with its centralized control, as described by Max Weber, with the humanistic form in which lower-level persons make more independent decisions, described by Joseph Litterer.

The dispersal of profit responsibility in many places simply makes it impossible for the top executive to control all the activities of all the subordinate profit centers. Accordingly, the higher level of management must satisfy its domineering tendencies by defining results expected and measuring those results, meanwhile keeping its hands off the operations.

This is far less a matter of being persuaded of the virtues of delegation and participative management than a simple inability to see everything. When you run out of eyes, hours, and ability to see everything, you are naturally required to manage by objectives whether you like it or not.

Such exemplary managerial practices are likely to develop in organizations like conglomerates where the new units have been acquired in one bite. It is especially imperative when the acquired company was purchased on some kind of payout plan over the years with strict contractual arrangements allowing the founding management to retain its position as long as profits are satisfactory. Far better than a sophisticated training program is an installment method of acquiring new firms which promote MBO; the result is almost inescapably MBO. The idea, for example, that a corporate president can manage 100 divisions autocratically rather than by objectives is, on the face of it, impossible.

MBO also results in firms that are nationally dispersed (the Prudential Insurance Company, for example) with all but a few managerial functions distributed among the five or six large regional offices, each with a complete functional staff. The bank with 350 branches will probably manage them by objectives, even if it does not realize it is doing so. The alternative is an exorbitant computerized management information system (MIS) and communications system. It is far more economical and sensible to find good people, place them in jobs, get them committed to objectives, and control them by exceptions.

On the other hand, a centralized form with functional departments usually means that the MBO program is a form of artificial or arbitrary choice. Bosses who are in the same room or even the same building with all their employees may declare that MBO is their official style. However, they often are playing house with the employees and, in fact, do not manage by objectives at all, even when they talk a great MBO game.

The Effect of Alliances

Two or three divisions or departments, connected by a network of alliances, joint programs, mutual support, and interdependencies, can make or break an MBO program. The credit and sales departments, which share the task of keeping receivables under control, can make a shambles of capital management goals or they can make achievement seem effortless and natural. The industrial engineering department can team up with production to make MBO easy or difficult.

Alliances can be formed among groups that fear they would be weakened, and their joint resistance will benefit both. Hospitals are replete with examples of groups which might ordinarily find themselves in competition but are instead joined in coalitions in the face of threatening objectives. The surgeons and medical staffs competing for personnel and technician time will stand together against the administrator whose objective is to reduce technician costs.

Take the case of the controller who was committed to a computerized management information system. It was his intent to have an on-line, real-time, alphanumeric tube in every manager's office. Thus, he would have daily—even hourly—control over every important input or resource to be employed in every part of the business. The personnel department at the same time was pushing MBO, suggesting delegation, freedom of action, and goals management rather than control of detailed activity.

In another office, the corporate attorney had built up a "Merlin the magician" relationship with the president. The counsel was in and out of the president's office, reporting little stories and advising on all sorts of things. She too recognized MBO as a threat to her position as high counselor. She teamed up with the controller to condemn MBO as a spurious and probably risky adventure that was probably not fully thought through and perhaps basically unsound—if not downright illegal. MBO never stood a chance. Power is not something voluntarily relinquished; those who have it may see MBO as a shifting of power downward and will accordingly employ alliances and political power to fend it off.

Money is Power

Those who control money or produce it in large amounts have power and can sway all kinds of decisions. In one large electronics firm with ten divisions, one division produced 80 percent of the profit. The general manager of that division had far greater power over corporate policy than his rank would indicate. If he disagreed with or could not use a corporate policy, he would simply ignore it. Because he produced most of the profit, he was sometimes gently admonished but never severely crimped. Such a power center is able to block new programs which do not suit its mode of operation. On the other hand, if the general manager of such a center can be persuaded or educated to adopt MBO, it will probably become a corporatewide system.

In other instances, it is a single function that has major influence. Marketing is king in many firms where the "marketing concept" determines the basic strategic goals. In others, it is the technology center or the financial group. In highly unionized firms, the labor relations manager will have considerable influence, and often determines whether MBO will be given a hearing, to say nothing of its being implemented. Power is often rooted in the ability to affect revenues, expenses, or pricing.

Dealing with Conservatism

Kenneth Boulding has pointed out that change agents, liberals, and innovators are often characterized by high-intensity behavior, while conservators and persons opposed to change are low intensity in behavior.[4] The change-oriented person may have to be dramatic, shrill, strident, persuasive, and even flamboyant to get a full hearing. The best response for the conservative is to lower his or her voice and be rational, cautious, and meticulous.

It is the strategy of conservatism and calmness to propose that the change be examined in detail and be tried only in part, and to suggest that perhaps certain aspects have not been fully revealed. In the face of such a strategy of delay and obfuscation, the change agent must act with skill, upon occasion taking the organization by storm. If the top executive can be persuaded to give the directive and the change agent proceeds with a vigorous combination of advocacy and education to build a plurality in the organization, the innovation may succeed.

The true merits of education as a vehicle for change are seen here. Conservative critics can be isolated and quietly permitted to change their minds without engaging in high-intensity tactics, for the strength of a countermovement is often related to the intensity of the attack on the status quo.

In some instances, the value of outsiders is that they can provide the decisive voice of change to break the deadlock of inertia created by low-intensity opponents. When the outsiders have gone, the less-intense movements can begin. Once the silence has been broken, insider MBO advocates can restore quiet, deplore the excesses which they themselves introduced, and quietly proceed with their educational and persuasive efforts.

MBO has failed in many organizations because those in charge ignored the political considerations included in the implementation. MBO is logical, systematic, and so on, but it must deal with various problems and influences. This does not mean that politics is contrary to the management system known as MBO, and that where politics enters changes and a new system cannot be expected to flourish. Political behavior itself has purposes, and goals are the beginning point of politics as well as of business or administration. It does require, however, that the MBO implementer pay attention to political realities and discriminate among alternative approaches, in choosing the methods of implementation.

SUMMARY

It is apparent that MBO is more than a set of cookbook rules for doing performance reviews or dealing with salary administration. Rather it consists of a philosophy that suggests that purposes and aims are important in determining the major decisions in the management of people and resources. It is not simply a one-on-one discussion procedure, but includes many subsystems for handling a whole host of chronic concerns of managers. It is also a concept that supplants other concepts such as personality-based management, or class- and cult-based management. In addition MBO is a rational system that begins with expected outputs, governs the release of resources, and determines the value of the activities of the organization and its people. The reader should note that special attention to the coaching and counseling aspects of MBO follow in the Management Development chapter of this book.

NOTES

1 Appreciation is expressed to Richard D. Irwin for permission to reprint in modified form, commencing on page 109 and ending on page 122, material from George S. Odiorne, *Personnel Administration by Objectives* (Homewood, Ill.: Richard D. Irwin, copyright 1971), pp. 330–358.

2 Appreciation is expressed to *Business Horizons,* Indiana University, for permission to reprint in modified form, commencing on page 123 and ending on page 134, the article "The Politics of Implementing MBO," by George S. Odiorne, in the June 1974 issue.

3 Joseph Juran, *Managerial Breakthrough,* McGraw-Hill, New York, 1961.

4 Kenneth Boulding, *The Skills of the Economist,* World Publishing, Cleveland, 1959.

REFERENCES

Batten, J. D.: *Beyond Management by Objectives,* American Management Association, New York, 1966.

Beck, Arthur C., and Ellis D. Hillmar: *Making MBO/R Work,* Addison-Wesley, Reading, Mass., 1976.

Carroll, Stephen J., and Henry L. Tosi, Jr.: *Management by Objectives: Applications and Research,* Macmillan, New York, 1976.

Drucker, Peter F.: *The Practice of Management,* Harper & Row, New York, 1954.

Hughes, Charles L.: *Goal Setting: Key to Individual and Organizational Effectiveness,* American Management Association, New York, 1965.

McConkey, Dale D.: *How to Manage by Results,* American Managment Association, New York, 1967.

McGregor, Douglas: *The Human Side of Enterprise,* McGraw-Hill, New York, 1960.

Mager, Robert F.: *Goal Analysis,* Fearon Pitman, Belmont, Calif., 1972.

Mali, Paul: *Managing by Objectives,* Wiley Interscience, New York, 1972.

Morrissey, George L.: *Management by Objectives and Results*, Addison-Wesley, Reading, Mass., 1970.

Odiorne, George S.: *Management by Objectives: A System of Managerial Leadership*, Pitman, New York, 1965.

————: *MBO II: A System of Managerial Leadership for the Eighties*, Fearon Pitman, Belmont, Calif., 1979.

Raia, Anthony P.: *Managing by Objectives*, Scott, Foresman, Glenview, Ill., 1974.

Reddin, William J.: *Effective Management By Objectives*, McGraw-Hill, New York, 1971.

Scanlan, Bert K.: *Results Management in Action*, Management Center of Cambridge, Cambridge, Mass., 1969.

Schleh, Edward C.: *Management by Results: The Dynamics of Profitable Management*, McGraw-Hill, New York, 1961.

Stewart, Nathaniel: *Strategies of Managing for Results*, Prentice-Hall, Englewood Cliffs, N.J., 1966.

Valentine, Raymond F.: *Performance Objectives for Managers*, American Management Association, New York, 1966.

Wikstrom, Walter: *Managing by and with Objectives*, Studies in Personnel Policy No. 212, National Industrial Conference Board, New York, 1968.

4

Management Development

George S. Odiorne

Professor of Management
University of Massachusetts/Amherst

The line dividing Management by Objectives from Management Development is a thin one indeed, for most management development occurs on the job. People learn to do things better when they do them under guidance with feedback. However, there are certain specific programs and actions on the part of an employer which can accelerate that growth. That is the area of management development.

- It might be a course either on or off company premises sponsored and conducted by a trained specialist called the director of management development.
- It might be a seminar, course, or conference conducted by an outside organization in which people acquire fresh new ideas and advanced information from outside their company.
- It could include certain kinds of coaching and counseling done periodically by the boss or some special counsel or employed by the company or organization.

The purposes are all the same: to change behavior. Behavior is activity which can be seen or measured.

The following pages outline the major principles of management development through training and through coaching and counseling.

MANAGEMENT TRAINING BY OBJECTIVES

Over the years at conventions of training directors, the perennial favorite among topics has been that dealing with the question "How can we evaluate training?" Despite a plethora of proposals, the level of dissatisfaction among the audience customarily has been high. Why should it be so difficult to evaluate this function, especially in the light of the amounts of money which are devoted to it, and the significance it plays in the personnel administration function?

The Importance of Training

In the world in which the policy "hire qualified people" is being replaced with that of "hire—then qualify people for their jobs," the role of the training director and the contribution of the training department will be heightened considerably. The concepts of investment being applied to human capital and the new developments in human-asset accounting may well produce insights which will place a real economic value upon training efforts.

Training by Objectives

The greatest value of these economic measures, such as human assets accounting, is that they permit tangible criteria for the evaluation of training effort. And yet this is but the first step in managing the training function of personnel by objectives. There are other definitions involved:

1 A new definition of training is emerging from innovations in teaching. Under the heading of behavioral technology, training means "changing behavior." Training should shape behavior of individuals to some predetermined goal, the goal to be determined by the needs of the organization, organizational objectives, or the individual himself. Thus, if no behavior change occurs, then no success can be attributed to the training effort. If it occurs but is invisible, it must be considered to be an invisible result.

2 The training goal is always a subgoal of some larger goal, and not an end in itself. The company which needs a kind of behavior to achieve an organizational goal trains for that purpose.

3 The evaluation of training effectiveness then depends upon the achievement of behavior change which was predetermined and defined in advance of the release of the effort.

Since 1960 the field of training has been subject to considerable attention, unmatched since the early days of World War II. The emphasis upon human power development as a method of eradicating unemployment, the demand for more technically trained persons for high technology businesses, the decentralization of firms, earlier retirements and shorter work weeks for many public servants such as police officers and firefighters, and the development of numerous new forms of training have combined to produce a training revolution.

It became apparent early in the 1960s that unemployment at levels above 4 percent was becoming unacceptable, and politically explosive. It became further apparent that unemployment could be socially explosive as the civil rights movement turned from passive into active means. Riots in the cities were quickly attributed to unemployment and poverty in the ghettos, and the cause of the poverty and unemployment was attached equally firmly to lack of skills. The solution adopted for all these symptoms was more training.

This produced a drastic change in training objectives. In management development and management training, learning theory has become the slave and instrument of economics. In this chapter we'll look at these two influences in that order: first economics of training, and then applied learning theory. These will then be integrated into an approach to training.

For most managers of training, the second influence—learning theory—has all too often been the master plan around which training is prepared, planned, and presented. This doesn't mean that training has been wrong, but rather that it has often been misguided. The question "Which form of training should be applied to work best?" has often been answered in favor of the most effective form from the viewpoint of learning theory, rather than the most effective form to achieve a specific end purpose or a needed objective.

While the economics of the training programs are probably easier to figure out in the corporation, where profit is a form of economic discipline which is easy to understand, the same limiting conditions exist in nonprofit organizations and government. As the recent trend toward program budgeting (Planning-Programming-Budgeting Systems, or PPBS) in government has pointed up, there is an economic dimension to public service which sets the limiting conditions upon activity in that sector as well. Thus, this analysis is for corporate and governmental trainers as well as management development experts.

Is there a theoretical justification for this arrangement of priorities—economics first, then learning theory? Clearly this sequence adopts the assumption that intention, goals, and objectives determine the effectiveness of the means used. The motive for the training becomes a matter of some moment when we consider it from such a viewpoint. The firm has a charter, which justifies all its objectives. The government agency has a limiting condition in law, which comes to the same conclusion in many cases. The motive for government to train people, however, is less clear, and the forms of training and applied learning theory will not be centered in its limiting condition, even though they cannot be ignored. Political scientists have often chosen power as the major motive for people's actions. Senator Fulbright proposes that a genius of our system is an ability to start with people as they actually exist rather than as they should be. The major realities he recognizes are that the goal of corporations is profit and that ambition and power is the goal in governmental and political life.

The sixties have seen a rather close alliance between the ambitions of politicians and the profit of economic institutions. Unemployment, poverty, and inflation have become issues in politics as well as matters of direct concern to corporations. It is becoming reasonably apparent by now that industrial training has a poor record of survival when the earnings of the business decline. When profits disappear, so does the training department in many cases. While this failure can be explained in part by the limited vision of the general manager, this can't be a complete explanation. It is also possible that much of the training being done is prosperity-based, and under intense economic scrutiny comes out looking like so much purposeless nonsense. The time to turn an economic light onto training is before the crisis of survival of training (and trainers) is at hand. As a result, we may eliminate a lot of the pretentious nonsense which some of the more experimental schools of social scientists have been selling to trainers. Learning theory and psychology can tell us how to teach. Economic analysis can tell us whether or not we should train at all.

The Future Demand for Training Is High

Labor market statistics are all in favor of the training function being an important one in the future. The work of the trainer is an important one to the firm, and should be accorded status in keeping with its importance. Let's look at the big training jobs that lie ahead for our profession during the coming decade:

1   The induction training of 26 million people will be required simply to get new persons on the jobs to replace those leaving the labor force in the next decade.

2   The training of 6 million new skilled craftspersons to replace those

retiring, as well as training present workers in new crafts, will have to be undertaken.

3   The upgrading of an additional 3 to 4 million managerial people faces us. One report states that 30 percent of the present managers will be replaced during this decade, and another 20 percent will move into lateral positions requiring new skills. The average age of company presidents is 59, and the average age of their assistants is slightly higher.

4   Job content is changing rapidly, which means much retraining must be done to keep abreast of these changes.

5   The urban crisis of the sixties has highlighted the explosive potential of the contrast between two societies: one white, educated, and employed; the other black uneducated, and unemployed. Retraining is a key remedy here.

The total cost of such on-the-job training in all its forms has been estimated at around $30 billion annually. In the face of such a challenge, training professionals have every reason to be optimistic about the economic potential of their field both as a career site and as a professional challenge.

Where does the economics of this field find its roots?

Investment in Human Capital as a Base Point

The president of the American Economic Association has pointed up the necessity for a new look at on-the-job training. In his presidential address in 1961, Professor Schultz said, "Although it is obvious that people acquire useful skills and knowledge, it is not obvious that these skills and knowledge are a form of capital, that this capital is part of a deliberate investment that has grown in Western societies at a faster rate than conventional (nonhuman) capital, and that this growth may well be the most distinctive feature of the economic system."

This provocative idea has had a sizable impact on the thinking of others since it was stated. Some have concluded from this view of investment that companies should therefore never fire anybody! Others have concluded that since the Internal Revenue Service accounting procedures don't accommodate themselves to this kind of thinking, it really isn't an investment at all. J. K. Galbraith notes that since companies don't hold title to their people, government training must take over.[1]

Only part of the investment in educational expenditures has tangible effects but we should not overlook the intangible effects, which have benefits as well. While the tangible effects of education, such as more productivity, can be equated to producers' goods, it may well be the intangible ones (creating better citizens, for example) which have greatest impact.

For one thing, education is good for the whole economy, as many studies have shown. In agriculture, for example, the higher educational level of farmers because of land-grant colleges has been credited with much of the improved agricultural productivity which characterized this country from 1940 to 1960. Southern economists have studied the effects of human-capital investment on the economic health of the region.

The training director has an important argument to present to potential learners in the studies showing that trained workers receive personal benefits that are denied the untrained. David and Morgan estimate that investment in education by the individual pays 4 to 6 percent return, as figured on a national basis. Professor Hansen reports that the return to individuals from schooling as private beneficiaries actually exceeds the social return.

And yet, far too few training directors have shown any awareness of this important economic facet of their work, that it does indeed add to the capital of the firm in the form of investment in human capital, and few have guided their efforts to accelerate this growth.

How does one begin? Figure 4-1 shows a worksheet to help you make a quick economic classification of your training program. This worksheet

Part I	Estimated total costs	
	Direct expense (paid out)	____
	Indirect (staff salaries, space, etc.)	____
	Participant salaries	____
	Total cost of program	____
Part II	Economic classification (state as percentage of above $)	
	Profit-improvement training (1-year period)	
	Sales: increase volumes, cut selling costs	____%
	Manufacturing: cut costs	____%
	Service: lower unit costs	____%
	Staff: improve program lower budget expense	____%
	Added human working capital	____%
	Investment in human capital	____%
	Fails to fit any economic classification	____%

Fig. 4-1 Worksheet.

can help you classify your training costs into economic categories. It has two major sections: Part I, identify the major segments of costs: Part II, by percentage identify how much of that cost would be classified as profit improvement, human working capital, and investment in human capital. The following sections show how this is done.

Profit Objectives as a Takeoff Point   The reason so many training departments find themselves come upon hard times—even when it is apparent that their function is necessary and will continue to be in the future—often lies in the specific economic relation they hold to their organization. (Not all organizations are profit making, but all are economic in part.) The training function is not necessarily an organization of reform, but it is an organization of change. Of all the personnel and industrial relations functions, the training function alone has the function of being change agent. (The failure of many especially created change agent programs is probably explainable in their failure to adopt and be consistent with the training staff role.)

What is the economic takeoff point for training? The diagram in Figure 4-2 spells out economic objectives for different parts of the firm. This diagram represents the different kinds of economic measures of organization performance. Each organization unit has a unique economic characteristic. Thus, the general manager level is the lowest possible level at which profit-producing training is of immediate importance, since it is the lowest level which has responsibility for profit. It is the lowest level which controls both revenue and expense. Sales personnel are contributors to profit through the control of two variables under their control: sales volume and selling expense. (The combination of these is "contribution to profit.")

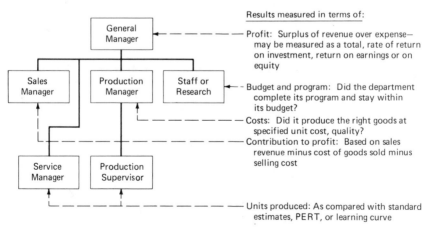

Fig. 4-2 Economic measures of organization performance.

The manufacturing manager is primarily measured by cost of goods sold, with side conditions of quality, delivery, and the like. Subordinates, manufacturing or service supervision, are measured by units produced as compared with certain engineered or historical standards.

Training or change programs which unqualifiedly purport to "improve productivity" are naïve in many respects. They aren't attuned to the economic end measurements or to the specific language of the firm in its economic division of labor.

Sales training programs should produce new volume or cut selling expense. Manufacturing management courses should aim primarily at cost reduction. Little else is significant in this branch of the business. Manufacturing supervision courses or programs should increase units produced against standards, reduce scrap, eliminate accidents, reduce downtime on machines, or prevent machine damage. Service supervision should provide units of service at standard costs or below.

It should be noted that all these kinds of training objectives are profit-centered, and probably will pay off for the firm within the immediate accounting period. Such training should be classified as profit-improvement training.

Is all training in this category? No, this is merely the takeoff point and basic program for training which is economically oriented. Two other economic kinds of training are possible.

Training as Addition to Human Working Capital   A second major economic classification of training functions includes those which pay off in relatively short time, but not within the one-year period in which profits are ordinarily measured. Periods of from one to three years' return on the costs of training can be expected. Training expenses for such purposes as training understudies for people going on vacation and for managers who will retire in a couple of years, training to have backstops for key personnel, or prior training for planned expansion of plant or sales force would be expenses which would not contribute to profit during the immediate accounting period at hand, yet would be sound economic expenses for the firm since they would enhance profit and pay back the costs within a one- to three-year period. Such training expenses are in the same category as inventories and receivables.

Training as Capital Budgeting   The third category of training is that which falls into the same economic category as major replacements or additions to plant and takes several years (up to 10) to return its cash outlay. This category includes such programs as sending executives to Harvard, rotation of junior executives through various departments in preparation for key jobs many years hence, upgrading workers in key crafts, and many other executive and managerial development programs upon which immediate cash return in this accounting period cannot be predicted.

Capital Budgeting for Investment in Human Capital

Having thus classified our training plans and programs as to how each will ultimately contribute to the profit of the firm, we'll probably discover that we've created some new problems in handling the long-range human investment portion of the budgets. To adequately prepare and justify such expenses the training director must be prepared to answer these questions as they apply to training programs for the forthcoming year.

Demand for Funds How much money in total will we need for expenditure in long-range investment in human capital during the coming period? The need here will be weighed against the prospective profitability of the alternative possibilities which are available. Shall we send three executives to executive development schools, and rotate six others, at a cost of $25,000, or should we run 40 weeks of education in political action for supervision for 300 supervisors at the same cost? Should we make a young executive assistant to the president for training purposes for two years at $25,000 or should we conduct a cadet training school for 15 college recruits at the same cost? The answers to such questions of investment alternatives must always be based on a comparison of alternative profitable uses. The money also competes with demands for capital for physical equipment or for research, and there must be some basis for screening alternative uses.

Supply of Funds Unlike the competing demands for capital funds for conventional training, human-capital investments are never—to my knowledge—raised through conventional capital-raising methods in business. Usually such capital comes out of operating income before it goes through profit—or reinvested earnings—channels. In many instances it may come through depreciation allowances which are automatically reinvested in the business. Perhaps one of the needs of business in the future will be for the setting aside of such allowances.

Guides for Construction of Trainer's Objective Statements

When the training manager or members of the training staff prepare to establish training objectives, they will find that a convenient kind of classification system of objectives statements for training can simplify their preparation of such statements. As shown in Figure 4-3, these three

	High	
	(3)	Innovative training objectives
	(2)	Problem-solving training objectives
	(1)	Regular training objectives
Training manager	Low	Classes of training objectives

Fig. 4-3 Training objectives.

classes of objectives comprise an ascending scale of excellence in training administration.

1   The minimum requirement for training departments is that they should conduct the regular, recurring, or routine kind of objectives in training. These might include such training objectives as induction training for new employees, supervisor training for new supervisors, new product training for salespeople, or sales-system training for new retail employees. These objectives should be based upon realistic figures drawn from history (the same quarter last year, for example) and should provide for such trade-off objectives as measures of numbers of trainees, hours of training, cost per trainee, time required for trainee to come up to standard levels of performance, and similar statistical indications of performance for the training department. These should be reality-based and should include a range of possible outcomes, including the highest and lowest possible outcomes permissible, plus a reality base from history. Such data establish a general base for administration of training, and constitute the minimum standards of performance for the training manager.

The training manager who performs all regular objectives within past limits is entitled to the same job for the same pay for another year. Excellence for the manager of training is performing problem-solving training or introducing innovative forms of training.

2   The second category, and one which comprises the major kind of goals for trainers, is problem-solving objectives. The manager of training whose department is finding and solving human behavior problems through applied training skills is worth more than the training department which merely performs last year's courses as before. This is a never-ending process, for this year's problem analysis and course designed to alleviate the problem becomes next year's standard or recurring course in many instances.

The manager of training who sees problems that really exist and solves them through training is of a higher level of excellence. This area of training is often the major point of emphasis in the system approach to training.

3 Innovative goals comprise the highest level of excellence for the training manager and his staff. Innovation can take the form of special training projects which have as their purpose the achievements of breakthrough to new higher levels of excellence through added kinds of behavior, new techniques to improve the quality or cut the cost of training, or assurance that the effects of training can be more certainly achieved.

Innovation goes beyond problem solving, for it assumes higher levels of achievement than problem solving, which often does nothing more than restore the status quo through eradicating causes of deviations from norms.

The difference between problem solving and innovation in training can be illustrated by the following case. The training manager, in addition to conducting regular courses, discovers that because of new orders and new products quality control is slipping in a plant. He conducts a new course in statistical quality control for all operating managers. The quality of the product is improved; that is, it is restored to previously former high levels. The problem is solved.

In another plant the submission rate of new ideas to the suggestion plan has reached a new level. The training manager, desiring to see it go even higher in order that even greater breakthrough to high levels of creative suggestion can be reached, plans and presents a work-simplification course which teaches systematic skills in innovative behavior to managers and operators. As a result the plant moves beyond the highest exception of anyone involved. The added earnings are a result of sharpening the creative behavior of many people, and are based upon some new forms of training.

Nobody had decided that a problem existed; in fact, they were well satisfied that the suggestion-system performance of the people was excellent. Yet the trainer saw an opportunity to exploit the latent creativity of the people and moved the organization performance to higher levels than imagined feasible. This would illustrate an innovative goal.

Innovation might also include new forms of training technique to improve existing programs, even when the present programs seem to be working quite satisfactorily. Some examples of this would include such objectives as these:

Preparation of an instructor briefing guide

The application of videotape to conference-leader skills training

The use of programmed texts in retail clerical training where they had not been used before

Simplification and increased effectiveness of supervisory chalk talks on selling unwanted jobs

Reducing the paperwork without losing essential control in the tuition-refund plan for employee outside courses

The Goal-Setting Procedure

About one quarter before the beginning of a new training year every staff member of the training department is required to set forth objectives, using the three major categories involved. These objectives are discussed individually with the manager of the training department, and the final training plan for the year is fixed in almost final form. The training staff then meets a couple of weeks prior to the beginning of the budget or training year, and each staff member presents training plans for the coming year. Jurisdictional conflicts are discussed, and areas of possible collaboration on objectives are discussed, as shown in Figure 4-4.

The first step is a dialogue confirmed by a memo (1) between the manager of training and departmental members. The dialogue and memo formalize a commitment by each staff member to deliver on regular goals, to try to solve certain problems, and, one hopes, to conceive innovations. (2) The staff meeting is the final commitment of all members of the team to their plan for the year.

The Follow-Up   Clearly stated objectives are the basis for regular review during the year. Perhaps quarterly staff meetings, with reports of results achieved against each objective stated with reasons for exceptions, will serve to keep progress moving. At the end of the year the goal-setting progress is repeated, except that last year's plans are reviewed, differences in achievement from stated goals are discussed, and the new goals for the forthcoming year are once more presented and discussed.

Fig. 4-4   Preparation of training plans.

Measuring the achievement of results against objectives is the purpose of the review and follow-up process. Since they are in writing there should be no disagreement as to the content of the objectives. If conditions change during the year, knock-out discussion confirmed by change memos is permissible if mutually agreed upon. These can be coverd in quarterly review sessions as well as individual discussions between the manager and staff.

The staff member should also feel perfectly free to discuss the possibility of knocking out inappropriate goals when conditions change during the year so that goals which looked sensible at the start prove no longer sensible or feasible. The purpose is not to set up a punishment system, but to gain a commitment system from every staff member. The training manager summarizes the goals, and these constitute the commitment to his or her boss.

Despite the nonpunitive nature of goals, they can be used for performance appraisal of staff members for such purposes as raises, promotions, coaching, self-development, and the training of trainers. Goals setting also provides some insights for the manager into which trainer can best complete the tough new jobs, and it is a form of organization planning, managerial control, and departmental planning. It also has numerous motivational effects upon staff performance and becomes the major communications vehicle for departmental operation.

Classifying Training Needs according to Objectives

It should be noted here that much prior discussion of training needs has centered around problem-solving goals. While it is true that training should solve problems, it is also true that this does not satisfy the total requirements of training departments. The term "training need" has been treated in the literature in the past as being a single unified item of concern. Usually this has been limited to problem solving.

Problem-solving objectives merely restore normality, and training should do more than merely solve problems. It should serve as a change agent, to improve the already satisfactory, to make breakthroughs to newer levels of performance, and to have improving and innovating effects on the organization through enlarging and altering behavior of people in the organization.

Thus, the use of the term "training need" should be dropped and the term "training objective" substituted for it. These training objectives or goals are statements of the behavior change hoped for as a result of training.

Thus, training needs—or objectives—should be classified into three major categories at the time choices and decisions are being made about activities being planned and resources being allocated. These three as outlined here include:

1   Regular training objectives
2   Problem-solving training objectives
3   Innovative or change-making training objectives

Such goals and objectives are not isolated from the real world, but are a product of an environment or context. Identifying and analyzing this context becomes the first step in identifying training objectives.

Training as a Force for Change

Because training in the systems approach means moving toward an objective from some previous position, this can be called training by objectives. It also means that training achieves objectives or should attempt to do so. This is a kind of discipline which liberates training from the many kinds of activities which it could become bogged down in, and makes it purposeful, meaningful, economic, and possible to evaluate. The most important training objectives are those which solve problems and introduce change. The best way to achieve this is to define a behavioral objective you intend to achieve through training, and when the training is complete check to see if you have reached it.

What Is a Problem?   Professor Herbert Simon has made an immense contribution to the science of decision making and problem solving in his small book *The New Science of Management Decisions,* published in 1960.[2] A computer man, Simon worked many years attempting to simulate on the computer the thought processes of the human mind. As a result of this research he has proposed a systematic definition of a problem. It suggests that a problem is a deviation from some standard. This implies that there are two dimensions to a problem, the present level and the desired level (or standard). If you don't know where you are, then you can't know what your problem is, or even if you have one. If you know where you are and like it there, you don't have a problem. If you know where you are and wish you were elsewhere (at another objective), then you have the distance to travel to get there, which constitutes the problem. It's easy to see why this would fit a computer analyst's mode of thought. The computer, in making management decisions, is essentially a user of comparison. There is no need, however, for you to be a computer, since the computer is merely simulating what you do when you think clearly.

In an earlier book,[3] this writer spelled out some further extensions of that definition, proposing that a "problem is a deviation from a standard, important enough to be solved, and to which somebody will be committed to a solution."

It has been suggested that Simon's definition of a problem is too limiting. The problem that is merely a variance from a standard leaves much undone in terms of achieving new goals. Management expert Joseph Juran has proposed that "breakthrough" to newer and higher levels of excellence, heretofore thought beyond the realm of the possible, is a more germane concern.[4] Peter Drucker adds that managers should be more concerned with exploiting opportunities than merely solving problems.[5] The distinction can be useful at the same time that it exploits the systematic and logical methods of systems analysis proposed by Simon. This is done by dividing problems as objectives for training purposes into two major categories.

1 *Problem objectives which restore the status quo.* These are problems caused by some change which has produced a deviation from a norm, important enough for somebody to think the variance should be closed up. Someone then is made responsible for closing the gap.

2 *Innovative or breakthrough objectives which move the present level to new levels of excellence.* The use of objectives is similar to plain problem solving; define the present level, then choose a new desired level. This sought-after level of behavior becomes the training objective.

If the difference between the two kinds of objectives seems subtle, their differences in results are gross. The training program that merely restores the status quo never improves things, it merely prevents them from getting worse. Innovative and breakthrough objectives make quantum leaps in performance even though the present level is considered satisfactory.

If this kind of specific definition of a problem seems to be a trifle esoteric, we should hasten to note that actually it is a great time-saver in the end. All too often the average person, asked to define a problem, will respond by stating its cause, rather than specifying the problem exactly.

"What is your training problem?"

"Motivation of workers."

"What problem does that cause?"

"Our people don't come in on Monday."

The second question indicates that the problem as originally stated isn't the problem, but the cause of the problem, which apparently is absenteeism. What the exact level of Monday absenteeism may be, and what a desirable or objective level might be, is not stated. To innovate, we ask: "What condition would exist if the training were successful?" An answer to this question would be required before an effective statement of the training objective could be made. It would also be needed if the effect of training were to be evaluated later.

Specific definition of a behavior change objective requires that present level and desired levels be defined. In training, the difference between the two becomes the objective of training, sometimes called the "training need."

"Task analysis" means defining present and desired behavior of a specific population of trainees; in other words, it means a very detailed and specific spelling out in behavioral terms of the rpesent behavior and the desired behavior. This analysis applies to either problem solving or innovative training. Let's use the example of a trainer who wants to do a task analysis upon a proposed course which will improve the delegation skills of some middle managers.

A Model for Task Analysis—Using a Systems Approach

1 Behavior to be changed:
   Managerial delegation to subordinates to be increased.

2 Nature and size of the group to be trained:
   a Nature and size of the group: about 30 middle managers ranging in age from 30 to 55, most having college degrees, usually in engineering, chemistry, or business administration, often accounting or finance.
   b Prior training or coaching: little if any, except for some possible outside reading. Several have taken management courses in colleges, but this was at least seven years ago. Few, if any, have been coached by their superiors.
   c Situational facts: strongly technical business, frequent changes due to product short run, technical obsolescence of product. Supervisors must work frequently with nontechnical personnel such as pipefitters, millwrights, and the like.

3 Present level of condition:
   a Supervisors are often seen (ratio delay study shows 50 percent frequency of occurrence) doing work themselves while their subordinates are standing by or doing other work.
   b Few, if any, coaching and instructing actions by the supervisors are observed. Subordinates never seem to be instructed in procedures which are repetitive, and which supervisors perform for them.
   c Supervisors often omit reports and other administrative re-

quirements of their job. Fifty percent of supervisory reports are late. Supervisors report themselves too busy to prepare reports, and do them at home or on Saturday.

4 Desired condition:

   a Supervisors should be observed in less than 10 percent of observations doing work of technicians and mechanics, and then for instruction only.

   b Supervisors should be seen engaged in coaching workers in procedures which are repetitive, using Job Instruction Training (JIT) technique for teaching. At other times they should be supervising and directing, not doing.

   c All supervisory reports should be prepared on the operating day scheduled, and emergency reports only done at home.

5 What would be the favorable end operational results if the training were successful?:

   Productivity would increase and down time between production runs would be reduced 50 percent. Turnover among skilled people would be reduced 20 percent. Amount of actual work done by technicians would increase, freeing supervisory time by 50 percent. All supervisory reports would be in on the day prescribed, making administrative decisions and upward reporting more timely by 20 percent.

6 What indicators could be used to determine changes from present level to desired level?:

   a Do ratio delay studies of activities of supervisors and note percentage of time engaged in technical work that is part of job descriptions of lower-ranking persons.

   b Do ratio delay study of supervisors (same study) and note percentage of time being spent in teaching, coaching, or JIT.

   c Count frequency of late reports from supervisors as percent of total report due by day.

   d Count frequency of delays in outgoing higher-level reports, and show what percentage are delayed because of late supervisory reports.

Presuming that you had previously analyzed the situation behaviorally to determine that the cause of the behavior you are studying was not in the situation itself, nor simply a matter of enforcement, but lay in the fact the managers didn't know how to, or couldn't, delegate these chores, your task analysis prepares the stage for breaking the training down into steps with criteria of achievement for each. As we noted earlier, this appears to be a training objective because it involves the behavior of people (the supervisors) which is caused by lack of knowledge, insufficient skills, wrong knowledge, or insufficient information. In a more narrative style this would read somewhat as follows:

Most of our supervisors were hired from college with emphasis upon technical education for plant supervision, and accounting or finance for the office and administrative tasks. After a tour of duty in technical engineering or staff accounting work, they are promoted to supervisory positions. In the past we have done little to prepare these people for the change in duties from technical expert to supervision of others. Their experience has been rewarding when they excelled at technical matters, and this technical excellence has often been the reason for their promotion. It is not surprising that they continue to pursue the very things which led to their immediate success, that is, promotion into management.

We find, however, that they cling to technical work, rather than teaching technical work to others and doing the supervisory planning and administrative work which is necessary in their departments, and this leads to two ill effects. The first is that they usurp all the technical work in the departments while the aids and assistants stand around watching. This has produced some quitting among technicians and mechanics who feel that they are not being well employed. The second effect is that the necessary work of reporting, and doing similar managerial tasks is being left undone.

Not an uncommon story. In such cases, what is the value of task analysis, what are the key ingredients, and how is this task analysis used?

1   It describes in specific, quantitative terms, in places where that is possible, what the present behavior consists of (part 3 of the model).

2   It describes the desired behavior in terms of quantitative differences, and the quantification of the behavior change comes out something like this:

   a   A reduction of 40 percent observed instances of supervisors working.
   b   More observable instances of coaching and training. (This rate of observations would be a declining curve, since the early evidence of coaching would permit tapering off and permitting the subordinates to be working independently once they have been trained. This could be described as a learning-curve rate of observation.)

ACTION TRAINING TECHNIQUES

Since the end of World War II, the race has been on to discover new techniques of teaching managers and employees. Conference and discussion methods were probably the first departures from straight lectures—or even more traditionally—papers read by executives. The trend was undoubtedly needed, and may well have prevented training from being inundated under a great wave of boredom. Whatever else might be said about special methods of presentation which are akin to the theater, unless the class is willing to stay through the whole session and pay reasonable attention to the proceedings in the room, the chances of affecting any behavior change are diminished.

Despite the ever-present possibility that training can become a form of managerial entertainment on company premises, there are volumes to be spoken in favor of such devices as role playing, management games, incident processes, and the like for presenting instruction. The major virtue can be summarized in the common element which runs through all of them: they require some simulated behavior on the part of trainees and thus feedback on the effects of this behavior is provided for both trainers and their peers.

We will now move from the behavioral objectives uncovered in the task analysis to scrutinize the optional kinds of training which might affect job behavior through a planned effort.

What Is Action Training?

To make action training effective there are certain essential ingredients in the training session itself. This may take the form of a class, or it might just as well be a coaching session between a single trainer and single trainee. The key ingredients are these:

1 The desired terminal behavior of the trainee has been specifically defined.

2 The trainee's present levels of behavior and performance are specified.

3 Through task analysis the specific behavior changes needed have been clearly defined.

4 During the training session the trainee engages in some action such as talking, writing, walking, or conferring.

5 The action engaged in simulates the behavior sought back on the job.

6 The course of change in behavior comprises some orderly progression of small steps.

7 At each stage of training feedback is obtained which makes it known whether the action is successful or unsuccessful.

8 The learning is under the instructor's control.

9 A summary evaluation, measuring actual outcome with stated objectives, is possible.

The forms that action training takes include most of the major innovations in training such as role playing, certain uses of case studies, management games, incident process, in basket training exercises, as well as practice sessions and workshops. The range of these applications is wide and grows steadily. If you understand the basics of action training, development of new forms to fit the training need is easily undertaken.

The essentials of action training are illustrated in Figure 4-5, which shows the time stages and the important ingredients of the flow in which the training is presented to the trainee. This isn't necessarily the way in which the trainer plans the action training, however. The first step is identifying the terminal behavior sought, though it appears as the final outcome on the action training diagram.

The Forms of Action Training

The specific forms of action training break down into different kinds of simulation. The common element is that all of them simulate the situation in which the trainees must operate in the real world, and require them to behave in a way that they might behave back in that environment if they were to apply the new behavioral skills desired.

Simulation doesn't necessarily mean faithful, complete, and accurate reproduction of all details of the job. Completeness of simulation could

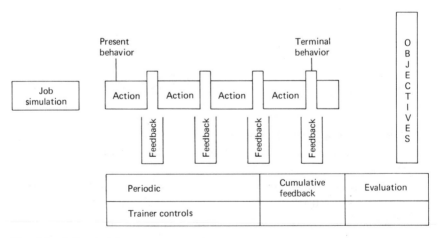

Fig. 4-5 Action training.

only be achieved by taking the individual right back to the department, the people, the machines, the problems, the pressures of the real job. Adding to details doesn't necessarily add to the certainty of behavior change. Plausible resemblance in important details is more desirable than exhaustive attention to little detailed touches. The overdoing of reality usually leads only to "cuteness" in the exercises.

These things become clearer as we look at some examples which illustrate the alternative methods of action training which are often used. These methods, all simulation of life, include:

Role playing

Case studies (with variation)

Management games

Demonstrations

Sticking with these main families of action training methods permits us to use variations of them in profusion, and to master a few key tools rather than become overinvolved in making choices among too many specific techniques.

Evaluation of Training Effectiveness

Being systematic in evaluation doesn't mean that you throw out old methods of testing; you merely supplement them by having a firmer set of criteria in mind. The systems approach suggests that the criteria for measuring training effectiveness is the set of objectives you started out to achieve.

The Futility of Ordinary Testing

One of the more fruitless activities of the customary classroom teaching is based on the folklore that somehow testing is a necessary part of the learning process. The teacher lectures to the students, assigns readings, and periodically sits the class before a blue book, away from books and notes, and tests students' ability to reproduce what their memory and reading skill have produced as a residue. Where the course consists of certain skills such as performing an experiment, students may actually perform such an experiment in the presence of the instructor. The vast majority of tests, however, are required demonstrations of verbal (oral or written) behavior, which may or may not reflect itself into some visible and productive behavior at a later time outside the classroom environment.

While this may serve many useful purposes in the school and college, it serves far fewer useful purposes in management training. The standard variations of verbal behavior testing—essay questions, true/false, multiple choice, comparison, definition, and the like—when applied to a subject such as human relations are most unlikely to prove anything more than the student's ability to recognize certain written symbols dealing with the language of human relations. Since human relations or other managerial training is most apt to be a complex kind of behavior, or repertory of behaviors, success on the verbal or pencil-and-paper test can hardly be described as proof of learning or a measurement of the degree of learning.

The systems approach to evaluation of training starts with a definition of behavior change objectives sought through a conscious development effort. This definition then remains a yardstick for measurement throughout the course, and achievement against the stated goals is the measure of success. All other forms of evaluation measure the internal character of activity itself, not the effectiveness of training.

Behavior and Its Consequences

One of the procedural hitches that can occur in evaluating the effect of a training effort is in sorting out behavior change from the results produced by that behavior. This can be illustrated in Figure 4-6, in which there are shown three separate ingredients of the behavior change process.

A training program (2) is conducted which is designed to change the behavior of the trainee from old behavior (1) to new behavior (3). As a result of the course or training effort the new behavior actually ensues. This new behavior affects something else in the environment (4) of the trainee.

We note that the fourth effect was desired before we started; that's why we organized and planned and executed the training effort. And yet, a limitation on the evaluation of training effectiveness lies in the possible existence of other forces (A and B) which might have occurred at the same time, or in concurrence with the training. Thus, the effect cannot be wholly or accurately ascribed to the training unless we can be certain that no other influences were at work. For example, if we con-

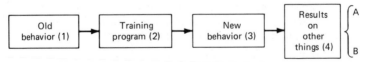

Fig. 4-6 Behavior change process.

duct a cost-reduction course for supervisors and costs go down, we can't assume that the result was wholly caused by the training. It may have been caused by better purchasing, longer runs in production, an easier product to make, better engineering, or a change in suppliers. Neither can we call the course in cost reduction a failure if after the course costs rise. They may have risen for any of the reasons which are cited above or other influences at work. It may also be true that costs went up but would have risen more if the cost-reduction course hadn't been conducted and the skill brought back to the job and applied.

From Figure 4-6 we might reasonably conclude that the best way of evaluating training would be to confine the evaluation to items 1, 2, and 3. Evaluations of item 4 might well be done, but if the first three have been used and proved effective, then 4 must be used cautiously. Perhaps it can give insights into whether or not the course objectives were properly designed; but even here there are many limitations. If a course defines its intentions as changing specific old behavior to specific new behavior and this change actually occurs, the training must be considered successful. The evaluation of training is limited to assessing or measuring as accurately as possible how much of the desired (objective) behavior was actually attained and applied, first in the class, and second, back on the job.

If training actually changed behavior in the class, then it must be considered a training success from the class standpoint and instruction-technique standpoint. If it fails to convert back to the job, then the analysis of system support of that behavior may be at fault; in that case not the training but the prior planning and task analysis is probably at fault.

COACHING AND COUNSELING FOR MANAGEMENT BY OBJECTIVES AND MANAGEMENT DEVELOPMENT

It is apparent that MBO is a logical process, and the temptation for logical and systematic managers is to presume that it is wholly logical. The face-to-face nature of MBO is an essential feature, however, for it personalizes an otherwise depersonalized and bureaucratic world of work. Many MBO programs have failed because the management of the organization did not persist in making it a personalized, face-to-face coaching process. There are many things that cannot be done by cold memoranda, unaccompanied by the personal processes of coaching and counseling.

1   You cannot strike a fair bargain by memo alone.

2 You cannot resolve disagreements by memoranda alone.

3 You cannot change behavior which is already under way by memoranda alone.

All three of these conditions exist when the boss and subordinate are engaged in an MBO process which has as its aim the development of subordinate performance, the production of change, and the resolution of agreements. Thus the counseling and coaching aspect of MBO is an integral part of its nature.

Cooperative leadership depends for its success upon principles of motivation. It is based upon tools for achieving mutual understanding and mutual goals. Interviewing is one of these tools; counseling is another, closely related one. Counseling is both a catalytic ingredient and a humanizing agent. In authoritarian management, control results from the power to impose punishment given the supervisor or executive by the organization. In cooperative leadership the executive uses human relation tools to develop a desire on the part of the worker or peer to work toward shared goals.

We have seen that the authoritarian style is characterized by nonparticipation on the part of the fellow worker and that cooperative partnership requires, as one of its features, participation.

This section will discuss the background and purpose of the cooperative counseling interview as a cooperative leadership tool; its basic principles; attitudes and attitude change; listening as a counseling technique; counseling and executive training; and postappraisal counseling.

Background and Purposes

Personnel counseling is one of the more important techniques of the cooperative, constructive, creative executive. It is to individual relationships what the participative, nondirective conference is to the relationship between the leader and the small group.

The general purposes of employee counseling are twofold. The first has to do with communications per se. The second has to do with morale, motivation, and adjustment of the counselee.

Several kinds of counseling programs have been identified. One kind provides information for employees; another gives assistance to supervisors in handling special problems; another type provides information regarding attitudes and morale of workers to help management take corrective action; yet another has as its purpose better personal and job adjustment of employees.

A survey by the National Industrial Conference Board of 519 firms found that most companies provide informal counseling of some sort.

Forty-seven percent had no formal counseling for men, and 43 percent had none for women. The proportion of firms having formal programs with full-time counselors was just under 10 percent.

A central philosophy of the counseling interview is that it should meet the need in large organizations for a "humanizing agent" to encourage teamwork and less formal, cold relationships between managements (of both business and unions) and the rank-and-file members of employees.

Employee counseling has been used to a considerable extent by some companies, notably the Western Electric Company and Sears, Roebuck, for the purpose mentioned above. Discussions between supervisor and employee are set up on a systematic basis to enable management to learn more about the attitudes of employees and to take any necessary remedial action. If employee counseling were used for this purpose alone, as it sometimes is, employee counseling would differ little from an employee attitude survey.

Employee attitude surveys are usually conducted by questionnaire. Questions concerning how the employee feels about the company as a whole and about the specific aspects of her or his job are asked. An appropriate questionnaire survey was conducted in the various offices of a national public accounting firm. One question concerned the feelings of the junior and semisenior accountants. It asked whether the partners showed favoritism. The question yielded the following information: 53 percent of the group felt that some or much favoritism was shown in the firm; 30 percent felt there was little; 7 percent said there was none. This favoritism as perceived by the group tended to lower morale.

The attitude survey by questionnaire given uniformly to all the employees in a group can yield a quantitative number or summary index that indicates the amount of discontent arising from various sources, for example, from favoritism. The survey enables comparison of a department with a company norm and also comparison with previous figures in order to uncover changes. The counseling interview, on the other hand, is at something of a disadvantage. The counselor might interview all the employees and tabulate the number who answer the question. This, however, is more likely to result in a general picture than a summary index. The judgment made as to the strength of feeling of the interviewee is subjective rather than quantitative. And of course it is more costly to use the interview than the questionnaire method.

One advantage of the counseling interview as a procedure for gathering information on employee attitudes is that additional information can be asked for; this additional information may be clarified during the interview. Interpretations can be requested, and they frequently throw additional light on interviewees' attitudes and feelings. The questionnaire procedure attempts to attain similar interpretative data by asking for free comments. A space is sometimes provided under the question for the respondent to clarify the checkmark response.

"Depth" procedure is not possible by use of the questionnaire. The depth interview is a clinical device requiring a considerable amount of specialized training on the part of the interviewer. When used by a clinician, it can reveal hidden feelings and attitudes that the interviewee often will not reveal in a short-term interview or in a questionnaire. The proponents of the depth interview hold that barriers to communication are broken down through "knowing the interviewee" and establishing a superior bond of rapport. This, of course, is not at all feasible in the questionnaire survey or in the typical short interview lasting from 10 to 30 minutes.

The depth interview is often used appropriately in exit interviewing when a job incumbent resigns or decides to leave the employ of the company. A constructive management would like to know the reasons (assuming that the employee is efficient) so that it can correct deficiencies. Usually human relations reasons, such as status, are involved.

We may take an illustration from the experience of the Western Electric Company. A middle-level executive decided to quit the company and submitted his resignation. When interviewed, he responded with rather vague reasons, such as desire to seek a job in another company, desire for a career suited to his skills and background, and family pressure to move from the locality. None of the reasons given seemed very realistic to the interviewer. After three sessions of interviewing, totaling about five hours, the real reason for his resignation was somewhat dramatically revealed.

The depth interview revealed that the executive have been allocated a single-pedestal desk while other executives on his same level, with the same salary, amount of responsibility, and authority in the hierarchical arrangement, had double-pedestal desks. This executive simply could not stand the symbol of inferiority; he had been brooding over this condition for a long time before he submitted his resignation; he was embarrassed by it to the extent that he could not, in casual conversation with his fellow workers, bring this grievance out into the open—it took a depth interview to reveal his difficulties. Once revealed they were easily overcome.

All employees are acutely aware of their self-perceived level in the organization; they are vividly mindful of status symbols. For example, during a certain period of its history, the Ford Motor Company had a well-known "mahogany row." Edsel Ford at that time had the largest suite of rooms in the corner of the executive building at the River Rouge plant near Detroit; other top bosses of the company had adjoining suites of rooms and single executive rooms done in plush furniture. There were several ways of noting status or, as Vance Packard has called it, "barnyard pecking order" in this organization. One was the distance away from the offices of Edsel Ford; another was the size and degree of magnificence of the office of the executive. These are human relations factors.

Interviewer-counselors are concerned with a specific kind of information, that which bears upon human relations. In striving to improve relationships, they are employee-centered rather than production-centered. Their interest in production is secondary, although excellence of employee relations indirectly tends to increase motivation of employees, which in turn may yield higher productivity.

In the Western Electric Company the counseling program, managed by W. J. Dickson, had two purposes: to study the employees' attitudes so that management could do something about improving them, and to increase motivation of employees. At one period in this program a number of counselors were used; each handled counseling interviews with about 300 employees. The employee usually initiated the interview. The interviewers did not give advice, nor did they take any remedial action. When they transmitted information upward to management, they did so without revealing the identity of the counselee who had a grievance or complaint that revealed a condition needing correction.

Basic Principles

During the early stages of the program for employee counseling, the interviewers developed a number of rules of the game. A brief abstract of these, adapted from Roethlisberger and Dickson, follows:[6]

1 The interviewer should treat what is said in the interview as an item in a context.

    a The interviewer should not pay exclusive attention to the manifest content of the intercourse.

    b The interviewer should not treat everything that is said as being at the same psychological level.

    c The interviewer should not treat everything that is said as either fact or error.

2 The interviewer should listen not only to what a person wants to say but also what he or she does not want to say or cannot say without help.

3 Using the preceding rule as a guide, the interviewer should seek the personal reference that is being revealed.

4 The interviewer should keep the personal reference in its social context.

a The interviewer should remember that the interview is itself a social situation and that, therefore, the social relation existing between the interviewer and the interviewee is in part determining what is said.

b The interviewer should guard against contagious bias by resisting the temptation to identify with the speaker's sentiments.

The interviewers in the Western Electric program recognized that the past history of each employee as well as forces outside the company affect the employees' behavior and attitudes. They wanted to examine all the forces that affect employees and determine their attitudes, which in turn determine their motivation. The counselors were instructed not to usurp any of the prerogatives or responsibilities of the supervisor. Some difficulties resulted because some supervisors at first misunderstood and mistrusted the motives of the counselor.

In most companies the supervisors are the only ones available to do counseling and thus in an authoritarian plant are required under this scheme to be both disciplinarian and nondisciplinarian. They use the directive form of management at some times; they then put on other hats and become nondirective counselors to engender cooperation and get information concerning morale and attitude.

At the Western Electric Company, each interviewer was assigned to a certain area of the plant. The interviewers coordinated their activities with the supervisors but, of course, did not divulge the results of the interview. Other principles in the counselors' manual that were found to be effective, especially in the relationship of the interviewer to the counselee, were:

1   The interviewer was to explain to the employee the purpose of the interview.

2   The employee was to be told how the interviews were to be used. For example, any complaints the employee had to make with regard to working conditions would be investigated together with those of the other employees and, insofar as possible, remedial action would be taken. The manner in which material gathered from the interviews would be used in supervisory training conferences was also to be explained.

3   The interviewer was to make clear to each employee that the interviews were to be kept strictly confidential; the employee could say anything to the interviewer, no matter how bad it was, without getting anyone into trouble, including supervisors, coworkers, or the employee giving the information. The interviewer was to explain that no names or organization numbers would be used.

4   The employee was to be told that the company was as interested in the things liked as in those things which caused dissatisfaction and which, in the employee's opinion, needed to be corrected.

5   The interviewer was to take almost verbatim notes as the employee talked. The interviewer was to explain to the employee that what was said was being written down word for word, to avoid any possible chance of misrepresenting or forgetting anything.

6   The interviewer was to be sympathetic, to listen well, and to convey genuine interest in the employee's problems and complaints.

7   Strict care was to be taken not to express any agreement or disagreement with the complaints that the employee made. The interviewer was to let the employee know that he or she was in no position to judge the correctness or incorrectness of what the employee said.

8   The interviewer was not to inform the employee of the nature of the complaints made by other employees.

9   The interviewer was not to give the employee advice as to what should be done. In rare cases the employee might be advised to see his or her supervisor, or information about the various benefit plans might be passed on. However, the interviewer was not to hesitate to offer encouragement to any employee if it seemed that it would do any good.

10   The interviewer was to write up the interview under six headings. The opinions of the employee were first to be divided into three categories—working conditions, supervision, and job. Under each of these headings two subclassifications, likes and dislikes, were to be added.

Attitudes and Attitude Change

Attitudes have been called "durable regulators." They are at least somewhat permanent regulators of behavior; they are difficult to change. The counseling interview is one way of changing them.

A psychological set is a regulator of behavior, but it differs from an attitude in that a set is temporary and regulates a specific kind of behavior, whereas attitudes are more permanent and more general and inclusive in their nature and they regulate a number of kinds of behavior. Thus, if we have an unfavorable attitude toward the Democratic party, this attitude is apt to be somewhat permanent. It is unlikely to change in a half-hour by listening to a political rally or an address or a discussion among friends at home. It would pervade much of our behavior with respect to political matters. Attitudes are made up of fact mixed with emotion. Prejudice is different only in that it is made up of very little fact or no fact at all; it is almost all feeling or emotion. We think of opinion as an attitude containing a large amount of fact, and prejudice as an attitude containing little or no fact.

Figure 4-7 is a schematic picture of several constellations or sets of forces that affect attitudes and behavior. The counseling interview is designed to reveal these forces so that interpretation of them can (1) guide corrective efforts by management and (2) guide the self-adjustment of the counselee. Another way of saying the same thing: management needs to know what these influences are, and the workers need to be aware of them so that they can get insights into their problems and find solutions themselves. The counseling interview is thus seen to be a double-barreled process.

Attitudes result from a multiplicity of forces so complex as almost to defy analysis. The scheme depicted in Figure 4-7 is oversimplified; it does, however, aid us to see that all behavior is caused and that the causes, however subtle, are both real and remediable.

Neither management nor the employee can alter the set of forces of the subject's previous learning (number 3 in the figure). These are the forces that have played upon the subject before and since birth; they include all the learning experiences that make the person we have today. However, present forces, including company conditions (number 1) and outside forces (number 2) are amenable to change. And present experience (number 4) is changed when either 1 or 2 is changed. Furthermore, present experience is changed by thinking or by gaining new insights whether or not 1 or 2 is changed.

Company conditions include both the physical and the myriad social conditions that impinge on the employees. The social milieu provides forces both powerful and influential as determiners of attitude. A double-pedestal desk is a social status symbol. Of itself it has little influence; only when it becomes meaningful when interpreted as a social force is it seen to affect attitudes and performance in any significant way.

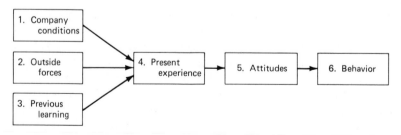

Fig. 4-7   Forces influencing attitude and behavior.

Listening as a Counseling Technique

The nondirective interview, unlike the directive interview, utilizes listening on the part of the interviewer-counselor as its basic technique. The directive interview, giving information, requires the interviewer to do most of the talking. A usual face-to-face conversation is not a monologue; on the average each party must listen 50 percent of the time.

We found in the section on interviewing that the interviewer, even in the personnel selection interview, tends to talk a great deal more than 50 percent of the time. This is unfortunate. The interviews would be more effective if the interviewer arranged the situation so that the interviewee would do most of the talking. In a nondirective interview this is even more crucial.

Skills in listening are, therefore, important to the creative leader. Such skills are of less consequence to the authoritarian. For example, the authoritarian father does not listen, he directs. Often he fails because authority exists only when orders are obeyed. Sometimes however, if the setting has been arranged by a skillful leader, listening to the problems of a child may be quite fruitful, because most people, including children, want to conform to the behavior norms of their group. Continuing group membership is a powerful motivating force. Conformity to group behavior norms tends to ensure continuing group membership; listening can increase conformity.

Listening is a tool that tends to increase the factual content of the talker's opinion and reduce its emotional loading. It may reduce prejudice. When prejudiced persons talk out their prejudices, they tend to get keener insight into their own thinking; they become more objective, less emotional. Through listening, the constructive manager is able to learn approaches which may correct a situation. If these changes can be made, shared goals may be the result.

We have said in previous chapters that only the learner can learn and that it is the responsibility of the trainer to help the learner arrange the situation so that learning can take place. Attitudes are learned behavior tendencies, and as such they can be changed just as habits are changed. This objective approach is helpful in dealing with wrong attitudes. Not only attitudes but also opinions and prejudices are learned. The nondirective counseling situation can be used by the skillful manager to aid a coworker to acquire attitudes that are fruitful to both the worker and the organization. Nondirective counseling is counseling by helpful listening. We have said elsewhere that counseling by listening is at once a device used by leaders, a tool for training people, and a point of view that will help develop further a philosophy of leadership.

In nondirective counseling the awareness of the counselee that the counselor is listening to and understanding his or her problems is crucial. Otherwise rapport is destroyed at once. Psychologists have studied the listening relationship with diligence. Some of their studies have been concerned with the effect of certain monosyllabic sound responses made by the counselor to signify understanding or agreement or both.

The "uh-huh" or "mmm-hmm" response of the counselor has been found to act as a reward or reinforcement of the counselee's responses. An experimental group in which this reinforcement was used responded with more multiple-word responses—they talked more—than did a control group. This has implications in nondirective counseling; the skilled counselor is aware that it is necessary to reinforce selectively the behavior of the counselee. Urging the counselee to talk more and interpreting what is said are ineffective in obtaining more verbalization; on the other hand, clarification (helping counselee to clarify thinking) and tentative analysis (presenting a new approach to the problem in a tentative manner) are effective.

Counseling and Executive Training

Supervisory training as a formal procedure has traditionally included such topics as the supervisor's job description, employee training methods, and employee rating. More recently such programs have included various aspects of human relations. In one such program, used by several companies in Michigan and New Jersey, the trainees meet in small groups for two hours each week for 10 weeks and cover the following topics:

- Introduction: causes of behavior
- Communications: speaking, listening, and reading
- Tension and frustration
- Group problem-solving
- Conference skills
- Role playing
- Merit rating methods
- Interviewing and counseling
- Postappraisal counseling
- Principles of motivation

This program emphasizes cooperative techniques and stresses counseling. About a fifth of it is devoted to counseling.

Counseling can be used as a training device in two ways. One way is to use typescripts or write-ups of counseling interviews in supervisory training; the second is for supervisors to do the counseling. Interview write-ups from provided case materials for training supervisors and executives have been used by some companies. Such materials are used in systematic group training. This was done at the Hawthorne plant of Western Electric Company. Use was made of the classic interview material collected by the interview specialists. An example of a condensed interview used in this way is presented below.

Interviewer: Perhaps you might like to give me an idea of what you think a good supervisor should be like.

Employee: I think first of all he should be able to handle his men right, and should know how to show them courtesy. He should never bark at a man or talk in such a way that a man doesn't feel like taking it. You know, some men, there's no getting away from it, are quick-tempered, and they must be approached in the right way, and if they are, they will do anything for a supervisor, but if someone barks at them—well, then it is time to look out.

You hear employees say that this place is a jail, but it isn't, it's the supervisors every time. . . . Another thing: Supposing a man gets hurt. Maybe he lifts up something and slightly bruises his hand or makes a scratch or something like that. Well, you have to tell your boss about it or go to the hospital. You tell the boss about it and he growls, "Why are you so clumsy?"

You understand, of course, that he fills out a big report for some small scratch. You know how easy it is for blood poison to set in, and all you have to do is to have them bandage it up or put some antiseptic on it or something. The supervisor, as perhaps you know, has to make out a report of time lost through accidents.

Here is something else: In regard to this personnel department, I don't know whether that department is a bluff or a disgrace to the company. A man goes for a transfer and the first day that he goes up there they tell him that they will line something up for him, and then the next day they will say, "No we are sorry that we haven't got anything." I don't know whether they have a conversation with the bosses over the telephones or not; but if they do, I think that is all wrong.

If you follow the rules, why you get bawled out for it because the rules aren't right; and if you don't follow them, you get bawled out. So . . . it makes a fellow wonder just what he should do. Why not have one rule which everyone abides by?[7]

This is a selected interview write-up used in supervisory training by Western Electric Company. It has the advantage of yielding concrete human relations problems for group discussion by supervisors in training. There are disadvantages of this method. The supervisor gets the material secondhand; the interview reports are condensed and lack the warmer qualities of the actual face-to-face contact experienced by the interviewer.

The disadvantages of the method disappear when the supervisor-trainee actually conducts counseling interviews. This alternate method of training provides experiences in which the problems in human relationships are live, vivid, real. Some of the favorable aspects of action research are present in this alternative procedure.

Action research is a kind of research in which those who perform the research study are the ones who use its products. They then say to themselves, "These problem solutions are real to me—I participated in working them out." No selling of ideas is needed because the authors of the ideas are the very people who are to use them. Discovery and application are accomplished by one and the same person; thus neither lost motion nor lag occurs between learning and using results of the learning. And learning through action research goes forward swiftly since the problem situation provides motivation. Action research is, therefore, a device for motivation.

The use of the counseling interview as action research, in which the executive trainee actually performs the counseling, is thus seen to be a training procedure. Since less than 10 percent of companies have formal programs in which specifically trained counselors do the work, most counseling is done, in actual practice, by supervisors and executives. Supervisors and executives may look upon such counseling as a fruitful self-training situation for which they plan and prepare with self-improvement as a goal.

Postappraisal Counseling

Two big questions all employees want answers to are, "What's my job?" and "How and I doing?" Personnel at all levels need and want continual answers to the last question. Some get answers from day-to-day supervision; many do not. Few people ask the question; they wait, often apprehensively, hoping someone will tell them. They need this information so that they can improve their skills; they need to feel someone cares about them to the extent that their good points will be recognized. More important, they need to have their deficiencies brought into proper perspective and discussed objectively so that anxiety, tension, and worry about them can be allayed.

A postappraisal counseling program is designed to provide this information and to give cooperation in correcting deficiencies. It yields both training and a participative, helpful climate in which personnel can grow. In this section we will define postappraisal counseling, look into its purposes, and discuss the adequacy of the appraisals on which it is based and how these appraisals are used.

Postappraisal is the face-to-face discussion and review of an employee's or supervisor's job performance in a nondisciplinary, nondirective, cooperative counseling interview. It enables comment upon, and thus rewards and reinforces, favorable aspects of job performance; and it clarifies unfavorable aspects of performance with a view to their improvement. Obviously, the success of a postappraisal counseling program depends upon the basic adequacy of the appraisals.

Since objective criteria of job performance is only availabe for a small percentage of all managerial positions, subjective judgements of supervisors, superiors, or peers must be used. Such judgments of performance are merit ratings. These may also be called performance valuations, performance reports, job reports, job scores, assessment of employees, job standards, achievement appraisals, or merely ratings.

Merit ratings are of two general kinds: absolute and relative. The absolute ratings attempt to show how well the position incumbent is doing in terms of absolute scale, such as 0 to 100 with 70 as adequate or "passing." Relative merit rating differs in that it employs one of a variety of person-to-person comparison techniques. When different rates are ranked from lowest to highest, this is a relative rating system.

Either the absolute or the relative systems can yield a single rating or many ratings on the same person. A single rating is usually designed to reflect overall value to the company. Multiple scales require the rater to rate the employee on several characteristics, such as industry, accuracy, efficiency in planning, and effectiveness in communications.

We have said that the value of postappraisal counseling depends upon the adequacy or goodness of the appraisals—the ratings—themselves. Before discussing this kind of counseling, we must consider adequacy of ratings and ways of assessing this adequacy.

Most top and middle managers believe they can evaluate personnel performance with accuracy and dependability. However, when data are collected on reliability of ratings, ratings are always found to be less than perfect; indeed, as much as half of the rating programs in business and industry are so contaminated with favoritism, lenient tendency, bias, and halo that they are worse than useless. Any counseling program based on them would do more harm than good. Improvement is needed.

Several arrangements are used by organizations in rating. One is simply to have the immediate supervisor do the rating. Another, more commonly used, is to have the immediate supervisor and another manager one step removed, usually the supervisor's boss, also rate the incumbent. Thus, the supervisor would be rated by a general supervisor, and then the general supervisor's boss, perhaps the department head, would also rate the supervisor. Sometimes these two people rate the employee independently without knowing each other's rating and then confer and reconcile the ratings. In other companies the department head will merely review the immediate supervisor's ratings and approve or disapprove the ratings on the various items. A method being used more and more is for an appraisal committee to make the appraisals in a group conference on each of the ratees.

Likewise, several methods exist for postappraisal counseling. The differences are based on who "plays back" the information to the ratee. Sometimes the ratee has a conference with the rating committee after the committee has decided upon the ratings. In other cases the ratee is asked to fill out a self-rating form, then in the counseling situation the employee compares the self-ratings with the committee's findings. In still other situations the supervisor who did the ratings "plays back" the ratings to the ratee and discusses them in a nondirective way.

The key aspect of effective postappraisal interviewing is its nondirectiveness. The nondirective counseling method is, as we have emphasized, quite different from discipline; the individual is not told what to do. In the nondirective counseling interview we have a clear example of the nonauthoritarian mode. Nondirective job counseling is one of the more important devices for melding the goal of management with the goal of the job incumbent. It is a device for establishing human interrelationships in such a way that goals will be mutual; it is a device used by the leader for arranging the situation so that mutual understanding will contribute to work toward shared goals. This type of counseling is used to change attitudes. Its skillful use can enable counselees to gain insights into problem solutions without being told what to do. The nondirective aspect has as its basic principle "Don't tell them, let them tell you." Use of a directive or disciplinary mode will often result in negative behavior; nondirective counseling is designed to result in positive behavior. If we can enable the counselees to see, to get insight into their problems, their insights are likely to be the same as or better than ours.

A characteristic of all life is that it tends to be self-repairing or self-remediating; a characteristic of all workers is that adjustments to problem situations tend to be made by them. Nondirective postappraisal counseling is based on the principle of use of these remediating properties by the individual self.

Several lists of suggestions are available as guidelines in postappraisal counseling. One of these, which gives useful pointers for the counselor, follows:

1 Look for a cue in the initial discussion to lead conversation into the employee's appraisal. If none develops in a reasonable period of

time, use your prepared plan for initiating discussion of the appraisal.

2 Review and get undersanding of the full concept of the job. This is frequently a source of misunderstanding.

3 Discuss the conditions which exist when the job is done well. Clarify the MBO standard of performance and the measure of performance which applies to this job—how you decide how well the job is performed.

4 Mention the committee's estimate of the employee's overall performance, but do not overemphasize the point.

5 Point out the areas of accomplishment in which the employee is doing a good job.

6 Point out the progress made in the past and the improvements you have observed since the last appraisal.

7 Discuss areas for improvement.

8 Use questioning which emphasizes the part the employee must play in self-improvement:

  a What are your ideas as the cause of the event?
  b What have you done to improve the situation?
  c If you were in charge, what would you do?
  d What steps would increase efficiency in this case?
  e What ideas do you have for improving your own effectiveness?
  f What prevents you from doing a better job?
  g To whom have you gone with your problems?
  h How does the future look to you in your present job?
  i How do you think we could best help you?

9 When direct criticism is to be presented, make sure that the employee will be able to "save face." Do not try to prove the employee wrong. State points of disagreement as questions which need further consideration. Don't give the impression of putting yourself on a pedestal as a judge of right and wrong.

  a Honest praise will help preserve self-respect.
  b Don't dwell long on past mistakes. Direct the discussion toward prevention of similar errors in the future and toward improved performance.
  c If you feel that part of any blame should be shared by you, say so.
  d Avoid antagonizing words such as "reason," "logic," and "common sense." Don't do the employee's thinking. Don't talk down.

10 Don't hurry employees who are slow at expressing their thoughts. Don't put words in their mouths. Don't cut them off before they finish what they apparently want to say. Try to grasp what they intend to say—they may have difficulty saying it. Listen also for cues to what they may be reluctant to say. Avoid showing impatience or antagonism regardless of what is said. Permit discussion of things relative to the job.

11   While being a good listener, control the conversation tactfully. Keep it out of insignificant areas. To draw the talk back into a desired direction, refer to a previously made point. Encourage employees to think through, plan, and take steps which they themselves can put into effect.

12   Never discuss for purposes of comparison a third person known to both yourself and to an employee. However, relating what others have done in improving themselves may show what can be done if properly motivated.

13   Explore employees' interests and goals, the types of work they are interested in or feel qualified to perform.

14   If promotability is raised, remember to avoid yes or no. Promotion depends on many things—ability, performance, rate of growth and improvement, competition, business conditions, and the like.

We discussed techniques of listening. Listening is at work in the nondirective counseling interview; here the counselor must listen most of the time. Simultaneously, the counselor must assure the counselee that he or she understands. Thus, we have in the skillful postappraisal counseling interview many pauses, some of long duration, even as long as a minute and a half; the use of "uh-huh" and the technique of paraphrasing are used a great deal to give the counselee a feeling of shared understanding.

Paraphrasing is an exchange in the counseling interview in which the counselor plays back, or reflects, what the counselee has said with slight changes here and there in wording. For example, the counselee will say, "I have difficulty in delegating work." The counselor might play this back in this way, "You believe you sometimes have difficulty in delegating the work?" This tends to reinforce the counselee's thoughts, for it emphasizes the counselors' feeling that this is one of the important aspects of the counselee's job. This paraphrasing suggests to the counselee that specific instances of difficulties in delegating might be brought up and talked out. The counselee is likely to say, "Yes, and here is an example of what I mean . . . ." Just such an objective was accomplished by a series of counseling interviews conducted by a skilled counselor.

In the first interview, the interviewer, Mr. Hill, greeted the interviewee, a manager named Art, and established rapport with him after a brief amount of chitchat or small talk. The interview progressed, quickly getting around to the excellent work Art had done on some aspects of his job. Art eventually brought up his thought that delegating work to his foreman was somewhat difficult for him.

After several long talks by Art, to which Hill listened attentively and frequently paraphrased to reinforce and show understanding, Art ended one of his discourses with, "I think I know how to do it—at least I will try." To this Hill replied: "Good. I'm confident you will do it, Art. And I am anxious to see you divide your workload with your subordinates." The postappraisal counseling interview ended on this positive accent.

Fortunately for us one of the basic properties of life is self-adjustment. We do better when we find out and correct for ourselves what is wrong. We often do better for ourselves than when someone else directs us. This is the principle on which nondirective counseling is based. It is also true that attitudes, which are fairly durable behavior tendencies, can be modified via nondirective, nondisciplinary counseling, in which counselor listening plays a major role.

We have seen that counseling is a cooperative training tool. It is done most systematically after job performance appraisals. Postappraisal counseling, to be helpful, must be based on dependable information. Nondirective counseling is recommended as one of the tools for the kit of the efficient, cooperative executive.

SUMMARY

While this chapter has dealt mostly with specific ways of conducting and managing management development, there is much more to it. Management Development is a form of investment in human capital. The growth companies are inevitably those which match their plowed-back revenues in research and market development with human resources development. It is not at all surprising that the "money tree companies," those with the highest levels of growth and profitability, are also those which expend more time and talent as well as adequate funding in management development. The rate at which companies grow is often determined by the rate at which they can provide competent management at all levels of the organization.While much of this expense is direct outlay for training in classes, the greatest expenditure is in the on-the-job training, where most management development occurs. This investment in human capital may be the most characteristic feature of modern industrial societies, especially in the West. It has business relevance, but it also has considerable social significance. Where opportunity and incentive are matched, they provide a kind of upward mobility for every youngster. The child of the laborer or the small merchant can become a titan or mogul, not just the offspring of the upper class. That in itself would be sufficient reason for management development to become a major objective of the modern corporation.

NOTES

Appreciation is expressed to Prentice-Hall, Inc., for permission to reprint selected portions from Bellows/Gilson/Odiorne, *Executive Skills: Their Dynamics and Development*, Chapter 8. Copyright 1962 by Prentice-Hall, Inc., Englewood Cliffs, N.J.

1   J. K. Galbraith, *The Liberal Hour*, Houghton Mifflin, Boston, 1960.

2   Herbert A. Simon, *The New Science of Management Decisions*, Harper & Row, New York, 1960.

3   George S. Odiorne, *Management Decisions by Objectives*, Prentice-Hall, Englewood Cliffs, N.J., 1969.

4   Joseph Juran, *Managerial Breakthrough*, McGraw-Hill, New York, 1964.

5   Peter F. Drucker, *The Effective Executive*, Harper & Row, New York, 1965.

6   F. J. Roethlisberger and William J. Dickson, *Management and the Worker*, Harvard University Press, Cambridge, 1939. Reproduced by permission.

7   Appreciation is expressed to *Journal of the American Society of Training Directors* for permission to reprint this interview from Cecil Garland, "Discussing the Appraisal with the Man," in the October 1969 issue. Copyright 1969 by American Society for Training and Development.

REFERENCES

Allen, Louis A.: *Management and Organization*, McGraw-Hill, New York, 1958.

Bursk, Edward C.: *How to Increase Executive Effectiveness*, Harvard University Press, Cambridge, Mass., 1954.

Cantor, Nathaniel: *The Learning Process for Managers*, Harper, New York, 1958.

House, Robert J.: *Management Development, Design Implementation and Evaluation*, Bureau of Industrial Relations, University of Michigan, Ann Arbor, 1967.

Kellogg, Marion S.: *Closing the Performance Gap: Results Centered Employee Development*, American Management Association, New York, 1967.

Merrill, Harwood, and Elizabeth Marting: *Development of Executive Talent*, American Management Association, New York, 1952.

Odiorne, George S.: *Management Training by Objectives: An Economic Approach to Management Training*, Macmillan, New York, 1970.

———: *Personnel Administration by Objectives*, Irwin, Homewood, Ill., 1971.

Planty, Earl G.: *Developing Managerial Ability: 600 Questions and Answers*, Ronald, New York, 1954.

Reigel, John W.: *Executive Development: A Survey of Experience in Fifty American Corporations*, University of Michigan Press, Ann Arbor, 1952.

Part 3
Techniques of Organizational Change—Organization Oriented

Organization Development

W. Warner Burke

Professor of Psychology and Education
Teachers College, Columbia University

Hardly anything can be done these days unless an organization does it. This is the conclusion of two people who have given a lot of thought and study to organizations. Hart and Scott[1] believe that in the United States we have moved gradually but most assuredly from an individualistic value base for our society to an organizational one. In fact, they label the current societal value system the "organization imperative." The era of the rugged individual, the independent, stand-on-your-own-two-feet type is now history. Our society is moved and shaped by organizations, not individual persons.

Hart and Scott make a strong and interesting case for their point of view; while you may not feel as strongly about the argument as they do, you probably will agree that organizations affect your life significantly and pervasively. And this effect is not likely to be a uniformly positive one. Organizations can easily become impersonal and bureaucratic—to use a term that now has become consistently pejorative.

The field of Organization Development (OD) has evolved, in part at least, as a consequence of this (1) "organization imperative" and (2) growing bureaucratization and impersonalization process. Organization Development represents change. The change direction is usually toward such goals as (1) the better utilization of human resources, (2) the design or redesign of structures and procedures that facilitate communication flow and decisions being made closer to the information source, (3) the development of reward systems that relate more directly and effectively to the so-called higher order needs in human motivation, (4) the involvement of people in decisions that directly affect them, and, in general, (5) the creation of a more humanistically oriented work situation.

The purposes of this chapter, therefore, are to explain thoroughly what OD is, where it comes from, how it is carried out, what the research about it indicates, and what its underlying value system represents.

TWO CASES

One of the best ways to explain anything, of course, is to use cases as illustrations. Consequently, we will review two relatively short examples of OD, one carried out in a manufacturing division of a business firm and the other in a medical school. A definition and discussion of OD follows these two cases. Then we review a longer case to show more of the details in an ongoing OD consultation. These cases lead us to the presentation of a model of Organization Development.

Case Example: A Manufacturing Division

A number of years ago I served as consultant to a division of a large United States manufacturing company. The division manufactured heavy electrical equipment in two different plants. I was called in because the division was in trouble. About a month prior to their contact with me a senior vice president from corporate headquarters had told the division's top management that unless they turned things around within six months, he would see to it that the division was closed down. That meant the possibility of a job loss for approximately 1000 people including the division's top management group—six people. The division's problems concerned complaints by two major customers (utility companies). Their orders were invariably late in delivery, and when the products did arrive they were poor in quality or did not meet adequately the product standards that were specified in the original sales.

Within the division everyone blamed everyone else for the problems. The marketing people complained that the design engineers took too long and had to do things too much "their way" instead of designing exactly what the customer wanted. The design engineers blamed the production people, who never seemed able to follow the design specifications. The production people, in turn, complained that the engineers designed the products for tolerances entirely too close for the antiquated machinery they had to use in the manufacturing process. And both the design engineers and production people yelled at the marketing and sales "hotshots" (as they frequently called them) for promising customers highly unrealistic delivery dates. And so the round robin of complaints went.

On my first consulting visit I spent several hours discussing the problems with the divisional general manager. He also showed me the entire operation, especially the manufacturing process. And we had a meeting with his subordinate managers at which I asked questions, they asked me questions, and we explored the issues. I proposed that the next step be individual interviews with each of them, after which I would report back to them as a group what the interview data indicated, and finally we would plan the next steps together. They agreed to the proposal, and two weeks later I spent a day interviewing each of the six members of the division's top management team (see Figure 5-1). On the following day we had a meeting in which my interview findings were discussed. Stated simply, it became clear that these people were not pulling together, especially with respect to trying to determine the primary causes of their problems. The blaming was not confined to the shop floor. Regardless of their level in the division, individual managers were certainly not "above" the mutual blaming process. We decided, therefore, to spend a few days off site to explore in more depth the issues that existed among them and to attempt to "get their act together." In OD language we call this activity "team building."

As a result of the off-site meeting the six managers became more cohesive as a group and greater clarity and priority was achieved regarding the division's problems. The highest priority, which became the next step in the consultation, was the conflict that existed between the design engineers and the manufacturing (production) group of managers and supervisors. To deal with conflict some weeks later, I arranged for another off-site meeting of three days. This time 12 people were involved, the top six managers within manufacturing and the equivalent six from the engineering design department. Although there were a

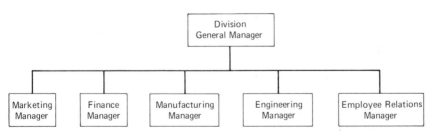

Fig. 5-1 Organization chart of the top management group of the manufacturing division.

number of differences or conflicts between the two groups, the main ones concerned the engineers' complaint about the manufacturing peoples' not following their design specifications closely enough, and the latter group's lament regarding the old and inadequate machines they had to work with. In other words, as the manufacturing persons put it, "Those design engineers just stay glued to their drafting boards and have absolutely no understanding or any concern about our problems on the shop floor."

In an attempt to surface as much of the conflict as possible and then to manage it toward some points of resolution, I used a technique that is considered fairly standard practice in Organization Development for dealing with conflict between two groups in an organization who have to work together effectively for the ultimate success of the organization (see Burke)[2]. The format for problem solving begins with the two groups exchanging perceptions with one another—how each group sees itself and the other group. After this exchange of perceptions the two groups, again working separately, then identify what they consider the problems to be within the interface, i.e., the domain of information exchange and relations in general between the two. Next, negotiation occurs regarding which problems they agree are most important to both groups. The final phase consists of forming cross-groups (in this case three groups of four persons each—two from engineering and two from manufacturing) with each one taking a different problem to plan action steps the two dissenting groups can take to resolve the conflict. A number of problems were indeed handled effectively and progress was made.

The most significant issue which emerged as a consequence of this intergroup meeting was the fact that the manufacturing group was not consistent in what and how they communicated with the design engineers. About two months later, therefore, I helped to conduct a teambuilding session with the top group of manufacturing. This meeting helped the manufacturing people to clarify as a unit what they needed from the design engineers (and other groups from within the division as well) and what their priorities were for dealing with some of their internal problems.

Summary   My consultative effort with this division lasted about nine months. By the end of that time the division had "turned around." The corporation's most recent quarterly report had shown that the division, compared with all the other divisions, was no longer at the bottom of the heap with respect to net profit and customer complaints. From the perspective of Organization Development two primary interventions had been made—team building for the top management team and for the manufacturing group and an intergroup conflict-resolution session between manufacturing and design engineering. Each intervention occurred quite naturally as a result of the previous one since such activities always produce further diagnostic information. In fact, as I gathered and analyzed more and more information I eventually came to the conclusion that a major cause of problems for the division was within its reward system. There was no basis for positive reinforcement, no incentive system of any kind; therefore, first-line supervisors relied heavily on punitive techniques (e.g., threatened layoffs) because they had few resources besides their individual ability to be persuasive. The system of pay for the hourly workers was based on equality (that is, for a given set of jobs all received the same pay—the only difference would be seniority), rather than equity (people paid as a function of their performance).

I recommended a change in this regard to the division general manager. He responded, "No way!" The particular reward system was corporatewide, and he explained that he did not have the power to change it. I further suggested that we go to his boss about the matter. He politely said no, and my consulting effort ended. There was further work that could have been done, but I was convinced that the effort would have been one of continuing to "put out fires" rather than dealing with underlying systematic causes.

Case Example: A Medical School

For well over three years an internal consultant within a medical school and I worked together in an Organization Development effort. We conducted team-building sessions (similar to the ones mentioned in the previous case) with a number of the academic and clinical departments over those years, and we also held an intergroup conflict-resolution session that was in response to a three-way problem. The conflict was among three subunits within the clinical pathology department—the medical doctors, the Ph.D. biologists and chemists, and the medical technicians. Although the procedure was more complicated, we followed essentially the same format I described in the previous case.

What made this OD effort different from the previous example was the major change that occurred in the school's internal structure. Prior to my arrival, a school curriculum-planning committee had been meeting on and off for two years. Its members believed that their plan for a new curriculum was excellent, but they couldn't seem to move toward implementation of the change itself. From interviews with a variety of people and from discussions with the committee I discovered that most of the faculty members were suspicious of the committee's work. Little or no communication outside the committee had occurred. The members of the committee were enthusiastic about their plan, but they feared that if it came to a faculty vote, which eventually was a necessity, they would lose. My data confirmed their fear.

After quite an effort my colleague (the internal consultant) and I persuaded them to run the risk of having their plan modified and involve a large number of other faculty in the planning process. We then organized a planned change process that eventually involved a hundred individuals, more than a third of the entire faculty. The original planning group became a steering committee, and numerous other committees were formed according to subject matter and year of medical school, from first year through the fourth. A year later the new plan was put before the entire faculty and was approved by a 4-to-1 vote. This approval moved us to the next stage—making it work. A structural change was required. The change was from an academic departmental structure as the main subunit of the school to two primary units—departments and four teaching groups each formed according to student school year. The new structure was a matrix with most faculty having two "home bases," their academic department and their teaching unit. The heads of each of the four teaching units were accountable to the Associate Dean for Education, and this structural entity within the school maintained a separate budget from the academic departments. Thus, the academic departments' mission was modified to that of exclusively (1) graduate training and (2) research, as opposed to the previous mission which included these two responsibilities plus classroom education for the four-year medical students. Implementation of the change spanned four years owing to the fact that it began with the next entering freshman class and continued sequentially rather than changing the curriculum of all four years simultaneously. Thus, the change was orderly and allowed plenty of time for "debugging" the new system.

I should point out that during this change effort my internal colleague and I regularly spent time with the dean and his immediate staff. We counseled the dean regarding his management strategy and style, and we worked with him in his relationships with the staff, particularly with the Associate Dean for Education. Trust between the dean and his associate was key to the success of the change. Also critical, of course, was the fact that a significant number of the faculty members were directly involved in planning the change, particularly those changes that each one of them would later be responsible for implementing.

Summary of the Cases

These two cases represent many of the more common elements and practices of Organization Development. They are (1) working collaboratively with the client rather than serving as an expert adviser only; (2)

intervening only after information has been collected which determines what the intervention will be; (3) using multiple interventions—team building, intergroup problem solving, structural modifications, training, counseling, and involvement techniques; and (4) in general, applying knowledge from the behavioral sciences.

DEFINING ORGANIZATION DEVELOPMENT

Beckhard's definition of Organization Development, stated more than a decade ago, remains the most popular and accepted one. He defines OD as "an effort (1) *planned*, (2) *organization-wide*, and (3) *managed* from the *top*, to (4) increase *organization effectiveness* and *health* through (5) *planned interventions* in the organization's 'process' using *behavioral-science* knowledge."[3] He goes on to explain further the italicized terms in his definition. The emphasis is obviously on the planned application of behavioral science knowledge for organizational improvement with top management remaining in charge.

While Beer and Huse[4] would agree with most of Beckhard's definition, they take issue with the "managed from the top" aspect. They contend that OD can start anywhere in the organization, the top, middle, or even with the rank and file. They agree that top management should not be opposed to an OD effort but that too strong a commitment to change on their part, especially in the early stages, could cause resistance lower down in the organization.

It is true that OD can and has started in levels of organizations other than the top. A caveat is necessary, however, if the organization in question is a hierarchically structured one, which most are, certainly within the domains of business-industry and government. In these pyramid-type organizations the OD effort must be managed from the top if it is to be implemented "organizationwide," to use Beckhard's term.

More important, the question really concerns *what* is managed from the top. In our case examples the "what" that was managed from the top was the *process* of change, not necessarily the *content* of what the new organizational state was to be. If top management had defined the desired state—not only for the overall organization but for all the organizational units as well—resistance would no doubt have occurred. When the process is managed in a manner that involves people, the content (or the substantive aspects of change) will not be resisted since those directly affected are making the decisions.

The emphasis in my definition of OD is on cultural change[5] and on the integration of the organization goals with the needs of its members.[6] Organization Development is synonymous with change but organization change is not always OD. Three criteria determine whether an organizational change is OD. If the intervention (1) responds to actual needs for change as experienced by organizational members, (2) involves organizational members in the planning and implementing of the changes, and (3) leads to change in the organization's culture, then the change effort is an OD one.[7] Not everyone in the field agrees with these criteria, particularly the third one—cultural change. Meeting this third criterion implies that the change is in a certain direction. And for me, most of the time it is.

Referring back to the case examples, the medical school example met all three of the above criteria, but consultation with the manufacturing division did not lead to cultural change, e.g., change in the organization's reward system. Even though OD techniques were used, the effort was not, in the final analysis, Organization Development. Adhering strictly to my three criteria, then, I consider this manufacturing division case to have been a short-term success, but for the purposes of Organizational Development, in the long run, a failure.

To be more specific about cultural change in an organization, the direction of change is typically toward developing an organizational culture where:

- Managers exercise their authority more participatively than unilaterally and arbitrarily.
- Cooperative behavior is valued more highly than competitive behavior.
- The growth and development of organizational members is just as important as making a profit or meeting the budget.
- Organizational members at all levels periodically receive feedback on their performance.
- Equal opportunity and fairness for people abounds—in recruitment, promotion practices, and in the organization's reward system.
- Organizational members are kept informed especially concerning matters that directly affect their jobs or them personally.

I could go on, but perhaps this short list gives a flavor of what the new culture would approach after OD had been underway for a while, at least a couple of years.

In an attempt to provide more than just a flavor, however, and to refer to other peoples' thinking about organizational culture, let me cite first the writing of Katz and Kahn.[8] They have contended that the culture of an organization is reflected in its (1) system of norms and values, (2) history of internal and external struggles, (3) types of people attracted, (4) work processes and physical layout, (5) modes of communication, and (6) exercise of authority. In a previous work[9] I used these six factors to compare three classical and traditional views of organizational culture (and the more prevailing culture of organizations today) with the desired organizational culture for purposes of Organizational Development. The three views are taken from the writings of Argyris,[10] Bennis,[11] and Massie.[12] Argyris uses the term "formal" to describe current organizational cultures, Bennis calls them "bureaucracies," and Massie refers to the characteristics of the "classical" (and still the prevailing) theory of organizational management. These three traditional descriptions are quite similar to one another and are in striking contrast to Beckhard's outline for what he calls a "healthy" organization and one that is aspired to in an OD effort.[13] Using the six factors of Katz and Kahn as a basis for the comparisons, Table 5-1 summarizes the three traditional/classical views and compares them with that of an organization that is involved in Organizational Development.

As stated earlier, complete agreement concerning a definition of what OD is or should be does not exist among professionals in the field. While most professionals would be willing to quote Beckhard's definition as perhaps the standard one, they would, at the same time, likely have their own version. This proliferation of definitions is due to at least three causes:

1 The field of Organization Development is new enough (about 20 years old as of this writing) still to be somewhat vague and unformulated.

2 Organization Development is anything but value-free. In fact, in some peoples' definition value change in the organization is specified. As in any other group of professionals, individual values differ. Moreover, what people in the field espouse and what they actually do differs.[14] Thus, variations in definitions reflect these value differences.

3 Related to the second cause is the contingency versus normative controversy. Some (perhaps most) experts believe that the direction of change for an organization *depends,* or is contingent, on a variety of factors, especially the outside environment (e.g., see Lawrence and Lorsch).[15] Two examples of definitions or Organization Development that reflect this viewpoint are:

a "any steps taken by managers to improve the effective and efficient functioning of the organization" (Lorsch).[16]

b "OD is all the activities engaged in by managers, employees, and

Table 5-1 Comparison of Contemporary Organizational Cultures with Culture of Organization Involved in OD

Factors reflecting culture of an organization	Type of Organization			
	Formal (Argyris)	Contemporary bureaucracy (Bennis)	Classical (Massie)	Involved in OD (Beckhard)
1. Norms and values	Individuality is repressed and no value placed on self-actualization.	Interpersonal relationships are impersonal and conformity is rewarded.	Activities of group are viewed on an objective and impersonal basis; highest value placed on productivity; people do not value the freedom of determining their own approaches to problems.	Individuality is stressed through norm of utilizing human resources to the maximum; feelings expressed as well as logic; collaborative efforts rewarded with less emphasis on competition; high value on democratic process of working and interacting.
2. History of internal and external struggles *a.* Classical conflict	The organization's demands and the individual's need to self-actualize usually differ considerably.	Interpersonal and organizational, since it is common in a bureaucracy to have bosses without technical competence and subordinates with it.	Between boss and subordinate since supervision is required to get work done.	No conflict; conflict among human beings is inevitable.
b. Style of conflict resolution	To submerge individual needs, since organizational demands come first.	To ignore it, since the boss will eventually retire or be "promoted."	Varies, but is in the hands of the boss; he handles it in any way he sees fit, typically autocratically.	To bring it into the open and work to manage it creatively.
3. Types of people organization attracts	Logical thinkers; highly rational persons who suppress their feelings.	Conditioned "organization men"; persons who desire order, structure, and stability in their lives.	Rational persons who do not like to work but if they have to, they prefer (1) the security of a	Persons with strong need for self-actualization.

			definite task, (2) to be directed, and (3) money as their primary incentive.	
4. Work processes and physical layout	Logical, systematic, i.e., according to scientific management principles.	Division of labor based on functional specialization.	Clear-cut patterns of work established and predicted; simple tasks are stressed because they are easier to master and lead to higher productivity.	Form of organizational structure follows function; self-renewing, viable system which organizes in a variety of ways depending on tasks.
5. Modes of communication	Conforms to what organizational charts and manuals prescribe.	Follows well-defined system based on rights and duties of employees.	Restricted to limits of the specific job and hierarchical channels, otherwise members will tend to be confused and to trespass on the domains of others.	Freedom of communication upward, downward, and laterally with emphasis on openness and candor.
6. Exercise of authority	Authority-obedience principle.	Follows well-defined hierarchy of authoritative positions.	Authority has its source at the top of a hierarchy and is delegated down; coordination will not be achieved unless it is planned and directed from above; members in a cooperative endeavor are unable to work out the relationships of their positions without detailed guidance from their superiors.	Authority is a function of knowledge and competence as well as role; decision making is on the basis of information source rather than organizational role.

SOURCE: H. A. Hornstein, B. B. Bunker, W. W. Burke, M. Gindes, and R. J. Lewicki, *Social Intervention: A Behavioral Science Approach*, Macmillan, New York, 1971, pp. 348-349. Used by permission.

helpers which are directed toward building and maintaining the health of the organization as a total system" (Schein).[17]

These definitions, with their uses of terms such as "any" and "all" activities or steps that would improve things, reflect the notion of *anything* that works and will help. Thus, installation of a new computer system would qualify as OD.

Normative, on the other hand, means that there is a standard or model to follow, a direction that is better than others. For OD, this norm is based on a combination of certain values, largely humanistic in nature, and selected principles from the applied behavioral sciences. These "selected principles" vary somewhat from practitioner to practitioner, but they stem from research and theory that have credible applicability. That is, in some areas enough is known to be advocated as a valid step for the organization to take. An example may help. Behavior modification, the application of B. F. Skinner's research and theory in psychology, is a proven quantity. It works. Reward systems in organizations would be improved if they were based more on Skinner's principles of positive reinforcement. *How* these principles would be applied in the organization is, of course, critical. Here is where the addition of humanistic values comes in. In other words, the application would never be coercive and would follow the three criteria for an OD intervention that I listed earlier: respond to a need for change, involve the people directly affected, and lead to change in the organization's culture (i.e., institutionalize the change). Job enrichment is another example of a proven quantity. Where it has failed has been in the *process* of application.[18]

It is no doubt obvious that as an OD consultant I take the normative side and therefore define Organization Development as a process of applying knowledge from the behavioral sciences toward changes in an organization's culture so that individual needs and organizational goals can be integrated more effectively.

Even though definitional differences remain, most people in the field would agree that OD (1) involves change, (2) is a continuing process, not a program or discrete event, (3) uses behavioral science technology, and (4) follows an action research model (to be explained in the section to follow).

Where Did OD Come From?

Organization Development as we know it today has three historical roots—all of which are characterized by certain change methodologies and associated with particular institutions:

1 Sensitivity or T-Group training, associated with the National Training Laboratories, now called the NTL Institute for Applied Behavioral Science

2 Sociotechnical systems, associated with the Tavistock Institute of London

3 Survey feedback, associated with the Institute for Social Research, University of Michigan

Sensitivity training, the application of group dynamics for individual learning via interpersonal relations and feedback regarding the impact of one's behavior on others, evolved from the work of Kurt Lewin and his associates during the late 1940s. For a comprehensive explanation of the method and its beginnings, see Bradford, Gibb, and Benne.[19] Briefly, sensitivity training involves the analysis of interpersonal relations in small groups where the major source of information from which to learn is the behavior and feelings of the group members themselves. Facilitated by a trainer, participants give feedback to one another with respect to their behavior in the group, and this process becomes the learning source for individual growth and development. Group members also have the opportunity to learn about group behavior. During the latter part of the 1950's sensitivity trainers began to apply this learning methodology within organizations. That is, the training was used as an attempt to change certain aspects of an organization, especially managerial style (see, for example, Shepard).[20] Gradually, sensitivity training, or at least much of the methodology from it, was used to improve the interpersonal relationships among members of the same organizational unit or team. This type of applicability was the forerunner of what is known today in OD as team building. The current (and no doubt future) practice of OD encompasses much more than team building, but this important intervention remains popular and has its roots in sensitivity training.

Sociotechnical systems is the label given to change activities in an organization that account for both the technological requirements and the social relationships of the people directly involved. One of the early studies which provided the basis for what was later called the sociotechnical systems approach to organizational change was conducted by Trist and Bamforth.[21] Both were professional staff members of the Tavistock Institute, an organization in London involved in human relations training and organizational change. Trist and Bamforth were asked by a coal mining company in England to help with a technological change problem. The company had introduced a new technique for mining coal, but following the change, absenteeism had increased and productivity had decreased. Trist and Bamforth found that the company had ignored the social relationships of the miners and the importance of these relationships for morale and productivity. The technical change required a greater division of labor and thereby had broken up long-established work teams. Trist and Bamforth then showed the company how it could, without returning to the old method, modify the technical change by making the work more composite and could as a consequence also retain the social patterns so important to the miners. The conceptual framework guiding Trist and Bamforth, as well as their colleagues at Tavistock—Rice, Emery, Higgen, Bridger, et al.—was as follows: any organization is simultaneously a technical *and* a social system and to ignore either in a change process is to invite failure since the two systems are inextricably related. Interventions in OD that are used today, such as job redesign, autonomous work groups and structural design of organizations, especially manufacturing operations, have their roots in the sociotechnical way of thinking about and changing an organization.

Survey feedback, a method of diagnosing and intervening in an organization with the use of a questionnaire, was developed in the 1950s at the University of Michigan's Institute for Social Research by Rensis Likert, Floyd Mann, and their colleagues. Collecting information from organizational members via a questionnaire was not particularly unusual at the time. Surveying employees' attitudes and the state of their morale, while not pervasive among organizations of the day, was an established procedure. Using the survey results for effective organizational change would have been unusual, however. What these Michigan psychologists realized was that though organizational managers might find the survey results interesting and might even be concerned, rarely did anything change in the organization as a result of the survey. Moreover, in some cases organizations would experience greater rather than fewer problems as a consequence of the survey. The fact that a survey was conducted would raise employees' expectations that their opinions were important to management and that some action would be taken. When nothing different actually occurred, employee skepticism if not cynicism would increase. Mann, in particular, developed a procedure whereby the survey results would be summarized and reported back within "family" units of the organization, that is, to the people who worked together, often as a team.[22] By carefully following certain steps of problem solving for groups these family units would (1) analyze the survey results in light of their own domain of work and (2) plan and later take steps for resolving problems identified via the survey. Thus, the technique got its name, survey feedback, as a result of questionnaire results being "fed" back in a structured way to the persons who generated the data in the first place, giving them the opportunity of doing something about the problems they had collectively identified. Survey feedback is a common practice in OD today; a recent book by David Nadler is devoted entirely to this type of change methodology.[23]

Although these three historical roots of organization development differ, they have at least one common property, and this commonality has contributed to the fact that the methodologies associated with the three are all used today in OD. All three methodologies are based on an action research model of change. Action research literally means to take action as a result of research findings. Thus, action research is distinguished from "pure" research. Both may contribute to some body of knowledge, but this outcome is far more important for the latter than for the former. The primary objective of action research is ultimately to take some action. Just as important in the process is to take the action as a function of what data, objectively derived, would indicate. Action research as originally conceived followed the scientific method quite closely during the research phase.[24] As used in OD, however, the concept is interpreted more loosely. Acting as a consultant according to an action research model means that action is taken as a function of data collected and that, in turn, the action taken generates further data to be collected and acted on. French has briefly clarified how OD should be conducted within the framework of action research.[25] For a more comprehensive treatment of the relationship between action research and organization development, see Frohman, Sashkin, and Kavanagh.[26]

With the definition and discussion of Organization Development above as background, we will now review a somewhat longer case to illustrate many more facets of OD. This case will be followed with a general but detailed view of the OD process in model form.

Case Example: A Pharmaceutical Company

A colleague and I were recently invited by a pharmaceutical firm to explore the possibility of our consulting with them as an organization. Approximately a year prior to our initial visit a morale survey had been conducted throughout the company. All employees including management were surveyed—about 3000 people. An outside opinion-research firm was hired to conduct the survey. The results of the survey showed quite clearly that there was considerable dissatisfaction throughout the company, especially among the rank and file.

The major problem concerned managerial style and the general approach the various levels of supervisors took in the management process, particularly the management of people. The survey indicated that most managers were perceived as autocratic, rather rigid in their approach and style, and unilateral (top-down) in the decision-making process. Another serious problem was the employees' perception that the company lacked a sense of mission and purpose or, in any case, a sense of clarity regarding the organization's mission. Other problems were identified, but these two represented the primary ones and reflected the general nature or characteristics of the organization at that time.

In their final report, the opinion research firm recommended that the pharmaceutical company hire an outside consultant—they used the term "change agent"—to help them deal with the major problems that had been identified in the survey. In other words, the opinion-research firm suggested that change was in order and the company could use some help in bringing it about.

The president of the pharmaceutical company followed this advice and appointed a top management committee to interview potential change agents and make a recommendation to him. My colleague and I met with this management committee for about three hours. We were shown the survey results and then asked what we might do as change agents. We asked many questions, but eventually we stated that we would want to conduct a further and continuing diagnosis of the organization since surveys usually reflected symptoms rather than causes of problems. We also stated that we would design a process or flow of events that would facilitate the development of a conceptual framework for change, that is, a sort of road map to clarify directions, targets, and priorities for change. We explained that this road map would also help us to determine exactly which action steps to take at what particular time. And, finally, we said that we would be particularly interested in studying in some depth the effectiveness of the human resource management function of their organization, i.e., such aspects as the compensation and overall reward system, training programs, the design (if any) of their career development effort, etc.

Following the meeting with the committee we had lunch with the president and in a summary fashion explained what we had just previously discussed and recommended. In both meetings, with the management committee and later with the president, we explained that we believed organizational change was a management responsibility and that in reality the managers of the company were the change agents. We stated further that we saw our function as being primarily a facilitative one, that the direction we would provide would be in terms of *how* to determine what needed changing and *how* to implement the change, not necessarily *what* to change.

Approximately one month following our "entry" meeting with the management committee and the company president we were told that they had selected us to consult with them. In our second meeting with the president, we had two primary agenda items. We wanted him to understand and agree to what we intended to do, and we wanted him to take certain steps. Following this meeting we sent the president a letter summarizing and specifying what we had discussed. He responded in writing, and though the process was relatively informal, we had established a consulting contract. The length of time for the initial contract was six months.

Our initial step was to establish an advisory committee for the change effort. The committee was composed (and still is) of the president as chairman and a vertical as well as cross section of the company, namely a member of the top management team, a department head who reported directly to the president, a representative from the next level of management but from another department, a first-line supervisor, a nonsupervisory administrator, two nonexempt employees, and a person from the personnel department who not only served as a member of this advisory committee but as internal consultant for the company with respect to the OD effort as well. The committee consisted, therefore, of 10 persons—eight from the company including the president and the two of us as external consultants. The committee met once a month and had the following purposes:

- To monitor the change effort
- To advise the president and the consultants about the efficacy of our plans
- To keep us informed and on track regarding the consequences of the various activities within the overall change effort
- To help with the overall communication process
- To suggest additional plans and activities

Our next step was to conduct individual interviews with each member of the top management team including the president. Figure 5-2 shows in organizational chart form the members of this management group. Our purposes for these interviews were to (1) determine more thoroughly the views of these top managers regarding their sense of need for organizational change, that is, to what extent they agreed with

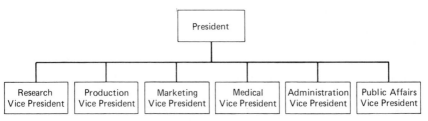

Fig. 5-2 Organization chart of the top management team of a pharmaceutical company.

the survey results, etc., (2) determine their degree of individual motivation for and commitment to a change effort, especially in light of the fact that each one of them would be integrally involved both personally and in the role of managerial change agent, and (3) establish some rapport between each of them and us as consultants.

The "ground rules" that we established with each manager at the outset of the interview were:

- The information that we collected would become public among the seven of them at a later "feedback" session but go no further.

- No person would be identified as the author of any specific statement; the control regarding who said what would be with each person.

- The information would be used (1) to clarify the top management team's view of the current state of the company and (2) as a basis for planning action steps for the change effort.

After the interviews were conducted, my colleague and I met to categorize and analyze the information we had collected and to plan the session where we would report back to the seven of them what the results of the interviews were and what seemed to be indicated—"diagnosis" in OD language. We categorized the interview data two ways: *first,* according to each of the questions that we asked. Even though we summarized the interviewees' responses, we attempted to stay as close to their actual words and phrases as possible. We listed these responses to each question according to how many of the seven persons mentioned the particular topic. For the *second* categorization we used a special model.

The Six-Box Model

The interview responses, therefore, were analyzed according to Weisbord's six-box model[27] (see figure 5-3). This model, which helps us to provide a road map, is a fairly simple, largely descriptive representation of what Weisbord considers to be the primary dimensions of any organization. There are, of course, other models, but in this case Weisbord's model sufficed, for it provided a quick and easy way of (1) tying interview responses to some organizational frame of reference, thereby enabling the managers to diagnose for themselves their situation in system terms, and (2) establishing some priority to those parts or dimensions of the organization that needed the most or most immediate attention. Thus if a predominance of the responses from the interviews could be categorized (with all seven managers agreeing) within the leadership box, which was the case in this company, then direction and priority would become clearer.

A further word of explanation regarding Weisbord's six-box model is in order at this point. Weisbord visualizes the model (again, see Figure 5-3) as a radar screen. "Just as air controllers use radar to chart the course of aircraft—height, speed, distance apart, and weather—those seeking to improve an organization must observe relationships among the boxes and not focus on any particular blip."[28] Any organization is situated within an environment, as Weisbord notes in the figure, and in the case of our pharmaceutical firm, we can describe its environment in such terms as the marketplace the company serves (primarily physicians), government regulations (federal standards the company's products must meet as determined by the Food and Drug Administration; there are state regulations as well), and the parent company's demands (the pharmaceutical firm is a subsidiary of a larger corporation). As the

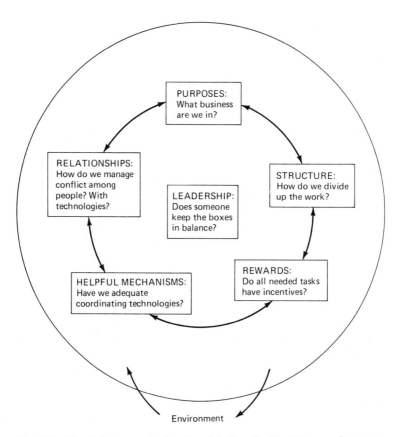

Fig. 5-3   The six-box organizational model. Visualize Fig. 5-3 as a radar screen. Just as air traffic controllers use radar to chart the course of aircraft—height, speed, distance apart, and weather—those seeking to improve an organization will observe relationships among the boxes and not focus on any particular blip.

arrows in Figure 5-3 indicate, the company is influenced by these various facets from the environment and in turn has an impact on, and to some extent shapes, its environment.

The organization itself, or radar screen, is represented by the six boxes. For each box, Weisbord believes that the organization should be diagnosed both in terms of its formal system and informal system. A critical element of any organizational diagnosis is the degree of gap between the formal aspects, e.g., organization chart (the structure box), and the organization's informal properties, e.g., how authority is actually carried out—who goes to whom for what. For the *purposes* box, the two most important factors are goal clarity—to what extent are organizational members clear about the organization's mission and purpose—and goal agreement—e.g., do people support the organization's purpose? For *structure* the primary question is whether there is an adequate fit between the purpose and the internal structure which is supposed to serve that purpose. Weisbord contends that three types of work *relationships* are the most important: (1) between individuals, (2) between units (departments) which perform different tasks, and (3) between people and the nature and requirements of their jobs. With respect to this relationships box, Weisbord argues that the OD consultant should "diagnose first for required interdependence, then for *quality of relations,* and finally for modes of conflict management."[29]

In determining possible blips for the *rewards* box the consultant should diagnose the similarities and differences between what the organization formally rewards—the compensation package, incentive systems, etc.—and what organizational members *feel* rewarded or punished for doing. Weisbord places the *leadership* box in the middle because he believes that a primary job of the leader is to watch for "blips" among the other boxes and to maintain balance among them. Moreover, Weisbord refers to an important, and perhaps classic, book of some years ago written by Selznick[30] to help the OD consultant further diagnose the leadership box. In other words, the consultant should determine the extent to which organizational leaders are (1) defining purposes, (2) embodying purposes in programs, (3) defending the organization's integrity, and (4) maintaining order with respect to internal conflict—the four most important leaderships tasks according to Selznick.

The last box, *helpful mechanisms,* refers analogously to "the cement that binds an organization together to make it more than a collection of individuals with separate needs."[31] Thus, helpful mechanisms refer to those processes which every organization must attend to in order to survive—planning, control, budgeting, and other information systems which help organizational members get their respective jobs done and meet organizational objectives. Again, the OD consultant's task is to determine which mechanisms (or which aspects of them) help members accomplish organizational purposes and which seem to hinder more than help. When an originally intended helpful mechanism becomes red tape, the likelihood is that it is no longer helpful. Table 5-2 should now serve as a helpful mechanism for summarizing the six-box model and the diagnostic questions to ask.

The Three-Stage Model

In this OD consulting effort my colleague and I used one other model. Like the six-box model, the three-stage model has the virtue of being descriptive and simple to understand and use. With respect to organizational change there is obviously an "actual state of affairs," or a present diagnosis of the organization, and a "desired state" for the organization's future. When a change in the organization is launched, most of the problems occur in the transition stage—between the actual state and the desired one. Actually, most top managers when deciding on a change

Table 5-2 Matrix for Survey Design or Data Analysis

	System	
	Formal (work to be done)	Informal (process of working)
1 Purposes	Goal clarity	Goal agreement
2 Structure	Functional, program, or matrix?	How work is actually done or not done
3 Relationships	Who should deal with whom on what? Which technologies should be used?	How well do they do it? Quality of relations? Modes of conflict management?
4 Rewards (incentives)	Explicit system What is it?	Implicit, psychic rewards What do people *feel* about payoffs?
5 Leadership	What do top people manage? What systems in use?	How? Normative "style" of administration?
6 Helpful mechanisms	Budget system Management information (measures?) Planning Control	What are they actually used for? How function in practice? How are systems subverted?

NOTE: Diagnostic questions may be asked on two levels:
1 How big a gap is there between formal and informal systems? (This speaks to the fit between individual and organization.)
2 How much discrepancy is there between "what is" and "what ought to be"? (This highlights the fit between organization and environment.)

rarely plan how the change process will be implemented. They may announce the change, say a new organizational structure, on Friday and expect it to be in place and operating the following Monday. The transitional stage, therefore, amounts to no more than a weekend when employees are expected to get over their shock and be ready to go to work making the new structure operable first thing Monday morning. But, as most experienced managers know, making the desired state work, especially if the change occurs practically overnight, takes a long time, and sometimes the change is never fully implemented. In other words, managers experience what social psychologists and others call "resistance to change." Thus, in their change model (this second model which we used with the pharmaceutical company) Beckhard and Harris[32] place as much if not more emphasis on the change process itself as on diagnosing present condition and planning the new one. Generally, then, to follow the thinking of Beckhard and Harris, organizational change can be depicted as a three-stage process:

Stage I	Stage II	Stage II
Actual state	Transition state	Desired state

The depiction above illustrates the process that occurs over time, but in planning and implementing organizational change the desired state is, of course, determined before the transitional state is defined. More specifically, to quote Beckhard and Harris, the change process has the following six aspects:

1 Diagnosing the present condition, including the need for change

2 Setting goals and defining the new state or condition after the change

3 Defining the transition state between the present and the future

4 Developing strategies and action plans for managing this transition

5 Evaluating the change effort

6 Stabilizing the new condition and establishing a balance between stability and flexibility[33]

As consultants to the pharmaceutical company's change effort, my colleague and I summarized this model to help the top management group track in an orderly fashion the sequence of change events and to highlight the points where most organizational change efforts fail, i.e., the transition stage. We presented this summary in a meeting which followed the interviews—in Organization Development language, the feedback session.

Approximately one week following our interviews my colleague and I arranged a meeting with the top seven managers of the company. The agenda for this half-day session included (1) reporting back to the team of seven our summary of the one-hour interviews with each one, and (2) presentation of the two models we wished to follow for diagnostic (Weisbord's) and planning (Beckhard and Harris's) purposes.

Having obtained agreement with the top management team that (1) their interview data were summarized accurately, (2) our way of analyzing those data (Weisbord's six-box model) was useful, and (3) our plan for the steps to take in moving toward a more desired state for the company was appropriate (the three-stage model), we then began the process of more directly intervening into the routine of the organization itself. This intervention process consisted of steps 2, 3, and 4 of Beckhard and Harris's change model—defining the new state, defining the transition state, and developing strategies for managing the transition.

My colleague and I recommended to the president that essentially the same survey, which was administered approximately a year before we began our consultation, be administered again two years later. The following table summarizes what I mean:

Year 1	Year 2	Year 3	Year 4
Survey conducted	Change effort (OD) begins	Survey conducted again	Organization reaches desired state

By year 4 we may recommend that the survey be administered for yet a third time. A number of large companies in the United States routinely conduct annual surveys of their employees' opinions, attitudes, and general morale. So our recommendation, while atypical for this company, would not necessarily be out of the ordinary. In any case, we shall collect other comparative data to determine if the company is performing better in such areas as net profit, return on investment, number of new products in the works and recently introduced into the marketplace, and relative standing among its competitors (e.g., the company's percentage share of the market).

Summary

Our activities as consultants to the pharmaceutical company generally followed the flow of events outlined by Beckhard and Harris. We placed particular emphasis on establishing processes and mechanisms for managing the transitional state between (1) diagnosing the organization's present state and (2) defining its future, desired state. *Three* steps were key to this transitional management. *First,* we established an advisory committee representing all hierarchical levels of the organization to help with the communication process and, generally, to keep us on track. *Second,* we conducted a two-day, offsite meeting with the top 40 managers of the organization to define the desired state for their organization and to plan the specific and necessary steps for reaching that future condition. This event was followed by individual units, with our help, planning and implementing activities that helped them to determine more specifically what their desired state should be. For example, during the transitional period, it is often wise to try a new plan—for example, a different incentive system—on a pilot basis, to see how workable and appropriate it will be before actually making the change permanent. In fact, this is one of the primary purposes of a transitional period, that is, to "try on things for size" before making a more permanent move. *Finally,* we insisted that we be called organizational consultants, not change agents. Even though in the Organizational Development literature reference is occasionally made to change agent as synonymous with OD consultant (e.g., see Tichy),[34] my colleague and I wanted to ensure that the president understood that he was the primary agent of change and the one most responsible for managing the overall Organization Development effort. Our role was to *help* him and others in the organization to plan and bring about the change. Thus, our expertise was primarily one of *process.* We provided (1) models for mapping the organizational terrain and facilitating an orderly management of change, (2) the design and structure for meetings and events that would ensure involvement of organizational members in making decisions that would directly affect them, thereby gaining commitment to change rather than resisting it, and (3) a plan (and we gradually acted on it) for developing in-company expertise in the type of consultation that we represented. Although it was somewhat secondary to the activities described above, we also provided *substantive* expertise in the domain of human resource management such as ideas and plans for career development, improvement of management education and development, changes in the reward system, assessment of managerial talent, and appraisal of manager performance. And since the company was unionized, we also offered suggestions for working with the union more effectively.

In this consultative effort, two primary factors guided us: our knowledge of the behavioral sciences and what is applicable to organizations especially in the arena of change, and our personal value of wanting to influence the organization to move in the direction of becoming a more humanistic place of work. While we were not missionaries, our intent with respect to this value was clear and, I might add, acceptable to the client.

STEPS IN THE OD PROCESS

The six primary steps in any OD process are entry, contract, data collection and diagnosis, feedback, intervention, and evaluation. We shall now proceed through these steps, explaining each one in turn.

Entry

Typically, the initial contact for an OD effort is initiated by the client. While "marketing one's services" is important for the survival of an OD consultant, whether internal to the organization or outside it, the consultant is more often than not asked by the client to discuss the possibilities of help. Also typically, the client calls for the assistance of an OD consultant because organizational members are experiencing pain.[35] However, it is *not* typical for the client to identify the problem in any systemic fashion, that is, in terms that follow some model of how organizations function; according to Goodstein, "rather, the client system presents 'symptoms' that may suggest to the consultant some underlying problem in one or more of the organizational models."[36] Thus, it is critical that the OD consultant have at least one working model of how organizations function—or are supposed to function for optimal efficiency and effectiveness.

Sometimes the OD consultant will be contacted by the client with a request to conduct a management development program, a negotiation skills workshop, or supervisory training. But even requests such as these should not necessarily be taken at face value. For example, Goodstein and Boyer[37] report a case in which the initial request was for a "communications workshop." These consultants quickly learned that their client organization was experiencing turmoil characterized by considerable anger and suspicion. They concluded that to conduct such a workshop would have led to open warfare. Eventually, the consultants moved with their client toward dealing with the underlying problems directly rather than attempting to "fix" the organization with a communications workshop.

Thus, in OD work this initial step, entry into the client organization, may be the most difficult one. Simultaneously, the OD consultant is attempting to reach two objectives: the establishment of rapport with the client—will the interpersonal "chemistry" mix adequately?—and the attainment of enough valid information to determine accurately the nature of the organization's problem(s) and whether organization development is appropriate. With respect to the first objective, establishing rapport, the most significant ingredient in this process is trust. Establishing some basis for interpersonal trust is important for any consultant-client relationship, but it is particularly important for OD consultation. There are at least three reasons for this emphasis on trust:

1   Since OD is rather vaguely defined, the client must believe more in the expertise of the consultant as a person than in certain techniques, packages, or programs the client may already know about. In other words, it is not always clear exactly *what* the client is buying. Moreover, a guaranteed outcome is typically not possible.

2   A client accepting consultation frequently experiences defensive feelings. The acceptance of help can be perceived as a failure on the part of the client, whose defensive feelings can be especially keen in an OD situation since the consultation is largely in the "people" domain of organizational activities.

Many client managers believe that while it is okay not to know a particular technology—say, something concerning electronic data processing—somehow it is less acceptable not to know how to handle organizational behavior problems, e.g., "motivating my people." In the entry process, it is therefore essential that the OD consultant be sensitive to the potentiality of these feelings.

3   Both the consultant and client know that because of the nature of their work together in this potential OD effort, it is highly likely that they will delve into sensitive areas. It is also likely that the top boss in the situation will hear some things that he or she would rather not. The client quite naturally wants some assurance that the consultant will treat these potentially sensitive areas with care and discretion. It should be added here that cultural,[38] ethnic, racial, or even gender[39] differences between the client and consultant become magnified during entry. Obviously, the greater the differences between client and consultant, the more potential distrust there is to overcome.

The second objective in entry is for the consultant to "get a fix" on the organization, that is, to obtain as quickly as possible enough information to determine whether an OD effort is warranted. Moreover, since OD involves change the consultant must assess the client's "readiness" for change. Pfeiffer and Jones[40] have developed a readiness checklist for the consultant. Some examples of the 15 indicators that they deem important are (1) whether the organization is experiencing a crisis, (2) the nature of the organization's culture—how amenable is it to change? (3) the organization's resources—can it afford the cost involved in an OD effort? (4) structural flexibility—how easily can reporting relationships be changed? and (5) internal consultants—are they available or is there potential for development of certain people for this role?

Another way of considering an organization's readiness for change is to conceptualize the potential in terms of what the social and psychological costs would be. David Gleicher's formula (referred to by Beckhard and Harris) for determining these costs is:

$$C = (ABD) > X$$

where C = change, A = level of dissatisfaction with the status quo, B = clear desired state, D = practical first steps toward the desired state, and X = cost of change. In other words, there has to be enough dissatisfaction with the current state of affairs (A) for someone to be mobilized for the change. The various subsystems need to have clear enough goals (B); otherwise, the "cost" (X) is too high. For each subsystem, there needs to be some awareness of practical first steps (D) to move, if movement is to take place.[41]

Both clarity of change direction *and* motivation are necessary. In our consultation with the pharmaceutical company it soon became clear to my colleague and me that they were experiencing pain and were dissatisfied with the status quo, but with respect to *where* to move and *how* to get there they were floundering. Thus, we concentrated our early efforts on establishing the directions for change. Beckhard and Harris, on the other hand, report a case where "we discovered and he (the client) discovered that although he had been dissatisfied with the status quo and had a clear picture of what he wanted to do and had instituted some practical first steps to carry out the change, he was not in fact *that* dissatisfied."[42] Beckhard and Harris go on to state that when the client became aware of his relative lack of motivation, he changed some of his behavior and plans so that eventually the change occurred satisfactorily.

To summarize: At entry consultants have two objectives—(1) to determine the efficacy of the interpersonal "chemistry" between themselves and their clients, and (2) to determine whether OD is appropriate. With respect to this latter objective the consultant must (1) discriminate between problem symptoms and causes—or communicate to the client as quickly as possible a way of getting at the causes—and (2) discern the client's readiness for change.

Contract

There usually is a formal contract between the consultant and client and also an informal one. The formal contract may be a simple letter of agreement which states briefly and in general terms what the consultant will do, how frequently the client will be billed (if the consultant is an external one), and when the contract will terminate. Or the contract may be a formal document whereby the consultant agrees (perhaps even swears), among other things, not to divulge information obtained during the OD process. I once consulted with a company that contracted with the Department of Defense from time to time; not only did I have to sign a legal contractual document for the corporation but I had to meet standards for a "secret" clearance from the federal government as well.

In OD consultation the informal contract with the client is perhaps the more important one. Adhering to values which underlie and, I might add, undergird Organization Development, the consultant establishes an agreement with the client whereby they (1) will keep one another informed as much as possible, (2) will be open with one another in their communications, especially regarding concerns either party may have, (3) will clarify what each expects to get from the relationship, and, in general, (4) will determine the ground rules of how they will operate with one another.[43]

Data Collection and Diagnosis

There are four primary modes of collecting information about an organization:

1   Observation—perhaps the most obvious mode. The consultant should not only record what he or she sees and hears but attempt to "sense" the organization from a feeling perspective. Does the organization "feel," for example, (a) warm or cold, (b) close or distant, (c) like a pleasant or fun place to work, (d) open or guarded.

2   Documents. The consultant may learn a lot by studying the typical records kept by the organization—such as absenteeism data, the current annual report, the number of grievances (if the organization is unionized)—and by reading recent reports from important committees or task forces.

3   Questionnaires. Surveys of organizational members' perceptions and attitudes about a variety of factors may be conducted by using an outside standardized questionnaire or by constructing one especially for the client organization. An example of the former type of questionnaire is Likert's "Profile of Organizational Characteristics."[44] This instrument surveys organizational members' attitudes about management practices from the standpoints of what they perceive the current state to be and of what they would desire as a more ideal state. Questionnaire results are then "profiled" according to the differences between the perceived, actual, and ideal states and according to the

degree of participative management practiced by the organization's managers. The degree of profiled participation ranges from auto-cratic—no participation—to consensual group decision-making—considerable participation.

Likert's profile as well as other standardized questionnaires may not completely suit an organization's requirements, especially when information needs to be collected in areas other than management practices. In these cases, a specially tailored questionnaire may need to be constructed. Before actually composing such a questionnaire, it is usually best to conduct a number of interviews, selected but ran-domized within the organization, so that the more salient dimensions for questionnaire items can be determined.

Time permitting, it is often wise to administer some combination of both an outside standardized questionnaire (so that useful compari-sons may be made) and a tailor-made internal one. For more informa-tion regarding the use of questionnaires in OD, see Nadler.[45]

4 Interviews. This is the most popular mode of data collection among OD consultants. Interviews may be conducted with one person at a time or in small groups. In the privacy of a manager's office a consultant can usually get more information than from a group inter-view, at least at the outset of an OD effort; but if time is limited, interviewing people in groups may indeed suffice. Unless I am at-tempting to gain information about a specific matter I normally ask the following four open-ended questions in an interview:

a What is going well in the organization; what are its strengths or positive qualities?

b What is not going well in the organization; what are the prob-lems, weaknesses, issues that need attention?

c What is satisfying about your particular job; what is rewarding?

d What are the barriers, hindrances, or blocks that prevent you from doing the kind of job you would like to do or think you should be doing?

The first two questions concern organizational matters, and the third and fourth address the individual and his or her job. The first and third questions focus on the positive while the second and fourth ask about problems, the negative side. Of course, these are not the only questions asked; additional and more specific questions are raised within each of the four categories. With the negative questions I am looking for areas in need of change but with questions 1 and 3 I am looking for areas that need strengthening and reinforcing, not neces-sarily changing. Also with these latter questions I am trying to demon-strate that OD is not a change activity merely for the sake of change but, rather, an effort toward intervening in areas where people in the organization feel a need for change.

To help with diagnosis—and particularly to avoid as much as possible the consultant's bias about what *should* be "corrected" in an organization or what is "proper" regarding managerial practice—a model and/or theoretical approach to analyzing or making sense out of the information collected is a must. Explicitly, and if not, certainly implicitly, every consultant (whether in OD or not) has a "model" or particular way of looking at and analyzing an organization. It is probably true that anyone who has lived and/or worked in an organization for some length of time has notions about what makes an organization the way it is and what should be done to make it better. My views are steeped in social psychology, the field of my graduate education. I pay particular attention to the norms and values that exist in the organization—what people conform to and what they feel is right and wrong about behavior in the organization. I am also interested in power and rewards—how decisions get made, how influence is exercised, and what behavior people *feel* rewarded and punished for doing in the organization. Other consultants have different views or pet areas for diagnosis. Thus, it is important to use a model for diagnosing an organization; and while the model may reflect one's bias, it should be comprehensive enough to ensure that significant domains of organizational life and functioning will not be overlooked.

Feedback

The next step in the OD process is the consultant's provision of a summarized and analyzed version of data collected during the previous step. This reporting back to the client is termed "feedback" in Organization Development since the consultant, in a manner of speaking, is "holding a mirror before the client" and, consequently, the client organization is "viewing a reflection" of what members have said about *their* organization. This feedback may be extensive and fairly complicated (i.e., in need of interpretation) when it is a summary of a major survey. As noted earlier, Mann[46] developed a process whereby considerable data may be "fed" back and handled in a participative way. His survey feedback method uses naturally existing "family" units in the organization. These units receive feedback regarding the overall organization, information with respect to their unit, and comparative data from other units which are comparable to them organizationally. For more detailed and current methods of dealing effectively with the feedback process of survey data see Nadler.[47]

The way my colleague and I provided feedback from our interviews in the pharmaceutical company is fairly standard (see especially, Golem-biewski).[48] Although OD consultants differ slightly, for me, the feedback process has three parts:

1   A summary of the interviews is provided, organized according to the questions asked. As much as possible, verbatim phrases from the interview are used, particularly those that tend to summarize what others also said. A number follows each phrase, indicating how many of the interviewees referred to that topic.

2   The interview data are then categorized and analyzed according to some model of organizational functioning. This analysis is discussed with the client group so that accuracy and agreement can be reached. An alternate step for this part of the feedback process is to present a model and then involve the client group themselves in the categorization and analysis. In any case, the objective of this part of the feedback is to provide a conceptual framework which uses systematic and organizational terminology so that a better understanding of the nature of the problems can be achieved and a priority for action planning can be established. The purpose of emphasizing organizational and systematic language here is to ensure that the change effort will be directed toward the organization as a system rather than toward individuals per se.[49]

3   As a final part of the feedback I give the client a synthesis of my observations, impressions, and emotional reactions. I make sure that this part of the feedback process is distinct from the previous two parts so that greater clarity can be maintained between what they have said (the more objective part for consultative purposes) and my subjectivity.

Intervention

In Organization Development intervention means "a planned response to a diagnosed need for change." Sequentially, then, the intervention follows data collection, diagnosis, and feedback. It should, however, be clarified. Perhaps it is obvious that while it is logical to explain the OD process as an orderly sequence of events, in reality an intervention is made the moment management decides to use a consultant. Interventions occur thereafter, some considerably before even the feedback step. In the pharmaceutical company case, for example, my colleague and I made an intervention in advance of data collection and diagnosis by persuading the president to appoint an advisory committee. (Incidentally, that intervention had a profound impact on the company because it signaled that management was beginning to do things differently—

involve people lower down in the organization in important matters.) Generally, the interventions, or series of planned change activities, occur after and as a response to a thorough diagnosis. I might add that even though I use the adjective "thorough," no diagnosis can be complete since organizations are never quite the same from one day to the next. And the longer the consultant waits between data collection and feedback, the more out of date the diagnosis will be. Thus, it is imperative that action be taken as soon as feasible—a time lapse of a month between data collection and feedback is a long time for fast-moving organizations, like those dealing directly with consumers. Moreover, any intervention provides more information for diagnosis. Besides, as Kurt Lewin, the theoretical father of OD, has pointed out—to paraphrase—the best way to understand an organization is to try to change it.

To be effective, according to Argyris[50], an intervention must meet three conditions: (1) generate valid information, (2) provide free, informed choice for the client, and (3) create an internal commitment on the part of the client to the choices made. These conditions are considered by Argyris to be "integral parts of any intervention activity, no matter what the substantive objectives are . . . for example, developing a management performance evaluation scheme, reducing intergroup rivalries, increasing the degree of trust among individuals, redesigning budgetary systems, or redesigning work."[51] As Argyris indicates, an OD intervention may take a variety of forms as long as it meets his conditions. As noted earlier, I add one other condition: the intervention must lead to cultural change.

Thus, interventions in OD may come in all shapes and sizes. A number of years ago, Hornstein and I[52] lumped all OD interventions into six categories:

- team building
- managing conflict
- survey feedback
- technostructural
- training
- miscellaneous

As you can readily see, we easily covered ourselves with the sixth category. Since that time others have developed more comprehensive and sophisticated categories. After our rather simple scheme came the Schmuck and Miles[53] OD cube. Their three classifiers were (1) diagnosed problems (e.g., goals, communication, leadership role definition); (2) focus of attention—from person to dyad, to team, to intergroup, to total organization; and (3) mode of intervention, such as training, process consultation, confrontation, and technostructural activity. Blake and Mouton[54] have also conceived of OD interventions and the consultative process as three-sided. Their Consulcube (see Figure 5-4), as they call it, is similar to the Schmuck and Miles cube but differs with respect to the nature of two of their dimensions: (1) focal issues, which are social and psychological, and (2) kinds of interventions, which range from "acceptant"—the least form of *intervening,* as such—to "prescriptive" and "theory and principles," which provide advice and direction for the client.

Bowers, Franklin, and Pecorella have a cube: *precursor conditions* (problem causes) by *problem behaviors* (more like symptoms) by *impingement modes* (types of intervention, e.g., survey feedback);[55] and so do Lippitt and Lippitt: *client* (individual to total system) by *change agent* (from "reflector" to "advocate") by *intervention phase* (from entry to action taking).[56] French and Bell[57] have a scheme (not a cube) and so do White

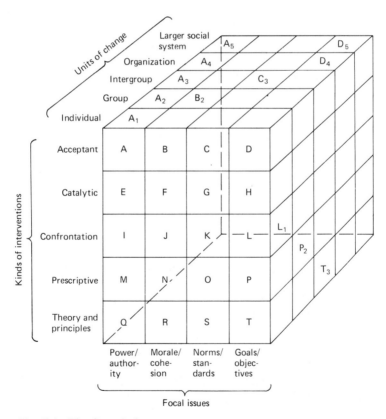

Fig. 5-4 The Consulcube℠.

and Mitchell[58] which *is*, alas, another cube. Obviously the field of OD is not lacking for categories of interventions. One typology that has proved more useful than most is Harrison's "depth" of intervention categories.[59] His categories form a continuum of emotional involvement. The greater the depth of intervention the more the focus of change is toward areas of the personality or self; the less the depth the more the focus of change is toward areas external to the person—the more formal and public aspects of one's role. Huse[60] has categorized most of the current interventions in OD according to Harrison's continuum beginning with *systemwide approaches* which fall at the "surface" end of the depth dimension. Interventions in this category include:

- change in the organization's structure
- survey feedback
- confrontation meeting (e.g., Beckhard)[61]
- quality of work life programs
- grid organization development (see Blake and Mouton)[62]

The next level concerns *individual-organizational interfaces* such as:

- job design
- role analysis
- management by objectives

Concern with *personal work style* is the next level, representing greater depth:

- process consultation (see Schein)[63]
- team building
- role negotiation
- intergroup conflict resolution

The final level, of greatest depth, is *intra- and interpersonal:*

- life and career planning
- sensitivity training
- personal consultation/counseling

Harrison suggests two criteria for choosing an intervention, that is, its degree of depth. He states that the consultant should "intervene at a level no deeper than that . . .

- "required to produce enduring solutions to the problems at hand"[64]

- "at which the energy and resources of the client can be committed to problem solving and to change"[65]

Some of the interventions my colleague and I chose with the pharmaceutical company were the transition model of Beckhard and Harris[66] as a format for managing the change effort, process consultation, and team building, especially with the top management group of seven; a modified version of the confrontation meeting;[67] the nominal group technique;[68] and management training which emphasized the diagnosis of one's style and approach as an individual manager.

As a way of summarizing this myriad of OD interventions, let us return to OD history. As noted earlier, OD grew from three roots, and most, if not all, interventions in use today came from these beginnings.

The *sensitivity training* root spawned interventions which deal with *personal* concerns and *relationships* such as career development, team building, intergroup conflict resolution, and training, especially management development programs which emphasize superior-subordinate relationships.

The *survey feedback* root is manifested in practice today in much the same way as it began. However, the contribution this approach has made to OD is considerably broader than the method itself. The emphasis on systematic data collection and diagnosis has influenced OD practice significantly. Furthermore, the fact that survey feedback is based largely on organizational members' perceptions has helped to put into perspective the importance of understanding that organization behavior is a function of how people *perceive* reality, not reality itself.

The *sociotechnical* root has helped OD practitioners, typically people oriented, to be cognizant of an organization's technology, whether it be manufacturing or service, and to understand better the relationship between the people and technological dimensions of an organization. A second, but no less important, contribution the sociotechnical professionals have made is the result of the attention they have given to structure both from the standpoint of the dimensions of a given job and the organization's overall design. It is only in recent years that OD professionals have finally awakened to the fact that the way jobs and organizations are designed and therefore structured, especially in the domain of authority, has pervasive effects on peoples' behavior.

Space does not permit an explanation of how each of these interventions is actually done. For example, what do you do when you serve as a process consultant? How is team building implemented? What is the design for an intergroup conflict resolution session? What is job enrichment and how do you do it? For answers to these particular questions I can refer you respectively to Schein,[69] Dyer,[70] Burke,[71] and Hackman.[72]

For other more general sources on how to conduct interventions in OD see, for example, Fordyce and Weil,[73] Golembiewski,[74] Merry and Allerhand,[75] and the annual publications of University Associates—The *Annual Handbook for Group Facilitators* and *A Handbook of Structured Experiences for Human Relations Training* (now eight volumes).

Evaluation

The sixth, but not necessarily the final, step in Organization Development is evaluation. While last in the sequence, evaluation efforts will produce more information for diagnosis and the cyclical process continues. In fact, it is prudent to begin evaluation at the data collection stage so that "before and after the intervention(s)" assessments can be made. If a survey has been conducted at the data collection stage, a repeat of the survey after one or more interventions have been made can provide useful, comparative information.

The major problem with OD evaluation, at least from a research standpoint, is the fact that it is practically impossible to arrange for a control group. Rarely, if ever, are any two organizations comparable; similar maybe, but with distinct differences. These differences are difficult to control. Often the best one can do is to take two or more assessments within the client organization over time and make comparisons accordingly. Since so many factors cannot be controlled for optimal research purposes, it is wise to use multiple methods of assessment. A before and after survey is rarely sufficient. In addition, measures should be taken over time in such areas as rates of absenteeism, turnover, grievances, productivity, and related performance indices, for example, the extent to which objectives are met.

These assessments, typically in numerical form, are necessary for a sound evaluation of OD. In the final analysis, however the OD effort will stand or fall as a consequence of what the client, usually the organization's managers, thinks and feels. And these behavioral reactions may or may not jive with the numbers. Managers are normally very pragmatic people, and if they "feel" like the OD effort is paying off, the chances are that it is.

Summary

These six steps—(1) entry, (2) contracting, (3) data collection and diagnosis, (4) feedback, (5) intervention, and (6) evaluation—represent the primary phases of the Organization Development process. Most OD efforts follow, in general, this sequence even though portions of the six steps often occur "out of phase." The formation of the advisory committee in the pharmaceutical company's change effort is a good example of an "early" intervention.

The focal point for change is systematic, or the organization itself rather than individuals per se. If an OD effort has been successful, organizational members' behavior will have changed, but these changes are not, as a rule, modifications in individuals' personalities. What has changed is the "personality" or culture of the organization as reflected in such behavioral activities, to name only a few possibilities, as new conforming patterns, a modified reward system (not necessarily increases in pay but different criteria for how raises are determined), greater participation in decision making, and a more open communication process.

THE OD CONSULTANT/PRACTITIONER

At the risk of describing a person who can walk on water, I shall list the competencies in terms of knowledge and skills an OD consultant should have whether internal to an organization or external. (These lists are not in any particular order, nor are they exhaustive, but they do represent some of the more important areas.)

Knowledge

The OD consultant should be knowledgeable in the following areas:

- the behavioral sciences and their applicability
- the design and management of organizational change
- self-awareness—one's motives, strengths, limitations, biases, values, and the behavioral consequences of one's feelings
- the nature and characteristics of organizations
- the nature of human behavior, especially personality, motivation, and principles of learning and development
- evaluation research

Skills

The OD consultant should have the ability to:

- listen actively and empathetically
- form relationships based on trust and honesty
- collaborate
- design and conduct learning activities

- perceive others' behavior accurately
- communicate articulately (OD is vague enough as it is; not being able to express "what this is all about" is a serious limitation)
- work with groups in a variety of activities
- counsel effectively, especially in a one-on-one situation
- diagnose problems, whether organizational or individual

Since OD represents certain values it is also important that the consultant hold similar ones. On several different occasions, usually as part of a training program, I have conducted sessions on values for OD consultants. As we have wrestled with the difficult process of trying to understand and articulate the values we hold, I have found that most people in the field seem to lean toward the individual. That is, most express their values in such terms as "freedom from coercion: having choice, opportunities to learn and grow, and a deep concern for human worth and dignity." These OD consultants (and my sample was certainly not random) expressed these and similar values as those they hold for themselves and the ones they hope they can help others maintain in organizational life. I'm not certain, of course, but if these value statements are indeed representative, there doesn't appear to be much concern about helping organizations qua organizations. For me, at least, since organizations are such a pervasive part of our lives, it is valuable to see that many survive and operate effectively so that human needs can be met both individually and societally.

As noted several times before, there are external consultants and those who are employees of the organization and, therefore, internal consultants. A word now about the latter. Internal OD practitioners are usually in staff positions located somewhere within the personnel or human resource management area. There are exceptions, such as the OD group within General Motors. Eventually they and the personnel people report to a common boss in the hierarchy, but their functions are separate. The OD responsibilities in GM include both consulting and research but not personnel as such. For most organizations, however, being within the personnel area is appropriate for OD practitioners since their mandate concerns primarily the people domain.

Ideally, OD should be conducted by a combination of external and internal consultants, especially at the outset. The external consultant can bring (1) additional knowledge and skill to supplement or complement the internal consultant as well as (2) a more objective viewpoint. The external consultant, on the other hand, cannot know and understand the organization as thoroughly as the internal person. The key role of the internal consultant is that of *sustaining* the OD effort once it has begun. A major objective of the external consultant, therefore, is to arrange for an internal counterpart if none exists. In the case of the pharmaceutical company no internal consultant was in place; therefore, my colleague and I worked with the president to locate someone for this role. Fortunately, there was a person within personnel who had the potential and was already trained to some extent. This internal consultant is now playing a major role in the change effort.

THEORETICAL FOUNDATIONS OF ORGANIZATION DEVELOPMENT

As mentioned already much of OD practice is based on the original thinking of Kurt Lewin. Both sensitivity training and survey feedback emanated from Lewin's theoretical influence. He conceptualized change for a group or organization as a three-step process: unfreeze, move, and refreeze. Before an organization can change it must be "unlicked" or "unfrozen" from its present state. *Unfreezing* may occur as a result of any one of several activities or interventions. The most common one is when the organization is confronted with information that is negative and arousing. To learn that we are not doing as well as we thought can have an unfreezing effect—"we need to do something!" Unfreezing can also occur as a result of some key managers being exposed to a "different way of doing things." While the organization is still in an unfrozen state, the second step must be taken. The *movement* step is the act of changing something, e.g., the organization's structure, the planning process, the way people work together in groups, etc. Once movement has occurred and the new behavior is underway, the final step, refreezing, takes place. This step often becomes one of determining the appropriate reward system so that the new behavior will be reinforced and maintained.

Lippitt, Watson, and Westley[76] extended Lewin's three steps into five:

1   Development of a need for change (unfreezing)

2   Establishment of a change relationship with the client

3   Work toward change (movement)

4   Generalization and stabilization of the change (refreezing)

5   Termination of the relationship

Most of their elaboration of Lewin's steps was with number 3, the movement or change step. They conceptualized this step as having three substeps or phases—diagnosis, examination of alternative change goals, and transformation of these goals into action.

It should be clear that the more modern versions of organizational change, such as the one by Beckhard and Harris,[77] still reflect the original ideas of Lewin and the later elaboration by Lippitt et al.

There is no single all-encompassing theory of Organization Development. Lewin's three steps is the closest. These steps are based on Lewin's original field theory in social psychology (see Deutsch),[78] but the steps themselves are nothing more than a model for OD consultants to follow. Most consultants know these steps and some of the principles behind them, but few have actually studied Lewin's field theory. Nevertheless, most consultants also know how to conduct one of the frequently used techniques in OD that is based on Lewinian field theory, the "force field analysis" technique. When conducting a force field analysis one is considering both those forces within a larger field of forces which *push* toward change (e.g., management pressure), and those which *restrain* movement toward change (e.g., group norms regarding level of productivity). Using this technique the consultant and client are in a better position to know how to deal with peoples' resistances to change. One of the earliest and best examples of this use is the classic study and change effort by Coch and French.[79]

Lewin's theoretical influence on OD is no doubt the heaviest, but others have helped to shape the field as well. Theorists who have contributed to the predominantly individual approaches to organizational change include:

- Maslow—motivational approaches, value orientations, and career development
- Herzberg—job enrichment
- Skinner—incentive systems and behavioral modification

The following theorists have contributed mostly to group approaches to change:

- Bion—diagnosing collusion (see Harvey),[80] autonomous work groups, sociotechnical systems, and team building
- Lewin—group decision making, managing change via groups, participation and involvement techniques using groups
- Argyris—sensitivity training and interpersonal competence (he has helped to operationalize McGregor's Theory Y)

Those theorists who have contributed more to total system approaches are:

- Likert—survey methodology and feedback, group decision making, and participative management

- Lawrence and Lorsch—organization design and structural change
- Levinson, H.—diagnosis of organization's history and current functioning, particularly with respect to psychoanalytic theory
- Blake and Mouton—grid organization development

If my three categories of these theorists' approaches are reasonably accurate, it is easy to see that OD has been influenced in diverse ways. Most if not all of these theorists have the following in common, however: their interests are or have been concerned with change, particularly organizational, and they have favored action research as a way of understanding what is appropriate to change.

RESEARCH ON ORGANIZATION DEVELOPMENT

Does OD pay off, does it work? In a limited fashion, yes. With perhaps one exception (see Seashore and Bowers),[81] there is no evidence that OD has been responsible for a large organizational change over a sustained period of time. Another possible exception is the long-term OD effort at TRW Systems, but there is no empirical evidence, only a case report (Davis, 1967).[82] There is evidence that OD works, however. Beckhard and Lake[83] have validated OD effects empirically and over time. But this study and OD effort were done with a unit of a larger organization.

The six statements in the previous paragraph reflect the nature of research on OD. It's a mixed bag. French, Bell, and Zawacki have summarized the situation very well:

> The majority of the research consists of case studies . . . many discussed only in anecdotal or impressionistic terms. Next there are a large number of investigations . . . or field experiments, that have some of the trappings of the scientific method-questionnaire responses analyzed with statistical techniques, and so forth—but they lack pre- and postmeasurement, control groups and control over extraneous variables to such an extent that they are of questionable scientific validity. And finally, there are a small number of research efforts that reflect generally accepted standards for social science research, and they thereby constitute a valid, reliable, and reproducible body of knowledge concerning the effects of OD. . . .[84]

There are several comprehensive reviews of the OD research literature. One of the best is by Friedlander and Brown,[85] which includes thoughtful commentary and a fine synthesis of the field. Other more recent ones include those by Alderfer,[86] Porras,[87] Porras and Berg,[88] and White and Mitchell.[89] For a review of OD research in schools, see

Fullan and Miles.[90] And, finally, for an excellent article on the methodological problems and issues of research in OD, see the award-winning paper by Golembiewski, Billingsley, and Yeager.[91]

CONCLUSION

I shall conclude the chapter by addressing briefly the future of Organization Development. Does OD indeed have a future? An analogous answer comes from Shakespeare: "What's in a name? That which we call a rose by any other name would smell as sweet." In other words, OD may not last forever in name, but its elements and characteristics will be around for quite some time. It's possible that OD will be subsumed within QWL—the quality-of-working-life movement (for a definition, see Walton)[92]—since both are more similar than different and both have common values. Or it could be vice versa, QWL within the overall framework of OD. Whatever the label, there will continue to be a need for knowledge and expertise regarding human behavior in organizations in general and the management of change in particular. In short, there will continue to be a client need.

To some extent, however, the future of OD rests with the consultants themselves. The issue of whether OD consultants will follow a normative versus a contingency model is yet to be resolved. Tichy[93] has indicated that some OD consultants are either disenchanted or, in any case, no longer adhere to the values OD represents, at least not in their consulting roles. It's difficult to say how representative of the field these consultants are since Tichy's sample was neither random nor very large. If the trend of these few is representative, however, OD will eventually be no different from any other type of consultation. After all, OD techniques may be used by anyone and in response to a variety of situations. The underlying value system is what makes OD distinct.

NOTES

1   D. K. Hart and W. G. Scott, "The Organizational Imperative, "*Administration and Society,* vol. 7, no. 3, 1975, pp. 259–284.

2   W. W. Burke, "Managing Conflict between Groups," in J. D. Adams (ed.), *New Technologies in Organization Development,* vol. 2, University Associates, La Jolla, Calif., 1974, pp. 255–268.

3   R. Beckhard, *Organization Development—Strategies and Models,* Addison-Wesley, Cambridge, Mass., 1969, p. 9.

4   M. Beer and E. F. Huse, "A Systems Approach to Organization Development," *Journal of Applied Behavioral Science,* vol. 8, 1972, pp. 79–101.

5 W. W. Burke, "A Comparison of Management Development and Organization Development," *Journal of Applied Behavioral Science,* vol. 7, 1971, pp. 569–579.

6 W. W. Burke and W. H. Schmidt, "Primary Target for Change: The Manager or the Organization?" in W. H. Schmidt (ed.), *Organizational Frontiers and Human Values,* Wadsworth, Belmont, Calif., 1970, pp. 151–169.

7 W. W. Burke and H. A. Hornstein (eds.), *The Social Technology of Organization Development,* University Associates, La Jolla, Calif., 1972.

8 D. Katz and R. L. Kahn, *The Social Psychology of Organizations,* Wiley, New York, 1966.

9 H. A. Hornstein, B. B. Bunker, W. W. Burke, M. Gindes, and R. J. Lewicki, *Social Intervention: A Behavioral Science Approach,* Free Press, New York, 1971.

10 C. Argyris, *Integrating the Individual and the Organization,* Wiley, New York, 1964; Argyris, *Interpersonal Competence and Organizational Effectiveness,* Dorsey, Homewood, Ill., 1962; and Argyris, *Personality and Organization: The Conflict between System and the Individual,* Harper and Row, New York, 1957.

11 W. G. Bennis, *Changing Organizations,* McGraw-Hill, New York, 1966.

12 J. L. Massie, "Management Theory," in J. G. March (ed.), *Handbook of Organizations,* Rand McNally, Chicago, 1965.

13 Beckhard, op. cit.

14 N. M. Tichy, "Demise, Absorption or Renewal for the Future of Organization Development," in W. W. Burke (ed.), *The Cutting Edge: Current Theory and Practice in Organization Development,* University Associates, La Jolla, Calif., 1978, pp. 70–88.

15 P. R. Lawrence and J. W. Lorsch, *Developing Organizations: Diagnosis and Action,* Addison-Wesley, Reading, Mass., 1969.

16 J. Lorsch, "Definitions of OD by the Experts," *OD Newsletter,* Academy of Management, Winter 1978, p. 3.

17 E. H. Schein, "Definitions of OD by the Experts," *OD Newsletter,* Academy of Management, Winter 1978, p. 3.

18 D. Sirota and A. Wolfson, "Job Enrichment: What Are the Obstacles?" *Personnel,* vol. 49, no. 3, 1972, pp. 8–17.

19 L. P. Bradford, J. R. Gibb, and K. D. Benne (eds.), *T-group Theory and Laboratory Method,* Wiley, New York, 1964.

20 H. A. Shepard, "Three Management Programs and the Theory behind Them," in *An Action Research Program for Organization Improvement,* Foundation for Research on Human Behavior, Ann Arbor, Mich., 1960.

21 E. Trist and K. Bamforth, "Some Social and Psychological Consequences of the Long Wall Method of Goal Setting," *Human Relations,* vol. 4, 1951, pp. 1–8.

22 F. C. Mann, "Studying and Creating Change: A Means to Understanding Social Organization," in C. M. Arensburg et al. (eds.), *Research in Industrial Human Relations,* Harper, New York, 1957.

23 D. A. Nadler, *Feedback and Organization Development: Using Data-Based Methods,* Addison-Wesley, Reading, Mass., 1977.

24 I. Chein, S. Cook, and J. Harding, The Field of Action Research, *American Psychologist,* vol. 3, 1948, pp. 43–50.

25 W. French, "Organization Development: Objectives, Assumptions, and Strategies, *California Management Review,* vol. 12, 1969, pp. 23–34.

26 M. A. Frohman, M. Sashkin, and M. J. Kavanagh, "Action-Research as Applied to Organization Development," *Organization and Administrative Sciences,* vol. 7, nos. 1 and 2, 1976, pp. 129–142.

27 M. Weisbord, "Organizational Diagnosis: Six Places to Look for Trouble with or without a Theory," *Group and Organization Studies,* vol. 1, no. 4, 1976, pp. 430–477; Weisbord, *Organizational Diagnosis: A Workbook of Theory and Practice,* Addison-Wesley, Reading, Mass., 1978.

28 Weisbord, "Organizational Diagnosis," p. 431.

29 Ibid., p. 440.

30 P. Selznick, *Leadership in Administration,* Harper & Row, New York, 1957.

31 Weisbord, "Organizational Diagnosis," p. 443.

32 R. Beckhard and R. T. Harris, *Organizational Transitions: Managing Complex Change,* Addison-Wesley, Reading, Mass., 1977.

33 Ibid., p. 16.

34 N. M. Tichy, "Agents of Planned Social Change: Congruence of Values, Cognitions, and Actions," *Administrative Science Quarterly,* vol. 19, 1974, pp. 164–182.

35 H. Levinson, *Organizational Diagnosis,* Harvard University Press, Cambridge, Mass., 1972.

36 L. D. Goodstein, *Consulting with Human Service Systems,* Addison-Wesley, Reading, Mass., 1978, p. 78.

37 L. D. Goodstein and R. K. Boyer, "Crisis Intervention in a Municipal Agency: A Conceptual Case Analysis," *Journal of Applied Behavioral Science,* vol. 8, 1972, pp. 318–340.

38 F. Steele, "Is the Culture Hostile to Organization Development? The U.K. Example," in D. N. Berg and P. H. Mirvis (eds.), *Failures in Organization Development and Change,* Wiley, New York, 1977, pp. 23–31.

39 D. N. Berg, "Failure at Entry," in D. N. Berg and P. H. Mirvis (eds.), *Failures in Organization Development and Change,* Wiley, New York, 1977, pp. 35–55.

40 J. W. Pfeiffer and J. E. Jones, "OD Readiness," in W. W. Burke (ed.), *The Cutting Edge: Current Theory and Practice in Organization Development,* University Associates, La Jolla, Calif., 1978, pp. 179–185.

41 Beckhard and Harris, op. cit., pp. 25–26.

42 Ibid., p. 27.

43 M. Weisbord, "The Organization Development Contract, *OD Practitioner,* vol. 5, no. 2, 1973, pp. 1–4.

44 R. Likert, *The Human Organization,* McGraw-Hill, New York, 1967.

45 D. A. Nadler and M. L. Tushman, "A Diagnostic Model for Organization Behavior," in J. R. Hackman, E. E. Lawler, and L. W. Porter (eds.), *Perspectives on Behavior in Organizations,* McGraw-Hill, New York, 1977, pp. 85–100.

46 Mann, op. cit.

47 Nadler, op. cit.

48 R. T. Golembiewski, *Approaches to Planned Change,* Marcel Dekker, New York, 1979.

49 Burke and Schmidt, op. cit.

50 C. Argyris, *Intervention Theory and Method,* Addison-Wesley, Reading, Mass., 1970.

51 Ibid., p. 17.

52 Burke and Hornstein, op. cit.

53 R. A. Schmuck, and M. B. Miles (eds.), *Organization Development in Schools,* National Press Books, Palo Alto, Calif., 1971.

54 R. R. Blake and J. S. Mouton, *Consultation,* Addison-Wesley, Reading, Mass., 1976.

55 D. G. Bowers, J. L. Franklin, and P. Pecorella, "Matching Problems, Precursors, and Interventions in OD: A Systemic Approach," *Journal of Applied Behavioral Science,* vol. 11, 1975, pp. 391–410.

56 R. Lippitt and G. Lippitt, "Consulting Process in Action," *Training and Development Journal,* part 1, vol. 29, no. 5, 1975, pp. 48–54; part 2, vol. 29, no. 6, 1975, pp. 38–44.

57 W. L. French and C. H. Bell, Jr., *Organization Development,* 2d ed., Prentice-Hall, Englewood Cliffs, N.J., 1978.

58 S. White and T. Mitchell, "Organization Development: A Review of Research Content and Research Design," *Academy of Management Review,* vol. 1, 1976, pp. 57–73.

59 R. Harrison, "Choosing the Depth of Organizational Intervention," *Journal of Applied Behavioral Science,* vol. 6, 1970, pp. 181–202.

60 E. F. Huse, *Organization Development and Change,* rev. ed., West Publishing, St. Paul, 1980.

61 R. Beckhard, "The Confrontation Meeting," *Harvard Business Review,* vol. 45, no. 2, 1967, pp. 149–155.

62 R. R. Blake and J. S. Mouton, *Corporate Excellence through Grid Organization Development,* Gulf Publishing, Houston, 1968.

63 E. H. Schein, *Process Consultation,* Addison-Wesley, Reading, Mass., 1969.

64 Harrison, op. cit., p. 190.

65 Ibid., p. 198.

66 Beckhard and Harris, op. cit.

67 Beckhard, "Confrontation Meeting"; and R. T. Golembiewski and

A. Blumberg, "Confrontation as a Training Design in Complex Organizations: Attitudinal Changes in a Diversified Population of Managers," *Journal of Applied Behavioral Science,* vol. 3, no. 4, 1967, pp. 525–555.

68   A. L. Delbecq, A. H. Van de Ven, and D. H. Gustafson, *Group Techniques for Program Planning,* Scott, Foresman Glenview, Ill., 1975.

69   Schein, *Process Consultation.*

70   W. G. Dyer, *Team Building: Issues and Alternatives,* Addison-Wesley, Reading, Mass., 1977.

71   Burke, "Managing Conflict."

72   J. R. Hackman, "Work design," in J. R. Hackman and L. J. Suttle (eds.), *Improving Life at Work,* Goodyear, Santa Monica, Calif., 1977, pp. 96–162.

73   J. K. Fordyce and R. Weil, *Managing with People,* Addison-Wesley, Reading, Mass., 1971.

74   Golembiewski, op. cit.

75   U. Merry and M. E. Allerhand, *Developing Teams and Organizations,* Addison-Wesley, Reading, Mass., 1977.

76   R. Lippit, J. Watson, and B. Westley, *Dynamics of Planned Change.* Harcourt, Brace, New York, 1958.

77   Beckhard and Harris, op. cit.

78   M. Deutsch, "Field Theory in Social Psychology," in G. Lindzey and E. Aronson (eds.), *The Handbook of Social Psychology,* 2d ed., vol. 1, Addison-Wesley, Reading, Mass., 1968, pp. 412–487.

79   L. Coch and J. R. P. French, "Overcoming Resistance to Change," *Human Relations,* vol. 1, 1948, pp. 512–532.

80   J. B. Harvey, "Consulting during Crises of Agreement," in W. W. Burke (ed.), *Current Issues and Strategies in Organization Development,* Human Sciences Press, New York, 1977, pp. 160–186.

81   S. E. Seashore and D. G. Bowers, Durability of Organizational Change, *American Psychologist,* vol. 25, March 1970, pp. 227–233.

82   S. A. Davis, "An Organic Problem-Solving Method of Organizational Change, *Journal of Applied Behavioral Science,* vol. 3, 1967, pp. 3–21.

83   R. Beckhard, and D. G. Lake, "Short- and Long-Range Effects of a Team Development Effort," in H. A. Hornstein, B. B. Bunker, W. W. Burke, M. Gindes, and R. J. Lewicki, *Social Intervention: A Behavioral Science Approach,* Free Press, New York, 1971, pp. 421–439.

84   W. L. French, C. H. Bell, and R. A. Zawacki (eds.), *Organization Development: Theory, Practice and Research,* Business Publications, Dallas, 1978, p. 407.

85   F. Friedlander and L. D. Brown, Organization Development, *Annual Review of Psychology,* vol. 25, 1974, pp. 313–341.

86   C. P. Alderfer, "Organization Development," in M. R. Rosenzweig and L. W. Porter (eds.), *Annual Review of Psychology,* vol. 28, 1977, pp. 197–223.

87 J. I. Porras, "The Comparative Impact of Different OD Techniques and Intervention Intensities," *Journal of Applied Behavioral Science,* vol. 15, 1979, pp. 156–178; Porras, "The Impact of Organization Development: Research Findings," *Academy of Management Review,* vol. 3, no. 2, 1978, pp. 249–266.

88 J. I. Porras and P. O. Berg, "Evaluation Methodology in Organization Development: An Analysis and Critique," *Journal of Applied Behavioral Science,* vol. 14, 1978, pp. 151–173.

89 White and Mitchell, op. cit.

90 M. Fullan and M. Miles, "OD in Schools: The State of the Art," in W. W. Burke (ed.), *The Cutting Edge: Current Theory and Practice in Organization Development,* University Associates, La Jolla, Calif., 1978, pp. 149–174.

91 R. T. Golembiewski, K. Billingsley, and S. Yeager, "Measuring Change and Persistence in Human Affairs: Types of Change Generated by OD Designs," *Journal of Applied Behavioral Science,* vol. 12, 1976, pp. 133–157.

92 R. E. Walton, "Quality of Working Life: What Is It?" *Sloan Management Review,* Fall, 1973, pp. 11–21.

93 Tichy, op. cit.

REFERENCE

Kast, F. E., and J. E. Rosenzweig: *Organization and Management: Experiential Exercises,* McGraw-Hill, New York, 1976.

6

Management Auditing

Spencer Hayden

President
The Spencer Hayden Company, Inc.

What do these organizations have in common: *Playboy,* the Roman Catholic Church, and Sinclair Oil Company? The answer: each has been analyzed by outside consultants—undergoing what is called a Management Audit or "general business survey."

Now consider a few others: International Telephone and Telegraph Company, Borden, Inc., and Barnes Engineering Company. These also conducted surveys, but used their own staffs rather than outsiders.

Why would any company want such a top-to-bottom analysis in addition to its usual accountants' audits? Obviously it is because those in charge feel a need for a change in organization or direction, and want to get a more penetrating look at the whole picture before taking any steps that might go wrong.

Take Sinclair Oil Company as an example. In the late sixties New York's Sinclair had annual revenues of $1⅓ billion and was a conspicuous corporate figure in the East. Its dinosaur symbol was well known at gas pumps; it had its own refining, marketing, and transportation divisions; it was about 56 percent self-sufficient in crude oil; and it operated one of the nation's largest pipeline systems.

Because the company's earnings lagged the industry, however, its management felt the need for a review of all its operations and planning. They brought in a management consultant who, working with an in-house task force of young managers, conducted a Management Audit that raised an array of red flags, many having to do with the lack of enough professional managers to handle prospects for future growth. Shortly thereafter, in 1968, the directors voted to merge Sinclair Oil into highly-profitable Atlantic Richfield Company, helping to make ARCO a giant in its field. Sinclair as an independent entity simply faded away.

What, exactly, goes into such Management Audits? Who uses them? Why are they authorized in the first place—especially if they may trigger all sorts of painful consequences?

How exactly are they conducted? Who does the brainwork? How long does it take? How much do they cost? Can they be done cheaper and better by in-house corporate staff? These are questions that have a direct bearing on organizational change.

WHAT ARE MANAGEMENT AUDITS?

Business strength or weakness, in terms of money, is traditionally measured by the financial audit with its resulting balance sheet and profit-and-loss statement. But these two documents tell only the firm's *financial* position as of a given date—how much money was made or lost over the reporting period, and whether accounting procedures are in good order. Actually such an audit does not give an adequate picture of how well a company is *managed*. Moreover, it does not tell what, if any, corrections in management procedures are needed to produce maximum efficiency in the future.

One insurance company asks these questions of its corporate policyholders:

> How productive is your management? Does it measure up to present day requirements?
>
> Most progressive companies make it a point to audit their accounts at least once a year in order to establish the adequacy and accuracy of such accounts and to reveal fiscal weaknesses that may need correction. The periodic inventorying and appraisal of physical assets is also an accepted practice.
>
> There is need for the same sort of stock-taking as applied to the management of a business. This can be accomplished through the medium of a Management Audit. Through this device, a business executive undertakes, in effect, to back off and survey his company critically and objectively. A comprehensive management checklist is helpful in this connection.

Management Audits thus seek to probe beneath the *surface* appearance of a business, focusing on the internal harmony and dynamics that lie beneath. As one financial analyst has said, "A management judged solely by the dollar results achieved may be sorely misjudged." Good results may come from a piece of good luck rather than from management efficiency.

Scope of Audits

Figure 6-1, "Sixty-nine key factors of the business-survey dimensions," illustrates the scope of a Management Audit. It was developed by the author and used as a framework by a number of analysts. But the true heart of any survey lies in the detailed section-by-section checklists for data collection *plus* the professional ability of the investigator.

Some tend to confuse Management Audits with the more limited but highly popular process called "organization studies." Management Audits do include a critical review of organization, but they go well beyond mere structure and reporting relationships. Whereas an organization specialist primarily seeks to determine if good staffing design is followed (e.g., "There must be clear lines of authority running from the top to the bottom of the organization. . . . No one in the organization should report to more than one line supervisor"), the more general management auditor asks questions such as, "Is this company in the right business?" "Are its market shares increasing or decreasing?" "Are costs out of line and what can be done about it if they are?"

Another misunderstanding has to do with thinking that "department studies" are management audits. While departmental evaluations often are valuable, they are not comprehensive. A "marketing audit" or "industrial relations audit" does not meet our criteria for a bona fide general survey. The *real* needs of a company typically cut across all or several departments and functions, and these needs have to be assessed by someone who can look at *all* segments—and then compare, rank, break down, and eventually synthesize a myriad of facts.

Variety of Audits

There is no universally accepted or "standard" outline for a general survey of this kind, though the Checklist for a Management Audit which concludes this chapter is fairly typical. Some of the more interesting variations deserve recognition here.

The granddaddy of all general management checklists and survey outlines is the excellent one developed by the founder of McKinsey & Company, the consulting firm. A recent biography of McKinsey, *Man-*

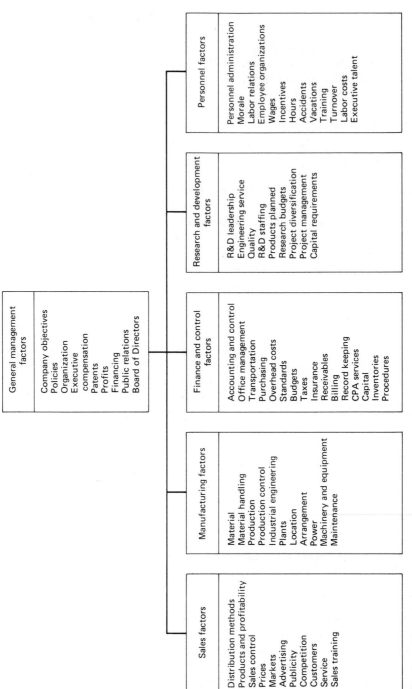

General management factors

Company objectives
Policies
Organization
Executive compensation
Patents
Profits
Financing
Public relations
Board of Directors

Sales factors

Distribution methods
Products and profitability
Sales control
Prices
Markets
Advertising
Publicity
Competition
Customers
Service
Sales training

Manufacturing factors

Material
Material handling
Production
Production control
Industrial engineering
Plants
Location
Arrangement
Power
Machinery and equipment
Maintenance

Finance and control factors

Accounting and control
Office management
Transportation
Purchasing
Overhead costs
Standards
Budgets
Taxes
Insurance
Receivables
Billing
Record keeping
CPA services
Capital
Inventories
Procedures

Research and development factors

R&D leadership
Engineering service
Quality
R&D staffing
Products planned
Research budgets
Project diversification
Project management
Capital requirements

Personnel factors

Personnel administration
Morale
Labor relations
Employee organizations
Wages
Incentives
Hours
Accidents
Vacations
Training
Turnover
Labor costs
Executive talent

Fig. 6-1 Sixty-nine key factors of the business-survey dimensions.

230

agement and Consulting, by William B. Wolf of Cornell University, graciously provides this entire document, giving the reader a priceless tool. It is claimed by some that the McKinsey staff still uses this outline, with only minor revisions. If true, it would be nothing to apologize for. Of course, a checklist is only as good as the investigator who uses it.

One might also obtain a copy of *Management Audit for Small Manufacturers,* published by the Small Business Administration and available from the Superintendent of Documents, U.S. Government Printing Office, Washington, D.C. This is a do-it-yourself appraisal that covers (in 15 categories) the vital areas of a business. In the booklet's words, "If the owner-manager can supply the proper answers to the questions, he may be sure that he is running his business efficiently." Not bad for a primer but not good enough for a complicated situation.

The present writer occasionally refers to *The Scientific Appraisal of Management* by Jackson Martindell, published by Harper & Brothers. The book is remarkably good, yet relatively unknown. Any reader can profit from studying the entire text and then using the 301 specific questions in the book's appendix for an individual survey. (Incidentally, this is the audit that was used to survey the management of the Roman Catholic Church. It got a very high score on it—just below that of Procter & Gamble!)

Martindell's appraisal system assigns points for excellence in ten categories (maximum attainable = 10,000), as follows, revealing a strong emphasis (2400 points) on quality of executives:

400	Economic Function
500	Corporate Structure
600	Health of Earnings Growth
700	Fairness to Stockholders
700	Research & Development
900	Directorate Analysis
1100	Fiscal Policies
1300	Production Efficiency
1400	Sales Vigor
2400	Executive Evaluation

One interesting variant of the general business survey is what I call the "Drucker Model." Quite simply, it involves a conference leader (usually an outsider) conducting management workshops in which the participants study and apply the key ideas of Peter F. Drucker, the guru of modern management. Typically, executives are required to read one of his books and, in a series of perhaps 10 half-day sessions, identify where *their* company is failing to measure up to Drucker's "principles." (This can become an informal in-house survey.) They then propose, in writing, a set of improvements which are referred to the chief executive officer. If the committee writes well, avoids offending, and has a president who admires Peter Drucker, some good can come out of the shoestring effort.

Sometimes this has the added advantage of being quite an exercise in executive development. A few years ago Barnes Engineering Company used Drucker's classic book *The Practice of Management* for such an audit; their managers came up with a series of solid top-to-bottom recommendations that helped change corporate direction. Howmet Corporation in 1975 built a program on Drucker's book *Management: Tasks, Responsibilities, Practices.* A group of 10 bright young managers spent five consecutive afternoons working out an analysis of their company based on the 27 "best chapters" in Drucker's ponderous 61-chapter tome. They submitted a summary for top management. In their words, "this report is an indication of those management areas which were collectively regarded as important to the participants. We hope that some thoughts or suggestions could result in overall improvements within our company."

Finally, you might want to skim the *Outline for a Management Audit* and *A Management Audit for the Small Company,* both published by the Policyholders Service Bureau of Metropolitan Life Insurance Company. These are two more do-it-yourself surveys, but they show their age; however, they could be helpful to beginners searching for materials to go into their own first checklists.

THE AUDITING PROCEDURE

Let us assume that you are a management consultant or an inside staff expert who has been asked to conduct a comprehensive Management Audit. It has also been agreed that the report will cover the following usual subjects (though, of course, some may be excluded or others—such as corporate social responsibility and computer operations—added):

1 Nature and history of the business
2 Ownership and corporate structure
3 Financial condition
4 Management control
5 Products and markets

6 Manufacturing

7 Research and development

8 Organization

9 Personnel/human resources

(At the end of the chapter the reader will find a fairly typical checklist for this particular Management Audit, which provides a detailed road map.)

Your procedure in conducting such a Management Audit would consist of five steps: preparation, data collection, analysis, development of recommendations, and report writing. None of these is simple; each requires a high level of professionalism.

The following suggestions can make your task easier if you are auditing. If you are merely an observer it's still a good idea to understand the steps. And, of course, if it is *you* who is sponsoring this study, you'd better become comfortably familiar with those methods—and anticipate possible problems. To keep discussions straightforward, these suggestions are addressed to the potential auditor of a manufacturing company as one common type of example.

Preparation

The first step is a review of any written proposal and/or authorization letter followed by a full discussion of the job to be done with the person who prepared that proposal. From this discussion, you should learn three things: the probable problem areas and factors to be stressed in conducting the survey; probable attitude of personnel toward the Management Audit and where there may be difficulties; and any special sources of information you can use, such as files.

Before moving ahead, all available data about the company should be reviewed. Both outside and inside investigators can profit from this mundane desk work. *Poor's Register* and *Moody's* are normally good sources of company history, corporate and financial structure, earnings, and basic products. For unlisted companies, Dun and Bradstreet reports usually supply most of the same basic information. Company annual reports and underwriter reports should be consulted also, if available. It goes without saying that inside investigators should have a head start at this stage, but a surprising number of employees are unfamiliar with some of the published reports on their company. Do your homework well right at the start.

In addition, it's a good idea to review published reports on the industry in general and on competitors in such periodicals as *Business Week, Fortune,* and *The Wall Street Journal.* Such review not only gives hints of the kind of problems the Management Audit may turn up, but also provides valuable background on the general nature of the business. It's helpful to put copies of any really important articles in the appendix to the report, to help stress a point with the client or sponsor.

The information obtained in this preparatory period should be sufficient for you to write the first three of the nine sections of the final report—Nature and History of the Business, Ownership and Corporate Structure, and Financial Condition. In fact, it is a good idea actually to write these early chapters *immediately*, as part of your preparation for the Management Audit, as it fixes this information firmly in mind and can usually be used for final report copy with only minor changes or additions later.

At this time, sketch out a weekly and monthly schedule to allot proper amounts of time to each part of the survey. A preferred order of interviews should also be set up. Normally, the order is as follows:

Meet the sponsor(s)

Tour of facilities, if one is unfamiliar with them

Accounting and finance

Sales/marketing

Manufacturing

Engineering/research and development

Personnel/human resources

Data Collection

Normally, when conducting a Management Audit, the outside consultant's first contact at the client base is with the president, board chairman, or other top official of the company. But as one may imagine, this can be a little bit sticky for an in-house investigator who is an employee. Outsiders seem to get more respect at the top.

This official should be able to give you a *broad* picture of the company and its sales, manufacturing and financial problems, company policies and goals, the corporate setup, organization, reporting relationships of immediate subordinates, control methods, and probably more important, key people in the company who can be depended on for full cooperation in the survey. It generally pays to have two or more investigators conduct this meeting, as a team, and not to rush the interview. This beginning can easily make or break the entire Management Audit. Outsiders have a clear advantage here and can probe; this briefing is often much less frank when the interviewer is a company employee and clearly subordinate.

During this session it should be determined also whether the Management Audit has been announced to all appropriate members of the organization. Come to the meeting prepared to suggest ways in which the announcement can be made, or even bring a sample letter that can be sent to the managers.

At this first meeting, describe your approach to the survey, outlining briefly the kind of information you need and the key personnel to be interviewed. You might use this session to request office space and/or clerical help—though it's better to specify such needs in the original proposal or agreement letter. Sometimes I arrange for the appointment of task forces of suitable employees to help in my data collection and impress the official with the benefits in training which these participants get.

At the close of this critical interview if you are an outsider doing the audit, arrange for a tour of the facilities. This affords an excellent opportunity for you to meet the key figures on an easy basis and get a firsthand impression of the company. Ask for a very senior, highly respected guide. Getting some junior to take you around will unfavorably influence everyone's first impression. And it's tough enough to get accepted without *that* extra handicap.

In order to obtain a complete picture of the overall operation you'll have to collect the following information, which will normally appear in your final report:

Balance sheet, 10-year period

Operating statement, 10-year period

Ownership character and concentration

List and rating of important distributors

List and rating of important accounts

List and rating of important competitors

Analysis of manufacturing cost

Current organization chart

The above items should be asked for and obtained early in the study, the first day if possible, for they form the basis for determining the course of the remainder of the study. The accounting department is the source of most of this data and should be the *first* point of contact after the introductory conference. Department members doubtless will promise—probably sincerely—to provide this data to you promptly, but you won't get it promptly. This, of course, tests your ability to be an effective consultant. Lots of adroitness may be needed in handling the accountants. But don't capitulate.

The accounting department can also answer many of the points covered in your outline and checklist, but it is much wiser for you *first* to analyze the operating statements, balance sheets, and manufacturing cost reports *before* getting into detailed discussions or probings with accounting or any other department. You can be sure the accountants will spread the word quickly on how smart you are. Being well prepared is the best guarantee of their respect.

Analysis

Analysis begins with the first data you obtain from the company. As additional data are obtained, their effects on and interrelation with what you have already collected or observed should be noted. Why, where, when, what, and who questions should be answered about each situation. The answers you get in interviews to these questions plus your own professional training and experience in other organizations will usually indicate a clear course of action to overcome the weaknesses that surface. Actually persons you interview will volunteer more suggestions than you'll ever need. Your job at this stage is to collect, compare (especially conflicting data or ideas), and sift such information.

It is important to the overall success of the Management Audit that you *quickly* come to a clear-cut decision as to the adequacy of company performance for each major item in the checklist. Don't wait until you have nearly finished. Such procedure prevents spending too much time on minor investigations or side issues, and permits a quick positive summation of "findings to date" for whoever is the sponsor. You're being paid to give an evaluation, so start taking positions! Some decisions *will* be reversed later as additional data in other areas are uncovered, but your arriving at *early* preliminary judgments assures straightforward progress of the survey.

The major problems that face the enterprise should then be listed and documented, by the nine section headings or by importance, or both. Now you're ready to recommend.

Development of Recommendations

Your analysis by now should suggest to you *several* ways to overcome each of the listed major problems of the enterprise. One or more of these should stand out as being better than the others. Selection of the one *best* way for eventual recommendation to the study's sponsor depends upon a number of factors, such as cost of the improvement, capability of company personnel to carry it out, and time elements. Sometimes quick action is essential, as in potential bankruptcy or takeover situations.

Here's an important tip: in most cases the better alternative solutions should be discussed confidentially and in a preliminary way with carefully selected client personnel involved. Previously overlooked difficulties with the attractive solution will thus be turned up, and, depending on the reaction, the best method for selling the final recommendations can be figured out. A caution: this testing of the waters will provoke some gossip and fuel some hopes and fears. Don't get yourself quoted until you're ready.

Report Writing

The audit's final report is normally the only physical item the sponsor or client receives from your work. It is the physical representation and record of all your analysis. But probably far more important to the "customer," it should be the instrument which clinches the adoption of all your recommendations. It has to stand on its own, even after you have walked away.

Thus, your report should be organized to present a clear, concise, and constructive representation of the state of the business. Recommendations for future action should be practical, timely, and above all convincing.

Your method of presentation should depend to a large extent upon the attitudes of the sponsors and how well the recommendations have been presold to them. Occasionally the "customer" has a stated preference as to method (speech with slides, open discussions, or just a document). Some even have keen preferences concerning typeface, paper used, and binders! In such cases, follow their lead—unless it detracts from the professional look of the presentation. Most consulting firms have style manuals that are quite good and effective.

An unemotional, straightforward presentation is generally best, perhaps following the general order of the Management Audit at the end of this chapter. Carefully and systematically describe the company's strengths and weaknesses in each area. However, if it has been decided in advance that a more tailored or selective approach is needed, some of the analytical parts can be relegated to an appendix and the report pointed directly at the major weaknesses. This gives a shorter, blunter presentation. Some investigators rely upon a series of punchy flip charts for their report, featuring headlines and subheads only, and talk from them. If you do that, make sure you leave behind a fuller, more complete record.

Here is another practical tip for the busy investigator: consider *distributing a questionnaire* to those managers whom you won't have time to interview, soliciting their views and perhaps supporting data on what's right and what's wrong in the company. These can be anonymously returned to you if the managers don't want to sign their names. You'l find this to be a gold mine, for it expands your contacts remarkably well It also pleases the respondents. The present writer has found especiall) valuable three pages of questions contained in the book *Practical Busines: Planning* by Charles E. St. Thomas (American Management Association) The following is a small sample of his list, which makes a good question-naire:

> Is our reputation for quality, delivery, service, and quotation really as good as it should be? How do we know? Do we make occasional opinion surveys, and so on? Is our product line really as complete as it should be, or are we losing profitable orders because we force the customer to go to a competitor whose offering is more complete? Is our distribution system really appropriate for our product line, or is it outdated, no longer able to serve the function for which it was originally intended? Do we know the impact that market, industry and economic growth can be expected to have on our existing products? Have we studied new products we could produce to satisfy forecast shifts?

It should be obvious by this time that (1) Management Audits can serve a very valuable function in spelling out the need for improvements and change and (2) they're not easy to do well. Maybe an experienced consultant should be brought in. But what are management consultants *really* like, and how does one go about using them?

MANAGEMENT CONSULTING

According to the Association of Consulting Management Engineers:

> The ultimate purpose of every consulting engagement is to *make something happen* in the client organization that will improve its performance. *Change*—for the better—is the ultimate measure of success. It doesn't matter how astute consultants are in analyzing the problem, nor how ingenious is the program or procedure they devise. Unless the consultant can persuade the client to *act* upon his recommendations, he has done him no service; indeed, he may have done him a disservice.

Robert Townsend once described a management consultant as a person who borrows your watch, charges a fee to tell you what time it is, and then walks off with the watch![1] But 98 percent of a sample of United States firms surveyed by one researcher said they used consultants—and typically they used several different ones. These companies can't *all* be asking for the time of day.

Another swipe is, "A consultant is someone brought in to find out what has gone wrong, by the people who made it go wrong, in the expectation that he will not bite the hand that feeds him by placing the blame where it belongs." Of course such obvious game playing would soon kill the profession. Management consulting is very much alive and well—growing at a rate of about 20 percent a year.

Actually, there are two general classes of "management consultants"—the independent outsiders and special in-house staff employees. Anyone considering having a Management Audit better know something about each group.

No one really knows how many outside (independent) "management consultants" there are, largely because there's no agreement on a definition of consultant. Management consulting is an unlicensed, unregulated profession.

In 1975 by one count there were approximately 3500 consulting firms in the United States, most comprised of 2 to 5 persons, with another 2000 or so individuals also active.

In 1976 one of the standard directories of consultants listed 5315 firms, organizations, and individuals, but probably not more than 5 percent of them conducted the sweeping Management Audits described here. In fact, much of the profession is dominated by certified public accountants and college professors, who consult in 146 different fields including cost reduction, industrial testing, investment counseling, consumer credit, and advertising. There is even a new directory called *University Consultants Network Register*.

Last year an estimated $2.5 billion was spent by organizations on outside management consulting services. The Big Eight accounting firms alone employ a total of 6400 consultants and bill about $340 million annually for "management advisory services," which is their euphemism for management consulting.

In addition to the outside "independent" practitioners there are probably more than 12,000 in-house ("internal") management consultants, well established in about 800 United States companies and other organizations. The typical staff seems to be about 15 persons, performing work that outsiders would charge more than $500 million for. Inside management consultants go by many names within their companies:

Organization Planning

Management Consulting

Industrial Engineering

Staff Services

Management Services

Corporate Systems

Administrative Systems

Corporate Planning

For example, W. R. Grace calls its 35 in-house consultants its Management Services Group. Mobil Oil Corporation's head of in-house consulting holds the title of Manager of Human Resources Consulting Services.

By 1977 about 200 of these insiders had become individual members of the Association of Internal Management Consultants (AIMC). About 93 percent of them have a bachelor's degree, 41 percent hold graduate degrees, and most report either to Finance or Administration.

This in-house consulting business also is prospering. AIMC membership is growing at about 15 percent a year.

Who Usually Conducts the Management Audit?

Most Management Audits are conducted by outside consultants, not inside corporate staffers. The main reasons for using external ("outside") consultants rather than internal ones are as follows:

* Objectivity of the outsider, especially for politically sensitive projects—which nearly all Management Audits are or turn out to be.
* Need for heavy manpower commitments which cannot be handled internally, especially in auditing a far-flung multiplant organization.
* Requirement for some technical expertise that may be lacking in-house, such as familiarity with all functions in a company or with their performance, including appropriate standards for each.
* Lack of top management respect for its own in-house teams, which may have been assigned to lower-level studies in the past, or which may have made some poor recommendations which have not been forgotten.

Internal consultants might be used well on Management Audits when the above situations do not exist. But their real worth probably lies in performing other types of projects, less sweeping or controversial.

If, as is most common, *outsiders* are retained to conduct the Management Audit, they can and sometimes should work closely with any inside consultants that may exist. Real cooperation is possible (but unusual). The internal consultant can, if willing, provide a great deal of information obtained in previous company work. Later, the in-house consultant often gets the job of implementing the external consultant's recommendations. A frustrated, by-passed staffer can neutralize much of the value of a good Management Audit if so inclined. But the cooperative insider can often work effectively *in parallel* with the outsider—though perhaps at a lower or supportive level in the study. And the outsider, if giving credit where due, can build up the image and reputation of the inside staff in the eyes of top management.

Management Consulting as a Profession

At the time of this writing, the Arthur D. Little Company, with 1050 professionals and 950 regular free-lancers, is the largest in the field, followed by Booz, Allen & Hamilton, Arthur Andersen (accounting firm), Coopers & Lybrand (also accounting), and McKinsey & Company.

Consulting firms tend to locate their offices in the East and Northeast, followed by the Midwest, West, and Southeast. Only a relatively small number are found in the Southwest.

The large, prestigious firms tend to get their staffs from the top graduates of good business schools—including Harvard and Stanford. Newcomers are usually males in their late twenties with at least a few years of business experience. Top candidates may be hired at a salary of $30,000 to $40,000 to start.

McKinsey & Company, with revenues of $100 million in 1979, reports a staff of 48 working directors and 85 principals (corresponding to senior and junior partners in a law firm), 520 associates who carry out most of the day-to-day assignments, and 125 staff researchers. Top directors there earn more than $400,000 a year. And at giant Arthur D. Little, President John F. Magee earned $256,380 in 1978, and had $687,826 retirement credit to date. Big money tends to attract top-quality personnel, another contrast with in-house staffs.

When charging for services a traditional rule of thumb for independent management consultants is to bill the client three times the consultant's salary for the period assigned full time to a project. One consulting firm describes where the revenues go as follows:

Professional salaries and fringes	50%
Office services, rent, insurance	15%
Selling and promotion	15%
Taxes	11%
Profit	9%

According to a recent survey the average per diem billing rates of consultants to their clients are as follows:

Partner	$679
Principal	502
Senior	416
Consultant	363
Junior	265

Those in the top echelons of larger firms tend to charge as much as 50 percent higher than those in smaller firms.

Choosing a Management Consultant

It used to be easy to choose an outside consultant—there were fewer of them, their leaders were well known to readers of business publications, and there was a single respected association that was happy to refer client inquiries to member firms.

Those days are gone. There are now thousands of consultants, many good and some bad; considerable puffery by public relations agents; direct mail promotion campaigns; and a bewildering proliferation of consulting associations and varying certification arrangements.

Some trade associations are quite professional, but others can be criticized as mail-order fakes or just assemblages of persons with differing degrees of ability. None speaks effectively for the profession as a whole. Even the good old Association of Consulting Management Engineers (ACME) no longer includes in its membership professional leaders such as McKinsey, Arthur D. Little, or Booz, Allen & Hamilton. There are various brotherhoods such as the Institute of Management Consultants, the Society of Professional Management Consultants, American Society of Business Management Consultants, Certified Management Consultants Association, International Consultants Foundation, and so on. Proliferation of such associations makes it hard for a client to zero in on a good supplier.

Says the president of the Boston Consulting Group, as quoted in *Consultant News,* "I do not believe there is any way to accredit a management consultant, any more than there is a way to accredit certified politicians and certified businessmen. . . . consultancy associations legitimatize the marginal consultant."

Nevertheless, in choosing a consultant for a Management Audit, some of ACME's suggestions are worth noting, as follows:

1   A prospective client should prepare a statement outlining the nature, general scope and purpose of the assignment to be undertaken prior to contacting prospective consultants. Such a statement will assist the client in selecting for interviews the consultant(s) most suitable for the assignment. It will also help potential consultants to present their qualifications and capabilities to undertake the work. [Author's note: Better clear this statement with others in your firm; you'll find they'll make changes in it.]

2   Consider the general qualifications of a number of management consultants who appear to be capable of meeting the requirements of the assignment and select for interview one or more (probably not more than three) who appear to be the best qualified for the proposed assignment.

Reference checks on general reputation should be a normal part of your preliminary search for consulting help. [Author's note: Ask your Board members for nominations or contact others in your industry.]

3 Preliminary discussions should be held with each of the consultants selected to discuss the project and their approach to it, and they should be asked to submit proposals. [Author's note: A top management team should handle this, not just one key person.]

4 The client should then study the proposals in terms of their understanding of the problem, approach, probable benefits, cost and the particular experience and ability of each consultant to meet the requirements of the engagement. In weighing this experience, care should be taken to consider the qualifications of the personnel who will actually be working on the project. [Author's note: Be sure to ask for the detailed biographies of each consultant to be assigned, plus number of hours each will work on the project.]

5 References of those consultants being seriously considered should be checked in depth. [Author's note: Consider hiring an independent consultant to help you select who will conduct the Management Audit. Forbid any fee-splitting.]

6 The final selection should be based on a careful weighing of the above factors. Final negotiations should follow the selection of the consultant. [The top management team can help here.]

For those who want to help bring about healthy change in their organizations, and are seriously interested in learning more about management auditing or management consulting as a profession, a Checklist for a Management Audit follows.

CHECKLIST FOR A MANAGEMENT AUDIT
1   Nature and History of the Business

Field of Business—manufacturing, sales, engineering, etc.

Specific Industry—steel, food, radio, etc.

Volume of business and geographical areas covered, including size and location of plants, sales offices, laboratories, etc.

Product lines and their relative amount of sales

Original company name and purpose

Changes in company name and purpose

Unusual events affecting the past or present situation

2   Ownership and Corporate Structure

Classes of stock or other securities, total shares and current price

Class and amount of stock or other securities held by each board member, company officers, and other important individual or group

Corporate control of the business—who controls the business and how is it controlled? How much stock does each officer have?

Market price of shares

Attitude of investors

3 Financial Condition

Operating statements for last 10 years, from which are developed trends and current position in regard to:

Profits or losses from operations by year and for period

Earnings as a percent of sales

Earnings per share

Earnings on invested capital

Percent of earnings paid out as dividends

Trend as a percent of gross sales of:

Returns for credit and allowances

Manufacturing cost, costs of goods sold

Net profit on operations

Other income

Gross profit on sales

Selling expense

Net profit on sales

General administrative expense

Deductions, other expenses

Net income

Earnings paid out as dividends

Return on investment

Financial statements last 10 years—from which are developed trends and current position with regard to:

General

Cash and cash items

Marketable securities

Investments

Trade notes and accounts receivable

Reserve for bad debts

Other current receivables, officers' and employees' loans, etc.

Inventories

Property, land and equipment

Intangible assets such as patents, trademarks, franchises, and goodwill

Deferred charges as prepaid insurance, supply items, experimental costs and discounts, and commissions on capital stock

Liabilities

Notes payable

Amounts due on long-term debts

Deferred income

Funded debt

Contingent liabilities

Capital stock

Earned and capital surplus

Dividends in arrears

Equity debt ratio

Current ratios

Special reports and investigation in the accounting area:

History of financing. Record of mortgage or other long-term debt, preferred and common stock issues. Performance on payment of interest and installments on debt

Debt and debt service requirements. Terms of outstanding long-term obligations—maturity dates, interest rates, call premiums. Restrictions regarding working capital, dividends, additional debt, etc.

Bank loans, amount, dates, sources, seasonal reductions, cleanups, and rates, past two years

Long-term lease obligations. Terms of all major leases, rentals, expiration dates, lease-purchase arrangements

Seasonal financial requirements. Short-term loans required for raw material purchases, finished goods accumulation, financing receivables, hedging

Cash position, monthly, past two years

Inventories:

Amount and balance of raw material in process and finished goods in relation to production and sales needs

Turnover, relate cost of sales to inventory, trend 10 years

Policy and extent of forward commitments on raw material

Vulnerability of the business in rapid price change in materials

Important raw material item and cost trends

Receivables—age analysis, trend, bad debt experience, and reserve

Sources and applications of funds, 5–10 years

Investments—kinds, condition and basis of evaluation

Officer and employee loans—amount and condition

Costs of compliance—OSHA, EEOC, ERISA

Actuarial analysis of pension liability, present and future

Properties:

Operating and nonoperating

Extent depreciated and depreciation rate

Net value to sales volume

Goodwill—basis of evaluation

Accounts payable—conditions and policy on discounts

Special reserves—kinds and amounts

Contingent liabilities:

Existing and threatened lawsuits

Guaranteed notes and obligations

Liability under large purchase contracts, etc.

Break-even points—overall and/or by major project, safety factors

Selling, general and administrative expenses. Define items included. Methods of allocation, to divisions, to products

Method of burden allocation

Patent situation:

Patents or licenses owned, age and importance to the business

Patent pools and licensing agreements

Royalties paid or received

Past and pending litigation

Future outlook

4   Management Control

Practices regarding budgeting, sales, production, costs, profits, etc.

Kind of cost system used

Quality, quantity, and cost

Sales

Capital expenditures

Sales, general and administrative expenses

Adequacy of internal control checks

List control reports issued, to whom and extent used

Degree of mechanization of accounting procedures

5 Products and Markets

Completeness and extent of sublines

Brand and trademark policies

Adaptability

Quality

Style and packaging

Competitive rating

Market acceptance

Trade standing

Volume in dollars and profit by major product line—5-10 years

Markets by major product line:

Type, location, and extent

Percent of total market supplied

Competition—list principal competitors

Stability

Economic factors influencing the market

Seasonal characteristics

Vulnerability from competition and technical advances

Concentration of sales among important accounts

List and rating of important customers

Advertising and sales promotion methods

Customer acceptance

Trade standing

Pricing:

Pricing policy

Stability of pricing structure

Factors influencing price

Future outlook

Distribution:

Distribution policies including method for selecting distributors

Growth of distribution, recent years

Types of distributors used

Number and location of distributors

Terms of sale including trade discounts

Distributors' and/or customers' attitude toward client

Miscellaneous data:

Extent of industry or other cooperation

Competitive practices and trade abuses

6 Manufacturing

Facilities, condition and adequacy

Location in respect to labor supply, raw material, and markets

Methods:

Type of shop, job, line production, etc.

Sequence of operations

Efficiency of layout

Methods for handling raw material, work in process, and finished goods

Housekeeping and safety

Bottlenecks

Basis for determining manufacturing volume—immediate orders, advance orders, inventory position

Break-even volume total and major product line

Costs:

Ratio of cost elements—raw material, direct labor, indirect labor, burden, uncontrollable charges to manufacturing

Major items and trends in labor costs—direct and indirect

Trends in burden costs, variable and fixed

Factory profit by product classes

Factory profit by popular or representative makes or models

Possible economies

7 Research and Background

Kind of research, basic, product, process, etc.

Facilities, condition and adequacy

Location with respect to manufacturing

Responsibility for product development, design, specifications, quality

Ratio, time spent on current production problems

8 Organization

Plan of organization—name, title, major duties and responsibilities of directors; officers; division, department, or branch heads; and key individuals reporting at these levels. Include management committees

Name, purpose and number of employees in divisions, departments, branches, or units

Exactness of duties and responsibilities

Accountability

9 Personnel/Human Resources

Overall adequacy of the management staff

Evaluation of all persons with managerial responsibility

Morale—all supervisory levels

Age spread of management and supervisory personnel

Areas of friction

Personnel policy

Labor relations:

Past difficulties

Current situation

Unions and employee associations

Method of hiring, transfer, upgrading, demoting, and discharging

Job classification and wage rate setting

Method of payment

Working conditions

Note: Also, if possible, evaluate the effectiveness of the company's strategic planning in the past, and its present planning sophistication and data base.

NOTE

1 Robert Townsend, *Up the Organization*, Knopf, New York, 1970.

REFERENCES

Albert, K. J.: *How to Be Your Own Management Consultant*, McGraw-Hill, New York, 1978.

Dobson, Edward L.: "The Management Audit," *Journal of Management*, vol. 4, 1976, pp. 3–6.

Drucker, Peter F.: *Management: Tasks, Responsibilities, Practices,* Harper & Row, New York, 1974.

————: *The Practice of Management,* Harper & Row, New York, 1954.

"How to Appraise a Management," *The Corporate Director,* vol. 1, no.3, 1951.

Hunt, Alfred: *The Management Consultant,* Ronald, New York, 1977.

Klein, Howard J.: *Other People's Business: A Primer on Management Consultants,* Mason/Charter, New York, 1977.

Kubr, M.: *Management Consulting: A Guide to the Profession,* International Labour Office, Geneva, 1976.

Martindell, Jackson: *The Scientific Appraisal of Management,* Harper & Brothers, New York, 1950.

"New Shape of Management Consulting," *Business Week,* May 21, 1979, pp. 98–104.

Policyholders Service Bureau: *Outline for a Management Audit,* Metropolitan Life Insurance Co., New York, 1947.

St. Thomas, Charles E.: *Practical Business Planning,* American Management Association, New York, 1965.

Wasserman, Paul, and Janice McLean (eds.): *Consultants and Consulting Organizations Directory,* Gale Research Company, Detroit, 1976.

Wolf, William B.: *Management and Consulting,* Cornell University, New York School of Industrial Relations, ILR Publications Division, Ithaca, N.Y., 1978.

7

The Control Cycle

Stephen R. Michael

Professor of Management
University of Massachusetts/Amherst

Footsteps were muffled by the plush rug in the conference room as the members of the Operations Committee trooped in punctually. They sank into the well-padded swivel chairs and rested their arms on the mahogany table after depositing their papers on it. After a bit of good-natured banter among committee members, Joseph Bitters, President of Arcane Gadgets, Incorporated, coughed and called the meeting to order.

"I'd like to depart from the usual format of our meetings by calling upon Ed to report to us the progress on the new plant."

Edward Arnold, Vice President of Engineering, cleared his throat and said, "We've really been making lots of progress. The building is now completely closed in and, if necessary, we can have the plant operational in about six months, provided we get delivery of machinery on time."

"I'm afraid that won't be necessary, Ed. Perhaps you've already heard that Tom [Thomas Ehard, Marketing Vice President] and I have just completed the final step of a review of sales. As you know, sales had been increasing over the years and we kept expanding our production capabilities to match. When we decided to go ahead with the new plant, demand was high and increasing. But in the last few months, sales have reached a plateau and may even decline. It looks now as if we will not need the new plant. Our problem this morning is to decide exactly what we're going to do."

Investigation of this situation would have disclosed that Arcane Gadgets had done two quite different things which were responsible for its predicament. The company's executives had prepared a detailed and meticulous plan for the construction and equipping of the new plant. But they had done little or no planning nor had they taken related control measures to assure themselves of the increased demand which they expected to supply from the new plant!

The fictionalized incident with which this chapter begins has its counterpart in real life quite often. Firms frequently find themselves overwhelmed by unexpected events. More often than not, a contributing factor is the lack of, or the presence of inadequate, controls.

Of course, there are many factors beyond the control of managers which have both positive and negative consequences for a firm. It is difficult not to turn a profit in an extended sellers' market and much harder to survive in a buyers' market. Sudden, unforeseeable changes in the economic, political, and social environment can play havoc with even well-laid plans and controls. But the absence of plans and controls can only turn potential trouble into impending disaster.

No doubt the bankruptcy of the Penn Central Railroad could be attributed in considerable part to the difficulties attendant on the merger of its two predecessors, the Pennsylvania Railroad and the New York Central Railroad. The managers of the resulting organization could not even agree on some common corporate purpose and squandered their assets and talents by diversifying into unrelated businesses. But consideration of its routine operations suggests that Penn Central did not have properly functioning controls.

Perhaps the major reason for trouble was that rail transportation is a dying industry. But then how account for prosperous railroads like the Union Pacific? Furthermore, trouble can strike companies in growing industries, too.

Take the case of Pan American Airlines. Pan Am had a number of problems—lack of management depth, a divided hierarchy, low employee morale—but a major one was lack of control. Apparently no serious attempt was made to anticipate competition in its business, and the company tried to deal with its changing economic environment simply by reacting to events. For example, as demand for its airline seats fell, the company did little to find out why but instead went on a cost-cutting spree which reduced supply capabilities at a time when overall demand for air flight was increasing!

Penn Central and Pan Am are only two of many business enterprises during the last decade or so which failed to maintain an appropriate control system to monitor their operations. To the list can be added Lockheed and Rolls Royce, the Ling-Temeo-Vought conglomerate, Chrysler Corporation, the Great Atlantic and Pacific Tea Company, and the New York Telephone Company, without exhausting the number of large candidates. Small firms have had equally big, but less publicized, problems of control.

Nor need we restrict ourselves to business enterprises to find examples of poor organizational controls. Municipalities (New York City), universities (New York University), and other nonbusiness organizations have all experienced difficult times of late as their control systems (to the extent that they had them) failed to permit them to adapt to problems and opportunities in their environment.

The impact of the environment on organizations takes many forms. Cluett, Peabody and Company has had to contend with a long-term trend of men's increasing preference for sport as against dress shirts. Because of the impending curtailment of its natural gas supplies, Public Service Company of New Mexico has begun to plan for the use of solar energy. Gillette Company has brought out a new shampoo aimed specifically at the new unisex market. Such diverse foreign firms as Canadian Tire Corporation, Henkel of Germany, and Industrie Pirelli of Italy are expanding or diversifying into American markets because of lagging domestic economies. Prodded by the decrease in American outer-space activity, Rockwell International Corporation is diversifying into consumer goods to get a better balance between government, industrial, and consumer sales. American firms, as a whole, have not yet responded positively to the opportunities for exporting that have developed because of the declining value of the dollar.

PLANNING AND CONTROL

The words "planning" and "control" have been used in the illustrations above, and their relevance to our subject requires a short discussion.

Planning is a part of the management technique which can be identified as the Control Cycle. The cycle as a process consists of the steps identified as (1) *planning* operations, (2) *directing* implementation of plans, and (3) *evaluating* the results by comparing them to the requirements of the plan. The Control Cycle is essentially a *control mechanism* for bringing about organizational change. The third stage (evaluating), which cycles back into the first (planning), affords the opportunity to take corrective action when the results are not acceptable. Figure 7-1 illustrates the Control Cycle.

The main purpose of the Control Cycle generally is to anticipate changes in the environment which will affect the demand for the organization's products, programs, and services so that the supply capabilities of the organization can be *adapted* to most efficiently and effectively supply the outputs required and to make *innovations* in its products,

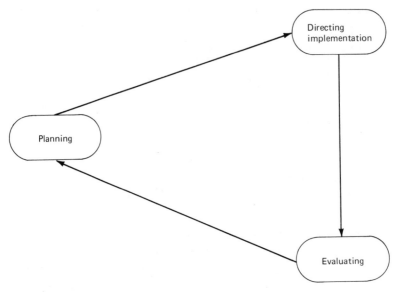

Fig. 7-1   The Control Cycle.

programs, and services when opportunities arise. The anticipation characteristic of the Control Cycle also makes it possible to secure *lead time* in which to adapt and innovate so that the organization's outputs are available when the demand for them materializes.

A final major reason for planning is that it permits the organizational members to develop *mutual expectations* about changes that will occur in the future. The important point here is that people become accustomed to behaving in certain ways; if their behavior has to be changed, there is a need to understand and agree on the changed behaviors in advance.

The rationale behind the concept of control as a mechanism for adjusting the organization to its environment is as follows:

1   Organizations exist to supply the demand for products, programs, and services.

2   Organizations must relate in some way to the environment in which the demand originates.

3   Organizations consist of resources, the most important of which is their personnel, whose efforts must be coordinated and integrated.

4   Organizations need control mechanisms to coordinate and integrate the behavior of organizational members and to adjust the organization's supply and other responses to the economic, political, and social demands made upon it by its environment.

In its simplest version, control is described as managerial behavior which consists of setting an objective, measuring and comparing the work accomplished with the targeted objective, and taking corrective action if the accomplishment is deemed inadequate (negative feedback). Figure 7-2 illustrates this sequence.

FEEDFORWARD VERSUS FEEDBACK CONTROL

During the last decade or so, however, a distinction has been made between *feedback control* and *feedforward control*,[1] and it is possible on the basis of this dichotomy to identify the following varieties of control mechanisms:

1 *Homeostatic feedback control*—maintaining a steady or unchanging state of affairs on the basis of interim results

2 *Adaptive feedback control*—adjusting organizational operations to changes in the environment on the basis of interim results

3 *Internal feedback control*—adjusting organizational operations on a short-term basis in advance of actual deviation of results from objectives on the basis of *intra*organizational information about changes in the environment

4 *External feedforward control*—adjusting organizational operations on a long-term basis in advance of actual deviation of results on the basis of *extra*organizational information about changes in the environment

These models will now be discussed in some detail to indicate precisely how the Control Cycle operates in the total pattern of organizational controls. Suffice it to say at this point that internal feedforward

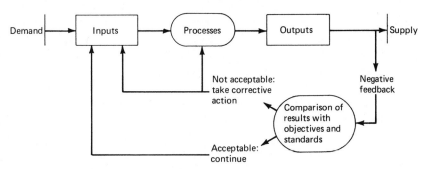

Fig. 7-2   Control of an operational system.

control is essentially short-range planning and external feedforward control is long-range planning.

Homeostatic Feedback Control

The most basic control system is homeostatic in nature. That is, it is a *steady state system,* one in which we want the result to be constant or to fluctuate only within predetermined limits. Two illustrations of such systems come readily to mind. One is the ability of the human body to maintain a steady body heat of 98.6 degrees. If the body temperature drops, the heart pumps blood faster; if the body temperature increases, sweat glands moisten the body to cool it off. The other example is the governor on an engine which increases or decreases fuel input as the engine loses or gains momentum.

Figure 7-2 also illustrates the homeostatic feedback control system which can be used to govern organizational operations. Perhaps the first thing to note is that it is, on balance, a closed system. Only limited information is available ordinarily. This information consists of communication from the environment essentially indicating the state of the environment *at that time.* The indicators conveying this information, however, are entirely within the system. Some of these indicators consist of purchase orders (demand) and of information concerning the organization's ability to supply the demand. For example, information concerning the inability of the system to supply the demand is considered unfavorable or negative in character and is called negative feedback.

Feedback means after the fact; in this case it means that we know that the system is not supplying the demand or cannot supply the demand at the time that demands are made upon it. In effect the control action is a *reaction.* It reacts to the present unfavorable situation—it is a *real time* system—and there is a *time lag* between discovering that the system is in an undesirable condition and taking corrective action. Time lag generally is not a problem so long as the system is responsive and able to correct deviation from standard within a reasonable period of time.

The homeostatic feedback control system is simple, and it can be efficient and effective for certain kinds of situations. One obvious example, in addition to those given above, is a "Mom and Pop" grocery store. Both merchandise and demand come in from the environment. "Mom and Pop" go through certain processes in retailing the merchandise. In terms of outputs and results, they keep a watch on their inventory and the level of sales. As stocks are depleted they reorder; if the level of sales falls below an acceptable level—one which gives them an adequate living—they may treat their customers with greater courtesy, place a small ad in the local newspaper, and perhaps have special sales. If the demand for merchandise exceeds the normal supply, they simply cannot handle it and lose sales. The business stays in a state of *static equilibrium* overall. Family-owned firms are often managed in this fashion.

Some specific operations in organizations are controlled by use of homeostatic systems. One such is the maintenance of existing policies and procedures. Managerial concern is to enforce them and to take corrective action whenever there are deviations from them. The formats of management information systems—for example, accounting systems—also are controlled homeostatically. Variations in accounting practices and reports would render the systems useless and therefore are not readily tolerated. Another operation under homeostatic control is the quality control function. The reason, of course, is that ordinarily neither excessive nor inadequate quality is desirable.

Adaptive Feedback Control

Whenever there is a need to continually adapt an organization or some part of it to its environment, however, a homeostatic control system is inappropriate. Then managers may have recourse to an *adaptive feedback control system.* The essential difference is that instead of attempting to maintain a static equilibrium by adjusting demand to supply as in the "Mom and Pop" grocery, the adaptive system is designed to adjust the supply to demand, in effect, to maintain a *dynamic equilibrium.* Figure 7-3 illustrates an adaptive feedback control system.

Whereas the homeostatic system utilizes only negative feedback, the adaptive system depends upon both negative and positive feedback. As

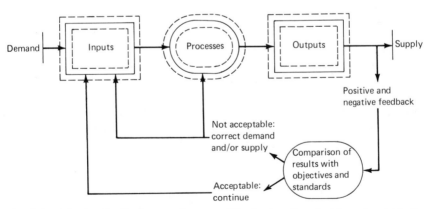

Fig. 7-3 Adaptive feedback control system. The broken lines inside and outside the system components indicate that the system parameters can decrease or increase, respectively, in response to feedback.

negative feedback provides information which is unfavorable for the organization, so positive feedback provides information which is favorable for the organization. A note about meanings of these terms is in order here. In a homeostatic system, any information reporting a deviation from the standard is called negative feedback. However, for an adaptive system, negative feedback is defined as information which reports a decrease in demand given established supply capabilities or the inability of the system to function at the existing level in the presence of demand adequate to take normal supplies. Conversely, positive feedback is any information which reports an increase in demand over the existing level of supply or an increase in supply capabilities for which demand can be promoted. The consequences of acting upon each kind of feedback are quite different. The results of properly reacting to negative feedback are reduced supply capabilities or a return to a previously existing level. The results of properly reacting to positive feedback are increased supply capabilities or increased demand to take up idle capacity.

The use of negative feedback only in a homeostatic system to maintain an organization in a steady state—versus the use of both negative and positive feedback in the adaptive feedback system to adjust its supply capabilities to demand or demand to supply capabilities—constitutes the essential difference between the two kinds of controls. This means that adaptive controls also operate in what is basically a closed system, that adaptive controls are also reactive in nature, that they also operate in present or real time, and that there is still a time lag between the receipt of positive or negative feedback and the taking of corrective action.

This control technique makes it possible to adapt the organization by changing its boundaries or parameters. As negative feedback is received (for example, if demand is decreasing), managers recognize that they may have to lay off workers, reduce purchases of raw or semifinished materials, close down fabrication departments and assembly lines, and take other similar actions with regard to operational factors if they cannot reverse the trend in demand. Conversely, as positive feedback is received (that is, if demand is increasing), additional workers are hired, purchases of raw or semifinished materials are increased, and additional fabrication and assembly lines are activated or established.

The ability of managers to function with an adaptive feedback control system is largely a function of (1) the production of standardized products, programs, or services and (2) a mildly fluctuating if not completely stable environment. These two factors enable the managers to master both the subtle and gross aspects of their operations and to react to changes in demand seasonally or annually. Gasoline station operators know, for example, that demand for gasoline increases every summer.

Hotel and motel operators expect crowds on holidays. Butchers know that people eat more, and more expensive cuts of, meat on weekends. Experience also indicates whether the long-term trend in demand for products is increasing, stable, or decreasing. The demand for refrigerators will probably continue indefinitely and the market is quite stable, whereas the demand for color television is still increasing.

It is possible, then, to control an organization relying upon an adaptive feedback system to provide standardized outputs in a relatively stable environment with predictable fluctuations. The major difficulty is that the organization must experience something before it can react to it. It is difficult or impossible under such a system to anticipate unexpected changes in the environment that trigger unexpected changes in demand for established products or to determine potential demand for new products or new uses for old products. Unable to predict what is unpredictable in such a system, the managers are generally faced with an unreasonable time lag during which they must frantically attempt to change the capabilities of the organization. If demand has dropped suddenly, they are stuck with an excess of resources which drive up costs; if demand has increased suddenly, revenues are lost unless sales can be back-ordered or filled from inventory. Whether costs go up or revenues down—or both—the effects on profit and/or survival quickly become obvious for an organization.

Feedforward Control and the Control Cycle

To overcome the difficulties described above, a control system is needed which helps to anticipate changes in demand. Such a system should provide information from the environment in advance so that this lead time can be utilized to change the organization's capabilities in time to cope with the altered demand for its outputs. We can call such a control mechanism a *feedforward control system.*

Its operation can be seen most clearly by considering the ubiquitous American central heating system. At first sight it resembles a homeostatic control system in that it appears to have a set standard for output. However, the standard can be changed easily. During the day the thermostat is set at the temperature that is comfortable to move around in; at night it is usually turned down a few degrees. The setting may also be changed to cope with considerable changes in outside temperature or to meet different demands for comfort at any time. Hence, the central heating system is really an adaptive feedback control system.

It works well as such because typically it is designed to cope with the maximum demands made upon it—demands which are fairly predictable based upon experience. Suppose, however, that because of unusual climatic changes the demands upon the system begin to fluctuate excessively and unpredictably and the system cannot respond within the normal time lag. How can we cope with such a situation?

One solution would be to put a temperature sensor *outside* the building in which the heating system is operating. Such an arrangement would constitute an early warning system. This sensor would pick up temperature changes in the environment before their full impacts were felt inside the building. This information could, for example, be used to activate the furnace to build up heat in anticipation of a great drop in temperature. The system would now be able to cope much better with unanticipated changes in demand. We would have changed the heating system from an adaptive feedback control to a feedforward control system.

In the same way we can change an organizational adaptive feedback control system into a feedforward control system; all we need is a control technique which includes the equivalent of an environmental sensor.

This technique is the Control Cycle which consists of the processes of planning operations, directing the implementation of plans, and evaluating the results.

More specifically, planning consists of a number of steps. The most important ones for our present discussion are: (1) *scanning and assessing the environment* to find out in what possible ways it will change; (2) using that information to *forecast demand* for products, programs, and services, to see how the demand will change; (3) *developing strategies* which will most efficiently make the transition to the new parameters of the organization so the altered demand can be supplied; and (4) *establishing standards and objectives* for the new levels of achievement.

Directing the implementation of plans means that those responsible for approving plans also must see to it that the necessary changes in organizational capabilities are made. This is done by communicating requirements of the plan, authorizing and or approving actions and resource commitments, and requiring subordinates to report back as they implement the plan.

Evaluating entails measuring results, comparing results with standards and objectives set in the plan, and taking corrective action when unacceptable deviations from standards and objectives occur.

In discussing homeostatic feedback and adaptive feedback systems, there was the implicit assumption that, in terms of any one area of organizational jurisdiction, they are mutually exclusive ways of controlling organizational operations. Either the one or the other is used. The case is different with respect to adaptive feedback control and feedforward control systems. Instead of being alternatives, they are complementarities. Adaptive feedback controls can be utilized alone, but feedforward controls are *added to* adaptive feedback controls. Figure 7-4 illustrates the superimposition of feedforward onto feedback controls.

There are a number of reasons for the superimposition. One reason is that the plans from the Control Cycle—the feedforward system—*do not include all the information* necessary to manage all organizational operations. Plans are concerned primarily with how operations will *differ* this year from last. Except as noted in the plans, policies and procedures will not change from one cycle of control to the next. For example, if the economic order quantity formula is used to control inventory, that formula will continue to be used and no mention need be made of it in the plan. However, the plan may call for increasing the *level* of the inventory because of expected increases in demand.

Another reason for separation of the two control systems is that they cover different kinds of operations—one present-oriented and the other future-oriented. Planning and the rest of the Control Cycle typically are the ultimate concern of higher authority. They must sanction changes in

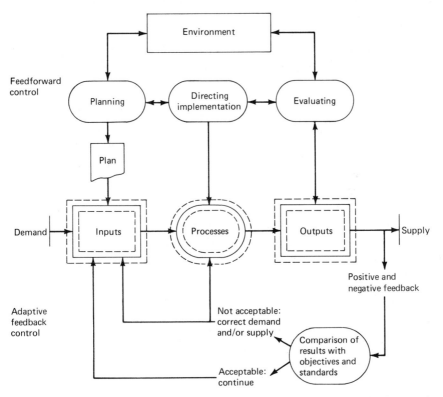

Fig. 7-4 Feedforward control system superimposed upon adaptive feedback control system.

the level of operations and assure themselves that the changes are made. Although lower levels of authority have contributed toward the establishment of plans, they are concerned primarily with implementing plans. Indeed, as we shall see, participation is useful and necessary because it leads to great efficiency and effectiveness in organizational operations. As higher authority is responsible for the feedforward controls—the Control Cycle—so lower-level participants in the organization are responsible for feedback controls. Whenever a new plan is approved, they substitute, for example, the new standards for the old and then control operations with feedback.

Finally, there are differences in how accurately the two kinds of controls can determine the amount of change required at some point. Feedforward control involves *estimates* only of the required change, since the future cannot be predicted accurately. Therefore, the most that can be done with feedforward control is to reduce the future gap between desirable and actual operations. To the extent possible, the remaining gap is closed by the use of feedback control when the results are in.

A short review of how the feedback and feedforward systems work should show that they are complementary. The planning process results in a plan which becomes an input into the feedback system and is the basis for making changes in the level of resources, in processes (production, marketing, research and development, and other functions), and in other organizational matters. Higher-level authority directs and monitors activities that implement the plan. As outputs are produced they are measured and compared to the standards established in the plan. If deviations from plan are within acceptable limits, operations continue and no corrective actions are taken. However, if unacceptable deviations are discovered, one or both of two kinds of action are taken. If an unacceptable deviation is found to be caused by faulty implementation of the plan or of a routine operation—perhaps inadequate training of new workers—the corrective action is taken in the feedback system by the managers in charge of operations. However, if unacceptable results appear to be caused by a changing environment or a faulty plan—perhaps an overoptimistic forecast of demand—the corrective action is taken by the planners and generally the plan is partially or wholly revised.

As already noted, feedforward control can take two forms, internal and external.

Internal Feedforward Control—Short-Range Planning

Internal feedforward control is based upon the use of information already available to the organization. That is, in the normal course of events, in the procurement of resources and in the selling of its outputs, the organization gathers and accumulates data. The data is a by-product of its operations. For example, the organization continually gets information about the ability of its vendors to deliver inventory materials and senses trends in demand for its products as it processes sales orders.

Thus, it is not necessary to await the full, final impact of delayed deliveries of raw materials—or the buildup of sales orders beyond the supply capabilities of the organization—as is the case in using only adaptive feedback control. Instead, as information about the organization's input and output situations suggests constraints and opportunities, that information is fed forward so that corrective action can be taken with respect to operations or to established standards and objectives. Hence, if a strike at a vendor will postpone deliveries of raw materials, alternative sources of supply can be canvassed. If alternative vendors cannot supply, then production schedules can be changed and allied remedial action taken in advance.

Annual budgeting, as practiced in large numbers of organizations, is perhaps the best, all-inclusive example of internal feedforward control. In the absence of a budget, the expense report constitutes an adaptive feedback control. When expenses seem to be getting out of line, cost-cutting measures are taken. Sometimes, of course, it is too late. The annual budget reduces the problem to a very great extent. Expenditures are planned and the budgeted amounts become the standards for costs. Although there are departures from the standards established in the budget, the variances are less than they would be without the influence of the predetermined benchmarks. The periodic budget-and-expense report combines the feedforward and feedback information managers need to control operations in the short term.

But an annual budget and the other planning activities associated with it have a limited time frame. They amount to short-range planning. Infinitely superior to adaptive feedback control, internal feedforward control still has the inherent deficiency of a short-range perspective.

External Feedforward Control—Long-Range Planning

External feedforward control is the answer to this deficiency. The essential difference is this: whereas in internal feedforward the organization relies upon information already available internally, in external feedforward the organization deliberately seeks information in the external environment. For example, it is possible to detect trends in the marketplace on the basis of sales orders placed with the organization. But such information has only a short-term validity, since no cause can be imputed to the detected trend. However, by carefully scanning the external environment, the organization may discover any one or more of a variety of events which are influencing the changes in sales: increases in personal disposable income, long-term changes in the region's population, switches in competitors' strategies, and the like. By carefully assessing such environmental information, the organization can make long-range projections of the consequences of events and trends in the external environment. "Long-range," of course, will mean different periods in different industries. The demand for refrigerators can be projected for a longer period of time than the demand for video-cassette recorders. Depending upon the industry, the range of projections may be from a few years to a few decades.

On the basis of information secured about changes in the environment—secured through routine transactions in the internal feedforward system or through specific scanning of the environment via the external feedforward system—operational standards and/or organizational objectives are modified in advance of the actual impact of the events and trends on the organization.

Unlike homeostatic and adaptive feedback controls, which are mutually incompatible, internal and external feedforward controls are complementary and supplementary. Internal feedforward control may be used alone or in conjunction with external feedforward. The latter, however, is not likely to be used without the former. Either or both, of course, must be coupled to a feedback system of control.

Contrasts in Controls

Table 7-1 summarizes the characteristics of the four kinds of management control systems described above: homeostatic feedback, adaptive feedback, internal feedforward, and external feedforward. The essential differences are as follows. The homeostatic approach is used to control operations we do not want changed. The adaptive feedback system is used to control situations where we expect changes in demand which can be accommodated in terms of the organization's past or present experience. The feedforward system is used to anticipate and prepare for changes in the environment which require longer lead time to bring about changes and demands for the organization's products, programs, and services. Internal feedforward control (short-range planning) is used when managers employ a short-time perspective; external feedforward (long-range planning) is used, in addition to internal feedforward, when managers want to utilize an optimum time perspective, often three to five years. Feedforward control is superimposed upon the adaptive feedback system because its major concern is changes, rather than the details of all operations.

Table 7-1 Comparison of Control Systems

Type of control system	System parameters		System information boundary		Nature of information		Control actions		Time frame		Timeliness	
	Fixed	Flexible	Closed	Open	Negative	Positive	Reaction	Anticipation	Real time	Future time	Time lag	Lead time
Feedback:												
Homeostatic	X		X		X		X		X		X	
Adaptive		X	X		X	X	X		X		X	
Feedforward (Control Cycle):												
Internal (short-range planning)		X		X	X	X		X		X		X
External (long-range planning)		X		X	X	X		X		X		X

265

Since it would appear that feedforward control is better able to adjust the organization to its environment, we might well ask why managers do not use it always in conjunction with one of the two feedback alternatives. The first point to note is that adaptive feedback controls are costlier than homeostatic feedback controls, while feedforward controls have higher costs than adaptive feedback. The reason for higher costs is that adapting or changing the organization always involves additional costs. Furthermore, feedforward control entails a cost in addition to the cost of feedback control. Unless additional benefits can be expected with a high probability of occurrence, there will be a tendency not to utilize feedforward control.

For this reason, many organizations prefer to remain whatever size they are by using homeostatic control and avoiding additional costs. The choice may also be a value preference; small may be seen as "beautiful," especially in the case of a family-owned firm. Also, in some specific organizational operations stability—such as constant heat in an oven, or the maintenance of established policies and procedures—may be a necessity, and homeostatic control will be used in such situations.

However, homeostatic controls may be dangerous for survival of an organization as a totality if the environment is dynamic or turbulent. Organizations that rely upon adaptive controls can more easily bring about an equilibrium between demand and supply and therefore a better balance between revenues and expenses. Consequently they perform better than organizations that rely upon homeostatic controls. That is one reason why supermarket chains have displaced most of the "Mom and Pop" grocery stores.

Feedforward controls exemplified by the Control Cycle are, as already noted, an incremental cost when they are added to an adaptive feedback system. They are an added cost and an added burden of activity—visibly so, as they compete for a manager's time. It is often said that operations drive out planning. What is meant is that the real time demands of the adaptive feedback system governing routine operations, which require immediate attention when anything goes wrong, take time away from planning the feedforward control system. All of this merely illustrates the simple fact that a feedforward system requires an additional investment of money and time. Only the benefits secured from anticipating environmental, and therefore organizational, change can justify the cost.

Going back to the incident with which this chapter opened, we can see that Arcane Gadgets, Incorporated, was using the two basic models of control we have described. For the building of a new plant, its managers utilized feedforward control by planning, directing the implementation of the plans, and evaluating the results such as cost, deadline dates, and other criteria of results for building a new plant. But to control the relationship between demand and supply for the products, they were relying on adaptive feedback controls, and they got the message too late.

What some of the reports of organizational responses to challenges in the environment cited above do not show is how the Control Cycle can be utilized to mobilize the organization to deal with its environment. That becomes the subject matter of what follows.

BUREAUCRATIZATION AND INNOVATION

At the beginning of this chapter we stated certain assumptions about the way an organization relates to its environment. We will now elaborate on this process of accommodation. Organizations are founded and survive because they serve a purpose in the larger environment. That environment is a cauldron of demands, actual and potential, to which an organization responds by fulfilling some of the demands. The provision of products, programs, and services by an organization to its environment we call, in total, the organizational "mission." The firm's outputs are the specific manifestations of its mission. In return for its outputs, the organization receives money and other compensations and the organization is then able to satisfy what are termed organizational "needs." They include, for example, profitability and market share (all to be discussed in detail later), and satisfaction of these needs makes it possible for the organization to survive and prosper.

If nothing were ever to change, managing an organization would be a fairly simple process and most managers could go fishing or golfing most afternoons. But in every organization there are two impersonal processes at work which continually bring about change. These are *bureaucratization* (or formalization of tasks and relationships to standardize intermediate and final outputs) and *innovation* (or deliberate attempts to change tasks and relationships so as to change intermediate or final outputs).

Bureaucratization

Like individual human beings, organizations as collections of people learn to behave in certain ways. We call such organizationally induced habitual behavior "structure." Its most obvious aspects are the jobs or roles which are depicted in organization charts. Resulting from the division of labor, jobs or roles limit the range of behavior of organizational members so that each becomes specialized and proficient through such limitation. In addition, organizational norms—mission, objective, policies, procedures, standards, and rules—specify how tasks are to be carried out and also specify some of the relationships between role incumbents.

So far bureaucratization or formalization would appear to dampen the possibility of change in operations and that is one of its major functions. Bureaucratization makes for predictability. Nothing works perfectly, however, and at least two factors conspire to prevent perfection. One is that organizational members learn to do their work better over time. Skills improve and shortcuts in task completion are found. These deviations eventually are incorporated into job descriptions and organizational norms, thus causing formal change. Despite such changes, however, the net effect of bureaucratization is to standardize operations.

The second factor impairing standardization is that organizational members quit, retire, die, or are fired. Turnover has certain implications. Human beings are imperfect substitutes for one another; thus personnel replacements cause considerable change in jobs and norms, initially due to lack of experience and later because of personal inclinations. Despite this factor also, however, new personnel hired today are put to work with more efficient procedures and methods than those hired yesterday.

Like people, organizations learn to do things better over time. Of course, it is people who embody the skills at any point in time. But the skills are really just the counterpart of the knowledge that accrues to the organization through the experiences of its members. Such knowledge is embodied in the structure of the organization. What to do and how to do it are encapsulated in the organizational norms. As defined earlier, these include the mission, objectives, policies, procedures, standards, and rules which govern the behavior of organizational members. As personnel have experience with their tasks, they develop improved skills and find more efficient and effective ways to accomplish them. These improved procedures replace earlier, less efficient ones.

The organization also learns how to divide the work to be done at a given volume among organizational members. Changes in the division of labor also occur. As output increases, the additional volume of work is subdivided, with each organizational member assigned a smaller segment of the total task as long as worker motivation is not impaired seriously. Up to some point, such additional subdivision results in additional output per labor hour.

A final factor which brings about change in the bureaucratization of routine operations is the substitution of some resources for others. The obvious substitution is machinery for labor but can include replacement of one raw or semifinished material by another.

The totality of what an organization learns about the production of its outputs is referred to as the *experience curve,* depicted in Figure 7-5. It has certain predictable qualities; for example, each time volume of output doubles, costs can be reduced 20 to 30 percent.[2]

Since learning is a function of feedback, we should not be surprised to discover that the bureaucratization or formalization of an organization is carried out largely under the aegis of adaptive feedback controls. As organizational members engage in their tasks, they improve their skills as a consequence of seeing the results of their efforts. As new techniques and methods are tried and found to improve production, they are incorporated in policies and procedures. As demand increases and supply capabilities are expanded, the division of labor becomes more specialized and is reflected in the organization chart. And to achieve economies of scale and otherwise reduce costs, resource substitution takes place, with changes in plant and equipment and input materials.[3]

Thus we see, overall, that even as an organization increasingly becomes more structured and routinized, it nevertheless appears to be undergoing fairly constant change so long as environmental demands fluctuate and such changing demands can be accommodated to some degree by adaptive feedback controls. Indeed, there will always be a need for feedback controls because it is simply impossible to anticipate and predict everything that can happen to an organization.

On the other hand, it would be foolish not to anticipate all that can be predicted with some degree of certainty. For example, it is possible to anticipate changes in the demand for a product in terms of the *product life cycle* (PLC) concept—which shows that products typically go through various stages based upon changes in demand—and then to anticipate cost changes in the different stages. Figure 7-6 illustrates the PLC. Such anticipation should remind the planners and other managers that changes in demand present opportunities for innovation in production. Reduced costs as volume increases is not at all an automatic result but is the consequence of rational management, given the opportunities.

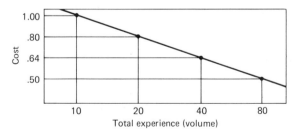

Fig. 7-5 The experience curve (on a log-log scale). Copyright Bruce D. Henderson, 1974. Reproduced by special permission.

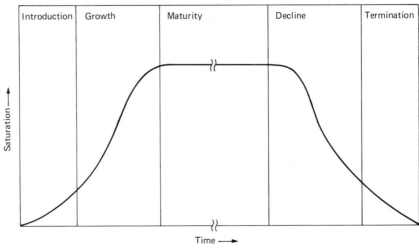

| Introduction | Growth | Maturity | Decline | Termination |

Fig. 7-6. The product life cycle.

Innovation and the Control Cycle

The fact that much of the change in demand for outputs can be anticipated makes the Control Cycle a desirable feedforward system to foster
innovation. This is equally true of (1) adjusting the supply capabilities
for existing products and (2) developing new products which have a
potential demand in the marketplace.

In the final analysis, the Control Cycle as a feedforward system is
superior to adaptive feedback controls only because it permits a better
equation between the demand and supply for the outputs of an organization. For it is a *continuous* process of adjusting the organization to its
environment through *anticipation* of changes and the affording of lead
time to make the necessary changes in resource quantities and mixes to
meet altered requirements. The alternative is the time lag inherent in
feedback controls which can result in idle resources until supply capabilities are reduced to equal decreased demand or lost revenues, or until
supply capabilities are increased to take care of increased demand.

Our emphasis upon demand and supply might suggest that production facilities are the only or primary object in planning the enterprise's
future and controlling events as they unfold. The production function
may indeed be the focal point of planning if only because the resources
loom large in terms of the firm's total assets. They are also highly visible.
Product demand in the form of sales orders are also conspicuous by their
presence and require some production planning and scheduling to produce the supply.

Less visible but equally important is the provision of financial resources for capital investments and operational expenses. The peaking of outlays for capital budget items and the steady drain of payments for production inputs contrast with the irregular receipt of revenues from sales. Therefore, cash flows must be anticipated and plans made to borrow on short- and long-term bases to cover financial needs.

Demand for the company's products does not engender itself, so it must also be planned. Sales, new product development, market research, distribution, and other marketing activities must be carefully thought out. Research and development, manpower planning, engineering, and public relations are other functions that must be planned to cope with the possible impacts of the environment on the different activities of the firm. Ideally, the Control Cycle should cover all activities of the organization.

KINDS OF PLANS

Like most things in this world, plans can be categorized. The three types can be described in terms of *continuity, time duration,* and *certainty of use.*

Continuity

Continuity suggests (1) single-use plans and (2) cyclical plans. *Single-use plans,* as the name clearly suggests, are used to achieve some specific, limited objective such as the building of a plant or the development of a new product. *Cyclical plans,* by contrast, are used to anticipate and control operations on a continuing basis. Instead of being tied to discrete units such as the building of a plant, cyclical plans are related to successive time periods. Most of this discussion is geared to an exposition of cyclical plans because they cover the essentials of single-use plans also.

Time Duration

Time duration—short-range versus long-range plans—applies only to cyclical planning. Short-range plans (the product of internal feedforward control) typically cover one year of operations, while long-range plans (the product of external feedforward control) may cover three, five, ten, or more years, depending upon the industry and its environment. The three- or five-year plan generally consists of that many one-year plans, each successive year's plan somewhat less concrete because of the greater uncertainty involved in the longer-term future. Each year the expired plan is dropped, the remainder are updated, and an additional year's plan is tacked on at the end. Figure 7-7 shows a five-year

Five-Year Plan				
Year 1	Year 2	Year 3	Year 4	Year 5
—	—	—	—	—
—	—	—	—	—
—	—	—	—	—
—	—	—	—	—
—	—	—	—	—
—	—	—	—	—
—	—	—	—	—
—	—	—	—	—
—	—	—	—	—
—	—	—	—	—

Fig. 7-7 A composite five-year plan. SOURCE: Stephen R. Michael and Halsey R. Jones, *Organizational Management,* Intext Educational Publishers, New York, 1973, p. 361. Reproduced by special permission of copyright holder, Harper & Row, Publishers, Incorporated.

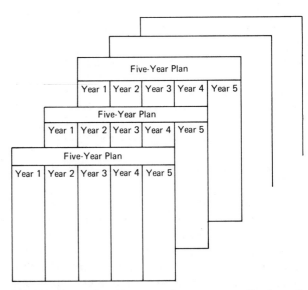

Fig. 7-8 Successive five-year plans. SOURCE: Stephen R. Michael and Halsey R. Jones, *Organizational Management,* Intext Educational Publishers, New York, 1973, p. 361. Reproduced by special permission of copyright holder, Harper & Row, Publishers, Incorporated.

plan as a composite of one-year plans. Figure 7-8 shows successive five-year plans, indicating the dropping and adding of one-year plans.

Certainty of Use

With respect to certainty of use, plans are categorized either as definite or contingent. *Definite plans* are those which managers expect to implement because of an expected state of the environment; *contingent plans* are to be used if the environment changes to some other state which has a lower probability of occurring than the expected state but which, nevertheless, can occur.

THE PROCESS OF PLANNING

Planning is a process which also has a structure and a product. The *process* is a bundle of activities consisting essentially of gathering and evaluating various kinds of information and making decisions related to each of the activities. *Structure* is the division *of* labor which describes the allocation of duties and responsibilities for the planning activities among the organization's personnel. The *plan* is the output *or* product of the planning process.

The process of planning as it unfolds here will appear relatively simple when compared to ongoing planning activities in any one organization. Indeed, there will be differences as well as similarities in planning activities in comparing any two organizations.

The reasons for the differences are not hard to find. First of all, management's perception of the need for the various kinds of planning activities will vary and more emphasis will be put upon some activities than others. For example, budgeting may be considered the most important planning activity in one firm, and only activities required to prepare a budget will be carried out. In addition, management's allocation of planning duties and responsibilities will vary as organizational structure varies and will also be influenced by its perceptions of planning abilities and interests in organizational members. In the former case, functional as against product organization of the firm will affect the division of planning labor. In the latter case, experience with the planning activities of managers may determine whether planning will be decentralized to all managers or centralized in top management, just to indicate the two extreme choices available.

Figure 7-9 is a preview of the activities or stages in the planning process. The sequence assumes cyclical planning. In the event that the product is to be a single-use plan, the review of the previous plan is dropped.

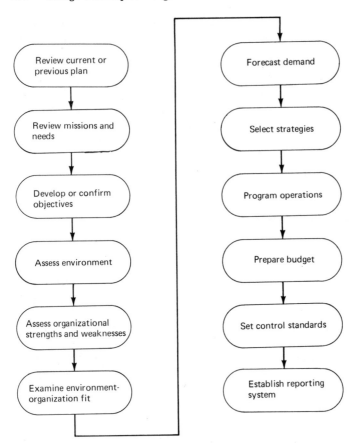

Fig. 7-9 Stages in the planning process. Activities that parallel the planning process: communication, coordination. SOURCE: Adapted from Stephen R. Michael and Halsey R. Jones, *Organizational Management,* Intext Educational Publishers, 1973, p. 363. Reproduced by special permission of copyright holder, Harper & Row, Publishers, Incorporated.

This sequence is not meant to be rigid. Rather, it is a series of activities in approximately correct chronological order. The situation confronted may permit or require the planner to change the sequence, engage in two or more stages simultaneously, or add or delete some activities. Furthermore, work at one stage may require references to changes in earlier stages, anticipation of later stages, or even recycling a series of activities. This is the familiar effect of feedback on ongoing activities.

There will also be a lot of *parallel* activity. That is, planning will be going on more or less simultaneously at different hierarchical levels of the organization and in all organizational units at any one level, such as departments, at the same time.

We move now to a consideration of the stages in the planning process. Because the Control Cycle is intended to be a continuous process, we will elaborate on planning as the preparation of cyclical rather than single-use plans.

Review Current or Previous Plan

The first step in the planning process will be a review of the previous or present plan. The reason for beginning at this point is that there is bound to be considerable continuity and carry-over from one cyclical plan to the next. Although activities are scheduled by the calendar, organizational operations and events do not fit such schedules perfectly or even very well. As a result, the production of a batch of goods or the building of a plant may overlap from one planning period to another.

Another reason for review of the present or previous plan is that we can only reap the full benefits of the Control Cycle by including in future plans the lessons we have learned (feedback) from implementing past or present plans. We may have done a poor job of communicating in the past, or have failed to measure work done correctly, or have been overly optimistic in thinking how much we could accomplish in a certain period of time. How important such learning is will become clearer in the discussion of the evaluating process in subsequent considerations.

Review Organizational Mission and Needs

Organizational mission and needs, respectively, involve what the organization is trying to do—that is, the reason for its existence—and what organizational requirements must be met for it to survive and fulfill or carry on its mission.

With respect to the mission, has it changed? Should it be changed? In what ways? To what extent? For example in the late 1960s and early 1970s, many organizations had changed from single or limited missions tied to one or a very few industries to multifaceted missions in many industries which earned them the name of "conglomerates." Others integrated vertically, forward or backward, so as to give them some control over a segment of an "upstream" or "downstream" industry—for instance, a paper manufacturing company bought forests so that it would not have to buy wood pulp on the open market. Similarly, divisions and departments in a company can review and change their missions. For example, should the administrative division expand its service to the rest of the firm by offering dictating/transcribing services over the telephone?

Organizational needs are satisfied by setting objectives which if achieved will enable the organization to survive. For example, a company may set a profitability objective of 15 percent after taxes. If achieved, its financial survival will be reasonably well assured. As described by Peter Drucker in *The Practice of Management,* organizational needs and their objectives include profitability, innovation, productivity, physical and financial resources, market standing, manager performance and development, worker performance and attitude, and public responsibility.[4] As a result of complete or partial implementation of previous or present plans, some organizational needs may have been satisfied to a greater extent than others. For example, previous plans may have included the objective of providing backstops for all positions above the level of first-line supervisors to meet the need for manager performance and development. If the objective has been achieved, attention may shift to some other aspect of management development, or it may be possible to emphasize other objectives to a greater extent.

Develop or Confirm Objectives

In the light of achievements accomplished through earlier plans and having reviewed the organizational mission and needs, it is possible realistically to begin to confirm established *objectives* and/or to develop new ones. Attention needs to be directed to two concerns at this point. One is to establish priorities among objectives which will satisfy the most pressing organizational needs in the correct order. This is necessary because organizational needs change in nature and intensity over time. It is also necessary because the organization cannot do everything at once and must state its priorities.

The other major concern is possible conflicts among objectives. Conflicting objectives lead to what is called "suboptimization." This means that if we attempt to maximize the achievement of an objective like market standing, we may tend to minimize the achievement of another objective like productivity. To illustrate further, one way to maximize market standing is to have a full line of products. The line will include some products which sell in small quantities, and this will mean smaller production runs and higher unit costs. Organizational units within the firms have exactly the same problems of priorities and optimization.

Assess Environment

The external environment in which an organization exists sets the boundaries for its activities. Demand for its products, programs, and services originates in that environment, as do demands for various other kinds of responses. The internal environment of the organization—the nature and quality of its structure, processes, and behaviors—determines how well it can respond to challenges by supplying economic outputs and fulfilling political and social obligations laid upon it.

In short, the external environment poses opportunities and problems and the organization exhibits strengths and weaknesses. The match between these two sets of factors determines the viability of the organization.

Scanning and assessing the external environment should yield information in at least three categories:

1 Potential demand for *existing* products, programs, and services

2 Opportunities for developing and marketing *new* products, programs, and services

3 Identification and understanding of events and trends that are, or could become, beneficial or troublesome for the organization and its outputs

From the perspective of a business enterprise, the external environment can be viewed as having economic, political, and social components.

The *economic* component of the environment has the most direct and immediate impact on the firm, and its assessment requires very special consideration. The central datum in the economic sphere is the gross national product (GNP). Forecasts of changing levels of GNP are made by the federal government, nonbusiness organizations such as the National Planning Association and private universities, and larger organizations for their own use. From a business standpoint, the major ultimate impact of GNP is on the standard of living of consumers. Increases or decreases in GNP not only affect most consumers, but may also affect them disproportionately. Hence, consumption patterns may change.

The availability of resources in the so-called factor markets is also an important aspect of the economic environment. The factor market is focused on the major inputs into business activity: investment capital, labor, business location, capital equipment and plant, and raw and semi-finished materials. The availability of these factors is crucial for the firm.

Another important consideration from an economic viewpoint is the industry or industries in which the organization operates. Technological advances are the most dynamic part of an industry and have important—sometimes devastating—implications for products, prices, customers, and competitors.

Perhaps the greatest immediate economic impact on a firm is the behavior of competition. Consequently, there are many kinds of information that an organization seeks to find out about its competitors.

These include price changes, plans for expansion, promotional strategies, cost and sales data, product styling, and manufacturing processes. The importance of these kinds of information will vary by industry and organizational characteristics, of course. In a survey of marketing executives reported in 1975, the nature and intensity of competition was seen as the most important environmental influence on marketing strategy in the 1970s.[5]

The *political* component of the external environment can be summarized as the existence of government legislation and policy at national, state, and municipal levels. Typically relevant policies at the national level include monetary, fiscal, antitrust, civil rights, foreign relations, conservation, and labor policies. Policies of state governments concerning such things as sales and inventory taxes, public transportation, incorporation and other related laws governing the legal status of firms will have an impact on the production and distribution of goods within their boundaries. At the municipal level real estate and sales taxes as well as zoning laws will affect the conduct of the business enterprise or its branches.

Society is the all-embracing environment of an organization; although its impact is not always immediate and obvious, its influence can hardly be ignored. Population changes exemplify this. For example, the past 50 years have seen the "birth dearth" of the Depression, the "baby boom" after World War II, and the "baby bust" of the present period. There may be another baby boom in the offing.

Events, trends, and public attitudes will have varying effects upon the futures of organizations. OPEC oil-pricing changes; the relaxation of conventional standards of clothing, morality, and much more; and the opinions of people on a host of contemporary problems such as conservation, product quality, nuclear power, inflation, and performance of the business system illustrate these three kinds of factors which vary in their impact on different industries.[6]

For organizations operating overseas in different countries, the problem of environment is multiplied because of the cultural differences which characterize host nations. The only safe prediction here is that the environment will vary from a little to a lot.

Information about the environment is available from many sources. These include publications such as newspapers, books, and special reports; general, technical, and trade journals; professional and industrial contacts and conferences; consultants; and government documents and organizational personnel—to identify only a few.[7]

From the standpoint of the organization, we should note that the perception of environmental information is diffused among its members. Marketing information is sought most avidly by marketing personnel, technological information by production engineering personnel, and so on. Individuals perceive what affects their jobs most. Position in the hierarchy also affects interest and perception. The higher the position, the more time a person spends in scanning the environment. Also, the more dynamic the environment, the more time will be devoted to scanning. Controllable factors also deserve and get more attention than noncontrollable factors in the environment.[8]

There is one additional, important contingency in this step of the planning process. It is that an organization can make or buy much of the information it needs. Reports on any or all aspects of the environment can be purchased ready-made or on special order from a host of commercial organizations and consultants.

Assess Organizational Strengths and Weaknesses

Assessment of the internal environment has as its objective the identification of the organization's strengths and weaknesses. Analyzing and evaluating the internal environment of the organization should enable planners to highlight its strengths—those functions and activities it has done well in the past—and its weaknesses—those functions and activities that it has not performed well in the past. For example, the production department may have the lowest unit costs in the industry (an obvious strength) but the marketing department seems unable to mount an effective promotion campaign (a very bad weakness). Other findings might include the following examples: personnel may be highly trained and competent or relatively inexperienced; organizational structure may be just right or haphazard in nature; plant and equipment may be up-to-date or obsolete; the normative pattern of the organization—policies, procedures, standards—may be complementary or dysfunctional in its impact on work routines; communications may facilitate or impede cooperative behavior. These are only a few extremes of potential strengths and weaknesses that can be unearthed upon a close look at the organization. One technique for identifying the organization's strengths and weaknesses is to conduct a Management Audit as described in Chapter 6.

Examine Environment-Organization Fit

The next step in planning activity—after looking at the external and internal environment of the organization—is to consider the compatibility of the environmental problems and opportunities on the one hand and the strengths and weaknesses of the organization on the other.

Problems can be solved and opportunities exploited adequately only if there are organizational capabilities that are appropriate. For example, a new product opportunity cannot be followed through easily if the organization has no relevant skills in the production technology, marketing, or customer service necessary for the undertaking. Figure 7-10 illustrates some of the results of an examination of the external and internal environments.

Forecast Demand

The conclusions drawn from the assessment of the environment can be thought of as a series of *premises.* Personal income will continue to increase; consumers will continue to switch from larger to smaller cars; homeowners will cultivate their gardens more and vacation less; these are anticipations of what will occur in the future. The resulting premises become the bases for forecasts. The forecasts represent the anticipated demand for the products, programs, and services of the organization. Generally the forecasts for demand will follow one or some combination of the following patterns:[9]

1 *Horizontal* or constant value, for products with stable markets.

2 *Seasonal* changes for products tied to weather, holiday periods, and other changes which occur during the year.

3 *Cyclical* changes due to long-term, economic fluctuations of varying length and magnitude. Durable products such as major household appliances experience these kinds of changes.

External Environment		
	Problems	Opportunities
Organization — Weaknesses	Company has poor marketing capabilities for consumer goods for which demand is decreasing.	The company lacks experience in R & D contract work for which demand is increasing.
Organization — Strengths	Strong computer capabilities will enable company to meet increased demands of federal government for more information about product characteristics.	Company has improved technological capabilities for producing industrial goods which are in great demand.

Fig. 7-10 The matching of environmental problems and opportunities with organizational strengths and weaknesses.

4 *Trends* toward increasing or decreasing demand, especially notice-able with new products and old declining products, respectively.

Figure 7-11 illustrates the four data patterns. Additionally, forecasts should be made of all political and social trends and expected events that will have a direct or indirect effect upon the organization. For example, what is the probability that Congress will pass restrictive energy legislation?

An organization may be involved with up to three levels of forecasts in planning. They are (1) national indices of economic activity, (2) the demand for the products of the industry, and (3) the demand for the products of the firm.

National Forecast   If it operates in national markets, a company may prepare its own forecasts of national economic activity. Alternatively, it may use forecasts prepared by public and private agencies. The most important national forecast is that of gross national product (GNP), as noted earlier. GNP forecasts are issued by the Department of Commerce, among other organizations.

In addition to GNP, other coincident indicators (factors which correlate directly and immediately with the level of economic activity) include corporate profits, industrial production, the unemployment rate, and help wanted ads. Leading and lagging indicators are also of interest in predicting the national level of economic activity. The former (which tend to foreshadow future economic activity) include business failures data published by Dun and Bradstreet, Inc., and data on new orders

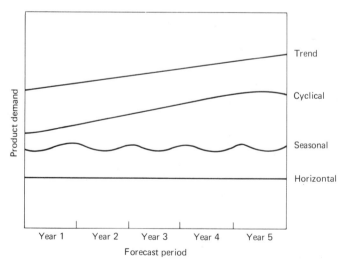

Fig. 7-11   Data patterns in forecasting product demand.

published by the Department of Commerce. The latter (which tend to reflect changes in economic activity some time after the changes take place) include personal income and sales by retail stores. The Department of Commerce publishes both forms of data.

The present and forecasted values of the national economic indicators cited above are used to establish correlations with the industry's and/or the firm's demand. Then the forecasts for national economic activity can be used to extrapolate the demand in the industry or for the firm.

Industry Forecast   For many companies, it is necessary to go from the national level of forecasting to the industry level before reaching the firm's level. Industry forecasts are based largely upon what are called "input-output tables." These show relationships of various industries. The products or outputs of one industry are shown as the raw materials or semifinished input materials of one or more other industries. Figure 7-12 illustrates the use of input-output tables.

The Department of Commmerce and trade associations publish industry forecasts routinely. One problem in using such industry forecasts is that the firm may produce only some of the products identified in an industry. For this and other reasons, it is generally necessary to prepare a special forecast of the sales of specific company products and services.

Company Forecast   Preparation of the company forecast involves consideration of two constraints. One is that there is some minimum level of operations necessary to survive or to achieve an objective or accomplish a task. This concept is referred to as the "break-even point." The other constraint is that there is some maximum level of operations to which the firm can realistically aspire or to which it is restricted because of the quantity and quality of its resources. Within these constraints the forecast will reflect the consequences of forces already in motion and forces that will be set in motion during the period of the forecast. For example, the products of the firm may have high acceptance in the market, which will result in some level of sales in the future. In addition, the firm may be able to increase the level of acceptance through more promotion, better service, or some other way. Figure 7-13 illustrates this concept.

Within the limits illustrated in Figure 7-13, it is possible to forecast at four different levels.[10] We can call the first level "imperative forecasting." This is the amount of demand required to enable the firm to survive. It is the point at which—called "break-even"—the firm's revenues just match its expenses. The operational counterpart of imperative forecasting for an organizational unit would be the level of operations, however specified, that would enable it to just barely fulfill its function or justify its existence. That is, the benefits it provides just equal its costs.

Another forecast level is that which can be reached on the assumption

A section of a new input-output grid for electronics

1968 output (sales), millions of dollars

1968 input (purchases)		Equipment: Population-oriented electronics	Equipment: Information and communications systems (nonmilitary)	Equipment: Instrumentation	Equipment: Industrial electronics	Equipment: Military electronics	Components: Components	Components: Electromechanical devices and hardware
Equipment	Population-oriented electronics	•	•	•	•	•	•	•
Equipment	Information and communications systems (nonmilitary)	160	500	40	20	600	100	40
Equipment	Instrumentation	30	180	20	•	230	70	10
Equipment	Industrial equipment	•	•	•	•	•	•	•
Equipment	Military electronics	0	0	0	0	11,500	0	0
Components	Components	1,409	707	102	41	1,192	•	•
Components	Electromechanical devices and hardware	365	737	47	29	440	•	•

• Less than $10-million

and what it says about the industry's long-term growth

	1968 (Millions of dollars)	1972 (Millions of dollars)	Increase 1968-72, percent
Total electronic equipment sales	$27,840	$36,763	32.0%
Computer equipment	6,200	10,000	61.2
Broadcast equipment, consumer electronics, education equipment	906	1,429	57.7
Industrial electronics	380	510	34.2
Electronic test equipment, analytical instruments, nuclear instruments, and medical instruments	1,144	1,528	33.6
Business equipment, communications and navigation	4,480	5,820	29.9
Military electronics	11,500	14,000	21.7
Home entertainment	3,230	3,476	7.6

Fig. 7-12 Input-output diagram. SOURCE: *Business Week,* January 25, 1969, p. 62; data, Quantum Science Corp. Reproduced by special permission.

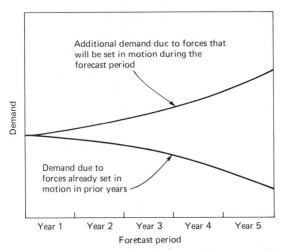

Fig. 7-13   Forces that affect the level of future demand.

that some mixture of forces similar or identical to those that affected the past will affect the future. We can call this "predictive forecasting." For example, a product has been promoted vigorously in the past and can be expected to be promoted vigorously in the future. If its sales have continued to rise in the past, we would expect them to increase in the future. Predictive forecasts are generally derived from a survey of customer expectations or from time series analysis, extrapolation of historical data.

"Determinative forecasting" introduces the idea that it is possible to reach a level of demand in terms of what management thinks the organization *should* achieve. Determinative forecasts are based upon the application of judgment to varied forms of information and experience. The forecaster must know the industry, the competition, the size and character of the markets, the idiosyncrasies of the customers, the differential impact of the various environments to which the market is subject, and the like. Sometimes a determinative forecast will be an extension of either an imperative or predictive forecast. For example, a construction firm may have calculated that it must sell 55 units of housing in the following fiscal year just to break even on revenues and expenses. Such an imperative forecast can be converted into a determinative forecast if company management decides that it will try to sell an additional 20 units of housing. A predictive forecast can be changed in similar fashion. In a sense, a determinative forecast represents a kind of self-fulfilling prophecy.

A fourth and final level of forecasting is reached when it is recognized that the firm could sell more of its products than it can produce. We can call this approach "constrained forecasting." Because resources are limited, they must be used in the most efficient way possible. For example, we might be able to sell 1000 desks and 2500 chairs, but that level of production would exceed production capacity by about 30 percent. What then is the best possible combination of desks and chairs to produce if they have different production costs and profit contributions? The answer to this problem can be found through the use of linear programming by setting up inequalities (rather than equations) which express the relationship and constraints on resources and outputs.

There is a suggestion in this description of four forecasting levels that each successive one details larger quantities of the firm's products. With the caution that this is possible but not inevitable, Figure 7-14 illustrates the suggested relationship.

Another implication in the above is that the basic data of a forecast are quantitative in nature and that the quantitative data are manipulated mathematically in the preparation of a forecast. However, some of the information relevant for forecasting is not quantitative in nature, though it may have quantitative implications. Examples include government legislation, actions by competitors, and technological advances. Usually, therefore, initial forecasts derived from quantitative data and manipulations are qualified by nonquantitative factors. In effect, there is a shift in the preparation of the forecast from a measurement approach to a judgmental approach, from a quantitative-mechanistic-logical framework to a qualitative-experiential-intuitive framework.

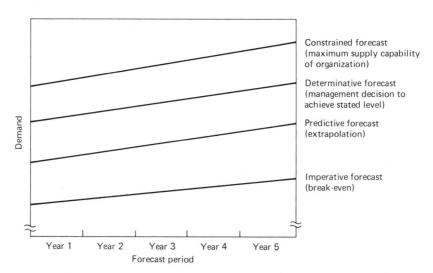

Fig. 7-14 Levels of forecasting.

For example, during an audit of the sales forecasting procedures in a medium-sized firm the author observed that after the sales forecaster extrapolated the past sales record using time series analysis, a top management committee consisting of the president and functional vice presidents reduced it by 10 percent based upon their knowledge and experience in the industry. The qualified, determinative forecast was closer to actual sales than the original predictive forecast.

How accurate are forecasts? The question is raised because very inaccurate forecasts may be more trouble than they are worth. The answer seems to be that the accuracy of forecasts can be increased with experience and accumulated historical data and that they are indeed worthy of preparation. Naturally, forecasts for next year tend to be more accurate than forecasts for the year after that.[11]

Select Strategies

The selection of strategies has to do with deciding upon the courses of action that will be taken to fulfill the forecast. A strategy in planning is the equivalent of a decision alternative. As in decision making, where alternatives are developed, evaluated, and selected, so also in planning managers review their missions, objectives, the environmental assessment, forecasts, and the specific end results they wish to accomplish; they ponder the various ways in which they can most efficiently and effectively carry out their operations to meet the demands made upon the organization.

Two general considerations should be noted here. First, it is important to develop an adequate range of strategies so that the one(s) selected will be most appropriate for the ends sought. Second, it is desirable to develop strategies that can be used *if* objectives or forecasts are modified drastically. These are contingent strategies. The overall result is an inventory of strategies which introduces flexibility into future operations since it is easier to change strategies if they are readily available.

As an example of the foregoing, assume that a marketing manager has just received a forecast which shows an expected 15 percent increase in sales for the following year. What strategies should this manager consider to reasonably assure that the increase will be realized? The following strategies might be developed:

- Improve customer service by responding within 48 hours to problems encountered with company products.
- Change advertising to take account of the growing leisure market.
- Increase the number of different-sized packages for the products.

- Offer a money-back guarantee to dissatisfied customers to entice new customers to buy.
- Use door-to-door selling as a supplement to mail order sales.

Whichever one is selected, the marketing manager would have the others as contingent strategies in the event of a drastic change in the forecast or if a competitor should come out with a new product.

The starting point for the development of strategies, as already suggested above, is the forecast. The organizational mission is both a general guide and a constraint in the search for strategies. It can be viewed as a common thread which should permeate all strategies that are given serious consideration. Review of organizational objectives will yield more specific guidelines for strategies since forecasts may have been modified to accommodate them. Premises developed during the environmental assessment, including the strengths and weaknesses of the organization, will indicate possible or necessary strategies. For example, the presence of a top-notch research and development department in the firm would facilitate the improvement and diversification of the product line to assure securing a forecasted increase in market share.

There are no substitutes for experience and creativity in the development of strategies. It is not only desirable but necessary to include all individuals who can make contributions by virtue of either qualifications. Experience will provide reliable ideas; creativity will provide new ideas.

In searching for strategic options, a major consideration is the question of how much time and effort should be expended in this activity. As in decision making generally, there is a human tendency to settle for the first reasonably adequate strategy that may occur to the planner. Such behavior is known as "satisficing." A more reasonable form of behavior is to search for the best or optimum solution. Since there are costs as well as benefits in searching, however, the search for options should be continued only so long as the marginal contribution of each additional strategy is greater than that of those already formulated.

When an adequate array of planning strategies has been developed, it becomes necessary to *select* the one(s) that will be most likely to assure achievement of the forecast and fullfillment of organizational objectives. Choosing the best or optimum strategies is similar to selecting an alternative in any decision situation. Costs and benefits of each relevant strategy must be projected in terms of its ability to facilitate the ends desired. Strategies given serious consideration must be compatible with the constraints imposed by organizational mission, needs, objectives, capabilities, policies, and existing problems and opportunities. Final decision criteria and the condition under which the strategy is likely to be implemented—certainty, uncertainty, risk, or conflict—must also be considered. This requirement is necessitated by the possibility that if the condition is other than certainty, the state of the environment may change and another (contingent) strategy may have to be substituted. To approach optimality, the development and evaluation of planning strategies should involve personnel representatives of the organizational areas that will be affected by them. The political advantages and disadvantages are more likely to be brought to the fore if they are reviewed by lower organizational levels.

Although it is often easy to do oral analyses of strategies in conference, it is especially helpful to record discussions in the form of minutes. Such minutes should stress resources required for implementation, the organizational units which will participate or be affected by strategies, the specific contributions they will make to solving problems and exploiting opportunities, unusual types of activities that may be required, special skills and talents needed, possible conflicts with existing policies, and the like. Wherever possible, the various options should be evaluated in terms of common denominators and calculated payoffs.

Program Operations

Programming is the translation of strategies into courses of action. The foreseeable implications for the organization are specified in considerable detail in terms of activities to be undertaken, resources that will be required, and the timing and sequence of events. For example, if the strategy selected to increase penetration of a market involves direct mail advertising in addition to other current promotional activities, the actions necessary to engage in direct mail advertising must be specified. Then the human, physical, and financial resources needed to carry on the advertising must be determined. These resource requirements should be broken down in terms of those the firm already has and those it will have to acquire. In turn, the acquisition of the additional resources will itself be an action detail of the plan and should be inserted as a step in the program prior to details involving their use.

The next step in programming is the preparation of a schedule to show the sequence of activities necessary to implement the strategy. The schedule should include the assignment of responsibilities for the required actions to the appropriate personnel. Such assignment is especially necessary for strategies that require new or modified forms of behavior since individuals with responsibilities for existing activities may not recognize their new duties. Furthermore, new assignments are a signal that special training may be required and this too should be scheduled.

The previous discussion has concentrated on new strategies developed for future planning periods; strategies which have been carried over from prior planning periods must also be programmed. Otherwise the program will not include all the operations necessary to implement the plan.

Because there will be a number of strategies for organizational objectives—and even multiple strategies for single objectives— scheduling all the strategies can become a complex task. It may thus be useful to employ network analysis for the sequence of activities. Two such techniques are *systems analysis* and *PERT* (program review and evaluation technique).

A few generalizations are in order about the scheduling and implementation of strategies. Those strategies and associated activities which have long lead times, a greater than usual amount of uncertainty attached to them, and/or special value or crucial significance to the plan should be scheduled as early as possible. Scheduling the commitments for acquisition of new resources should be delayed if possible—but not to the point of endangering any commitments—until their utilization is imminent. Although these two assertions may appear to be contradictory or self-canceling, they need not be. Good judgment can reconcile them since they are simply admonitions to carry out activities at the most propitious times. For important strategies it may also be necessary to determine points of no return. That is, once a certain point has been reached in an activity, it is difficult or impossible to disengage from or abandon it. Or if it is abandoned most or all the costs are "sunk" (irretrievable) and their consequences essentially irreversible. Attention should be directed to these points of no return during implementation of the plan to emphasize the finality of decisions which carry out the plan beyond these points.

Prepare Budget

The budget is a financial restatement of the programs. It is an allocation of organizational resources stated in financial terms. The budget is also a schedule, since the utilization of resources is to take place during specified periods of time. Next, the budget is a statement of managerial responsibilities because the allocation of resources is to *cost centers,* that is, specific organizational units. Thus the budget is a summary of the estimated costs associated with implementing the strategies of the plan. Finally, the budget is a feedforward control device. As the plan is carried out, actual financial costs (feedback) are presented along with the original budgeted figures for comparison and for control of operations.

The function of a budget, therefore, is to aid and control the implementation of the plan. A few thoughts are in order for the preparation and monitoring of budgets. Budgeting considerations should not dominate decisions in planning, though financial capabilities will clearly set bounds on decision making. This problem will be minimized if strategies have been realistically developed and selected and if the program has been worked out properly, seeking efficiency as well as effectiveness.

Perhaps the single most important thing to incorporate into a budget is *flexibility*. Flexibility is achieved in two areas: (1) in management's behavior; (2) in the form of the budget itself.

Flexibility in management's attitude and practice toward budgeting is achieved by having the budget accepted as a means of control and not an end in itself. This is easier said than done, admittedly. When changes in operations both require and justify different levels of expenditures from those projected, managers have to learn that the budget should be changed. Such learning can best be instilled by adopting flexible budgets, which may be variable, alternative, or supplemental.

Variable budgets include projections for different levels of operations. For example, the sales forecast may anticipate sale of 100,000 units of goods, plus or minus 5 percent. Then the budget shows the permissible level of expenditures for the three levels of 95,000, 100,000, and 105,000 units. If sales appear to be occurring at the 95,000 level, the budget for that amount is in effect automatically.

Alternative budgets would involve three separate schedules in the above example. The most likely schedule would be adopted and maintained unless another alternative appeared to be more in accord with the facts. If so, the other alternative would be formally adopted to replace the first.

A *supplemental budget,* as the term implies, is added to a single-schedule budget when the latter is meant to be a ceiling on expenditure. For example, the production department may have a capital budget of $100,000. Subsequently the production manager concludes that what is needed is a faster machine than originally had been planned as a replacement. The manager will then request an additional appropriation to cover the increased cost.

Set Control Standards

Since the purpose of planning is to bring about change, it is necessary to be able to determine whether anticipated changes are in fact taking place. To this end we must have reference points or indicators to tell us whether we are moving toward the new state of affairs or have arrived there. We see such indicators or standards in everyday life: "For a golfer, a good score is 72. For a runner, a mile in 4 minutes is a good run. For a bowler, 250 is a good game. For a salesman, 5 customer calls make a good day's work."[12] These standards represent par for the activities involved. If a golfer's score is 89, or a runner's time 4 minutes and 22 seconds, or a bowler's score 195, or a salesperson's average number of calls 3.75, the individual can see the amount of behavioral change needed to achieve par for the course.

Similar learning takes place in the managers of an organization. When they know their present score and are working toward a par or standard connected with their jobs, they can see the changes that are required to fulfill their responsibilities. The score improves as they increase the amount of resources involved in an operation, or change the resource mix, or take other action to change their operations.

Of course, setting standards for control does not of itself assure desired performance. Standards are like the gauges on the dashboard of an automobile. For example, if the water gauge signal flashes, the driver must take some action that will bring the temperature of the motor back to an acceptable level.

In an organization it is more difficult to find the *critical points* for which standards must be set than it is for an individual. The following comments indicate the more vital points and areas for consideration. First of all, standards should be set in terms of the desired results of the plan. For example, if we have forecasted a 10 percent increase in sales, we should set quotas of sales for each sales region, district, and salesperson to reflect that increase. Standards should be similarly set for other functions, activities, and tasks of the organizational plan.

In addition to new operations, another critical area for control standards are established operations that have proven difficult to contend with in the past. It is especially important to tie these standards to the duties of specific managers, to pinpoint the individuals responsible for the quality of the operations. Otherwise they cannot be held accountable and the standards will serve no useful purpose.

A word of caution is in order in setting standards: Standards should be set at some optimum level which provides adequate information for control and can be secured at a reasonable cost. There are in every organization a very large number of potential control points. Using them all would be very expensive and would tend to undermine motivation of personnel as well.

In general, standards should be established at critical points so that the information will provide warning of changes that will occur. Advance warning makes it possible to take corrective action to minimize deviation from standards. *Inputs* and *processes*, in addition to *outputs* of operations, constitute points at which standards can be established. These are in decreasing order of importance from the standpoint of advance warning.

An input standard specifies quantitative and/or qualitative characteristics of resources which are to be used to achieve the goals and/or outputs of the plan. They would include human skills, materials, money, space and related facilities, orders received, and policies and procedures which provide information about the transformation of the resources. Input standards are necessary where it is not possible to accommodate highly variable resources in the transformation processes; they also tend to be a harbinger of results.

A process standard generally designates desirable quantitative and qualitative characteristics of the behavior of people and things during the period of production of material or provision of services. Clerks should smile at customers; machines should be set at a certain speed; the oven should have a constant temperature of 500 degrees; and so on. Process standards are especially prevalent in production operations that are highly routine and complicated.

An output standard, as already indicated, generally designates desirable or required characteristics of an operation's outputs or results. The production line should turn out so many units each hour, day, or week; return on investment on new ventures should be not less than 12 percent after taxes; salespersons should realize $1000 sales per day; and so on.

Output standards are the most common since they indicate clearly whether the plan is being achieved and because results are easier to determine than the character of inputs and processes.

Quantitative standards are relatively easy to set with some experience. Qualitative standards are much more difficult because they involve judgment rather than measurement. As a consequence it is easy to settle for quantitative indicators and neglect the qualitative. However, qualitative characteristics of operations have a tendency to influence quantitative results. Therefore, neglect of the qualitative will ultimately have a deleterious effect on the quantitative.

Events and activities fluctuate both purposively and randomly over time, and this fluctuation poses a problem for the use of standards. To the extent that deviations are random and tend to be self-canceling, it is not necessary to take corrective action. Conversely, if no corrective action is taken when an operation is definitely but not obviously out of control, considerable losses can be incurred. What can we do to resolve the dilemma? One answer is to set *tolerance limits*. Tolerance limits can be set for any activity which has a measurable result. As long as deviations from standard fall within limits, no corrective action need be taken.

One of the most common standards used to judge progress in achieving planned outputs and target is budgets. Thus we see that budgeting is not only a step in the planning process, but the budget also constitutes a standard. Objectives and forecasts also usually serve as standards. Standard costs are another common indicator of progress—or the lack of it—in carrying out plans. However, they are limited in usefulness to production-type operations with high volume of identical outputs.

As a final word on standards, it is necessary to point out that there is a need for balance in setting feedforward control standards. That is, there may be a tendency to set standards only for the obvious aspects of operations, to oversubscribe these and neglect others. For example, a standard of 15 percent return on investment may be set for a product division, but other indicators of operations may be neglected. As a result, the profit standard may be oversubscribed at the expense of neglecting other critical areas such as machine maintenance and personnel development.

Establish Reporting System

The final step in the process of planning is the establishment of a reporting system. Provision should be made in the format for the routine reporting of two kinds of information: (1) the feedforward standards which reflect targets set for objectives, forecasts, outputs, and other characteristics of the plan; (2) data which show progress being achieved toward fulfilling the targets. The latter is the familiar concept of feedback, information made available about performance in order to keep operations under control.

For maximum usefulness, the format should include provision for showing unacceptable deviations from standards, the concept of *management by exception*. When these are shown, a manager who receives the report can quickly spot the operations that are out of control, take corrective action, and ignore operations which are performing as scheduled.

The above describes what is called a "management information system," or MIS. Since an MIS tends to focus on quantitative information, we should point out that completeness also requires the preparation of nonstandardized reports for operations whose results cannot be fitted into a quantitative framework (for example, research and development on new products or progress toward securing a government contract).

The management information system typically provides for sending routine, periodic reports to the managers responsible for specific operations, with copies to their superiors. Provision should be made in the reporting system for subordinates to explain to their superiors, where necessary, the meaning and significance of routine reports. For example, the reasons for unacceptable deviations from standards should be explained in such follow-up reports. In addition, corrective action taken or contemplated should be discussed.

Budget-expense reports are the most obvious and common examples of the reporting system described above. The feedforward control standards are the budgeted dollars for the acquisition and utilization of resources. As resources are acquired and utilized, the magnitudes of the transactions are summed and reported periodically, the feedback phenomenon. A properly prepared budget format should also make provision for showing variance of actual expenses from original appropriations, so that problem areas can be spotted easily among the mass of figures.

In general, one overall stricture must be kept in mind, especially in preparing an information system to report on the implementation of plans: The information must be relevant and must be made available with a frequency which makes it possible for managers to take remedial or facilitating action at the most propitious moment.

Activities That Parallel Planning

There are two additional activities in the process of planning—*communication* and *coordination*.

Communication takes place in conjunction with each step in the process of planning. The finished plan itself must be communicated to various units of the organization. Since communication is largely a function of organizational design, further details will be given in the discussion of the organization and management of the Control Cycle.

Coordination parallels the process of planning because planning labor is divided among line and staff personnel in the organization. This aspect of planning will also be detailed in a subsequent section.

THE PLAN AS THE PRODUCT OF PLANNING

Although it may appear that the plan as the product of planning would naturally be more important than the process itself, this is not the case necessarily. Rather, we can say that the process is more important than the product.[13] That is, the biggest single dividend that can be realized from the process of planning is not a series of statements about proposed future activities. Instead, it is the future-oriented perspectives to which the managers involved in planning become conditioned: the anticipation of uncertain events inside and outside the organization; the need to review the missions, objectives, and policies of the organization; definition of organizational strengths and weaknesses; practice in decision making about future operations; communications stressing organizational expectations; and the like. These attitudes and behaviors are incorporated into the manager's repertoire; if repeated and reinforced, they will persist beyond the usefulness of particular plans.

Yet it would be an error to conclude, in view of the preceding comments, that the plan itself is unimportant. For despite the uncertainties and even ambiguities that will be incorporated into the plan, it will still represent the best expectations of the planners. Its purpose, after all, is to guide future behaviors of organizational members.

The plan as a package should include some or all of the following, depending on whether it is a corporatewide plan or a plan for a unit of the organization.[14]

1 Statement confirming any of the existing missions and objectives and announcing changes in either

2 Summary of the external environment with emphasis on problems and opportunities

3 Statement describing the organization's capabilities in terms of strengths and weaknesses

4 Discussion of the environment-organization fit

5 Forecasts of anticipated demands

6 Specification of the strategies selected as guidelines for implementing the anticipated demand

7 A summary of the program: a statement about resource requirements (personnel, plant, money, machinery, and the like); changes in product offerings; schedules of activities and assignments of responsibilities

8 A budget giving the financial implications of the program, along with pro forma profit and loss statements and balance sheet

9 Control standards—financial, operational, and behavioral standards of performance established to monitor implementation of the plan

10 Preview of the information reporting system if it is to be different from the one in existence

11 Changes in organizational design—structure, policies, procedures, and the like

Figure 7-15 illustrates the contents of a company plan.

THE PROCESS OF DIRECTING
IMPLEMENTATION OF PLANS

Most of the discussion and writing about the Control Cycle emphasizes—and almost invariably is restricted to—the process of planning.

<table>
</table>

Company Plan

1 Mission and objectives
2 Assessment of external environment
3 Organizational strengths and weaknesses
4 Organization-environment fit
5 Forecast
6 Strategies
7 Program
8 Budget and other financial statements
9 Control standards
10 Reporting system
11 Changes in organizational design

Fig. 7-15 Table of Contents for a company plan. SOURCE: Adapted from Stephen R. Michael and Halsey R. Jones, *Organizational Management,* Intext Educational Publishers, New York, 1973. Reproduced by special permission of copyright holder, Harper & Row, Publishers, Incorporated.

Little or nothing is said of what is involved in directing the implementation of plans and only somewhat more about evaluating results and taking corrective action.

Planning is also the most glamorous of the three processes that constitute the Control Cycle, and it is the heart of the feedforward system. There may also be an intuitive belief or recognition that implementation and evaluation are, in practice if not in theory, left to the feedback system responsible for control of routine operations. As a consequence, final plans are approved and distributed to organizational members, and quite often no active monitoring is undertaken by those persons responsible for the feedforward component of organizational controls. The consequence can often be seen in poor results and low—or no—profits and even threats to organizational survival.

That is why this presentation has emphasized that planning is only one of three processes that enable the organization to help solve its demand and supply problems, fulfill its mission, and accomplish its objectives. That emphasis will be maintained.

The plan generated in the feedforward system, then, becomes an input into the feedback system governing routine operations. Managers who have been given specific responsibilities for bringing about organizational changes detailed in the plan are expected to accomplish them. However, people do what is inspected, not expected, according to an old Navy maxim, and that must be the watchword of the persons responsible for the Control Cycle.

In fact, the monitors of the plan must have two major concerns: (1)

the proper implementation of the plan, and (2) the evaluation of results and adjustment of plans when results are not as projected or not deemed satisfactory. The first concern constitutes the subject matter of this section. The second will be discussed in the following section.

Although this discussion will pose a dichotomy of monitors and implementers of plans, such distinctions do not always exist in all cases. It is true that higher-level managers have the ultimate responsibility for implementation through monitory action, but many managers are both monitors *and* implementers. They monitor some of the changes and directly implement others themselves.

For example, a department's plans may require hiring new personnel because of increased demand. The new positions may be at various levels in the department. The department manager will probably write the job description for the new managerial assistant but will only monitor the preparation of job descriptions for new personnel who report to section heads.

Behavioral Aspects of Implementation

The behavioral aspects of organizational change, discussed in Chapter 1, should be kept in mind during this exposition. It may be useful to reiterate some of the highlights of that material.

Meaningful organizational change always involves changing the supply capabilities of an organization. Although organizational change in the past few decades has emphasized increasing the supply capabilities of firms, in reality capabilities sometimes have to be decreased because of decline in demand. The latter requires "managing for negative growth," as one author has entitled his consideration of that problem.

Change as such is always somewhat of a burden, even if those involved eagerly desire it. When they do not, it can be traumatic. In large part, resistance to change stems from habituated behavior. After some experience, we learn to do work so well that it becomes a partly unconscious process. That is true for driving a car, tending a machine, typing, and even routine decision making. Fully conscious attention may, indeed, interfere with efficient accomplishment in some tasks.

To change habituated behavior, it is necessary to eliminate—or "unfreeze"—it, substitute new behavior, and become habituated to it— "refreezing."[15] The costs involved in motor and mental efforts can be considerable. In addition, there is the possibility of failure. Finally, the change may also be a demotion.

It is small wonder, then, that there is so much resistance to change. Resistance is likely even if the subjects have been participants in shaping the changes—though such participation is clearly a means of reducing resistance—and even if they are intended to benefit from the changes.

Other factors may also contribute to maintaining the momentum of existing routines and reinforcing the inertia often attendant upon changing conditions. These include the pressure of current work and supervisors who wish it to be done expeditiously. The peer groups of fellow workers will contain at least a few who may resist the changes, for whatever reasons, and pressure others to stand with them. Each situation is likely to have special, additional factors.

Knowledge of motivational considerations, of the dynamics of group behavior, and of a variety of leadership styles will be helpful to the monitor in overcoming resistance. A word is in order on these behavioral topics, though no justice can be done to their importance or to the scope of knowledge available.

In properly dealing with their followers, leaders will be aware of the differences as well as the similarities of their subordinates. They may be similar in age, length of experience, dedication to the organization's interests, and other ways. They will also differ in their interests, ambitions, abilities, perceptions, cognitions, values, attitudes, and conclusions about organizational means and ends.

The leader can effectively deal with subordinates on two planes: by recognizing individual personality orientations motivated primarily by achievement, security, competence, prestige, or affiliation drives and by dealing with subordinates differentially so as to complement their orientations.

With some knowledge of group dynamics, the leader can also deal with subordinates as *groups*. For example, cooperation can be encouraged among them in situations where cooperation is necessary to get the job done and competition encouraged where different levels of performance produce a higher level of organizational achievement. The leader should avoid some frequent failures of supervisors: encouraging one mode of behavior where another is required; encouraging both forms for the efforts required to reach a common goal when only one can be useful; failing to reward achievement and punish the lack of it.

The Problem of Power

As leaders, the managers must have some sense of how much power they have over their subordinates and the extent to which that power must be shared with them. Power can be seen as taking one of two major forms.[16]

Authority is that form of power in which leaders can issue orders and instructions because their subordinates think they have the right to do so, whatever the rationale for thinking so. Punishment for failure to comply is also seen as legitimate. Authority is the consequence of agreement between the leaders and followers.

Coercion, by contrast, is that use of power which results in followers obeying orders and carrying out instructions only because the leaders can punish their followers if they do not comply. Clearly, there is disagreement between leaders and followers in this use of power.

What is at issue here is attitude and behavior. In an authority relationship, both are positive; in a coercive relationship, attitude is negative but behavior is positive. In effect, in a coercive relationship the followers are saying: "We don't think you have the right to give us that order but we will follow it because we don't want to be punished." Figure 7-16 illustrates the concepts of authority and power.

The difficulty is this: followers are more likely to perceive orders and instructions about current tasks as being legitimate and proper than they are to perceive orders and instructions about new and different tasks as falling within the authority relationship or the "zone of acceptance," as it has been called. Yet many of the new behaviors required by planned organizational changes are likely to be seen as falling outside the zone of acceptance. What is a leader to do?

One action the leader should have taken was to have involved subordinates as much as economically feasible in the development of the plans which are to be implemented. What the leader should do now is attempt to rely upon authority and avoid the use of coercion except as a last resort.

If the leader senses that the authority relationship does not carry over into some organizational changes that must be implemented, then it is possible to resort to the use of *influence.* We can define influence as a

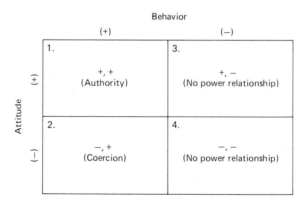

Fig. 7-16 Attitude and behavior of subordinate in power relationships with superior. The first symbol in the cell indicates attitude, the second behavior. SOURCE: Stephen R. Michael and Halsey R. Jones, *Organizational Management,* Intext Educational Publishers, New York, 1973, p. 414. Reproduced by special permission of copyright holder, Harper & Row, Publishers, Incorporated.

nonpunitive approach to getting agreement through persuasion and participation.

The leader can attempt to influence her or his followers by pointing out the costs and benefits of the old system of operation versus the costs and benefits of the new system. Of course, the leader can only win if the new system has a better cost-benefit profile than the old for the subordinates. If that is not the case, there may have to be a resort to coercion or the change may have to be canceled.

Participation in Decision Making

It is also possible to influence followers favorably by getting them to participate in the decisions required to implement organizational changes. There are four levels of participation possible.[17]

1 Some decisions will have to be made by the leader as supervisor who has to direct decision making to, and integrate it with, higher-level activities. Followers as subordinates participate only as they carry out the implications of the decision in their own jurisdictions.

2 Consultation with followers may be necessary for some decisions which affect them and concerning which they may be able to provide information and perspectives not available to the leader. The leader will still make the decision.

3 Some decisions may fall into the gray area between the leader and followers. The leader may, for motivational and learning purposes, request subordinates, singly or as a group, to recommend solutions to such problems. The leader retains a veto power but uses it sparingly.

4 In some cases, decisions can be delegated to followers, with the leader to be informed of the decisions after they are made.

Although an apparently infinite variety of decision situations may develop during the implementation of plans, it is possible to categorize most of these as problems of authorization and of supplementary changes.

Authorization decisions include:

1 Initiating changes. Scheduled or not, it is necessary for the manager to authorize specific changes necessary to implement plans. If scheduled, the date may have to be changed; if unscheduled, a date will have to be chosen.

2 Maintaining the momentum of change. Because change requires new and unlearned behavior, the manager must see to it that obstacles and barriers are dealt with expeditiously.

3 Terminating change efforts. The completion of the change may or may not be obvious. The manager must see to it that change efforts are terminated when the objective has been achieved.

Supplementary changes are necessary because no plan can anticipate all possible actions that need to be taken. Nor is it necessary to stipulate actions which are routine and clearly required to implement a plan. But such decisions need to be made during implementation. Some of the more common supplementary decisions include:

1 Tactics. These amplify the basic strategies that govern changes.

2 Scheduling. Actions that could not or need not be scheduled in the plans need to be scheduled during implementation.

3 Priorities. These may be changed during implementation.

4 Resource mix. Developments in technology or changes in factor markets may necessitate changes in resource mix.

5 Sequencing. The sequence of interdependent actions will have to be determined or may have to be rearranged.

As the manager involves subordinates in the decisions necessary to implement plans, a set of problems and opportunities has to be faced. The manager must choose, for example, between specifying the *means* or the *ends* sought in a decision; both cannot be specified.

As the manager issues orders and instructions or delegates power for decision making, subordinates who range widely in their reactions to superiors must be dealt with: some may expect unequivocal commands; others may prefer subtle suggestions; most will probably fall between the extremes.

Assuming that a manager will be sensible enough to order or request only those actions and goals that are possible of accomplishment, the problem of assigning them to persons who are capable of successful follow-through remains. At the same time, there may be the question of whether the assignment falls within the subordinates' zones of acceptance, and what to do if it does not. Furthermore, the manager must be prepared to reward and punish subordinates justly, thereby avoiding the extremes of favoritism and scapegoating, respectively.

Information for Control

To reinforce subordinates properly, the manager needs information about accomplishments; such information is not less important than the progress it reflects. This information, or feedback, will be the major ingredient for the third process in the control cycle: evaluating. The manager has three means of gathering information: personal inspection, oral communication, and written reports. Each of them can have positive motivational side effects, probably in decreasing order of importance. Ideally, all three are used.

Personal inspection of ongoing organizational changes enables the manager to see the context as well as the content of the changes. Given the known proclivity of subordinates to withhold bad news from their superiors, inspection visits permit the manager to observe all the facts of the situation. Implementation problems often can be more readily resolved at the site where they occur or persist.

Such visits also constitute a kind of deference on the part of the superior. In most superior-subordinate interactions, it is the subordinate who goes or is called to the superior's office or location. By reversing the pattern, the superior adds to the esteem of subordinates. Inspection visits are most important where considerable distance separates superior from subordinate—as in branch offices and regional plants—because they help to increase the normally low level of interaction.

Oral communication as defined here encompasses all superior-subordinate interaction other than inspection visits. The purpose is usually for the subordinate(s) to report progress and to secure authorization for organizational changes. The superior may meet individually or collectively with subordinates, depending upon the interrelatedness of subordinates' activities. Minutes or other records of the communication are helpful for future reference. Knowing that they will have to report progress at scheduled intervals to their superior stimulates subordinates to take action between meetings.

Written reports are best exemplified by management information systems, or MIS. The most obvious routine example is the budget-expense reports prepared periodically by accounting departments. MIS would also include any special reports provided for in the plans to transmit information not covered in existing routine reports.

EVALUATING THE CONTROL CYCLE

As already noted in the early pages of this chapter, the essence of evaluating the Control Cycle involves two steps. The first is a comparison of the results of operations with the standards that have been established. From the judgment made in the comparison, one of two conclusions is reached. One conclusion is that the results are *acceptable*. No further control action need be taken and operations can be continued. A second conclusion is that the results are *not acceptable* and corrective action must be taken. Figure 7-2 illustrates the two steps.

Information for evaluating the Control Cycle is generated in the feedback-controlled operations system. It is used first, however, to make necessary adjustments in routine operations. Subsequently, the information is used to evaluate the feedforward system.

For example, assume that an organization had forecasted revenues of X, plus or minus 3 percent for the next fiscal year. At the end of the first month, revenues are streaming in at the annual rate of X plus 1.4 percent. The positive feedback in well within the tolerance limits of plus or minus 3 percent, so no action need be taken. At the end of the second month, sales are down, the negative feedback shows that sales are now at the annual rate of X minus 2.2 percent. Although a decline from the midrange of the forecast, the results are still acceptable. However, by the end of the first quarter sales are at the annual rate of X minus 5.5 percent. The rate is not acceptable. What to do?

Review of Operations

Routine operations controlled by the feedback system should be reviewed first. The essential question here is: Were all operations carried out as planned? Assuming that the forecast was based upon a 10 percent increase in sales over the past year, did the production department produce the required output? Was it able to hire the additional people to take care of the additional production? Were the additional raw material inventory requirements secured on schedule? Did shipments reach destinations and retailers when needed?

If expectations of increased sales were predicated in part on increased promotional effort, were the planned promotional activities carried out successfully? Did competitors react to the marketing department's strategy as predicted? Did customer returns and complaints exceed the established standards?

Of course, it is more than likely that the manager—whether the president of a functional firm or the general manager of a product division—probably will have some information about the concerns addressed in the questions above. Presumably the manager has been in more or less continual contact with subordinates about these matters during the quarter. It is even possible that as the sales trend reversed itself, increasing attention was being paid to operations to identify causes, so that the trend could be altered if it exceeded tolerance limits. The manager in charge may—should—have been getting reports interpretive of the financial information routinely. Now that the trend has reached an unacceptable dimension, corrective action is required. Tighter production schedules, more finely tuned advertising, some quick market research to find some answers: these are all possible next steps to take in the feedback control system.

If shortcomings are found, they need to be corrected, preferably by the manager having immediate jurisdiction over the affected activity. If no deficiencies are discernible, an additional step is required.

Review of Control Cycle Activities

In the latter event it is necessary to take a look at the feedforward controls, the Control Cycle. The two places to inspect are the implementation of plans and the plan itself. With respect to implementation, to what extent were changes made in the program as unforeseen difficulties arose? If changes were made, did they have unexpected consequences that were not, or could not be, anticipated? For example, if late delivery of new machinery required subcontracting some of the production, were there quantity or quality problems that may have accounted for the shortfall in sales? Was a marketing strategy changed to accommodate a competitor's tactics—unsuccessfully? Many other questions can be posed, of course. If something on the order of the possibilities suggested above did happen in the implementation of the plan, remedial action taken at the time (if any) should be reviewed. If hindsight suggests that such action was insufficient, it should be supplemented at this time. If no prior corrective action at all was taken, the major consideration will now be whether it is still possible to overcome the deviation from planned results, or whether plans may have to be changed.

When the implementation of plans has been reviewed and there is still reason to believe that there is no complete answer to the unacceptable variations from standards, the plan itself must be reviewed. The review should take place in terms of (1) the extent to which the plan at the time it was prepared seems to have been an appropriate response to the environment that was predicated for the near term and (2) the extent to which the environment may have changed since the plan was implemented. The consequence of this evaluation of the plan may be the necessity to change objectives, forecasts, strategies, programs, budgets, or standards, singly or in any combination. Such changes are fed forward into the feedback-controlled operations system.

Review of Organizational Design

The final step in evaluating the Control Cycle—if the suspicion lingers that not all the causes of deviation from standard have been uncovered—is to review the design of the organization. By organizational design we mean the organization structure which guides and constrains behavior. Structure consists of two elements: the division and coordination of labor and the normative pattern of missions, objectives, policies, procedures, standards, and rules. For example, a company may have a great many products but a functional division of labor. The result can easily be a neglect of specific products, since the emphasis is on function. The solution: either a product division of labor at the corporate level or a product division of labor within some of the functions to establish responsibilities for specific products. As to the normative pattern, the company may have, for example, a policy which makes the firm a follower rather than a leader in the introduction of new products. It may, therefore, never be able to gain market shares it projects for its new products when it finally gets around to introducing them.

It has been implied, if not clearly suggested, in the foregoing that review of feedback and feedforward information to control organizational operations is a continual activity. The review is triggered periodically by routine reports prepared at scheduled intervals and occasionally on the basis of information generated or secured as a byproduct of organizational operations and continuous scanning of the external environment.

Whether or not these monthly, quarterly, and occasional evaluations of the Control Cycle result in any changes in operations or plans, a *thorough* reevaluation should be made of the feedforward controls annually. Such annual review serves two purposes. First, it encourages a reappraisal of the control activities undertaken in the periodic and occasional reviews during the past year to see what lessons can be learned from the corrective measures initiated. The second purpose, of course, is both to update the short-range plan for next year and the remaining years of the long-range plan and to add another year to compensate for the year ended.

Summary and Conclusions on Evaluating

Some points are worth reiterating about the evaluation of the Control Cycle. In analyzing feedback from operations, just as in forecasting and setting standards, the manager must be aware of data patterns and their relationships. As noted earlier, data patterns (1) can be horizontal or constant in nature and, conversely, (2) may show trends, either increasing or decreasing. Additionally, in the short run there may be (1) seasonal fluctuations and in the long run there may be (2) cyclical fluctuations. These fluctuations are often associated with both of the more basic horizontal and trend patterns.

Where relevant, awareness of relationships between results and environmental events is necessary to evaluate outcomes properly. For example, an increase in sales may have been predicated upon an increase in personal disposable income in the country or region. If the sales increase does not fall at, or within the tolerance limits of, the standard, there may be cause for concern—*unless* information from the environment shows a similar departure from the expected level of personal disposable income. Relationships of organizational indicators are important, too. For example, as sales of any one product increase, unit costs should decrease and *total* product costs should increase at a declining rate.

The above comments illustrate only some of the considerations that managers must keep in mind as they go about the process of evaluating. As they do so, their concern should be to avoid two basic kinds of errors:

1 Taking corrective action when it is not necessary, in cases where the fluctuations are random and self-canceling.

2 Not taking corrective action when it is necessary, in situations where there are specific factors that must be dealt with to overcome unexpected results.

ORGANIZATIONAL STRUCTURE FOR THE CONTROL CYCLE

Each manager is responsible for control activities, including planning, in the individual organizational unit, and the chief executive has the chief and ultimate responsibility for the total organization.[18] To permit discharge of this obligation, the chief executive has to structure the Control Cycle into the organization's design.

For example, the simplest division of labor is to have division and department heads completely responsible for making plans for their organizational units, with coordination through the chain of command which characterizes the hierarchy. To assure adequate consideration of plans at the top level, the chief executive may have the executive or other top management committee formally critique the plan and its implementation, and evaluate results.

If the chief executive senses that managers may not give enough devotion and time to this function because of pressing operational problems, a staff activity may be established. This is possible because a great many of the activities included in the Control Cycle consist of work other than decision making. These activities typically are generating, supplying, and analyzing information, deducing conclusions and implications, and developing decision alternatives. Staff personnel can do all these activities. Only the decision making itself must be reserved for line managers.

The board of directors must also play a part in the Control Cycle. This is because planning requires the allocation of resources—summarized in the budget—and the directors are charged by law with conserving the assets of their organization. The board's role may vary in practice. It may be little more than a rubber stamp for the chief executive; it may, conversely, take a dominant role in shaping plans and play a vigorous role in evaluating results. Where the board's role falls on the continuum illustrated by these two extremes depends upon the political relationships between it and the chief executive.

The chief executive may even go outside the organization to hire consultants to assist with the Control Cycle, especially planning. Consultants can act as resource people, providing information and suggestions as requested, work directly with managers, or act in a staff capacity. They may be especially helpful in initiating the Control Cycle and as resource persons.

RESEARCH DATA ON THE CONTROL CYCLE

Research on the control cycle has been in the mainstream of the search for knowledge about management generally, which had a major impetus following World War II. The research output has been especially heavy since the 1960s.

It would be difficult to do full justice in this limited presentation to the concepts, hypotheses, and theories which have resulted from the studies. Bias and prejudice may, therefore, be unavoidable in the selection of subjects to be discussed. An attempt will be made, nevertheless, to synthesize the research information available so that readers can form at least tentative conclusions about the usefulness of the Control Cycle. Notes and references at the end of the chapter provide additional material for readers interested in the Control Cycle.

The concept of the Control Cycle is a social invention—it is not an activity that is programmed in our nervous system. If it were, we would not have to learn it, just as we do not have to learn to breathe or blink our eyes.

However, the Control Cycle does appear to resemble human activities that are similar. For example, people learn to do things in part through the process of feedback control. They also learn to anticipate the requirements of changed circumstances, such as stockpiling firewood or other fuel for the winter season. They are anticipating increased demand for energy by bringing in a supply of fuel in advance. That is just like the idea of feedforward control.

Yet it is too big a jump from these personally controlled systems of behavior to organizationally controlled systems of behavior. That is why we call the Control Cycle a social invention. Since it is not clearly a natural phenomenon, it follows that there are no natural laws governing the use of the Control Cycle. Instead, there is a wide range of behavior, from no utilization whatsoever to varying degrees of complexity and sophistication.

General Considerations

The literature on the Control Cycle consists of complementary and contradictory knowledge about (1) what it is or should be, (2) the extent of its use, and (3) whether it makes a difference if it is utilized by organizations.

Writers disagree about exactly which activities properly come under the concept of the Control Cycle, especially those concerning the planning process. For example, the model of planning given in this chapter differs in varying degrees from models described by other writers. Such differences reflect different degrees of understanding and experience as well as different ways of segmenting and emphasizing the stream of activities which constitute the Control Cycle. As an example of the latter, some models distinguish between assessing the environment and forecasting demand in the planning process and some do not. The reason: forecasting as defined by some writers *includes* assessing the environment, and so they simply do not treat the subject separately.

One area of limited agreement concerns the basic nature of the Control Cycle as a mechanism of organizational change. Although all writers discuss planning activities as involving preparation for organizational change, most of them rely on the concept of feedback rather than feedforward control for explanation. One trio of writers concludes that feedforward controls are not used in management,[19] while some others advocate it and cite certain activities and approaches that are specifically identified as feedforward in character.[20]

There is a reluctance to recognize that the Control Cycle fulfills the definition of feedforward controls in *all* respects. The distinction is important only because if managers see the Control Cycle as just another technique of feedback control, they are unlikely to be attracted to it. Who needs one more control technique very much like the one already in use?

Although no one seems to know exactly how widespread the use of the Control Cycle is in the management of organizations, its use seems to be increasing. Like other social inventions, it is being diffused to the extent that it appears to meet the needs of its users. American organizations are preeminent in their use of the Control Cycle, and surveys over the past few decades testify to its spread. For example, surveys by the Stanford Research Institute in 1961 showed that 60 percent of the respondents of *Fortune*'s 500 largest industrial companies had formal planning programs in 1961, 72 percent had them in 1964, and 90 percent had them in 1968.[21] Lucado reported in 1974 that there was over a threefold increase in planning in 34 companies he surveyed from 1963 to 1973; that is, the incidence increased from 27 percent to 85 percent in eight years. The larger the revenues of the firm, the more likely it was to prepare annual corporation plans.[22] Smaller firms are also increasingly using the Control Cycle. Similar trends can be discerned in European countries. A survey of planning practices of companies in assorted United Kingdom industries showed that 80 percent of the respondent firms had been engaged in planning from 1 to 10 years.[23]

Variants of the Control Cycle also appear to be spreading to nonbusiness organizations. Attempts to install Planning-Programming-Budgeting Systems (PPBS) in the 1960s and Zero-Base Budgeting in the 1970s in American government attest to the interest and need for improved control practices. Advocacy of planning at universities and other nonprofit organizations is also increasing.

Benefits of Planning

In contrasting feedback and feedforward controls in an early section in this chapter, the additional costs of the Control Cycle were noted. What benefits are derived from the use of the Control Cycle? It is possible to suggest answers to this question at the individual, group, and organizational levels.

Hemphill's study showed that high school principals who stressed planning when given simulated administrative work were also those who earned high performance ratings for work on their jobs from their superiors.[24] Although this was only a correlation, there is an inference that the principals resorted to planning in both the simulated and real work.

In a 1955 study with groups of workers, supervisors, and foremen at the Lockhead Aircraft Corporation, planning was shown to have significant relationships with some criteria of organizational effectiveness.[25]

Studies conducted at the organizational level also suggest that utilization of the Control Cycle has positive results. For example, of 36 companies in six industrial groups studied by Thune and House and reported in 1970, 17 companies with formal planning programs outperformed 19 companies with informal programs of change. Formal planning and successful economic performance were most closely related in companies of medium size in dynamic markets.[26] Herold's study reported in 1972 confirmed Thune and House's work by showing that companies using the Control Cycle outperformed companies which had informal programs of change in sales and profits.[27] Ansoff investigated the acquisition behavior of American manufacturing firms and found that the planners outperformed the nonplanners on virtually all criteria of success.[28] However, Fulmer and Rue concluded in 1974 that there was no simple, direct relationship between economic success and the Control Cycle after analyzing the performance of 386 companies.[29] In fact, service companies which did *not* plan outperformed those that did. Kallman and Shapiro found by examining the performance of over 500 companies in the motor freight industry that planning did not pay. The reason: uncontrollable variables in the environment such as government regulation and unionized labor.[30] Finally, Malik and Karger reported in 1975 that 19 companies in three industries which used planning outperformed 19 companies in the same industries which did not plan.[31]

One reason that companies with formal planning systems may outperform those with informal systems is that to be done well, behavior involved in planning and the rest of the Control Cycle has to be differentiated from behavior devoted to routine operation, and, of course, has to be done prior to performance. To test this hypothesis, Shure and his associates did an experimental study in a laboratory setting. Three kinds of groups were set up. Members of the "separate planning" group were given separate and definite amounts of time for planning and working; members of the "contemporary planning" groups were given equal but undifferentiated times for planning and working; members of the "no planning" group were given no time for planning. The results: best performance in the "separate planning" groups; not as good in the "contemporary planning" groups; worst in the "no planning" groups.[32]

Planning seems to be better than no planning, but it also makes a difference who does the planning. Bass and Leavitt conducted experiments with managers which showed that productivity and morale were higher in groups that did their own planning than in groups which did not do any planning. But—the most significant finding—groups which were given plans to carry out turned in poorer results than groups that prepared their own plans and groups that had no plans.[33] The study was replicated using Scandinavian, Dutch, Belgian, British, American, and Indian managers, comparing groups with self-developed plans to groups with assigned plans only. The results were the same—managers who developed their own plans did better than those who were given ready-made plans.

Do the above experiments conclusively demonstrate that each person should plan his own work? Probably not. They do show that participation is a powerful motivating force in productivity. But in an *organizational context* there are some advantages to separating "planning" from "doing" structurally. These are (1) greater efficiency in the division of labor at different hierarchical levels and between line and staff; (2) individuals who have the skills to *do* may not have the skills required to *plan*—for example, the carpenter may not be able to prepare architectural plans for building a house; and (3) the doer may have no interest in planning.

Nevertheless, it is possible, says Bass, to separate planning and doing and still get motivational commitment and successful performance. This can be done by (1) clarifying objectives, (2) giving the doers a chance to critique plans, (3) providing flexibility for possible change by doers when required, (4) promoting understanding through the use of language understood by both planners and doers, (5) encouraging two-way communications generally, (6) permitting some decision-making discretion to the doers, and (7) minimizing competition between planners and doers.[34]

The Control Cycle as Organizational Change

The introduction of the Control Cycle into an organization is itself an example of organizational change because it involves new tasks, new behaviors, and a realignment of role relationships. Consequently, establishment of the Control Cycle can result in the problems typically encountered in changing organizations.

Henry studied the planning practices of 45 corporations in the mid-1960s. He found some differences in the behaviors, activities, and structures associated with the Control Cycle.[35] Leadership behavior of top executives appeared to be a crucial factor in planning effectiveness. In some cases, Henry concluded that lukewarm support from the top resulted in ineffectiveness. Attitudes toward change also affected the approaches as well as the results of planning activities. Initiation of, reaction to, or indifference to change (or some combination) characterized the firms. Timidity toward change sometimes had unfortunate results.

The primary focal points of planning activities also varied among the companies. In some firms, activities were concentrated on finance, marketing, or other functions; in others capital budgeting, growth, or acquisitions were in the limelight; the majority of the companies focused on organizationwide, comprehensive planning.

With regard to structure, the typical arrangement was a corporate staff (an individual or group) for coordinating the planning responsibilities of line managers. The balance of firms placed the responsibility for planning in a number of different positions in the organizational structure. In functionally organized companies, planning was highly centralized with staff in a more dominant role; in product-divisionalized firms, planning was decentralized, with line managers in the dominant roles in related activities. Approval of long-range plans was the prerogative of the president, executive committee, or board of directors. In a separate study reported in 1974, Lucado found that among 34 corporations in five categories of revenue ($10–50 million at one extreme and $1–20 billion at the other), 50 percent had planning committees and 62 percent had planning staffs. All the 14 firms, ranging in size from $350 million to $20 billion in revenues, had planning staffs.[36]

Ten years after his initial study, Heny did another survey and confirmed his earlier conclusion that top management support was crucial for effective planning.[37] For example, failure of top management to specify organizational goals, statements of mission, or corporate strategies led to considerable uncertainty at lower echelons.

Design of the planning system was also a problem. Both extreme formality and extreme informality in procedures and responsibility assignments led to troublesome situations, as did excessive centralization *and* decentralization. There was also often a failure to integrate strategic (long-range) and operational (short-range) planning efforts.

The third major problem area was system implementation. Difficulties arose from failure to consult and involve executives and managers, to train them for their new duties, to make allowances for the additional workloads, and from seemingly arbitrary methods of capital allocation.

All these difficulties are symptomatic of faulty organizational change practices. They were sufficiently prevalent that of the 29 firms surveyed, 18 redesigned their planning system anywhere from 5 to 15 years after the original introductions.

In a separate study of American and European firms, Eliasson confirmed Henry's findings concerning changes in planning systems: "Planning systems do not exhibit any particular stability. . . . Several of the U.S. companies revisited in 1973 and 1974 had reorganized their planning systems entirely."

Eliasson dichotomized the uses to which the Control Cycle was put as (1) a *remote control and guidance system* by top management to impose its views on lower echelons or (2) an *analytical system* in which lower echelons submitted numerical information on operations which was combined with forecasts of the economic environment. Concluded Eliasson: "Major decisions as a rule are neither shaped as a part of planning nor on the advice of planners."[38]

One of a number of pitfalls in planning that Steiner discovered, however, in a major study was top management consistently making decisions on an intuitive basis which were at variance with data in the formal plans. However, this pitfall manifested itself as a serious shortcoming primarily in firms with revenues under $100 million. Other pitfalls that Steiner found included top management's delegation of responsibility to planners while it concentrated on operations, inadequate formulation of corporate goals, failure to use standards generated in plans to measure results, failure to involve lower-level personnel in reviews of long-range plans, and the like.[39] In short, in some companies top management did a poor job of planning.

Subsequently, Steiner and Schollhammer replicated the study on the international scene, surveying companies in Canada, Japan, England, Italy, and Australia. They found the same pitfalls. Conclusion: planning can be done poorly in any country in the world.[40]

The international scene also confronts multinational corporations with a setting that is more diverse than that of a domestic corporation. Such diversity has consequences for the nature of planning systems. Lorange's analysis for example, suggests that a multinational corporation's situational setting interacts with organizational design factors (such as hierarchical involvement) resulting in three distinct patterns of planning systems for geographically oriented, product-oriented, and evolving-global firms.[41] To reiterate the main theme of this book, the correct solution to a problem is dependent upon the situation.

Research on Planning Activities

The preceding discussion has been about planning research concerning the Control Cycle as an entity. We will now discuss the separate activities involved in the processes of control. The process of planning has received the overwhelming portion of the attention of researchers. Little has been done about gathering knowledge concerning directing the implementation of plans and only somewhat more about evaluating results. Indeed, research about evaluation of results typically has been in the context of determining whether firms that plan do better than those which do not in terms of performance. Hence, most of what follows will be about research conducted on some of the activities involved in the process of planning.

One activity which has begun to get considerable attention in just the last 10 years or so is that of *assessing the environment.* An early study was by Aguilar who distinguished, among other things, four ways of scanning the environment. These were undirected viewing, conditional viewing, information search, and formal search. Aguilar also studied the types of information gathered, the sources of such information, and the rules for deciding which kinds of scanning should be used. He found that personal sources of information exceeded impersonal sources and that subordinates were the greatest single source of information, with superiors being very poor sources.[42] Keegan's and Collings's studies confirmed Aguilar's findings generally and also for the international business environment.[43]

In a study of 12 large business organizations, Fahey and King found that the firms in question resorted to scanning the environment to different degrees. The "irregular model" described the practices of companies which resorted to scanning in response to a crisis; the "regular model" reflected the practices of firms which scanned periodically for short-range planning implications; the "continuous model" was used by companies which apparently were not satisfied that occasional or even periodic looks at the environment would give them enough information for planning purposes.[44] According to Miles and Snow, based upon their research and literature reviews, organizations assume one of four stances toward the environment. Some companies—*defenders*—stake out a narrow market segment and do not search for information outside that area. *Prospectors* are firms that continually scan the environment for all possible opportunities. *Analyzers* are organizations which operatae in both stable and turbulent environments; they bureaucratize operations in the stable environment and imitate the innovative behavior of competition in the turbulent environment. *Reactors* are firms in which managements attempt to react to environmental change when they perceive it, but do not do so effectively.[45]

Kefalas and Schoderbek examined managerial practices with respect to scanning the environment and concluded that (1) higher-level managers spend more time scanning than lower-level managers, (2) managers in turbulent environments spend more time in scanning than managers in stable environments, (3) managers pay more attention to controllable as against uncontrollable factors in the environment, and, as one might expect, (4) managers look for information that complements their organizational responsibilities; for example, a marketing executive will stress gathering marketing information.[46]

Clearly the most important information in the environment for most organizations most of the time is information about the competition they face. Wall reported on changes toward this question by comparing the attitudes of *Harvard Business Review* readers in 1959 and 1973. He found that (1) the level of interest in competitive information had increased, (2) there was no tendency to formalize search procedures, (3) hiring key employees away from competition was an increasingly popular way of getting competitive information, (4) industrial espionage had increased, and (5) pricing information was the kind most wanted in both 1959 and 1973.[47] As a final point to be made about the scanning and assessment of the environment, Neubauer and Solomon developed an eight-step model for this activity.[48]

Forecasting activities have not received as much attention as the previous activity discussed from the standpoint of research. Much of the literature is mathematical in nature, involving techniques of forecasting, since forecasting activities conclude with a quantitative result derived largely from the manipulation of numbers. Some of the literature, aimed at practicing managers, is of the "how-to-manage-it" variety. However, Vancil examined the accuracy of five-year forecasts, corrected each year, of some companies for the years from 1964 to 1969. The forecasts for 1969 became progressively more accurate, with the 1968 forecast for 1969 equalling 99 percent of actual revenues for that year.[49] Wotruba and Thurlow studied participation of sales force personnel in forecasting and sales quota setting in 202 companies. Accuracy of sales force forecasts ("In general, my salesperson forecast just about right") was attested to by 38 percent of the sales managers.[50]

As already noted, a very great deal of the research on planning has focused upon strategy formulation, development, and selection. Some of this research will be highlighted.

Basic to the idea of strategy formulation is the search activity for developing alternative courses of action. Filley, House, and Kerr conclude, following an examinatin of the literature, that such behavior is positively related to planning success. Most of the laboratory experiments cited were done with groups, but presumably the results are relevant for individuals. For example, in one study, one group was told to produce as many solutions as possible for a problem while another group was told to develop only high-quality solutions. The first group produced about *twice* as many good solutions as the second.[51]

With respect to *kinds* of strategies used by organizations, Hofer studied the strategy choices of manufacturing firms and categorized strategic responses in 28 categories. One of his conclusions was that different challenges elicit different responses. For example, strategic responses to increased demand differed from strategic responses to decreased demand.[52] Glueck also studied strategic responses to environmental challenges and, among other conclusions, isolated some frequently followed basic strategies from 1930 to 1974 among 358 American manufacturing firms: *growth* (47 percent), *stability* (22 percent), *retrenchment* (17 percent), and combination (14 percent). These four strategies were a reclassification of Hofer's 28 types.[53]

Growth-through-acquisition strategies were studied by Kitching. One of his findings was that vertical and horizontal acquisitions were most likely to be successful; conglomerate and concentric marketing and technology acquisitions were more likely to fail. The sample consisted of 69 of 181 mergers and acquisitions made by 22 firms ranging in size from $25 million to $2 billion in 14 industries.[54]

Final Considerations and Conclusions

Hofer has summarized studies of strategic planning research; his data are reproduced in Table 7-2.[55]

In reflecting upon research results which suggest both that planning improves organizational performance and that it does not, Hofer concludes that it is not planning per se which improves performance but the quality of an organization's strategy. That is, some firms plan and some do not. Of those that do, some firms plan well and others plan poorly. The former show improved performance; the latter do not.[56] To state his conclusion once more in different terms: some organizations learn how to plan well; others do not.

It is tempting to go on and on, citing still more research studies about various aspects of the Control Cycle. For example, a considerable amount of research has been done on budgeting. Space does not permit the indulgence of reporting results here. However, in a spirit of compromise, two more items of reseach will be reviewed briefly because they pertain to the overall concept of control.

Tannenbaum[57] and others did a series of studies to ascertain the distribution of control in organizations. Control as defined in these studies seems to mean recognized power to influence others, with the implication of structural relationships. The definition seems compatible with the concept of control and the Control Cycle as expanded here, since for example, higher management has power (or control) over lower-level management in approving or disapproving plans prepared by the latter. Personnel in the organizations studied were asked to specify the amount of control resident in each level of hierarchy. The results indicated different *degrees* of control at different levels and different *total amounts* of control within the units of any one organization as well as between organizations.

These two factors were tested against standards of effectiveness. Conclusions: it did not matter what the relative degrees of control were at different levels of the hierarchy insofar as effectiveness was concerned. For example, an organization could be effective—or ineffective—whether it had centralized or decentralized control. What did matter was the perceived total amount of control in the organization; the more control, the greater the effectiveness.

Table 7-2 Strategic Planning Research

Types of research	Studies done by	Characteristics of research			
		Nature of studies	Types of organizations studied	Potential for future research	Suggestions for future research
(1) The nature of organizational strategies	Thompson*	Descriptive	Single, dominant and related product line businesses	Limited for businesses	Most future studies should focus on types of organizations not studied to date—e.g., hospitals, public agencies, or educational institutions—and on multiorganizational strategy. There is a need for a few more studies on multi-industry companies, however.
	Newell*	Descriptive	Single and dominant product line businesses	Large for nonbusiness organizations and for multiorganizational strategy	
	Scott*	Descriptive	Dominant and related product line businesses		
	Henry*	Descriptive	Dominant and related product line businesses		
	Litschert	Descriptive	35 firms in paint and varnish industry		
	Khandwalla	Descriptive/normative	79 U.S. manufacturing firms		
	Hanna*	Descriptive	Conglomerate businesses		
	Hosmer*	Descriptive	Graduate schools of management		
	Diffenbach*	Descriptive	Multiorganizational strategy and U.S. energy policy		
(2) The costs and benefits of strategic planning	Thune and House	Normative	Businesses: ≥ $75 M	Limited for businesses	Most future studies should focus on types of organizations not
	Herold	Normative	Businesses: ≥ $75 M		
	Ansoff et al.	Normative	Businesses mergers		

Table 7-2 (Continued)

			Characteristics of research		
Types of research	Studies done by	Nature of studies	Types of organizations studied	Potential for future research	Suggestions for future research
	Rue & Fulmer	Normative	Businesses: ≥ $10 M	Moderate for nonbusiness organizations and for multiorganizational strategy	studied to date and on multiorganizational strategy. There is also a need for several more studies on business
	Sheehan	Normative	Canadian businesses		
(3) Strategic planning information and analysis	Aguilar	Descriptive	Mostly chemical mfg. firms	Moderate for businesses	Most future studies on businesses should be normative in character. There is a need for a number of descriptive studies of this type on nonbusiness organizations and on multiorganizational strategy.
	Keegan	Descriptive	International mfg. firms		
	Collings	Descriptive	Businesses	Large for nonbusiness organizations and for multiorganizational strategy	
	Klein	Prescriptive	International mfg. firms		
	Stevenson	Descriptive	Concentrically diversified businesses		
(4) Organizing the strategic planning function	Naumes	Prescriptive	M.B.A. students	Moderate for businesses	Most future studies on businesses should be normative in character. There is a need for a number of descriptive studies of this type on nonbusiness organizations and on multiorganizational strategy. All future
	Wrapp	Descriptive	Businesses: ≥ $50 million		
	Warren*	Descriptive	15 large U.S. businesses		
	Myers	Descriptive/ normative	6 electronics companies: $25–$125 M	Large for nonbusiness organizations and for multiorganizational strategy	
	Aythreya*	Descriptive/ normative	2 large U.S. mfg. firms		
	Ringbakk	Descriptive	Fortune 500 companies		

			Comments
Litschert	Descriptive	Manufacturing businesses	studies in this area should pay some attention to the ways political and social systems' variables can affect the organizational aspects of planning.
Vancil et al*	Descriptive/ normative	Businesses: ≥ $100 M	
Shank et al.	Descriptive/ normative	Businesses: ≥ $100 M	
Steiner*	Descriptive/ normative	215 U.S. businesses	
Steiner and Schölhammer*	Descriptive/ normative	460 U.S. and foreign businesses	
Dobbie	Descriptive	50 large California firms	
Miller	Descriptive/ normative	North American businesses	
McArthur and Scott*	Descriptive	French National Planning System	

(5) The political and social systems aspects of the strategic planning process

			Sample	Comments
Berg*	Descriptive	Large, diversified mfg. firm	Large to very large for all types of organizations and for multiorganizational strategy	Most future studies should be at least comparative and preferably normative. All types of organizations, as well as multiorganizational strategy, should be studied.
Aharoni	Descriptive	International businesses		
Bower*	Descriptive	Large chemical company		
Ackerman*	Descriptive	Paper mfg. businesses		
Carter	Descriptive	Small computer business		
Gilmour	Descriptive	3 large dominant or related product-line firms		
Allison	Descriptive/ normative	Executive branch of fed. gov't		
Cook	Hypothesis testing	14 supermarket chains		
Trevelyan*	Descriptive	Consulting and manufacturing firms		

Table 7-2 (Continued)

Types of research	Studies done by	Characteristics of research			
		Nature of studies	Types of organizations studied	Potential for future research	Suggestions for future research
(6) The content of effective strategies	Dunn	Descriptive	Plastic pipe industry	Large to very large for all types of organizations and for multiorganizational strategy	Most future studies should be normative. Such studies should be structured so that conclusions can be developed about the appropriateness of various generic types of strategy for different sets of environmental circumstances. All such studies should differentiate clearly between levels of strategy: i.e., functional, business, corporate, or multiorganizational.
	Untermann	Descriptive	Life insurance companies		
(a) at a business level	Chevalier	Descriptive/ normative	Large, mature businesses		
	Boston Consulting Group	Descriptive/ normative	Medium-to-high technology industries		
	Fruhan	Descriptive/ normative	Large, mature businesses		
	Abernathy & Wayne	Descriptive/ normative	Manufacturing firms		
	Cooper et al.	Descriptive/ normative	Dominant product line mfg. companies		
	Utterback & Abernathy	Hypothesis testing	120 manufacturing firms		
	Udell	Descriptive	Medium & large U.S. businesses		
	Schoeffler et al.	Normative	Large, mature businesses		
	Kirchhoff	Descriptive/ normative	Capital intensive mfg. firm		
	Hatten	Descriptive/ normative	Beer companies		

(b) at a corporate level		
Gutmann	Descriptive/ normative	High growth businesses
Abbanat	Descriptive/ normative	23 small businesses
Hofer	Descriptive/ normative	U.S. manufacturing firms
Glueck	Descriptive/ normative	U.S. manufacturing firms
Rumelt	Descriptive/ normative	*Fortune* 500 companies
Schendel, et al.	Descriptive/ normative	S&P compustat tape turnaround firms
Nowill	Descriptive/ normative	Large, mature businesses
Kitching	Descriptive/ normative	Business mergers
Kitching	Descriptive/ normative	European business mergers

* These studies also looked at several other aspects of strategic planning, usually strategic planning information and analysis, organizing the strategic planning function, or the political and social systems aspects of the strategic planning process.

SOURCE: From Charles W. Hofer, "Research on Strategic Planning: A Survey of Past Studies and Suggestions for Future Efforts," *Journal of Economics and Business*, vol. 28, Spring–Summer 1976, pp. 282–283. Copyright 1976 by Temple University, School of Business Administration. Reproduced by special permission.

The significance of this research may be summarized as follows: *order is better than disorder.* The consequence of the exercise of control is that organizational members are paying attention to their responsibilities rather than neglecting them. The models of control discussed in the opening pages of this chapter illustrate what appear to be the major ways in which organizational personnel structure their control procedures.

Following a meticulous survey of the planning literature, Hofer concluded that:

1 More research has been done on strategic planning than is generally recognized.

2 Most of the research has been descriptive, comparative, or descriptive/normative in nature; what is needed is the testing of hypotheses such as: A is the cause of effect B.

3 Future studies will require larger samples of organizations, observed and measured over longer periods of time to adequately isolate cause-and-effect relationships.

4 Most research has been done with business organizations; similar studies of nonbusiness organizations are needed, to see if their control problems are similar.[48]

We might add a few more conclusions to the above:

5 Most research has been done on the planning process of the Control Cycle; needed are studies of the other two processes: directing implementation of plans and the evaluation of results.

6 Research depth on the activities involved in the planning process varies greatly; we know much more about developing, formulating, and selecting strategies than we do about programming strategies or setting standards for evaluation. Until we know more about the less-studied activities, it may be difficult for managers to properly learn the planning process and perform well.

7 We need to know more about the extent to which managers resort to the models of control described in this chapter and the conditions and situations in which they do so.

Meanwhile, however, in the absence of perfect knowledge, managers have to manage. The feedforward system of the Control Cycle should help them to anticipate and master change in their organizations.

NOTES

1 For example, see Harold Koontz and Robert W. Bradspies, "Managing through Feedforward Control," *Business Horizons,* vol. 15, June 1972, pp.

25–36, and Dale W. Merriam and Joseph W. Wilkinson, "Model for Planning and Feedforward Control," *Managerial Planning*, vol. 25, March–April 1977, pp. 31–36, 40.

2 "The Experience Curve—Reviewed, I. The Concept," *Perspectives*, The Boston Consulting Group, Boston, 1974.

3 "The Experience Curve—Reviewed, II. History," *Perspectives*, The Boston Consulting Group, Boston, 1973.

4 Peter F. Drucker, *The Practice of Management*, Harper & Row, New York, 1954, chap. 7.

5 Denis F. Healy, "Environmental Pressures and Marketing in the 1970's," *Long Range Planning*, vol. 8, June 1975, pp. 41–45.

6 See, for example, Marketing Concepts, Inc., *The Study of American Opinion: 1978 Summary Report*, U.S. News and World Report, Washington, D.C.: 1978.

7 Francis J. Aguilar, *Scanning the Business Environment*, Macmillan, New York, chap. 4.

8 Asterios Kefalas and Peter P. Schoderbek, "Scanning the Business Environment—Some Empirical Results," *Decision Sciences*, vol. 4, 1973, pp. 63–74.

9 Spyros Makridakis and Steven C. Wheelwright, *Forecasting Methods and Applications*, Wiley, New York, 1978, pp. 7–11.

10 Stephen R. Michael and Halsey R. Jones, *Organizational Management* Intext Educational Publishers, New York, 1973, pp. 369–372.

11 Richard F. Vancil, "The Accuracy of Long-Range Planning," *Harvard Business Review*, vol. 48, September–October 1970, pp. 98–101.

12 Ernest C. Miller, *Objectives and Standards of Performance in Marketing Management*, AMA Research Study 85, American Management Association, New York: 1967, p. 13.

13 E. Kirby Warren, *Long-Range Planning: The Executive Viewpoint*, Prentice-Hall, Englewood Cliffs, N.J., 1966, pp. 24–25, 29–30.

14 For a different and more detailed outline of a business plan, see Willian L. Brockhaus, "Professional Business Planning: Key to Enterpreneurial Success," *Journal of Applied Management*, vol. 3, January–February 1978, pp. 5–9.

15 Edgar F. Schein, "The Mechanism of Change," in Warren G. Bennis, Kenneth D. Denne, and Robert Chen (eds.), *The Planning of Change*, 2d ed., Holt, New York, 1969, pp. 98–107.

16 Michael and Jones, op. cit., pp. 413–415.

17 Stephen R. Michael, "Control, Contingency, and Delegation in Decision Making," *Training and Development Journal*, vol. 33, February 1979, pp. 36–42.

18 H. Edgerton and J. Brown, *Planning and the Chief Executive*, The Conference Board, New York, 1972, p. 19ff.

19 Alan C. Filley, Robert J. House, and Steven Kerr, *Managerial Process and Organizational Behavior*, 2d ed., Scott, Foresman, Glenview, Ill., 1976, pp. 462–463.

20 Koontz and Bradspies, op. cit.; Merriam and Wilkinson, op. cit.; F. A. K. Gul, "The Problem of Feedback in an MIS," *Management Accounting*, vol. 56, February 1978, pp. 62–63; Barry E. Cushing, "A Mathematical Approach to the Analysis and Design of Internal Control Systems," *The Accounting Review*, vol. 49, January 1974, pp. 24–41, and by the same author, "A Further Note on the Mathematical Approach to Internal Control," *The Accounting Review*, vol. 50, December 1975, pp. 151–154; B. P. E. Box, B. M. Jenkins, and J. F. MacGregor, "Some Recent Advances in Forecasting and Control," *Applied Statistics*, vol. 23, 1974, pp. 158–175; G. E. P. Box and G. M. Jenkins, "Discrete Models for Feedback and Feedforward Control," in D. G. Watts (ed.), *The Future of Statistics*, Academic New York, 1968, pp. 201–240; Akira Ishikawa and Charles H. Smith, "A Feedforward System for Organizational Planning and Control," *Abacus*, vol. 8, December 1972, pp. 163–179.

21 "Devising Acceptance of Corporate Strategy," *Stanford Institute Research Journal*, January 1965; James K. Brown et al., "The Status of Long Range Planning," *Conference Board Record*, September 1966.

22 William E. Lucado, "Corporate Planning—A Current Status Report," *Managerial Planning*, vol. 23, November–December 1974, pp. 27–34.

23 J. C. Higgins and R. Finn, "The Organization and Practice of Corporate Planning in the U.K.," *Long Range Planning*, vol. 10, August 1977, pp. 88–92.

24 J. J. Hemphill, "Personal Variables and Administrative Styles," *Behavioral Science and Educational Administration*, National Society for the Study of Education, 1964.

25 A. L. Comrey, W. High, and R. C. Wilson, "Factors Influencing Organizational Effectiveness: IV. A Survey of Aircraft Workers," *Personnel Psychology*, vol. 8, 1955, pp. 79–99.

26 S. Thune and R. House, "Where Long-Range Planning Pays Off," *Business Horizons*, vol. 13, August 1970, pp. 81–87.

27 David M. Herold, "Long Range Planning and Organizational Performance: A Cross-Valuation Study," *The Academy of Management Journal*, vol. 15, March 1972, pp. 91–102.

28 H. Igor Ansoff, "Does Planning Pay? The Effect of Planning on Success of Acquisitions in American Firms," *Long Range Planning*, vol. 3, no. 2, March 1970.

29 R. Fulmer and L. Rue, "The Practice and Profitability of Long Range Planning," *Managerial Planning*, vol. 22, May–June 1974, pp. 1–7.

30 Ernest A. Kallman and H. Jack Shapiro, "The Motor Freight Industry—A Case Against Planning," *Long Range Planning*, vol. 11, February 1978, pp. 81–86.

31 Z. Malik and D. Karger, "Does Long Range Planning Improve Company Performance?" *Management Review*, vol. 64, September 1975, pp. 27–31.

32 G. H. Shure, M. S. Rogers, I. Larson, and J. Tassone, "Group Planning and Task Effectiveness," *Sociometry*, vol. 24, 1962, pp. 263–282.

33 Bernard M. Bass and Harold J. Leavitt, "Some Experiences in Planning and Operating," *Management Science*, vol. 10, 1963, pp. 574–585.

34   Bernard M. Bass, "When Planning for Others," *Journal of Applied Behavioral Science,* vol. 6, 1970, pp. 131–171.

35   Harold W. Henry, *Long Range Planning Practices in 45 Industrial Companies,* Prentice-Hall, Englewood Cliffs, N.J., 1967.

36   Lucado, op. cit.

37   Harold W. Henry, "Formal Planning in Major U. S. Corporations," *Long Range Planning,* vol. 10, October 1977, pp. 40–45.

38   Gunnar Eliasson, *Business Economic Planning,* Wiley, New York, 1976, pp. 221–223.

39   George A. Steiner, *Pitfalls in Comprehensive Long Range Planning,* The Planning Executives Institute, Oxford, Ohio, 1972.

40   George A. Steiner and Hans Schollhammer, "Pitfalls in Multi-National Long Range Planning," *Long Range Planning,* vol. 8, April 1975, pp. 2–12.

41   Peter Lorange, "Formal Planning in Multinational Corporations," *Columbia Journal of World Business,* vol. 8, Summer 1973, pp. 83–88.

42   Aguilar, op. cit.

43   W. J. Keegan, "Scanning the International Business Environment: A Study of the Information Acquisition Process," unpublished doctoral dissertation, Harvard Business School, June 1967; R. L. Collings, "Scanning the Environment for Strategic Information," unpublished doctoral dissertation, Harvard Business School, June 1968.

44   Liam Fahey and William R. King, "Environmental Scanning for Corporate Planning," *Business Horizons,* vol. 20, August 1977, pp. 61–71.

45   Raymond E. Miles and Charles C. Snow, *Organizational Strategy: Structure and Process,* McGraw-Hill, New York, 1978, pp. 28–29.

46   Kefalas and Schoderbek, op. cit.

47   Jerry L. Wall, "What the Competition Is Doing: Your Need to Know," *Harvard Business Review,* vol. 52, November–December 1974, pp. 22–23.

48   F. Friedrich Neubauer and Norman B. Solomon, "A Managerial Approach to Environmental Assessment," *Long Range Planning,* vol. 10, April 1977, pp. 13–20. See also Eli Segev, "How to Use Environmental Analysis in Strategy Making," *Management Review,* vol. 66, March 1977, pp. 4–13.

49   Vancil, op. cit.

50   Thomas R. Wotruba and Michael L. Thurlow, "Sales Force Partcipation in Quota Setting and Sales Forecasting," *Journal of Marketing,* vol. 40, April 1976, pp. 11–16.

51   Filley, House, and Kerr, op. cit., pp. 457–459.

52   Charles W. Hofer, "Some Preliminary Research on Patterns of Strategic Behavior," *Proceedings of the Business Policy and Planning Division of the Academy of Management,* Paper No. 5, Academy of Management, Boston, 1973.

53   W. F. Glueck, *Business Policy: Strategy Formation and Executive Action,* 2d ed., McGraw-Hill, New York, 1976.

54 J. Kitching, "Why Do Mergers Miscarry?" *Harvard Business Review,* vol. 45, November–December 1967, pp. 84–101.

55 Charles W. Hofer, "Research on Strategic Planning: A Survey of Past Studies and Suggestions for Future Efforts," *Journal of Economics and Business,* vol. 28, Spring–Summer 1976, pp. 261–286.

56 Hofer, op. cit.

57 Arnold S. Tannenbaum, *Control in Organizations,* McGraw-Hill, New York, 1968.

58 Hofer, op. cit.

REFERENCES

Books

Aguilar, Francis J.: *Scanning the Business Environment,* Macmillan, New York, 1968.

Ansoff, H. Igor, R. P. Declerck, and R. L. Hayes (eds.): *From Strategic Planning to Strategic Management,* Wiley, New York, 1976.

Argenti, John: *Corporate Collapse: The Causes and Symptoms,* Halsted Press, New York, 1976.

Armstrong, J. Scott: *Long Range Forecasting: From Crystal Ball to Computer,* Wiley, New York, 1978.

Brickner, William H., and Donald M. Cope: *The Planning Process,* Winthrop Publishers, Cambridge, Mass., 1977.

Business Planning Guide, The Federal Reserve Bank of Boston, Boston, 1976.

Easton, Allan: *Managing for Negative Growth,* Reston Publishing Co., Reston, Va., 1976.

Eby, Frank H., Jr., and William J. O'Neill: The Management of Sales Forecasting, Lexington Books, Lexington, Mass., 1977.

Egerton, Henry C., and James K. Brown, *Planning and the Chief Executive,* The Conference Board, New York, 1972.

Eliasson, Gunnar: *Business Economic Planning,* Wiley, New York, 1976.

Henry, Harold W.: *Long Range Planning Practices in 45 Industrial Companies,* Prentice-Hall, Englewood Cliffs, N.J., 1967.

Hussey, David E.: *Corporate Planning Theory and Practice,* Pergamon, New York, 1974.

Lorange, Peter, and Richard F. Vancil: *Strategic Planning Systems,* Prentice-Hall, Englewood Cliffs, N.J., 1977.

Makridakis, Spyros, and Steven C. Wheelwright: *Forecasting Methods and Applications,* John Wiley, New York, 1978.

Miles, Raymond E., and Charles C. Snow: *Organizational Strategy: Structure and Process,* McGraw-Hill, New York, 1978.

Newman, William H.: *Constructive Control,* Prentice-Hall, Englewood Cliffs, N.J., 1975.

Ross, Joel E., and Michael J. Kami: *Corporate Management in Crisis—Why the Mighty Fall,* Prentice-Hall, Englewood Cliffs, N.J., 1973.

Rothberg, Robert R.: *Corporate Strategy and Product Innovation,* Free Press, New York, 1976.

Schendel, Dan E., and Charles W. Hofer: *Strategic Management,* Little, Brown, Boston, 1979.

Smith, Theodore A.: *Dynamic Business Strategy: The Art of Planning for Success,* McGraw-Hill, New York, 1977.

Steiner, George A.: *Pitfalls in Comprehensive Long Range Planning,* The Planning Executives Institute, Oxford, Ohio, 1972.

———: *Strategic Managerial Planning,* The Planning Executives Institute, Oxford, Ohio, 1977.

———: *Top Management Planning,* Macmillan, New York, 1969.

Strong, Earl P., and Robert D. Smith: *Management Control Models,* Holt, New York, 1968.

Warren, E. Kirby: *Long Range Planning: The Executive Viewpoint,* Prentice-Hall, Englewood Cliffs, N.J., 1966.

Weber, John A.: *Growth Opportunity Analysis,* Reston Publishing Co., Reston, Va., 1976.

Articles

Ansoff, H. Igor: "The State of Practice in Planning Systems," *Sloan Management Review,* vol. 18, Winter 1977, pp. 1–24.

Bass, Bernard: "When Planning for Others," *Journal of Applied Behavioral Science,* vol. 6, 1970, pp. 131–171.

Clifford, Donald K., Jr.: "Managing Your Product Life Cycle," *Marketing Times,* July–August 1976, pp. 20–24.

Currill, David L.: "Introducing Corporate Planning—A Case History," *Long Range Planning,* vol. 10, August 1977, pp. 70–77.

Giglioni, G., and A. Bedeian: "A Conspectus of Management Control Theory: 1900–1972," *The Academy of Management Journal,* vol. 17, June 1974, pp. 292–305.

Henry, Harold W.: "Formal Planning in Major U.S. Corporations," *Long Range Planning,* vol. 10, October 1977, pp. 40–45.

Hofer, Charles W.: "Research on Strategic Planning: A Survey of Past Studies and Suggestions for Future Efforts," *Journal of Economics and Business,* vol. 28, Spring–Summer 1976, pp. 261–286.

Kefalas, Asterios, and Peter P. Schoderbek: "Scanning the Business Environment—Some Empirical Results," *Decision Sciences,* vol. 4, 1973, pp. 63–74.

Kinnunen, Raymond J.: "Hypotheses Related to Strategy Formulation in Large Divisionalized Companies," *The Academy of Management Review,* vol. 1, October 1976, pp. 7–14.

Koontz, Harold, and Robert W. Bradspies: "Managing through Feedforward Control," *Business Horizons,* vol. 15, June 1972, pp. 25–36.

Leontiades, Milton: "What Kind of Corporate Planner Do You Need?" *Long Range Planning,* vol. 10, April 1977, pp. 56–64.

Lucado, William E.: "Corporate Planning—A Current Status Report," *Managerial Planning,* vol. 23, November–December 1974, pp. 27–34.

Paine, Frank T., and Carl R. Anderson: "Contingencies Affecting Strategy Formulation and Effectiveness: An Empirical Study," *Journal of Management Studies,* vol. 14, May 1977, pp. 147–158.

Pitts, Robert A.: "Diversification Strategies and Organizational Policies of Large Diversified Firms," *Journal of Economics and Business,* vol. 28, Spring–Summer 1976, pp. 181–188.

Schendel, Dan E., and G. R. Patton: "Corporate Stagnation and Turnaround," *Journal of Economics and Business,* vol. 28, Spring–Summer 1976, pp. 236–241.

Segev, Eli: "How to Use Environmental Analysis in Strategy Making," *Management Review,* vol. 66, March 1977, pp. 4–13.

Vancil, Richard F.: "The Accuracy of Long-Range Planning," *Harvard Business Review,* vol. 48, September–October 1970, pp. 98–101.

Wall, Jerry L.: "What the Competition Is Doing: Your Need to Know," *Harvard Business Review,* vol. 52, November–December 1974, pp. 22–23+.

Journals

Business Week. Has weekly feature entitled "Corporate Strategies." McGraw-Hill Publishing Co., 1221 Avenue of the Americas, New York, NY 10020.

Long Range Planning. Bimonthly journal of the Society for Long Range Planning and of the European Planning Federation. U.S. office: Pergamon Press, Maxwell House, Fairview Park, NY 10523.

Managerial Planning. Bimonthly journal of The Planning Executives Institute, P.O. Box 70, Oxford, Ohio, 45056.

Planning Review. Published bimonthly for the North American Society for Corporate Planning by Crane Russak & Co., 347 Madison Ave., New York, NY 10017.

Part 4

Review and Overview of Organizational Change

8

Techniques of Organizational Change: A Summary

Stephen R. Michael

Professor of Management
University of Massachusetts/Amherst

The manager who is prepared to take a contingency approach to organizational change has a variety of techniques from which to choose, as the preceeding chapters show. Which technique is chosen should depend, of course, upon the situation. The characteristics of the techniques need to be juxtaposed with the requirements of the problem or opportunity which is to be addressed and resolved. If that is done, the requirements of the contingency approach to management are satisfied.

To facilitate that task, we will (1) review the model of organizational change described in Chapter 1 (Figure 1-1) to show its compatibility with the techniques, (2) compare and contrast the techniques of organizational change in respect to their major characteristics, and (3) suggest an outlook that should facilitate a closer rapport between environment and organization.

THE TECHNIQUES AND THE CHANGE
MODEL

Chapter 1 provided a general model of organizational change—Figure 1-1 summarizes it—suggesting the major steps or stages that are involved in adjusting the organization to its environment. Although this model was not specifically used in elaboration of the various techniques of organizational change, it is explicit or implicit in those descriptions. Let us see how.

With respect to the opportunities and constraints contained in the *external environment,* only the Control Cycle has an explicit concern for scanning and assessing such phenomena. However, all the other techniques of organizational change have an implicit accommodation for the environment. This is most clearly noticeable in the examples given in the descriptions of the techniques. When an organization has a problem for which it resorts to one of the techniques, the problem is directly or indirectly the consequence of interaction between the organization and its environment. Perhaps the single greatest difference among the techniques is that, because of built-in characteristics of the Control Cycle, Management by Objectives, and Management Development (if there is an ongoing program), these three techniques permit the *anticipation* of environmental opportunities and problems and provide lead time for organizational change, the essence of feedforward control. Organizational Behavior Modification and Organization Development, by contrast, are *reactive* techniques; that is, they are resorted to as specific interventions in organizational processes when the organization is already faced with a problem. They rely upon feedback control. Management Auditing is different from these two categories in that it can be used as a feedforward *or* feedback control. It can be used to anticipate problems or to solve them, to prevent or to cure.

All six techniques can be used to identify organizational strengths and weaknesses. However, Organizational Behavior Modification, Management by Objectives (to some extent), Management Development, and Organization Development tend to focus primarily upon the *behavioral* strengths and weaknesses of organizational members. Hence, nonbehavioral problems may not be identified with these techniques until the symptoms of the problem become manifest in the personal and interpersonal behaviors of organizational personnel. For example, rapid environmental change may result in a poor fit between an organization and its environment. The organization may not be keeping up with market and technological changes, with the consequence that personnel notice that their performance is deteriorating, a conclusion obvious from their inability to maintain market share, productivity, and other objectives.

Interpersonal behaviors subsequently deteriorate also, and at some point it is necessary to resort to Organization Development to remedy the immediate behavioral problems and to investigate the more basic problem as well.

Once any technique of organizational change is invoked, it would appear to be capable of determining the compatibility of the organization and its environment in terms of the kinds of problems that it is designed to deal with.

It is in the problem definition that important differences can be noticed among the techniques of organizational change. As already suggested, the different techniques are not interchangeable, though as we shall see they tend to be complementary.

All the techniques demand a problem definition, but the definition for each is in terms of its capabilities. Organizational Behavior Modification, Management by Objectives, Management Development, and Organization Development define problems in terms of individual or interpersonal behavior. Behavioral problem definitions may or should lead to definitions of associated or more basic problems, of course. Conversely, Management Auditing and the Control Cycle tend to lead to problem definitions in nonbehavioral terms: new products have to be developed; an obsolescent plant should be closed. Behavioral problems are not generally assumed to exist or be likely to arise; however, they may become evident at any time.

Since these techniques deal with different kinds of problems, their strategic solutions are different also. Organizational Behavior Modification solutions are in terms of specifying individual behavior which will bring about desired results. This is also true for Management by Objectives and Management Development. Specific solutions are as varied as the tasks for which the individuals are responsible. By contrast, Organization Development solutions are somewhat more limited, since they focus upon sensitivity training, team building, group problem solving, and similar activities designed to improve interpersonal relationships, with less emphasis upon individual task performance. As to Management Auditing and the Control Cycle, the alternative solutions to problems are most likely to be concerned with the issues of demand for the products of the organization, its supply capabilities, the appropriateness of its mission and objectives, organizational structure (roles and role relationships summarized by the organization chart and policies and procedures), and organizational processes such as communications and decision making.

As the kinds of alternative solutions developed in the course of resolving the problems of organizational change vary considerably, so the bases for choosing solutions among the techniques vary also.

Selection of solutions for the behavioral problems associated with Organizational Behavior Modification, Management Development, Organization Development, and to some extent Management by Objectives, comes from the realm of behavioral theory. For example, the schedule of reinforcement chosen to bring about behavioral change under Organizational Behavior Modification would be the type found to be effective in similar prior situations, whether fixed ratio, fixed interval, or variable.

With Management Auditing, the Control Cycle, and to some extent with Management by Objectives, appropriate solutions are sought in terms of management theory or what are called principles of management. For example, Management Auditing may show that an organization's functional structure is inappropriate for its proliferating activities. If it has a continuing series of projects to conduct, knowledge of the characteristics of alternative structural forms would dictate a matrix structure; if the organization has a long line of stable, differentiated products, product organization would be appropriate. Similarly, if in the course of a Management by Objectives conference between superior and subordinate a mutual conclusion were reached that some of the subordinate's operations were out of control, an appropriate solution could be found in terms of management control theory.

Five of the six techniques of organizational change provide for implementation of the strategic solution(s). Organizational Behavior Modification, Organization Development, Management by Objectives, and the Control Cycle have specific provision for implementation activities by superiors and/or consultants. Although Management Development activities do not have a highly structured format of procedures, the responsibility of the Personnel or Training Department overall and the responsibility and interest of managers for their subordinates' development suggest an implicit concern if not explicit provision for implementation. Management Auditing alone does not seem to contain implicit or explicit provision for implementation, though some follow-up action is clearly needed after recommendations are accepted. The reason seems to be that important and/or organizationwide audits are normally done by outside consultants who do not ordinarily take the lead in bringing about the changes required by implementation. Those changes require the authority and presence of managers who have jurisdiction over the structural and processual areas involved. Consultants, therefore, can usually be little more than resource persons at the implementation stage of change.

All six techniques of change are clearly dedicated to bringing about an improved fit between organization and environment and all but Management Auditing provide specific steps and/or express the need to evaluate the results of organizational change that they bring about. Not that there is no need to with Management Auditing. But because of the assumption of responsibility by management when the consultant has made recommendations, the evaluation is left to the implementers.

From the foregoing discussion we can reasonably conclude that the techniques of organizational change are compatible with and reflect the components of the model of organizational change presented in Figure 1-1.

COMPARISON OF CHANGE TECHNIQUES

Similarities and differences among the techniques of organizational change have no doubt become evident in the separate and collective descriptions of them so far. It may be helpful, nonetheless, to emphasize these differences and similarities as a matter of record. Yet it will be possible to compare and contrast only their gross features and we must pass over many subtle characteristics that give each technique its unique flavor. In addition to the exposition presented here, readers are urged to examine some of the literature referred to at the ends of Chapters 2 to 7.

One of the simplest distinctions that can be made among the techniques of organizational change is the focal point or target of the technique: individual behavior as such or the organization as an entity. An organizational unit, such as a product division or functional department, would also come under the second category. This distinction was made in the presentation of the different techniques. Part 2 of this book presented the techniques which focus on individual behavior: Organizational Behavior Modification, Management by Objectives, and Management Development. Part 3 presented the techniques which have as their target the entire organization or some substantial portion of it: Organization Development, Management Auditing, and the Control Cycle. Table 8-1 summarizes the above and the following distinctions among these techniques.

A second distinction that can be made among the techniques of organizational change has to do with the *symptoms of problems* which become obvious. Organizational Behavior Modification, Management by Objectives, Management Development, and Organization Development are designed to deal with problems where the symptoms suggest that behavior of personnel is the underlying cause of organizational difficulties. But they do not deal with exactly the same kinds of problems. For example, Organizational Behavior Modification has been used largely in changing workers' behavior in tasks or situations that are primarily physical in nature. The work cycle in such cases is relatively short and it is possible to observe and record behaviors easily. Although

Table 8-1 Comparison of the Techniques of Organizational Change

Characteristic	Types of techniques					
	Organizational Behavior Modification	Management by Objectives	Management Development	Organization Development	Management Auditing	Control Cycle
Focal point	Individuals	Individuals	Individuals	Entire organization or part	Entire organization or part	Entire organization or part
Symptoms of problems requiring attention	Undesirable behaviors of workers resulting in substandard performance	Different expectations and interpretations by superiors and subordinates' performance	Deficiencies in performance of tasks requiring mental or social skills to do present job and/or lack of skills to do future job	Destructive conflict and lack of cooperation among individuals and groups	Existing or anticipated problems or opportunities: product demand and supply, structure, functions, processes	Inability to adapt organization to changing environment using feedback control on product demand and supply, structure, functions, processes
Kinds of Changes sought or achieved	Improved fit between individual and job at nonmanagerial levels primarily	Improved fit between individual and job at managerial and professional levels	Improvement in mental and social skills at managerial and professional levels	Improved interpersonal and intergroup behavior	Improvements in product demand and supply, structure, functions, processes	Improvements in product demand and supply, structure, functions, processes
Theoretical bases	Behavioral theory	Behavioral and management theories	Behavioral theory	Behavioral theory	Management theory	Management theory
Type of control	Feedback to resolve problems	Feedforward/feedback to forestall problems or exploit opportunities	Feedforward/feedback to forestall problems or exploit opportunities, or feedback to resolve problems	Feedback to resolve problems	Feedforward/feedback to forestall problems or exploit opportunities, or feedback to resolve problems	Feedforward/feedback to forestall problems and exploit opportunities
Continuity	Intermittent	Continuous	Intermittent or continuous	Intermittent	Intermittent	Continuous
Change agent	Superiors and/or inside and outside consultants	Superiors; inside and outside consultants can assist	Superiors, with Personnel or Training Department to coordinate	Outside and/or inside consultants with backing of higher management	Outside and/or inside consultants with backing of higher management	All managers, with assistance of staff group and/or outside consultants

adaptable to dealing with behavior that is primarily mental or social in nature, it has not been used extensively in such cases. Management by Objectives seems somewhat more suited for changing behaviors that require mental and social skills where behavioral inputs and the resulting outputs may have to be negotiated between superiors and subordinates. Situations where Management Development is appropriate are those where professional and managerial skills are inadequate or have to be extended in scope. In contrast to the three preceding techniques, Organization Development is used primarily in situations where the social process results in destructive interpersonal conflict or lack of cooperation between individuals and groups.

Symptoms that suggest the need for Management Auditing and the Control Cycle are quite different from the preceding. In these cases the difficulties are usually associated with organizational operations, and the symptoms may include decreasing product demand, deficient supply capabilities, problems of organizational jurisdiction, product obsolescence, low return on investment, technological change, and almost any other conceivable problem that does not originate in the inappropriate, separate behaviors of personnel with respect to each other and their respective tasks. In terms of dealing with problems *at any point in time* Management Auditing and the Control Cycle are virtually interchangeable. For example, a Management Audit can be used to examine and recommend changes in the product line of a company. But the Control Cycle is also used for the same purpose. A long-range plan developed with the Control Cycle might involve recommendations to restructure the organization; again the same recommendation could be developed in the context of a Management Audit.

The kinds of changes that are sought and can be achieved naturally follow from the kinds of problems appropriate for each technique. For Organizational Behavior Modification, Management by Objectives, Management Development, and Organization Development, the changes will be directly observable in the behavior of organizational members. In Organizational Behavior Modification, the result should be a better fit between the worker and the job; in Management by Objectives, greater consonance in the expectations, and subsequent interpretation, of the subordinate's performance; in Management Development, a better fit between the professional or managerial person and the present or future position; in Organization Development, improved relationships between individuals and groups. Changes sought and wrought with Management Auditing and the Control Cycle include organizational structure (roles and role relationships plus organizational norms: objectives, policies, procedures, standards and rules), functions (procurement, production, marketing, etc.), and processes (communication, decision making, controlling, etc.). Indirectly, changes in these categories usually result in behavioral change of organizational members. Results of change are generally sought in quantitative indicators: revenues, expenses, profit, productivity, market share, and the like.

Theoretical bases for the change techniques fall into two broad categories: behavioral theory and management theory. Organizational Behavior Modification, Management by Objectives to some extent, Management Development, and Organization Development are based upon behavioral theory; Management Auditing, the Control Cycle, and Management by Objectives (to some extent) are based upon management theory.

In the cases of Organizational Behavior Modification, Management by Objectives, Management Development, and Organization Development, there is a common reliance upon motivation and learning theories. That is, for change to take place in the behavior of individuals, it is necessary for people to want to change behavior and to be in a situation where they can secure knowledge and/or improve performance in response to feedback, including rewards. Organization Development relies additionally upon theories of perception and communication plus interpersonal and group dynamics.

In addition to behavioral theory, Management by Objectives is based upon management control theory; the latter is also a basis for the Control Cycle, which, like Management Auditing, relies upon the full gamut of management theory and knowledge about organizational structure, functions, and processes.

In a sense, all these techniques have a *control* characteristic involved in their applications in organizations. That is, they are vehicles to establish control over organizational change. They are used to forestall and/or to resolve problems. Some are used primarily to forestall; others, primarily to resolve. The kinds of control were discussed in Chapter 7.

Techniques to forestall problems are the Control Cycle, Management by Objectives, and Management Development. Hence, they are feedforward/feedback controls. As noted in Chapter 7, for optimal control feedforward requires feedback also. Management Auditing and Management Development are used both as feedforward/feedback or feedback-only controls. That is, they can be used to forestall and resolve expected problems or only to resolve existing ones. Organizational Behavior Modification and Organization Development by contrast are feedback-oriented only. A further word is in order here, however. There is nothing to preclude using both Organizational Behavior Modification and Organization Development as feedforward/feedback controls on the behavior of organizational members. These techniques could be used to prevent as well as cure problems. All that would be required is establishment of a scanning activity to anticipate behavioral problems.

The types of control involved in the techniques of organizational change have an effect upon the *continuity* of their use. Those which rely upon feedforward/feedback of necessity are institutionalized in the organization; they are, in effect, continuous processes like communications and decision making, and are assumed to be a part of each manager's job and/or the task of a specialized unit. Management by Objectives, Management Development, and the Control Cycle have this characteristic, as does Management Auditing if there is a staff group of internal management auditors. Organizational Behavior Modification and Organization Development, by contrast, are techniques which are superimposed intermittently on the organization as the need is perceived. These latter techniques could also, of course, become built-in processes of the organization.

The techniques vary as to who initiates and brings about the changes. We will call these people *change agents,* reiterating Burke's caution that the ultimate change agent is the top manager(s) in the organization or organizational unit. The choice is among managerial superiors, outside consultants, and inside consultants. Of course, consultants can be used to help install or help in the continued use of any of the techniques. We will identify them, however, only where they frequently are, or must be, utilized. Techniques which have been categorized as continuous, built-in processes, must of necessity be conducted by organizational managers, perhaps in conjunction with advice and assistance from outside or inside consultants, or a staff group. Application of the techniques labeled as intermittent can (in the case of Organization Development, must) be conducted by consultants. The use of all the techniques must be supported by higher management for effectiveness, of course.

Specifically, then, Organizational Behavior Modification and Management Auditing generally involve consultants and Organization Development requires their use. Management by Objectives and Management Development are the responsibility of all managers who have managerial subordinates; the Control Cycle, of all managers. Management Development is also the responsibility of all managers, with the Personnel or Training Department coordinating the activity.

One final point to be reviewed is the interrelationships of the techniques to each other. Perhaps it has already become evident that they are, or can be, mutually supportive. For example, an organization which has adopted Management by Objectives may recognize that it would be helpful to utilize the Control Cycle as an organizationwide technique to coordinate the separate plans prepared for each subordinate. Conversely, an organization depending upon the Control Cycle for organizationwide change may find it helpful to utilize Management by Objectives as a means of getting operational commitment to the master plan.

In the course of an Organization Development effort, consultants might uncover an unusual amount of misunderstanding between hierarchical levels and could recommend installing Management by Objectives to improve relations. Similarly, in preparing long-range plans under the Control Cycle, higher management might find the change required in the behavior of organizational members as individuals and groups to be so great that it required resorting to Organizational Behavior Modification, Organization Development, and Management Development. Finally, a Management Audit might well point to the need for one or more of these techniques to implement recommendations. No attempt has been made to show these relationships on Table 8-1 because the apparently complete compatibility of the techniques makes it unnecessary.

BECOMING SENSITIVE TO NEED TO CHANGE

As managers ponder these techniques of organizational change, they may conclude that the real problem is to *become aware* of the need to change the organization as the environment changes. But how does one become aware?

The answer is simple and may appear merely tautological: just think about it. *Perception* is a highly selective process and we tend to learn about those things we perceive. Perception requires interest. People who walk through the woods are not likely to notice differences among the trees if they do not glance carefully at the overall configurations, the barks, and the leaves of the trees. Distinctions such as oak, maple, and birch will not exist because they are not noticed. In the same way managers must look for signs that distinguish organizational operations that are going very well, those that are satisfactory, and those doing poorly. Concomitant attention to the environment is a necessity also, of course. That attention can be given by perusing trade journals, reading business books and articles, attending trade association meetings, and noting the practices of customers, competitors, and vendors.

Communication is a necessary follow-up to perception. A perceptive manager will talk to subordinates and superiors (the board of directors if the manager is the president) about organizational strengths and weaknesses and relevant phenomena in the environment. And although subordinates constitute a reservoir of insights and ideas about what is right and wrong about the organization, the most difficult kind of communication is from subordinate to superior. For that reason special efforts must be made to encourage upward communication.

The most comprehensive form of upward communication is the *attitude survey*, which elicits opinions of all personnel about organizational operations. The need for objectivity by those administering the survey and the need for anonymity by the respondents dictates that the survey be conducted by an outside consultant. These services are readily available.

There are other ways to encourage upward communication. Although much maligned and even ridiculed occasionally, a *suggestion system* can be a useful device for securing information from lower-level personnel about the improvement of operations. An *open-door policy* helps also, as does a *grievance system* in which nonunion personnel can appeal against adverse administrative actions.

To keep communications open and to achieve and maintain credibility, management must do two things as it gathers information about the organization and environment via organizational members. Both involve *taking action* on the basis of available knowledge.

The first action is to remedy minor problems and implement simple ideas for improvement at the earliest possible date. The temptation is at hand not to tinker with operations when really big changes may be impending. In a way, that attitude makes some sense. But it makes even more sense to reinforce the behavior and meet some of the expectations of organizational personnel by responding quickly to relatively minor matters. Like all other people, subordinates (and everybody but the chief executive officer is a subordinate in an organization) tend to judge on the basis of what is done, not merely what is said. By observing quick responses from higher management, they are reassured that there is more at stake than mere exercises in communication.

The second action that needs to be taken is initiation of an effort to bring about long-range changes that appear necessary, with follow-through until the organization is more compatible with its environment. Failure to follow through can have indeterminate or even disastrous consequences, as the following instances show.

In one case I was asked to conduct a Management Development program for first- and second-line supervisors. The request came from the local plant manager of a national company. Toward the end of the program, I reiterated to the plant manager the recognized view that after the program ended some kind of effort should be made to reinforce the learning that had taken place. I suggested a number of options—an occasional article on the subjects covered in the program, staff conferences focusing on efforts to use the knowledge and skills attained in the program, including standards of effective supervision in the performance appraisals to reflect improved capabilities, and so on. After a short interval of hemming and hawing, the plant manager finally told me in precise but polite language to mind my own business. I later learned that the program had been conducted mainly to impress the home office with the plant manager's availability for promotion, now that he had a well-trained group of subordinates. As far as I could tell, the program had little long-term effect upon performance at the plant.

In another instance, some colleagues and I were called in to conduct a Management Development program following an attitude survey. The survey results suggested that first- and second-line supervisors were quite insensitive to the workers, and top management felt that they needed training. As we got into the program, it began to be clear to us that the first- and second-line supervisors were largely responding to their treatment by higher management and following orders to "get the work out." We tested the perceptions of the hierarchy by asking the eight members of higher management if they considered themselves oriented by Theory X (people are lazy and have to be coerced to work) or by Theory Y (people are responsible and will get the work done without constant prodding). Of the eight top managers, seven labeled themselves as Theory Y–oriented; only one thought he was Theory X–oriented. Then we asked the 44 first- and second-level supervisors to indicate whether they thought the top managers were oriented according to Theory X or Theory Y. Their answer: seven of the eight managers were Theory X–oriented. Having compiled a long list of problems during the program, we approached the executive vice president and recommended a Management Audit to examine the structure, functions, and processes of the company to find solutions for its difficulties. Nodding sympathetically, the executive vice president explained that, much as he would like us do the audit, the firm's financial condition was such that they just couldn't afford it. A few years later all they could afford to do was to go out of business.

Embarking upon major organizational change poses immediate problems which require major decisions. The problems can be stated as:

1 How much time is available in which to bring about the desired changes?
2 Who are to be the change agents?
3 Which technique(s) of organizational change should be used?

The availability of time to change is largely a function of how urgently the need to change is felt. If sales are declining precipitately, or costs increasing astronomically, or key personnel quitting in droves, there is no time to be lost. At the other extreme—if product or technological obsolescence, or the simultaneous retirement of many top officers, or unfavorable demographic trends will begin to be troublesome in only a few years—a more leisurely pace is possible.

The time available will have an impact on who the change agents are to be. There is not likely to be much slack time among managers who are busily engaged in minimizing the impact of imminent disaster. In such situations, the time and effort of outside consultants would be needed to devise ways and means to counteract the environmental trends and events causing havoc to the organization. As Burke notes, however, top management must still be the primary change agents—consultants can only gather data, analyze it, and make recommendations. Nevertheless, consultants can, because of their ready availability and instant expertise (not to be taken for granted as Hayden suggests), make enormous contributions to lightening management's load.

If a more leisurely pace is possible, there is much to be said for developing capabilities internally. In the cases of Management by Objective and the Control Cycle, this is inevitable, since all managers will have to become proficient in the techniques eventually. Even here it is possible, indeed desirable, to have a staff person or group with special responsibilities for the technique. With a formal Management Development program, all managers will have some responsibilities for their subordinates, but the overall management of the program will normally be lodged in the personnel or training department. With respect to Organizational Behavior Modification, Organization Development, and Management Auditing, the specialized skills suggest the need for outside consultants, or internal consultants *if* the volume of activity and organizational size warrant it. The *Fortune* 500 companies can easily afford such internal consultants; other organizations need to weigh the decision more carefully.

Exposure to the various techniques of organizational change described in the preceding chapters should prevent the reader from making the most basic mistake in selecting a technique for his or her organization. That mistake is selecting on the basis of a current fad, as against selecting on the basis of what the organization needs. As suggested in the opening chapter, articles, books, and seminars about management tend to emphasize what is new, with less regard for what is useful in specific situations.

Hence, a reader selecting the technique to utilize may find it helpful to compare the nature of organizational change required with the characteristics of the techniques described in this book. If uncertainty persists, additional references can be consulted to clarify unresolved issues. As an alternative, or in addition, to further research, it is possible to request presentations by consultants in the techniques that, on the surface, would appear to be relevant. The consultants can be asked to show how their approach would help to resolve the problem at hand or forestall one on the horizon. A choice can then be made on the basis of the presentations.

In making the choice of technique, as in deciding to go ahead with organizational change, there are elements of risk. But then, the risk of not taking action may be even greater. Since all business decisions involve elements of risk, and managers are risk takers, the decision maker should feel reasonably comfortable in making the choice.

Index